RealtySchool.com

NEVADA
STATE
LAW

Fifth Edition

Including Two Practice Exams

NRS 645 and NAC 645

and the Nevada Law and Reference Guide

produced by JOSEPH R. FITZPATRICK

REALTYSCHOOL.COM
NEVADA STATE LAW

produced by Joseph R. Fitzpatrick

5th Edition
ISBN-13: 978-0615865638 (RealtySchool.com)
ISBN-10: 0615865631

Nevada Salesperson and Broker Content Outline

Effective January 1, 2017

The state-specific examination is made up of forty (40) scored items for salesperson candidates and fifty (50) scored items for broker candidates. The salesperson and broker examinations also contain five to ten (5-10) pretest items. The pretest items are not identified and will not affect a candidate's score in any way. The following examination content outline is applicable to both real estate salespersons and real estate brokers.

I. DUTIES AND POWERS OF THE COMMISSION (5%)
A. **Determining Misconduct**
 1. Investigations
 2. Hearings and Appeals
B. **Enforcement and Disciplinary Action**
 1. Sanctions and Fines
 2. Additional Education
 3. License Suspension
 4. Revocation
C. **Real Estate Education, Research, and Recovery Fund**

II. LICENSING REQUIREMENTS (10%)
A. **Types of Licensing and Permits and Requirements**
B. **Activities Requiring a License or Permit**
C. **License Maintenance**
 1. License Renewal
 2. Changes in License Status
 3. Reasons for Denial of a License or Renewal
D. **Required Timely Notifications to the Division**
 1. Conviction or entry of a guilty/nolo contendere plea
 2. Broker association
 3. Changes in personal information
E. **Branch Offices and License Display (Broker Only)**
F. **Cooperative Certificates (Broker Only)**

III. AGENCY (20%)
A. **Agency**
B. **Duties Owed by a Nevada Licensee**
C. **Consent to Act**
D. **Confirmation of Agency Relationship**

IV. LICENSE PRACTICE (20%)
A. **Licensee Responsibilities**
B. **Broker Supervision of Licensees**
C. **Commissions and other Compensation**
D. **Advertising**
E. **Rules for Broker Price Opinions**
F. **Handling of Monies**

V. DISCLOSURES (20%)
A. **Residential Disclosure Guide**
B. **Seller's Real Property Disclosure**
C. **Disclosure of Common-Interest Communities**
D. **Disclosure of licensee as principal**
E. **Other disclosures**

VI. CONTRACTS (15%)
A. **Brokerage Agreements, including listing and buyer representation**
B. **Preparation and Handling of Documents**
C. **Closing Statements**
D. **Advance Fees**
E. **Handling of Earnest Money Deposits**

VII. RECORD KEEPING (5%)
A. **Maintenance of Records**
 1. Timely submission of records to broker
 2. Required retention
 3. Protection of confidential information
B. **Inspection of Records (Broker Only)**
C. **Trust Account Records and Management (Broker Only)**

VIII. SPECIAL TOPICS (5%)
A. **Subdivisions**
B. **Time Shares**
C. **Environmental Issues**
D. **Water Rights**

TABLE OF CONTENTS

NRS 645

CHAPTER 645 - REAL ESTATE BROKERS AND SALESPERSONS

GENERAL PROVISIONS

ADMINISTRATION

REGULATION OF PRACTICES

ADVANCE FEES

LICENSES

PROHIBITED ACTS; PENALTIES; ENFORCEMENT

NOTE: Sections 3 to 40, inclusive, of chapter 517, Statutes of Nevada 2007, at p. 3105, have been codified as NRS 645G.010, 645G.020, 645G.030, 645G.050, 645G.060, 645G.070, 645G.140 to 645G.310, inclusive, 645G.330 to 645G.400, inclusive, 645G.500 to 645G.520, inclusive, and 645G.530 to 645G.900, inclusive.

GENERAL PROVISIONS

NRS 645.0005 Definitions.   As used in this chapter, unless the context otherwise requires, the words and terms defined in NRS 645.001 to 645.042, inclusive, have the meanings ascribed to them in those sections.
    (Added to NRS by 1985, 1260; A 1995, 2074; 1997, 956; 2003, 931, 1290; 2005, 648, 665; 2007, 1788)

NRS 645.001 "Administrator" defined.   As used in this chapter, "Administrator" means the Real Estate Administrator.
    (Added to NRS by 1963, 663)

NRS 645.002 "Advance fee" defined.   "Advance fee" means a fee contracted for, claimed, demanded, charged, received or collected for an advance fee listing, advertisement or offer to sell or lease property, issued for the purpose of promoting the sale or lease of a business or real estate or for referral to a business or real estate brokers or salespersons, or both, before the last printing or other last issuance thereof, other than by a newspaper of general circulation.
    (Added to NRS by 1957, 210; A 1985, 1260)

NRS 645.004 "Advance fee listing" defined.
    1. "Advance fee listing" includes, but is not limited to:
    (a) The name or a list of the names of the owners, landlords, exchangers or lessors, or the location of property or a business, or of an interest therein, offered for rent, sale, lease or exchange.
    (b) The name, or a list of the names, or the location at which prospective or potential purchasers, buyers, lessees, tenants or exchangers of property may be communicated with or found.
    (c) A brokerage agreement by which a person who is engaged in the business of promoting the sale or lease of businesses or real estate agrees to render to an owner or lessee of the property any services, to promote the sale or lease of the property, for an advance fee.
    (d) A brokerage agreement by which a person agrees to locate or promote the sale or lease of a business or real estate for an advance fee.

2. The term does not include publications intended for general circulation.
(Added to NRS by 1957, 210; A 1971, 681; 1979, 1534; 1985, 1260; 1987, 731; 1995, 2074)

NRS 645.0045 "Agency" defined.
1. "Agency" means a relationship between a principal and an agent arising out of a brokerage agreement whereby the agent is engaged to do certain acts on behalf of the principal in dealings with a third party.
2. The term does not include a relationship arising solely from negotiations or communications with a client of another broker with the written permission of the broker in accordance with the provisions of subsection 2 of NRS 645.635.
(Added to NRS by 2007, 1787)

NRS 645.005 "Brokerage agreement" defined. "Brokerage agreement" means an oral or written contract between a client and a broker in which the broker agrees to accept valuable consideration from the client or another person for assisting, soliciting or negotiating the sale, purchase, option, rental or lease of real property, or the sale, exchange, option or purchase of a business. The term does not include a property management agreement.
(Added to NRS by 1995, 2072; A 2003, 932; 2005, 648)

NRS 645.007 "Business" defined. "Business" means the tangible assets and goodwill of an existing enterprise.
(Added to NRS by 1985, 1260)

NRS 645.0075 "Business broker" defined. "Business broker" means a person who, while acting for another and for compensation or with the intention or expectation of receiving compensation:
1. Sells, exchanges, options, purchases, rents or leases a business that is sold, exchanged, optioned, purchased, rented or leased as part of an interest or estate in real property;
2. Negotiates or offers, attempts or agrees to negotiate the sale, exchange, option, purchase, rental or lease of a business that is or is intended to be sold, exchanged, optioned, purchased, rented or leased as part of an interest or estate in real property; or
3. Lists or solicits prospective purchasers of a business if a component of the listing or solicitation is an interest or estate in real property.
(Added to NRS by 2005, 646; A 2013, 2097)

NRS 645.009 "Client" defined. "Client" means a person who has entered into a brokerage agreement with a broker or a property management agreement with a broker.
(Added to NRS by 1995, 2072; A 2003, 932)

NRS 645.010 "Commission" defined. As used in this chapter, "Commission" means the Real Estate Commission.
[Part 6:150:1947; A 1949, 433; 1955, 131]—(NRS A 1963, 663; 1981, 1605)

NRS 645.013 "Designated property manager" defined. "Designated property manager" means a person who has the qualifications required by NRS 645.6055 to be a designated property manager and who is appointed as the designated property manager for an office pursuant to NRS 645.6055.
(Added to NRS by 2003, 1287)

NRS 645.015 "Director" defined. As used in this chapter, "Director" means the Director of the Department of Business and Industry.
(Added to NRS by 1963, 663; A 1993, 1891)

NRS 645.018 "Owner-developer" defined. As used in this chapter, "owner-developer" means a person who owns five or more lots within a recorded subdivision, shown on an approved parcel map, or the parceling of which has been approved by the county, on each of which there is a single-family residence not previously sold.
(Added to NRS by 1975, 1639; A 1979, 1535)

NRS 645.019 "Property management" defined. "Property management" means the physical, administrative or financial maintenance and management of real property, or the supervision of such activities for a fee, commission or other compensation or valuable consideration, pursuant to a property management agreement.
(Added to NRS by 1997, 954; A 2003, 932)

NRS 645.0192 "Property management agreement" defined. "Property management agreement" means a written contract between a client and a broker in which the broker agrees to accept valuable consideration from the client or another person for providing property management for the client.

(Added to NRS by 2003, 931)

NRS 645.0195 "Property manager" defined. "Property manager" means a person engaged in property management who, as an employee or independent contractor, is associated with a licensed real estate broker, whether or not for compensation.

(Added to NRS by 1997, 954)

NRS 645.020 "Real estate" defined. As used in this chapter, "real estate" means every interest or estate in real property including but not limited to freeholds, leaseholds and interests in condominiums, town houses or planned unit developments, whether corporeal or incorporeal, and whether the real property is situated in this State or elsewhere.

[Part 2:150:1947; 1943 NCL § 6396.02]—(NRS A 1973, 1097; 1975, 1541)

NRS 645.030 "Real estate broker" defined.

1. "Real estate broker" means a person who, for another and for compensation or with the intention or expectation of receiving compensation:

(a) Sells, exchanges, options, purchases, rents or leases, or negotiates or offers, attempts or agrees to negotiate the sale, exchange, option, purchase, rental or lease of, or lists or solicits prospective purchasers, lessees or renters of, any real estate or the improvements thereon or any modular homes, used manufactured homes, used mobile homes or other housing offered or conveyed with any interest in real estate;

(b) Engages in or offers to engage in the business of claiming, demanding, charging, receiving, collecting or contracting for the collection of an advance fee in connection with any employment undertaken to promote the sale or lease of business opportunities or real estate by advance fee listing advertising or other offerings to sell, lease, exchange or rent property;

(c) Engages in or offers to engage in the business of property management; or

(d) Engages in or offers to engage in the business of business brokerage.

2. Any person who, for another and for compensation, aids, assists, solicits or negotiates the procurement, sale, purchase, rental or lease of public lands is a real estate broker within the meaning of this chapter.

3. The term does not include a person who is employed by a licensed real estate broker to accept reservations on behalf of a person engaged in the business of the rental of lodging for 31 days or less, if the employee does not perform any tasks related to the sale or other transfer of an interest in real estate.

[Part 2:150:1947; 1943 NCL § 6396.02] + [2.5:150:1947; added 1955, 615]—(NRS A 1957, 337; 1959, 393; 1963, 330; 1973, 1097; 1975, 1383; 1977, 928; 1979, 1535; 1981, 1327; 1985, 312, 1261; 1997, 505, 956; 2005, 648, 665)

NRS 645.035 "Real estate broker-salesperson" defined.

1. Within the meaning of this chapter, a "real estate broker-salesperson" is any person who holds a real estate broker's license, or who has passed the real estate broker's examination, but who, as an employee or as an independent contractor, for compensation or otherwise, is associated with:

(a) A licensed real estate broker in the capacity of a salesperson, to do or to deal in any act, acts or transactions included within the definition of a real estate broker in NRS 645.030; or

(b) A registered owner-developer in the capacity of a sales manager in accordance with NRS 645.283 and 645.289.

2. In this chapter, the term "real estate salesperson" includes "real estate broker-salesperson" when applicable.

(Added to NRS by 1957, 337; A 1975, 793, 1541; 1977, 928; 1981, 1605; 1985, 312; 2005, 1286)

NRS 645.037 "Real Estate Division" and "Division" defined. As used in this chapter, "Real Estate Division" and "Division" mean the Real Estate Division of the Department of Business and Industry.

NRS 645.040 "Real estate salesperson" defined. Within the meaning of this chapter, a "real estate salesperson" is any person who, as an employee or as an independent contractor, is associated with a licensed real estate broker or registered owner-developer to do or to deal in any act, acts or transactions set out or comprehended by the definition of a real estate broker in NRS 645.030, for a compensation or otherwise.

[3:150:1947; 1943 NCL § 6396.03]—(NRS A 1971, 1410; 1973, 1763; 1975, 1541, 1639; 1977, 929; 1985, 313)

NRS 645.042 "Used manufactured home" or "used mobile home" defined. "Used manufactured home" or "used mobile home" means a manufactured home or mobile home, respectively, which has been:

1. Sold, rented or leased, and which was occupied before or after the sale, rental or lease; or

2. Registered with or been the subject of a certificate of title issued by the appropriate agency of authority of this State, any other state, the District of Columbia, any territory or possession of the United States, or any foreign state, province or country.

(Added to NRS by 2005, 664)

NRS 645.044 Use of terms "salesman," "saleswoman" and "salesperson" authorized.

1. A person licensed as a real estate salesperson may use the term "real estate salesman," "real estate saleswoman" or "real estate salesperson" in the course of doing business.

2. A person licensed as a real estate broker-salesperson may use the term "real estate broker-salesman," "real estate broker-saleswoman" or "real estate broker-salesperson" in the course of doing business.

(Added to NRS by 1999, 92)

NRS 645.0445 Applicability of chapter.

1. The provisions of this chapter do not apply to, and the terms "real estate broker" and "real estate salesperson" do not include, any:

(a) Owner or lessor of property, or any regular employee of such a person, who performs any of the acts mentioned in NRS 645.030, 645.040, 645.230 and 645.260, with respect to the property in the regular course of or as an incident to the management of or investment in the property. For the purposes of this subsection, "management" means activities which tend to preserve or increase the income from the property by preserving the physical desirability of the property or maintaining high standards of service to tenants. The term does not include sales activities.

(b) Employee of a real estate broker while engaged in the collection of rent for or on behalf of the broker.

(c) Person while performing the duties of a property manager for a property, if the person maintains an office on the property and does not engage in property management with regard to any other property.

(d) Person while performing the duties of a property manager for a common-interest community governed by the provisions of chapter 116 of NRS, an association of a condominium hotel governed by the provisions of chapter 116B of NRS, a condominium project governed by the provisions of chapter 117 of NRS, a time share governed by the provisions of chapter 119A of NRS, or a planned unit development governed by the provisions of chapter 278A of NRS, if the person is a member in good standing of, and, if applicable, holds a current certificate, registration or other similar form of recognition from, a nationally recognized organization or association for persons managing such properties that has been approved by the Real Estate Division by regulation.

(e) Person while performing the duties of a property manager for property used for residential housing that is subsidized either directly or indirectly by this State, an agency or political subdivision of this State, or the Federal Government or an agency of the Federal Government.

2. The provisions of this chapter do not apply to:

(a) Any bank, thrift company, credit union, trust company, savings and loan association or any mortgage or farm loan association licensed under the laws of this State or of the United States, with reference to property it has acquired for development, for the convenient transaction of its business, or as a result of foreclosure of property encumbered in good faith as security for a loan or other obligation it has originated or holds.

(b) A corporation which, through its regular officers who receive no special compensation for it, performs any of those acts with reference to the property of the corporation.

(c) The services rendered by an attorney at law in the performance of his or her duties as an attorney at law.

(d) A receiver, trustee in bankruptcy, administrator or executor, or any other person doing any of the acts specified in NRS 645.030 under the jurisdiction of any court.

(e) A trustee acting under a trust agreement, deed of trust or will, or the regular salaried employees thereof.

(f) The purchase, sale or locating of mining claims or options thereon or interests therein.

(g) The State of Nevada or a political subdivision thereof.

[5:150:1947; A 1955, 457]—(NRS A 1973, 1100; 1979, 1538; 1981, 1328; 1983, 151; 1985, 1262, 1507; 1987, 517; 1993, 2021; 1997, 957; 1999, 938; 2007, 2292, 3114; 2009, 35)—(Substituted in revision for NRS 645.240)

ADMINISTRATION

NRS 645.045 Administration by Real Estate Division. The provisions of this chapter shall be administered by the Real Estate Division, subject to administrative supervision by the Director.

(Added to NRS by 1963, 663)

NRS 645.050   Real Estate Commission: Creation; number and appointment of members; powers and duties; regulations; service of process.

1.   The Real Estate Commission is hereby created. The Commission consists of five members appointed by the Governor.

2.   The Commission shall act in an advisory capacity to the Real Estate Division, adopt regulations and conduct hearings as provided in this chapter. The Commission shall adopt regulations establishing standards for the operation of licensees' offices and for their business conduct and ethics.

3.   The Commission may by regulation delegate any authority conferred upon it by this chapter to the Administrator to be exercised pursuant to the regulations of the Commission.

4.   Service of process and other communications upon the Commission may be made at the principal office of the Real Estate Division.

[Part 6:150:1947; A 1949, 433; 1955, 131]—(NRS A 1963, 663; 1973, 1098; 1979, 1536; 1981, 1605)

NRS 645.060   Real Estate Commission: Limitation on consecutive service by member.   Members are eligible for reappointment, but shall not serve for a period greater than 6 years consecutively, after which time they are not eligible for appointment or reappointment until 3 years have elapsed from any period of previous service. If a successor is appointed to fill the balance of any unexpired term of a member, the time served by the successor shall not apply in computing the 6 years' consecutive service unless the balance of the unexpired term exceeds 18 months.

[Part 6:150:1947; A 1949, 433; 1955, 131]—(NRS A 1977, 1259)

NRS 645.070   Real Estate Commission: Oaths of members.   Each member of the Commission shall, before entering upon the duties of his or her office:

1.   Take the constitutional oath of office; and

2.   In addition, make oath that the member is legally qualified under the provisions of this chapter to serve as a member of the Commission.

[Part 6:150:1947; A 1949, 433; 1955, 131]

NRS 645.090   Real Estate Commission: Qualifications of members.   Each member of the Commission must:

1.   Be a citizen of the United States.

2.   Have been a resident of the State of Nevada for not less than 5 years.

3.   Have been actively engaged in business as:

(a)   A real estate broker within the State of Nevada for at least 3 years immediately preceding the date of appointment; or

(b)   A real estate broker-salesperson within the State of Nevada for at least 5 years immediately preceding the date of appointment.

[Part 6:150:1947; A 1949, 433; 1955, 131]—(NRS A 1981, 1605; 1987, 912)

NRS 645.100   Real Estate Commission: Residency of members.

1.   Of the five members appointed to the Commission pursuant to NRS 645.050:

(a)   Three members must reside in or have a principal place of business located in Clark County;

(b)   One member must reside in or have a principal place of business located in Washoe County; and

(c)   One member must reside in or have a principal place of business located in Carson City or Churchill, Douglas, Elko, Esmeralda, Eureka, Humboldt, Lander, Lincoln, Lyon, Mineral, Nye, Pershing, Storey or White Pine County.

2.   For purposes of appointing a member or filling a vacancy in the membership of the Commission, if no qualified person is willing to serve on the Commission from the region prescribed in:

(a)   Paragraph (a) of subsection 1, the Governor must appoint a qualified person who is willing to serve on the Commission from the region prescribed in paragraph (c) of subsection 1 or, if there is no such person, a qualified person who is willing to serve on the Commission from the region prescribed in paragraph (b) of subsection 1.

(b)   Paragraph (b) of subsection 1, the Governor must appoint a qualified person who is willing to serve on the Commission from the region prescribed in paragraph (a) of subsection 1 or, if there is no such person, a qualified person who is willing to serve on the Commission from the region prescribed in paragraph (c) of subsection 1.

(c)   Paragraph (c) of subsection 1, the Governor must appoint a qualified person who is willing to serve on the Commission from the region prescribed in paragraph (b) of subsection 1 or, if there is no such person, a qualified person who is willing to serve on the Commission from the region prescribed in paragraph (a) of subsection 1.

If there is no qualified person willing to be appointed or to fill a vacancy on the Commission from any region, the seat must be left vacant.

3. At the expiration of the term of a member who is appointed from outside a prescribed region pursuant to paragraph (a), (b) or (c) of subsection 2 or if that member vacates the seat, the Governor must appoint a qualified person from the prescribed region or, if no qualified person is willing to serve on the Commission from that region, appoint a qualified person pursuant to paragraph (a), (b) or (c) of subsection 2, as applicable.

4. The apportionment of members pursuant to subsection 1 is intended to give approximately proportional regional representation on the Commission to the residents of this State. In each regular legislative session following the completion of a decennial census conducted by the Bureau of the Census of the United States Department of Commerce, the apportionment of members on the Commission must be reconsidered to ensure approximately proportional regional representation is maintained. Any reapportionment of a seat pursuant to this subsection does not become effective until the expiration of the term of the member who holds the seat immediately preceding the date of the reapportionment.

[Part 6:150:1947; A 1949, 433; 1955, 131]—(NRS A 1959, 393; 1969, 343, 893; 1981, 1328; 2015, 2684)

NRS 645.110 Real Estate Commission: Officers.   The Commission, at the first meeting of each fiscal year, shall elect a President, a Vice President and a Secretary to serve for the ensuing year.

[Part 6:150:1947; A 1949, 433; 1955, 131]—(NRS A 1963, 161, 663; 1981, 1606)

NRS 645.120 Administrator: Qualifications; restrictions.   The Administrator shall:

1. Possess a broad knowledge of generally accepted real estate practice and be reasonably well informed on laws governing real estate agency contracts.

2. Not be interested in any real estate firm or brokerage firm, nor shall he or she act as a broker or salesperson or agent therefor.

[Part 6:150:1947; A 1949, 433; 1955, 131]—(NRS A 1957, 337; 1959, 394; 1963, 664; 1967, 931; 1975, 351; 1985, 1261)

NRS 645.130 Employees, legal counsel, investigators and other professional consultants of Real Estate Division; restrictions.

1. The Real Estate Division may employ:

(a) Legal counsel, investigators and other professional consultants without regard to the provisions of chapter 284 of NRS.

(b) Such other employees as are necessary to the discharge of its duties.

2. No employee of the Real Estate Division may be interested in any real estate firm or brokerage firm, nor may any employee act as a broker or salesperson or agent therefor.

[Part 6:150:1947; A 1949, 433; 1955, 131]—(NRS A 1963, 162, 664; 1967, 1503; 1971, 1442; 1981, 1285; 1985, 445, 1261)

NRS 645.140 Deposit and use of money received by Division; salary of members; per diem allowance and travel expenses of members and employees of Commission.

1. Except as otherwise provided in this section, all fees, penalties and charges received by the Division pursuant to NRS 645.410, 645.660 and 645.830 must be deposited with the State Treasurer for credit to the State General Fund.

2. The fees received by the Division:

(a) From the sale of publications must be retained by the Division to pay the costs of printing and distributing publications.

(b) For examinations must be retained by the Division to pay the costs of the administration of examinations.
☐ Any surplus of the fees retained by the Division for the administration of examinations must be deposited with the State Treasurer for credit to the State General Fund.

3. Money for the support of the Division must be provided by direct legislative appropriation, and be paid out on claims as other claims against the State are paid.

4. Each member of the Commission is entitled to receive:

(a) A salary of not more than $150 per day, as fixed by the Commission, while engaged in the business of the Commission; and

(b) A per diem allowance and travel expenses at a rate fixed by the Commission, while engaged in the business of the Commission. The rate must not exceed the rate provided for state officers and employees generally.

5. While engaged in the business of the Commission, each employee of the Commission is entitled to receive a per diem allowance and travel expenses at a rate fixed by the Commission. The rate must not exceed the rate provided for state officers and employees generally.

[Part 6:150:1947; A 1949, 433; 1955, 131]—(NRS A 1957, 547; 1960, 305; 1963, 162, 664; 1965, 1140; 1967, 931; 1973, 1098; 1975, 307; 1979, 1536; 1981, 1995; 1983, 332, 1544, 1546; 1985, 445; 1989, 1705; 1995, 161; 1997, 847; 2007, 2958; 2015, 2780)

NRS 645.145   Real Estate Commission: Fiscal year.   The Commission shall operate on the basis of a fiscal year commencing on July 1 and terminating on June 30.

(Added to NRS by 1963, 161)

NRS 645.150   Real Estate Commission: Meetings.

1. The Commission may hold at least two regular meetings annually, one of which must be held in the southern part of the State, and one of which must be held in the northern part of the State, at such place or places as the Commission designates for that purpose.

2. Additional meetings of the Commission may be held at the call of the President when there is sufficient business to come before the Commission to warrant such action, at any place convenient to the Commission, or upon written request of two members of the Commission. Written notice of the time, place and purpose of all meetings must be given to each member at least 3 working days before the meeting.

[Part 6:150:1947; A 1949, 433; 1955, 131]—(NRS A 1959, 394; 1981, 1606; 1983, 1448)

NRS 645.160   Real Estate Commission: Quorum; effect of vacancy; act of majority.

1. A majority of the Commission shall constitute a quorum for the transaction of business, for the performance of any duty, or for the exercise of any power or authority of the Commission.

2. A vacancy on the Commission shall not impair the right of the remaining members to perform all of the duties and exercise all of the power and authority of the Commission.

3. The act of the majority of the Commission when in session as a Commission shall constitute the act of the Commission.

[Part 6:150:1947; A 1949, 433; 1955, 131]

NRS 645.170   Real Estate Division: Principal and branch offices.

1. The Director shall designate the location of the principal office of the Real Estate Division. The Administrator shall conduct business primarily in the principal office of the Real Estate Division.

2. If the principal office of the Real Estate Division is located in:

(a) The southern district of Nevada created pursuant to subsection 3 of NRS 645.100, the Real Estate Division shall establish at least one branch office in the northern district of Nevada created pursuant to subsection 4 of NRS 645.100.

(b) The northern district of Nevada, the Real Estate Division shall establish at least one branch office in the southern district of Nevada.

3. The Real Estate Division may designate other convenient places within the State for the establishment of branch offices.

[Part 6:150:1947; A 1949, 433; 1955, 131]—(NRS A 1963, 664; 1995, 993)

NRS 645.180   Real Estate Division: Seal; general provisions governing public inspection and confidentiality of records; admissibility of certified copies of records as evidence.

1. The Division shall adopt a seal by which it shall authenticate its proceedings.

2. Except as otherwise provided in NRS 645.625, records kept in the office of the Division under authority of this chapter are open to public inspection under regulations adopted by the Division, except that the Division may refuse to make public, unless ordered to do so by a court:

(a) Real estate brokers' and real estate salespersons' examinations; and

(b) The criminal and financial records of licensees, applicants for licenses and owner-developers.

3. Copies of all records and papers in the office of the Division, certified and authenticated by the seal of the Division, must be received in evidence in all courts equally and with like effect as the originals.

[Part 6:150:1947; A 1949, 433; 1955, 131]—(NRS A 1963, 665; 1975, 1541; 1979, 1537; 2003, 3464)

NRS 645.190 Powers of Real Estate Division; regulations of Commission or Administrator; publication of manual or guide.

1. The Division may do all things necessary and convenient for carrying into effect the provisions of this chapter.

2. The Commission or the Administrator, with the approval of the Commission, may from time to time adopt reasonable regulations for the administration of this chapter. When regulations are proposed by the Administrator, in addition to other notices required by law, the Administrator shall provide copies of the proposed regulations to the Commission no later than 30 days before the next Commission meeting. The Commission shall approve, amend or disapprove any proposed regulations at that meeting.

3. All regulations adopted by the Commission, or adopted by the Administrator with the approval of the Commission, must be published by the Division and offered for sale at a reasonable fee.

4. The Division may publish or supply a reference manual or study guide for licensees or applicants for licenses, and may offer it for sale at a reasonable fee.

[Part 6:150:1947; A 1949, 433; 1955, 131]—(NRS A 1963, 1073; 1973, 1099; 1975, 1542; 1977, 91; 1979, 1537)

NRS 645.191 Authority for Real Estate Division to conduct business electronically; regulations; fees; use of unsworn declaration; exclusions.

1. The Administrator may adopt regulations which establish procedures for the Division to conduct business electronically pursuant to title 59 of NRS with persons who are regulated pursuant to this chapter and with any other persons with whom the Division conducts business. The regulations may include, without limitation, the establishment of fees to pay the costs of conducting business electronically with the Division.

2. In addition to the process authorized by NRS 719.280, if the Division is conducting business electronically with a person and a law requires a signature or record to be notarized, acknowledged, verified or made under oath, the Division may allow the person to substitute a declaration that complies with the provisions of NRS 53.045 or 53.250 to 53.390, inclusive, to satisfy the legal requirement.

3. The Division may refuse to conduct business electronically with a person who has failed to pay money which the person owes to the Division or the Commission.

(Added to NRS by 2003, 1288; A 2011, 17) *Cover This.*

NRS 645.193 Real Estate Division to prepare and distribute forms setting forth certain duties owed by licensees. The Division shall prepare and distribute to licensees:

1. A form which sets forth the duties owed by a licensee who is acting for only one party to a real estate transaction.

2. A form which sets forth the duties owed by a licensee who is acting for more than one party to a real estate transaction.

3. A form which sets forth the duties owed by a real estate broker who assigns different licensees affiliated with his or her brokerage to separate parties to a real estate transaction.

(Added to NRS by 1995, 2073) *—must Go over it with client.*

NRS 645.194 Real Estate Division to prepare booklet concerning certain disclosures required in sale of residential property.

1. The Division shall prepare a booklet that provides relevant information concerning the disclosures that are required by federal, state and local laws and regulations by a buyer and a seller in a transaction involving the sale of residential property.

2. The Division shall make copies of the booklet prepared pursuant to subsection 1 available to licensees which the licensee must distribute to prospective buyers and sellers in the sale of residential property in accordance with the regulations adopted by the Commission.

3. The Commission shall approve the format and content of the information that must be included in the booklet.

4. As used in this section, "residential property" has the meaning ascribed to it in NRS 113.100.

(Added to NRS by 2005, 1285)

NRS 645.195 Inspection of records of broker and owner-developer by Real Estate Division; regulations.

1. The Division shall regularly inspect the transaction files, trust records and pertinent real estate business accounts of all real estate brokers and owner-developers to ensure compliance with the provisions of this chapter.

2. The Commission shall adopt regulations pertaining to those inspections.

(Added to NRS by 1973, 989; A 1975, 1542; 1979, 1537)

NRS 645.200 Attorney General: Opinions and action as attorney.

1. The Attorney General shall render to the Division opinions upon all questions of law relating to the construction or interpretation of this chapter, or arising in the administration thereof, that may be submitted to the Attorney General by the Division or the Commission.

2. The Attorney General shall act as the attorney for the Division in all actions and proceedings brought against or by the Division pursuant to any of the provisions of this chapter.

[7:150:1947; 1943 NCL § 6396.07]—(NRS A 1963, 665; 1979, 1537)

NRS 645.210 Injunctions.

1. Whenever the Real Estate Division believes from evidence satisfactory to it that any person has violated or is about to violate any of the provisions of this chapter, or any order, license, permit, decision, demand or requirement, or any part or provision thereof, it may bring an action, in the name of the Real Estate Division, in the district court of the State of Nevada in and for the county wherein such person resides, or, if such person resides outside the State of Nevada, in any court of competent jurisdiction within or outside the State of Nevada, against such person to enjoin such person from continuing such violation or engaging therein or doing any act or acts in furtherance thereof.

2. If this action is in a district court of the State of Nevada, an order or judgment may be entered awarding such preliminary or final injunction as may be proper, but no preliminary injunction or temporary restraining order shall be granted without at least 5 days' notice to the opposite party.

[31:150:1947; 1943 NCL § 6396.31]—(NRS A 1963, 665; 1973, 1099)

NRS 645.215 Investigation by Real Estate Division of certain transactions relating to unimproved land or subdivision; injunction for fraud, deceit or false advertising.

1. If the Real Estate Division has reason to believe that fraud, deceit or false advertising is being, has been or is to be perpetrated in connection with the proposed or completed sale, purchase, rental, lease or exchange of any vacant or unimproved land or subdivision outside the corporate limits of any city, it may investigate the circumstances of such sale, purchase, rental, lease or exchange.

2. If such investigation reveals any evidence of fraud, deceit or false advertising which has influenced or induced or may influence or induce the sale, purchase, rental, lease or exchange, the Real Estate Division shall advise the Attorney General or the district attorney of the county in which the land or subdivision is located. The district attorney or, upon the request of the Administrator, the Attorney General shall cause appropriate legal action to be taken to enjoin any further sale, purchase, rental, lease or exchange until the fraud, deceit or false advertising is eliminated and restitution has been made for any loss.

3. Nothing in this section shall prevent prosecution of any person in a criminal action under the provisions of any other law.

(Added to NRS by 1961, 75; A 1963, 666; 1973, 1099)

REGULATION OF PRACTICES

NRS 645.230 Unlawful to engage in certain conduct without license or permit or without complying with certain provisions of chapter; power of Real Estate Division to file complaint with court and assist in prosecution of violation; prosecution by district attorney or Attorney General.

1. It is unlawful for any person, limited-liability company, partnership, association or corporation to engage in the business of, act in the capacity of, advertise or assume to act as, a:

(a) Real estate broker, real estate broker-salesperson or real estate salesperson within the State of Nevada without first obtaining the appropriate license from the Real Estate Division as provided for in this chapter;

(b) Property manager within the State of Nevada without first obtaining from the Real Estate Division as provided for in this chapter a license as a real estate broker, real estate broker-salesperson or real estate salesperson and a permit to engage in property management;

(c) Designated property manager within the State of Nevada without complying with the provisions of NRS 645.6055;

(d) Business broker within the State of Nevada without first obtaining from the Real Estate Division as provided for in this chapter a license as a real estate broker, real estate broker-salesperson or real estate salesperson and a permit to engage in business as a business broker issued pursuant to the provisions of NRS 645.863; or

(e) Designated business broker within the State of Nevada without complying with the provisions of NRS 645.867.

2. The Real Estate Division may prefer a complaint for a violation of this section before any court of competent jurisdiction and may assist in presenting the law or facts upon any trial for a violation of this section.

14

3. The district attorney of each county shall prosecute all violations of this section in their respective counties in which violations occur, unless prosecuted by the Attorney General. Upon the request of the Administrator, the Attorney General shall prosecute any violation of this section in lieu of the district attorney.

[1:150:1947; 1943 NCL § 6396.01]—(NRS A 1963, 666; 1973, 1100; 1981, 514; 1985, 1262; 1997, 166, 957; 2003, 1290; 2005, 649)

NRS 645.235 Administrative fine for engaging in certain conduct without license, permit, certificate, registration or authorization; procedure for imposition of fine; judicial review; exceptions.

1. In addition to any other remedy or penalty, the Commission may impose an administrative fine against any person who knowingly:

(a) Engages or offers to engage in any activity for which a license, permit, certificate or registration or any type of authorization is required pursuant to this chapter, or any regulation adopted pursuant thereto, if the person does not hold the required license, permit, certificate or registration or has not been given the required authorization; or

(b) Assists or offers to assist another person to commit a violation described in paragraph (a).

2. If the Commission imposes an administrative fine against a person pursuant to this section, the amount of the administrative fine may not exceed the amount of any gain or economic benefit that the person derived from the violation or $5,000, whichever amount is greater.

3. In determining the appropriate amount of the administrative fine, the Commission shall consider:

(a) The severity of the violation and the degree of any harm that the violation caused to other persons;

(b) The nature and amount of any gain or economic benefit that the person derived from the violation;

(c) The person's history or record of other violations; and

(d) Any other facts or circumstances that the Commission deems to be relevant.

4. Before the Commission may impose the administrative fine, the Commission must provide the person with notice and an opportunity to be heard.

5. The person is entitled to judicial review of the decision of the Commission in the manner provided by chapter 233B of NRS.

6. The provisions of this section do not apply to a person who engages or offers to engage in activities within the purview of this chapter if:

(a) A specific statute exempts the person from complying with the provisions of this chapter with regard to those activities; and

(b) The person is acting in accordance with the exemption while engaging or offering to engage in those activities.

(Added to NRS by 2003, 1289)

NRS 645.240 Persons to whom chapter does not apply. [Replaced in revision by NRS 645.0445.]

NRS 645.250 Power of cities and towns to license and regulate brokers and salespersons not affected. Nothing contained in this chapter shall affect the power of cities and towns to tax, license and regulate real estate brokers or real estate salespersons. The requirements of this chapter shall be in addition to the requirements of any existing or future ordinance of any city or town so taxing, licensing or regulating real estate brokers or real estate salespersons.

[32:150:1947; 1943 NCL § 6396.32]

NRS 645.251 Licensee not required to comply with certain principles of common law. A licensee is not required to comply with any principles of common law that may otherwise apply to any of the duties of the licensee as set forth in NRS 645.252, 645.253 and 645.254 and the regulations adopted to carry out those sections.

(Added to NRS by 1995, 2072)

NRS 645.2515 Broker's price opinion: Requirements; duties of licensee; regulations.

1. A person licensed pursuant to this chapter may prepare and provide a broker's price opinion and charge and collect a fee therefor if:

(a) The license of that licensee is active and in good standing; and

(b) The broker's price opinion meets the requirements of subsection 3.

2. A person licensed pursuant to this chapter may prepare a broker's price opinion for:

(a) An existing or potential seller for the purposes of listing and selling a parcel of real property;

(b) An existing or potential buyer of a parcel of real property;

15

(c) A third party making decisions or performing due diligence related to the potential listing, offering, sale, exchange, option, lease or acquisition price of a parcel of real property; or

(d) An existing or potential lienholder, except that a broker's price opinion prepared for an existing or potential lienholder may not be used in lieu of an appraisal for the purpose of determining whether to approve a mortgage loan.

3. A broker's price opinion must include, without limitation:

(a) A statement of the intended purpose of the broker's price opinion;

(b) A brief description of the real property and the interest in the real property for which the broker's price opinion is being prepared;

(c) The basis used to determine the broker's price opinion, including, without limitation, any applicable market data and the computation of capitalization;

(d) Any assumptions or limiting conditions used to determine the broker's price opinion;

(e) The date of issuance of the broker's price opinion;

(f) A disclosure of any existing or contemplated interest of every licensee who prepares or provides the broker's price opinion, including, without limitation, the possibility of a licensee representing the seller or purchaser;

(g) The license number, name and signature of every licensee who prepares or provides the broker's price opinion;

(h) If a licensee who prepares or provides the broker's price opinion is a real estate salesperson or a real estate broker-salesperson, the name of the real estate broker with whom the licensee is associated; and

(i) In at least 14-point bold type, the following disclaimer:

Notwithstanding any preprinted language to the contrary, this opinion is not an appraisal of the market value of the property. If an appraisal is desired, the services of a licensed or certified appraiser must be obtained.

4. If a broker's price opinion is submitted electronically or on a form supplied by the requesting party:

(a) A signature required by paragraph (g) of subsection 3 may be an electronic signature, as defined by NRS 719.100.

(b) A signature required by paragraph (g) of subsection 3 and the disclaimer required by paragraph (i) of subsection 3 may be transmitted in a separate attachment if the electronic format or form supplied by the requesting party does not allow additional comments to be written by the licensee. The electronic format or the form supplied by the requesting party must:

(1) Reference the existence of a separate attachment; and

(2) Include a statement that the broker's price opinion is not complete without the attachment.

5. A broker's price opinion that is submitted electronically is subject to any regulations relating to recordkeeping as adopted pursuant to this chapter.

6. A broker is responsible for all activities of a licensee who is associated with the broker and with the preparation of a broker's price opinion.

7. The Commission may adopt regulations prescribing the manner in which a broker's price opinion must be prepared in accordance with the provisions of this section.

8. As used in this section, "broker's price opinion" means a written analysis, opinion or conclusion that a person licensed pursuant to this chapter prepares for a person described in subsection 2 relating to the estimated price for a specified parcel of real property.

(Added to NRS by 2009, 1936)

NRS 645.252 Duties of licensee acting as agent in real estate transaction. A licensee who acts as an agent in a real estate transaction:

1. Shall disclose to each party to the real estate transaction as soon as is practicable:

(a) Any material and relevant facts, data or information which the licensee knows, or which by the exercise of reasonable care and diligence should have known, relating to the property which is the subject of the transaction.

(b) Each source from which the licensee will receive compensation as a result of the transaction.

(c) That the licensee is a principal to the transaction or has an interest in a principal to the transaction.

(d) Except as otherwise provided in NRS 645.253, that the licensee is acting for more than one party to the transaction. If a licensee makes such a disclosure, he or she must obtain the written consent of each party to the transaction for whom the licensee is acting before he or she may continue to act in his or her capacity as an agent. The written consent must include:

(1) A description of the real estate transaction.

(2) A statement that the licensee is acting for two or more parties to the transaction who have adverse interests and that in acting for these parties, the licensee has a conflict of interest.

16

(3) A statement that the licensee will not disclose any confidential information for 1 year after the revocation or termination of any brokerage agreement entered into with a party to the transaction, unless he or she is required to do so by a court of competent jurisdiction or is given written permission to do so by that party.

(4) A statement that a party is not required to consent to the licensee acting on behalf of the party.

(5) A statement that the party is giving consent without coercion and understands the terms of the consent given.

(e) Any changes in the licensee's relationship to a party to the transaction.

2. Shall exercise reasonable skill and care with respect to all parties to the real estate transaction.

3. Shall provide the appropriate form prepared by the Division pursuant to NRS 645.193 to:

(a) Each party for whom the licensee is acting as an agent in the real estate transaction; and

(b) Each unrepresented party to the real estate transaction, if any.

4. Unless otherwise agreed upon in writing, owes no duty to:

(a) Independently verify the accuracy of a statement made by an inspector certified pursuant to chapter 645D of NRS or another appropriate licensed or certified expert.

(b) Conduct an independent inspection of the financial condition of a party to the real estate transaction.

(c) Conduct an investigation of the condition of the property which is the subject of the real estate transaction.

(Added to NRS by 1995, 2072; A 2001, 2892; 2005, 649; 2007, 1788)

NRS 645.253 Licensees affiliated with same brokerage: Additional duties when assigned to separate parties to real estate transaction. If a real estate broker assigns different licensees affiliated with his or her brokerage to separate parties to a real estate transaction, the licensees are not required to obtain the written consent required pursuant to paragraph (d) of subsection 1 of NRS 645.252. Each licensee shall not disclose, except to the real estate broker, confidential information relating to a client in violation of NRS 645.254.

(Added to NRS by 1995, 2073)

> *Test Question*

NRS 645.254 Additional duties of licensee entering into brokerage agreement to represent client in real estate transaction. A licensee who has entered into a brokerage agreement to represent a client in a real estate transaction:

1. Shall exercise reasonable skill and care to carry out the terms of the brokerage agreement and to carry out his or her duties pursuant to the terms of the brokerage agreement;

2. Shall not disclose confidential information relating to a client for 1 year after the revocation or termination of the brokerage agreement, unless he or she is required to do so pursuant to an order of a court of competent jurisdiction or is given written permission to do so by the client;

3. Shall seek a sale, purchase, option, rental or lease of real property at the price and terms stated in the brokerage agreement or at a price acceptable to the client;

4. Shall present all offers made to or by the client as soon as is practicable, unless the client chooses to waive the duty of the licensee to present all offers and signs a waiver of the duty on a form prescribed by the Division;

5. Shall disclose to the client material facts of which the licensee has knowledge concerning the transaction;

6. Shall advise the client to obtain advice from an expert relating to matters which are beyond the expertise of the licensee; and

7. Shall account for all money and property the licensee receives in which the client may have an interest as soon as is practicable.

(Added to NRS by 1995, 2073; A 2007, 1788)

NRS 645.255 Waiver of duties of licensee prohibited. Except as otherwise provided in subsection 4 of NRS 645.254, no duty of a licensee set forth in NRS 645.252 or 645.254 may be waived.

(Added to NRS by 2007, 1787)

NRS 645.256 Broker who provides asset management services to client required to provide Real Estate Division with certain information annually; disciplinary action by Division.

1. A broker who enters into an agreement to provide asset management services to a client shall:

(a) Disclose annually to the Division any such agreements to provide asset management services to a client; and

(b) Provide proof satisfactory to the Division on an annual basis that the broker has complied with the requirements of NRS 645H.490.

2. In addition to any other remedy or penalty, the Division may take administrative action, including, without limitation, the suspension of a license or permit or the imposition of an administrative fine, against a broker who fails to comply with this section.

3. As used in this section:

(a) "Asset management" has the meaning ascribed to it in NRS 645H.030.

(b) "Client" has the meaning ascribed to it in NRS 645H.060.

(Added to NRS by 2011, 2831)

NRS 645.257 Action to recover damages suffered as result of licensee's failure to perform certain duties; standard of care.

1. A person who has suffered damages as the proximate result of a licensee's failure to perform any duties required by NRS 645.252, 645.253 or 645.254 or the regulations adopted to carry out those sections may bring an action against the licensee for the recovery of the person's actual damages.

2. In such an action, any knowledge of the client of the licensee of material facts, data or information relating to the real property which is the subject of the real estate transaction may not be imputed to the licensee.

3. In an action brought by a person against a licensee pursuant to subsection 1, the standard of care owed by a licensee is the degree of care that a reasonably prudent real estate licensee would exercise and is measured by the degree of knowledge required to be obtained by a real estate licensee pursuant to NRS 645.343 and 645.345.

NRS 645.258 Duties concerning transaction involving used manufactured home or used mobile home.

1. In any transaction involving a used manufactured home or used mobile home that has not been converted to real property pursuant to NRS 361.244, a licensee shall provide to the purchaser, on a form prepared by the Real Estate Division, the following disclosures:

(a) The year, serial number and manufacturer of the used manufactured home or used mobile home;

(b) A statement that the used manufactured home or used mobile home is personal property subject to personal property taxes;

(c) A statement of the requirements of NRS 489.521 and 489.531; and

(d) Such other disclosures as may be required by the Real Estate Division.

2. The disclosures required pursuant to subsection 1 do not constitute a warranty as to the title or condition of the used manufactured home or used mobile home.

3. A real estate broker who represents a client in such a transaction shall take such actions as necessary to ensure that the client complies with the requirements of NRS 489.521 and 489.531.

(Added to NRS by 2005, 665)

NRS 645.259 Liability of licensee for misrepresentation made by client; failure of seller to make required disclosures is public record. A licensee may not be held liable for:

1. A misrepresentation made by his or her client unless the licensee:

(a) Knew the client made the misrepresentation; and

(b) Failed to inform the person to whom the client made the misrepresentation that the statement was false.

2. Except as otherwise provided in this subsection, the failure of the seller to make the disclosures required by NRS 113.130 and 113.135 if the information that would have been disclosed pursuant to NRS 113.130 and 113.135 is a public record which is readily available to the client. Notwithstanding the provisions of this subsection, a licensee is not relieved of the duties imposed by paragraph (a) of subsection 1 of NRS 645.252.

(Added to NRS by 1995, 2074; A 2001, 2893)

NRS 645.260 One act constitutes action in capacity of broker or salesperson. Any person, limited-liability company, partnership, association or corporation who, for another, in consideration of compensation by fee, commission, salary or otherwise, or with the intention or expectation of receiving compensation, does, offers or attempts or agrees to do, engages in, or offers or attempts or agrees to engage in, either directly or indirectly, any single act or transaction contained in the definition of a real estate broker in NRS 645.030, whether the act is an incidental part of a transaction, or the entire transaction, is acting in the capacity of a real estate broker or real estate salesperson within the meaning of this chapter.

[4:150:1947; 1943 NCL § 6396.04]—(NRS A 1985, 1263; 1997, 166)

NRS 645.270 Allegation and proof of licensed status in action for compensation. A person, limited-liability company, partnership, association or corporation engaged in the business or acting in the capacity of a real estate broker or a real estate salesperson within this State may not commence or maintain any action in the courts of this State for the collection of compensation for the performance of any of the acts mentioned in NRS 645.030 without alleging and proving that the person, limited-liability company, partnership, association or corporation was a licensed real estate broker or real estate salesperson at the time the alleged cause of action arose.

[30:150:1947; 1943 NCL § 6396.30]—(NRS A 1985, 1263; 1997, 166)

NRS 645.280 Association with or compensation of unlicensed broker, broker-salesperson or salesperson unlawful; payment of commission other than through broker or owner-developer unlawful.

1. It is unlawful for any licensed real estate broker, or broker-salesperson or salesperson to offer, promise, allow, give or pay, directly or indirectly, any part or share of his or her commission, compensation or finder's fee arising or accruing from any real estate transaction to any person who is not a licensed real estate broker, broker-salesperson or salesperson, in consideration of services performed or to be performed by the unlicensed person. A licensed real estate broker may pay a commission to a licensed broker of another state.

2. A real estate broker-salesperson or salesperson shall not be associated with or accept compensation from any person other than the broker or owner-developer under whom he or she is licensed at the time of the real estate transaction.

3. It is unlawful for any licensed real estate broker-salesperson or salesperson to pay a commission to any person except through the broker or owner-developer under whom he or she is licensed at the time of the real estate transaction.

[26:150:1947; 1943 NCL § 6396.26]—(NRS A 1959, 394; 1975, 1542; 1979, 1538; 1985, 1263; 2005, 1286)

NRS 645.283 Owner-developers: Employment of licensed salespersons; association with qualified sales manager; registration.

1. Except as otherwise provided in subsection 2, an owner-developer who is registered with the Real Estate Division may employ one or more licensed real estate salespersons to sell any single-family residence, owned by the owner-developer and not previously sold, which is within the area covered by his or her current registration.

2. An owner-developer may not employ a licensed real estate salesperson pursuant to subsection 1 unless a licensed real estate broker-salesperson who is qualified pursuant to NRS 645.289 is associated with the owner-developer as a sales manager to oversee the activities of the real estate salesperson.

3. The area covered by an owner-developer's registration may be enlarged from time to time upon application and payment of the required fee.

4. Registration may be kept in force by annual renewal.

(Added to NRS by 1975, 1639; A 2005, 1287)

NRS 645.285 Owner-developers: Form and contents of application for registration. → *Read it.*

1. Application for original registration as an owner-developer shall be made on a form provided by the Division, and shall set forth:

(a) The limits of the area within which the applicant owns the residences proposed to be sold;

(b) The location of the applicant's principal place of business; and

(c) Any further information required by regulations of the Commission.

2. An application to enlarge the area covered by a registration shall set forth the limits of the area to be added.

(Added to NRS by 1975, 1639)

NRS 645.287 Owner-developers: Regulations concerning qualifications; principal place of business and records.

1. Regulations adopted by the Real Estate Commission shall not establish any educational qualification or require any examination of an owner-developer, but shall provide appropriate standards of good moral character and financial stability.

2. Each owner-developer shall maintain a principal place of business and keep there the records concerning salespersons employed by the owner-developer.

(Added to NRS by 1975, 1639)

NRS 645.289 Owner-developers: Qualifications and duties of person who acts as sales manager.

1. To qualify as a sales manager for the purposes of NRS 645.283, a licensed real estate broker-salesperson must have at least 2 years of experience during the immediately preceding 4 years as a real estate broker-salesperson or salesperson licensed in this State or any other state or territory of the United States, or the District of Columbia.

2. A real estate broker-salesperson shall:

(a) Before becoming associated with an owner-developer as a sales manager, notify the Division on a form prescribed by the Division that he or she will be acting in that capacity; and

(b) Upon the termination of his or her association with an owner-developer as a sales manager, notify the Division of that fact.

(Added to NRS by 2005, 1286)

NRS 645.300 Delivery of copy of written brokerage agreement; receipt. When a licensee prepares or has prepared a written brokerage agreement authorizing or employing the licensee to purchase or sell real estate for compensation or commission, the licensee shall deliver a copy of the written brokerage agreement to the client signing it at the time the signature is obtained, if possible, or otherwise within a reasonable time thereafter. Receipt for the copy may be made on the face of the written brokerage agreement.

[28:150:1947; 1943 NCL § 6396.28]—(NRS A 1979, 1539; 1995, 2074)

NRS 645.310 Deposits and trust accounts: Accounting; commingling; records; inspection and audit.

1. All deposits accepted by every real estate broker or person registered as an owner-developer pursuant to this chapter, which are retained by him or her pending consummation or termination of the transaction involved, must be accounted for in the full amount at the time of the consummation or termination.

2. Every real estate salesperson or broker-salesperson who receives any money on behalf of a broker or owner-developer shall pay over the money promptly to the real estate broker or owner-developer.

3. A real estate broker shall not commingle the money or other property of a client with his or her own.

4. If a real estate broker receives money, as a broker, which belongs to others, the real estate broker shall promptly deposit the money in a separate checking account located in a bank or credit union in this State which must be designated a trust account. All down payments, earnest money deposits, rents, or other money which the real estate broker receives, on behalf of a client or any other person, must be deposited in the account unless all persons who have any interest in the money have agreed otherwise in writing. A real estate broker may pay to any seller or the seller's authorized agent the whole or any portion of such special deposit. The real estate broker is personally responsible and liable for such deposit at all times. A real estate broker shall not permit any advance payment of money belonging to others to be deposited in the real estate broker's business or personal account or to be commingled with any money he or she may have on deposit.

5. Every real estate broker required to maintain a separate trust account shall keep records of all money deposited therein. The records must clearly indicate the date and from whom the real estate broker received money, the date deposited, the dates of withdrawals, and other pertinent information concerning the transaction, and must show clearly for whose account the money is deposited and to whom the money belongs. The real estate broker shall balance each separate trust account at least monthly. The real estate broker shall provide to the Division, on a form provided by the Division, an annual accounting which shows an annual reconciliation of each separate trust account. All such records and money are subject to inspection and audit by the Division and its authorized representatives. All such separate trust accounts must designate the real estate broker as trustee and provide for withdrawal of money without previous notice.

6. Each real estate broker shall notify the Division of the names of the banks and credit unions in which the real estate broker maintains trust accounts and specify the names of the accounts on forms provided by the Division.

7. If a real estate broker who has money in a trust account dies or becomes mentally disabled, the Division, upon application to the district court, may have a trustee appointed to administer and distribute the money in the account with the approval of the court. The trustee may serve without posting a bond.

[27.5:150:1947; added 1955, 76]—(NRS A 1963, 1073; 1975, 1543; 1979, 1539; 1981, 1606; 1983, 152; 1995, 2074; 1997, 958; 1999, 1538)

NRS 645.313 Other financial accounts: Investigation and audit involving insolvency of broker or enforcement by Division; regulations governing scope of audit; grounds for disciplinary action.

1. The Division may investigate and audit all financial accounts related to the business of a real estate broker, regardless of whether it is a trust account, if the Division has reasonable cause to believe that the broker is using or has used the account to operate or carry on the broker's business and the Division:

(a) Has reasonable cause to believe or has received a credible complaint that the real estate broker is insolvent or is in any financial condition or has engaged in any financial practice which creates a substantial risk of insolvency; or

(b) Determines that the investigation and audit are reasonably necessary to assist the Division in administering or enforcing any other provision of this chapter or any other statute that the Division is charged with administering or enforcing.

2. The Commission shall adopt regulations prescribing the scope of an audit conducted pursuant to this section.

20

3. The Commission may take action pursuant to NRS 645.630 against:

(a) Any real estate broker or other licensee who knowingly fails to cooperate or comply with or knowingly impedes or interferes with any investigation or audit conducted by the Division pursuant to this section; or

(b) Any real estate broker who is insolvent or who is in any financial condition or has engaged in any financial practice which creates a substantial risk of insolvency.

4. As used in this section, "insolvent" or "insolvency" means a condition in which a real estate broker is unable to meet the liabilities of the broker's business as those liabilities become due in the regular course of the broker's business and which creates a substantial risk of harm to the public or a consumer.

(Added to NRS by 2003, 1288)

NRS 645.314 Administrator may charge broker for costs and fees of audit under certain circumstances; additional grounds for disciplinary action.

1. The Administrator may charge and collect from a real estate broker an amount equal to the amount of the actual costs and fees incurred by the Division to conduct an audit of the financial accounts of the real estate broker pursuant to this chapter or any regulations adopted pursuant thereto if:

(a) The Division makes a request during the course of the audit for the real estate broker to produce, provide access to or grant authorization to the Division to inspect or obtain any documentation related to the business of a real estate broker which the broker is required to maintain pursuant to NRS 645.310 and any regulations adopted pursuant to this chapter;

(b) The real estate broker fails to comply with the request within a reasonable time established by the Division; and

(c) The Division has reasonable cause to believe that the requested documentation will assist it in investigating whether the real estate broker has committed any act or offense that would be grounds for taking disciplinary action against the real estate broker.

2. If the Administrator charges a real estate broker for the costs and fees of an audit pursuant to subsection 1, the Administrator shall bill the real estate broker upon the completion of the audit. The costs and fees must be paid within 90 days after the date the real estate broker receives the bill. Except as otherwise provided in this subsection, any payment received after the due date must include a penalty in the amount of 10 percent of the amount specified in the bill plus an additional penalty in the amount of 1 percent of the amount for each month, or portion of a month, that the bill is not paid. The Administrator may waive the penalty for good cause.

3. The failure of a real estate broker to pay any costs and fees as required by this section constitutes grounds for disciplinary action against the real estate broker.

4. Money received by the Division pursuant to this section must be:

(a) Deposited with the State Treasurer for credit to the appropriate account of the Division.

(b) Used by the Division only to offset the fees and costs incurred by the Division in carrying out the provisions of NRS 645.313.

(Added to NRS by 2005, 1285)

NRS 645.315 Conditions and limitations on certain advertisements; required disclosures; prohibited acts.

1. In any advertisement through which a licensee offers to perform services for which a license is required pursuant to this chapter, the licensee shall:

(a) If the licensee is a real estate broker, disclose the name of any brokerage under which the licensee does business; or

(b) If the licensee is a real estate broker-salesperson or real estate salesperson, disclose the name of the brokerage with whom the licensee is associated.

2. If a licensee is a real estate broker-salesperson or real estate salesperson, the licensee shall not advertise solely under the licensee's own name when acting in the capacity as a broker-salesperson or salesperson. All such advertising must be done under the direct supervision of and in the name of the brokerage with whom the licensee is associated.

(Added to NRS by 1999, 92; A 2003, 932)

NRS 645.320 Requirements for exclusive agency representation. Every brokerage agreement which includes a provision for an exclusive agency representation must:

1. Be in writing.

2. Have set forth in its terms a definite, specified and complete termination.

3. Contain no provision which requires the client who signs the brokerage agreement to notify the real estate broker of the client's intention to cancel the exclusive features of the brokerage agreement after the termination of the brokerage agreement.

4. Be signed by both the client or his or her authorized representative and the broker or his or her authorized representative in order to be enforceable.

[28.5:150:1947; added 1955, 18]—(NRS A 1995, 2075; 2003, 932)

NRS 645.3205 Dealing with party to real estate transaction in manner which is deceitful, fraudulent or dishonest prohibited. A licensee shall not deal with any party to a real estate transaction in a manner which is deceitful, fraudulent or dishonest.

(Added to NRS by 1995, 2074)

NRS 645.321 Discriminatory practices unlawful; penalty.

1. It is unlawful, on account of race, religious creed, color, national origin, disability, sexual orientation, gender identity or expression, ancestry, familial status or sex, to:

(a) Discriminate against any person:

(1) By denying the person access to or membership or participation in any multiple-listing service, real estate brokers' organization or other service or facility relating to the sale or rental of dwellings; or

(2) In the terms or conditions of such access, membership or participation.

(b) Discriminate against any person:

(1) By denying the person access to any opportunity to engage in a transaction regarding residential real estate; or

(2) In the terms or conditions of such a transaction.

2. Any person violating the provisions of subsection 1 shall be punished by a fine of $500 for the first offense and for the second offense shall show cause why his or her license should not be revoked by the Commission.

3. As used in this section:

(a) "Disability" means, with respect to a person:

(1) A physical or mental impairment that substantially limits one or more of the major life activities of the person;

(2) A record of such an impairment; or

(3) Being regarded as having such an impairment.

(b) "Familial status" means the fact that a person:

(1) Lives with a child under the age of 18 and has:

(I) Lawful custody of the child; or

(II) Written permission to live with the child from the person who has lawful custody of the child;

(2) Is pregnant; or

(3) Has begun a proceeding to adopt or otherwise obtain lawful custody of a child.

(c) "Gender identity or expression" means a gender-related identity, appearance, expression or behavior of a person, regardless of the person's assigned sex at birth.

(d) "Sexual orientation" means having or being perceived as having an orientation for heterosexuality, homosexuality or bisexuality.

(Added to NRS by 1971, 733; A 1991, 1983; 1995, 1994; 2011, 872)

ADVANCE FEES

NRS 645.322 Accounting of use of advance fee charged or collected; Division may demand accounting. Any person or entity who charges or collects an advance fee shall, within 3 months after the charge or collection, furnish to his or her client an accounting of the use of that money. The Real Estate Division may also demand an accounting by such person or entity of advance fees so collected.

(Added to NRS by 1957, 211; A 1963, 667; 1995, 2075)

NRS 645.323 License required for acceptance of advance fee listing. A person shall not accept an advance fee listing unless he or she is licensed as a real estate broker, broker-salesperson or salesperson pursuant to this chapter.

NRS 645.324 Forms of brokerage agreements; reports and forms of accounting; regulations; maintenance of agreements for review and audit; grounds for disciplinary action.

1. The Commission may require such forms of brokerage agreements which include provisions for the payment of advance fees to be used, and such reports and forms of accounting to be kept, made and submitted, and may adopt such rules and regulations as the Commission may determine to be necessary to carry out the purposes and intent of NRS 645.322.

2. A licensee shall maintain, for review and audit by the Division, each brokerage agreement that is entered into by the licensee.

3. Any violation of the rules, regulations, orders or requirements of the Commission constitutes grounds for disciplinary action against a licensee.

(Added to NRS by 1957, 211; A 1995, 2075; 1997, 959)

LICENSES

NRS 645.330 General qualifications of applicant; grounds for denial of application; eligibility for licensing as broker.

1. Except as otherwise provided by a specific statute, the Division may approve an application for a license for a person who meets all the following requirements:

(a) Has a good reputation for honesty, trustworthiness and integrity and who offers proof of those qualifications satisfactory to the Division.

(b) Has not made a false statement of material fact on his or her application.

(c) Is competent to transact the business of a real estate broker, broker-salesperson or salesperson in a manner which will safeguard the interests of the public.

(d) Has passed the examination.

(e) Has submitted all information required to complete the application.

2. The Division:

(a) May deny a license to any person who has been convicted of, or entered a plea of guilty, guilty but mentally ill or nolo contendere to, forgery, embezzlement, obtaining money under false pretenses, larceny, extortion, conspiracy to defraud, engaging in a real estate business without a license, possessing for the purpose of sale any controlled substance or any crime involving moral turpitude, in any court of competent jurisdiction in the United States or elsewhere; and

(b) Shall not issue a license to such a person until at least 3 years after:

(1) The person pays any fine or restitution ordered by the court; or

(2) The expiration of the period of the person's parole, probation or sentence,

☐ whichever is later.

3. Suspension or revocation of a license pursuant to this chapter or any prior revocation or current suspension in this or any other state, district or territory of the United States or any foreign country before the date of the application is grounds for refusal to grant a license.

4. Except as otherwise provided in NRS 645.332, a person may not be licensed as a real estate broker unless the person has been actively engaged as a full-time licensed real estate broker-salesperson or salesperson in this State, or actively engaged as a full-time licensed real estate broker, broker-salesperson or salesperson in another state or the District of Columbia, for at least 2 of the 4 years immediately preceding the issuance of a broker's license.

[Part 8:150:1947; A 1949, 433; 1955, 424]—(NRS A 1973, 1101; 1975, 794; 1979, 1540; 1981, 1607; 1983, 163; 1985, 1263; 1993, 2805; 1995, 993, 2477; 1997, 2165; 2003, 1499; 2005, 1287, 1288, 2773, 2807; 2007, 1474)

NRS 645.332 Applicants licensed in another jurisdiction: Exemption from certain examination requirements; issuance of license as broker or broker-salesperson by reciprocity.

1. An applicant for a license as a real estate salesperson is not required to pass the uniform portion of a national real estate examination otherwise required by NRS 645.330 and 645.460 if:

(a) The applicant holds a license in good standing as a real estate broker, broker-salesperson or salesperson issued by another state or territory of the United States, or the District of Columbia;

(b) The requirements for licensure as a real estate salesperson issued in that state or territory of the United States, or the District of Columbia, are substantially equivalent to the requirements in this State for licensure as a real estate salesperson; and

(c) The applicant has passed the examination in that state or territory of the United States, or the District of Columbia.

2. The Division may issue a license as a real estate broker or broker-salesperson to a person who holds a license as a real estate broker or broker-salesperson, or an equivalent license, issued by a state or territory of the United States, or the District of Columbia, if that state or territory, or the District of Columbia, has entered into a reciprocal agreement with the Commission for the issuance of licenses pursuant to this chapter and the person submits proof to the Division that:

(a) The person has been issued a license as a real estate broker or broker-salesperson, or an equivalent license, by that state or territory of the United States, or the District of Columbia; and

(b) At the time the person files an application with the Division, the license is in good standing.

3. The Division may refuse to issue a license as a real estate broker or broker-salesperson pursuant to subsection 2 to a person who has committed any act or offense that would be grounds for denying a license to an applicant or taking disciplinary action against a licensee pursuant to this chapter.

4. The Commission shall not enter into a reciprocal agreement pursuant to subsection 2 unless the provisions relating to the practice of real estate, including the requirements for the licensing of real estate brokers and real estate broker-salespersons in the other state or territory of the United States, or the District of Columbia, are substantially similar to the provisions relating to the practice of real estate in this State.

(Added to NRS by 2005, 1284)

NRS 645.335 Depository financial institution prohibited from being licensed.

1. For the purposes of this section, "depository financial institution" means any bank, savings and loan association, savings bank, thrift company, credit union or other institution which:

(a) Holds or receives deposits, savings or share accounts;

(b) Issues certificates of deposit; or

(c) Provides to its customers other depository accounts which are subject to withdrawal by checks, drafts or other instruments or by electronic means to effect payment to a third party.

2. The purposes of this section are to help maintain the separation between depository financial institutions and the business of real estate and to minimize the possibility of unfair competitive activities by depository financial institutions against real estate brokers and salespersons.

3. No depository financial institution or its holding company, parent, subsidiary or affiliate may directly or indirectly be licensed to sell real estate in this State.

(Added to NRS by 1985, 1507)   → 64 - 16 Magic number   1st photo

NRS 645.343 Educational requirements; regulations of Commission concerning standards of education.

1. In addition to the other requirements contained in this chapter, an applicant for an original real estate salesperson's license must furnish proof satisfactory to the Real Estate Division that the applicant has successfully completed a course of instruction in the principles, practices, procedures, law and ethics of real estate, which course may be an extension or correspondence course offered by the Nevada System of Higher Education, by any other accredited college or university or by any other college or school approved by the Commission. The course of instruction must include the subject of disclosure of required information in real estate transactions, including instruction on methods a seller may use to obtain the required information.

2. An applicant for an original real estate broker's or broker-salesperson's license must furnish proof satisfactory to the Real Estate Division that the applicant has successfully completed 45 semester units or the equivalent in quarter units of college level courses which include:

(a) Three semester units or an equivalent number of quarter units in real estate law, including at least 18 classroom hours of the real estate law of Nevada and another course of equal length in the principles of real estate;

(b) Nine semester units or the equivalent in quarter units of college level courses in real estate appraisal and business or economics;

(c) Nine semester units or the equivalent in quarter units of college level courses in real estate, business or economics; and

(d) Three semester units or an equivalent number of quarter units in broker management.

3. On and after January 1, 1986, in addition to other requirements contained in this chapter, an applicant for an original real estate broker's or broker-salesperson's license must furnish proof satisfactory to the Real Estate Division that the applicant has completed 64 semester units or the equivalent in quarter units of college level courses. This educational requirement includes and is not in addition to the requirements listed in subsection 2.

4. For the purposes of this section, each person who holds a license as a real estate broker, broker-salesperson or salesperson, or an equivalent license, issued by a state or territory of the United States, or the District of Columbia, is entitled to receive credit for the equivalent of 16 semester units of college level courses for each 2 years of active experience that, during the immediately preceding 10 years, the person has obtained while he or she has held such a license, not to exceed 8 years of active experience. This credit may not be applied against the requirement in subsection 2 for three semester units or an equivalent number of quarter units in broker management or 18 classroom hours of the real estate law of Nevada.

5. An applicant for a broker's license pursuant to NRS 645.350 must meet the educational prerequisites applicable on the date his or her application is received by the Real Estate Division.

6. As used in this section, "college level courses" are courses offered by any accredited college or university or by any other institution which meet the standards of education established by the Commission. The Commission may adopt regulations setting forth standards of education which are equivalent to the college level courses outlined in this subsection. The regulations may take into account the standard of instructors, the scope and content of the instruction, hours of instruction and such other criteria as the Commission requires.

(Added to NRS by 1960, 155; A 1963, 667; 1969, 1448; 1973, 987, 1591; 1975, 794, 1544, 1639; 1977, 610; 1981, 1032; 1983, 228; 1993, 419; 1995, 505; 1999, 180; 2005, 1288)

NRS 645.345 Regulations of Division concerning schools and courses of instruction in principles and practice of real estate; standard of instruction.   The Division, with the approval of the Commission, shall:
1. Adopt reasonable regulations defining what constitutes:
(a) A course of instruction in real estate principles, practices, procedures, law and ethics, which course of instruction must include the subjects upon which an applicant is examined in determining his or her fitness to receive an original real estate salesperson's license.
(b) A school offering such a course.
2. Adopt regulations providing for the establishment and maintenance of a uniform and reasonable standard of instruction to be observed in and by such schools.

(Added to NRS by 1960, 155; A 1969, 1448; 1975, 1545; 1981, 1034)

NRS 645.350 Application: Form and contents.
1. An application for a license as a real estate broker, broker-salesperson or salesperson must be submitted in writing to the Division upon blanks prepared or furnished by the Division.
2. Every application for a real estate broker's, broker-salesperson's or salesperson's license must set forth the following information:
(a) The name, age and address of the applicant. If the applicant is a partnership or an association which is applying to do business as a real estate broker, the application must contain the name and address of each member thereof. If the application is for a corporation which is applying to do business as a real estate salesperson, real estate broker-salesperson or real estate broker, the application must contain the name and address of each officer and director thereof. If the applicant is a limited-liability company which is applying to do business as a real estate broker, the company's articles of organization must designate a manager, and the name and address of the manager and each member must be listed in the application.
(b) In the case of a broker, the name under which the business is to be conducted. The name is a fictitious name if it does not contain the name of the applicant or the names of the members of the applicant's company, firm, partnership or association. Except as otherwise provided in NRS 645.387, a license must not be issued under a fictitious name which includes the name of a real estate salesperson or broker-salesperson. A license must not be issued under the same fictitious name to more than one licensee within the State. All licensees doing business under a fictitious name shall comply with other pertinent statutory regulations regarding the use of fictitious names.
(c) In the case of a broker, the place or places, including the street number, city and county, where the business is to be conducted.
(d) The business or occupation engaged in by the applicant for at least 2 years immediately preceding the date of the application, and the location thereof.
(e) The time and place of the applicant's previous experience in the real estate business as a broker or salesperson.
(f) Whether the applicant has ever been convicted of or is under indictment for a felony or has entered a plea of guilty, guilty but mentally ill or nolo contendere to a charge of felony and, if so, the nature of the felony.
(g) Whether the applicant has been convicted of or entered a plea of nolo contendere to forgery, embezzlement, obtaining money under false pretenses, larceny, extortion, conspiracy to defraud, engaging in the business of selling real estate without a license or any crime involving moral turpitude.
(h) Whether the applicant has been refused a real estate broker's, broker-salesperson's or salesperson's license in any state, or whether his or her license as a broker or salesperson has been revoked or suspended by any other state, district or territory of the United States or any other country.
(i) If the applicant is a member of a limited-liability company, partnership or association, or an officer of a corporation, the name and address of the office of the limited-liability company, partnership, association or corporation of which the applicant is a member or officer.
(j) All information required to complete the application.

3. An applicant for a license as a broker-salesperson or salesperson shall provide a verified statement from the broker with whom the applicant will be associated, expressing the intent of that broker to associate the applicant with the broker and to be responsible for the applicant's activities as a licensee.

4. If a limited-liability company, partnership or association is to do business as a real estate broker, the application for a broker's license must be verified by at least two members thereof. If a corporation is to do business as a real estate broker, the application must be verified by the president and the secretary thereof.

[Part 9:150:1947; 1943 NCL § 6396.09]—(NRS A 1963, 668; 1967, 932; 1975, 1545; 1979, 1541; 1981, 514, 1608; 1983, 164; 1985, 1264; 1995, 2478; 1997, 167, 2166; 2003, 1500; 2005, 2774, 2807, 2815; 2007, 1474)

NRS 645.355 Investigation of applicant's background; fees; fingerprints.

1. Each applicant for a license as a real estate broker, broker-salesperson or salesperson must pay a fee for the costs of an investigation of the applicant's background.

2. Each applicant must, as part of the application and at his or her own expense:

(a) Arrange to have a complete set of fingerprints taken by a law enforcement agency or other authorized entity acceptable to the Division; and

(b) Submit to the Division:

(1) A completed fingerprint card and written permission authorizing the Division to submit the applicant's fingerprints to the Central Repository for Nevada Records of Criminal History for submission to the Federal Bureau of Investigation for a report on the applicant's background and to such other law enforcement agencies as the Division deems necessary; or

(2) Written verification, on a form prescribed by the Division, stating that the fingerprints of the applicant were taken and directly forwarded electronically or by another means to the Central Repository and that the applicant has given written permission to the law enforcement agency or other authorized entity taking the fingerprints to submit the fingerprints to the Central Repository for submission to the Federal Bureau of Investigation for a report on the applicant's background and to such other law enforcement agencies as the Division deems necessary.

3. The Division may:

(a) Unless the applicant's fingerprints are directly forwarded pursuant to subparagraph (2) of paragraph (b) of subsection 2, submit those fingerprints to the Central Repository for submission to the Federal Bureau of Investigation and to such other law enforcement agencies as the Division deems necessary; and

(b) Request from each such agency any information regarding the applicant's background as the Division deems necessary.

(Added to NRS by 1981, 1616; A 1983, 165; 2003, 1290, 2862; 2005, 1289)

NRS 645.358 Payment of child support: Submission of certain information by applicant; grounds for denial of license; duty of Division. [Effective until the date of the repeal of 42 U.S.C. § 666, the federal law requiring each state to establish procedures for withholding, suspending and restricting the professional, occupational and recreational licenses for child support arrearages and for noncompliance with certain processes relating to paternity or child support proceedings.]

1. In addition to any other requirements set forth in this chapter:

(a) A natural person who applies for the issuance of a license as a real estate broker, broker-salesperson or salesperson shall include the social security number of the applicant in the application submitted to the Division.

(b) A natural person who applies for the issuance or renewal of a license as a real estate broker, broker-salesperson or salesperson shall submit to the Division the statement prescribed by the Division of Welfare and Supportive Services of the Department of Health and Human Services pursuant to NRS 425.520. The statement must be completed and signed by the applicant.

2. The Division shall include the statement required pursuant to subsection 1 in:

(a) The application or any other forms that must be submitted for the issuance or renewal of the license; or

(b) A separate form prescribed by the Division.

3. A license as a real estate broker, broker-salesperson or salesperson may not be issued or renewed by the Division if the applicant is a natural person who:

(a) Fails to submit the statement required pursuant to subsection 1; or

(b) Indicates on the statement submitted pursuant to subsection 1 that the applicant is subject to a court order for the support of a child and is not in compliance with the order or a plan approved by the district attorney or other public agency enforcing the order for the repayment of the amount owed pursuant to the order.

4. If an applicant indicates on the statement submitted pursuant to subsection 1 that the applicant is subject to a court order for the support of a child and is not in compliance with the order or a plan approved by the district attorney or other public agency enforcing the order for the repayment of the amount owed pursuant to the order, the Division shall advise the applicant to contact the district attorney or other public agency enforcing the order to determine the actions that the applicant may take to satisfy the arrearage.

(Added to NRS by 1997, 2163; A 2005, 2775, 2807)

NRS 645.358 Payment of child support: Submission of certain information by applicant; grounds for denial of license; duty of Division. [Effective on the date of the repeal of 42 U.S.C. § 666, the federal law requiring each state to establish procedures for withholding, suspending and restricting the professional, occupational and recreational licenses for child support arrearages and for noncompliance with certain processes relating to paternity or child support proceedings and expires by limitation 2 years after that date.]

1. In addition to any other requirements set forth in this chapter, a natural person who applies for the issuance or renewal of a license as a real estate broker, broker-salesperson or salesperson shall submit to the Division the statement prescribed by the Division of Welfare and Supportive Services of the Department of Health and Human Services pursuant to NRS 425.520. The statement must be completed and signed by the applicant.

2. The Division shall include the statement required pursuant to subsection 1 in:

(a) The application or any other forms that must be submitted for the issuance or renewal of the license; or

(b) A separate form prescribed by the Division.

3. A license as a real estate broker, broker-salesperson or salesperson may not be issued or renewed by the Division if the applicant is a natural person who:

(a) Fails to submit the statement required pursuant to subsection 1; or

(b) Indicates on the statement submitted pursuant to subsection 1 that the applicant is subject to a court order for the support of a child and is not in compliance with the order or a plan approved by the district attorney or other public agency enforcing the order for the repayment of the amount owed pursuant to the order.

4. If an applicant indicates on the statement submitted pursuant to subsection 1 that the applicant is subject to a court order for the support of a child and is not in compliance with the order or a plan approved by the district attorney or other public agency enforcing the order for the repayment of the amount owed pursuant to the order, the Division shall advise the applicant to contact the district attorney or other public agency enforcing the order to determine the actions that the applicant may take to satisfy the arrearage.

(Added to NRS by 1997, 2163; A 2005, 2775, 2776, 2807, effective on the date of the repeal of 42 U.S.C. § 666, the federal law requiring each state to establish procedures for withholding, suspending and restricting the professional, occupational and recreational licenses for child support arrearages and for noncompliance with certain processes relating to paternity or child support proceedings)

NRS 645.370 Issuance of license to certain organizations doing business as broker; restrictions.

1. Each limited-liability company doing business as a real estate broker must designate its manager, each partnership doing business as a real estate broker must designate one of its members, and each corporation doing business as a real estate broker must designate one of its officers, to submit an application for a broker's license.

2. Upon such manager's, member's or officer's successfully passing the examination, and upon compliance with all other requirements of law by the limited-liability company, partnership or corporation, as well as by the designated manager, member or officer, the Division shall issue a broker's license to the manager, member or officer on behalf of the limited-liability company, corporation or partnership, and thereupon the manager, member or officer so designated is entitled to perform all the acts of a real estate broker contemplated by this chapter; except:

(a) That the license entitles the manager, member or officer so designated to act as a real estate broker only as officer or agent of the limited-liability company, partnership or corporation, and not on his or her own behalf, except as otherwise provided in NRS 645.385; and

(b) That if in any case the person so designated is refused a license by the Real Estate Division, or in case the person ceases to be connected with the limited-liability company, partnership or corporation, the limited-liability company, partnership or corporation may designate another person who must apply and qualify as in the first instance.

[Part 9:150:1947; 1943 NCL § 6396.09]—(NRS A 1963, 669; 1975, 1547; 1979, 1543; 1985, 1265; 1997, 168)

NRS 645.380 Issuance of license as broker required for certain members and officers of certain organizations. Each member or officer of a limited-liability company, partnership or corporation who will perform or engage in any of the acts specified in NRS 645.030, other than the manager, member or officer designated for such purpose by the limited-liability company, partnership or corporation in the manner provided in NRS 645.370, must apply for and take out a separate broker's license in his or her own name individually. The license issued to any such member or officer of a limited-liability company, partnership or corporation entitles the member or officer to act as a real estate broker only as an officer or agent of the limited-liability company, partnership or corporation and not on his or her own behalf except as otherwise provided in NRS 645.385.

[Part 9:150:1947; 1943 NCL § 6396.09]—(NRS A 1983, 165; 1985, 1266; 1997, 168)

NRS 645.385 Waiver of requirements of NRS 645.370 **and** 645.380. The Division may waive the requirements of NRS 645.370 and 645.380 by adopting regulations authorizing real estate brokers to act on their own behalf as well as on the behalf of a limited-liability company, corporation or partnership.

(Added to NRS by 1973, 1105; A 1975, 1547; 1985, 1266; 1997, 168)

NRS 645.387 Issuance of license as broker-salesperson or salesperson to sole shareholder of corporation on behalf of corporation or to manager of limited-liability company on behalf of company; restrictions; duties; expiration.

1. Any natural person who meets the qualifications of a real estate broker-salesperson or salesperson and:

(a) Except as otherwise provided in subsection 2, is the sole shareholder of a corporation organized pursuant to the provisions of chapter 89 of NRS; or

(b) Is the manager of a limited-liability company organized pursuant to the provisions of chapter 86 of NRS,

☐ may be licensed on behalf of the corporation or limited-liability company for the purpose of associating with a licensed real estate broker in the capacity of a broker-salesperson or salesperson.

2. The spouse of the owner of the corporation who has a community interest in any shares of the corporation shall not be deemed a second shareholder of the corporation for the purposes of paragraph (a) of subsection 1, if the spouse does not vote any of those shares.

3. A license issued pursuant to this section entitles only the sole shareholder of the corporation or the manager of the limited-liability company to act as a broker-salesperson or salesperson, and only as an officer or agent of the corporation or limited-liability company and not on his or her own behalf. The licensee shall not do or deal in any act, acts or transactions included within the definition of a real estate broker in NRS 645.030, except as that activity is permitted pursuant to this chapter to licensed broker-salespersons and salespersons.

4. The corporation or limited-liability company shall, within 30 days after a license is issued on its behalf pursuant to this section and within 30 days after any change in its ownership, file an affidavit with the Division stating:

(a) For a corporation, the number of issued and outstanding shares of the corporation and the names of all persons to whom the shares have been issued.

(b) For a limited-liability company, the names of members who have an interest in the company.

5. A license issued pursuant to this section automatically expires upon:

(a) The death of the licensed shareholder in the corporation or the manager of the limited-liability company.

(b) The issuance of shares in the corporation to more than one person other than the spouse.

6. Nothing in this section alters any of the rights, duties or liabilities which otherwise arise in the legal relationship between a real estate broker, broker-salesperson or salesperson and a person who deals with him or her.

(Added to NRS by 1981, 513; A 1997, 169)

NRS 645.400 Additional information concerning applicants may be required by Division; regulations concerning applications.

1. In addition to the information required by this chapter, applications for brokers' or salespersons' licenses must contain such other information pertaining to the applicants as the Division may require.

2. The Division may require such other proof through the application or otherwise, with due regard to the paramount interests of the public as to the honesty, truthfulness, integrity and competency of the applicant.

3. The Commission may adopt regulations connected with the application for any examination and license.

[Part 13:150:1947; A 1949, 433; 1943 NCL § 6396.13]—(NRS A 1979, 1543; 1981, 1609)

NRS 645.410 Regulations concerning fees for examination; time for payment of fees.

1. The Commission shall adopt regulations establishing the fee for an examination for a license as a real estate broker, broker-salesperson or salesperson and all other fees necessary for the administration of the examination.

2. Every application for examination for a license as a real estate broker, broker-salesperson or salesperson under the provisions of this chapter must be accompanied by the applicable fees established pursuant to subsection 1. The applicant

must pay the original license fee and the fee for the Real Estate Education, Research and Recovery Fund at the time he or she files an application for a license.

[11:150:1947; 1943 NCL § 6396.11]—(NRS A 1963, 670; 1973, 1102; 1975, 795; 1979, 1543; 1981, 1609; 1985, 1266; 1995, 162)

NRS 645.420 Action on application by Division; additional investigation; invalidation of license for certain errors in issuance.
1. The Division shall notify each applicant in writing whether the applicant passed or failed the examination.
2. The Division shall act upon all applications for licenses as real estate brokers, broker-salespersons or real estate salespersons within 60 days from the date of receiving the completed application for a license.
3. If in the opinion of the Real Estate Division additional investigation of the applicant appears necessary, the Real Estate Division may extend the 60-day period and may make such additional investigation as is necessary or desirable before acting on the applicant's application.
4. The burden of proof is on the applicant to establish to the satisfaction of the Real Estate Division that he or she is qualified to receive a license.
5. Passing the examination creates no vested right in the applicant to hold a license pending an appeal of a denial of his or her licensing by the Division.
6. The Division, upon the discovery of any error in the issuance of a license which is related to the qualification or fitness of the licensee, may invalidate the license. The Division shall promptly notify the licensee, in writing, of the invalidation and the licensee shall surrender the license to the Division within 20 days after notice is sent by the Division. A licensee whose license is invalidated under this subsection and is surrendered within the time specified is entitled to a hearing as for a denial of application in accordance with the provisions of NRS 645.440.

[Part 13:150:1947; A 1949, 433; 1943 NCL § 6396.13]—(NRS A 1963, 670; 1973, 1102; 1975, 796; 1977, 611; 1981, 1329, 1609)

NRS 645.430 Restrictions on reapplication after applicant denied license on ground other than failure of examination. If an applicant shall have been denied a license except for failure to pass an examination, the applicant shall not be permitted to reapply until the Real Estate Division shall, in its discretion, upon petition of the applicant, grant leave to file such reapplication.

[Part 13:150:1947; A 1949, 433; 1943 NCL § 6396.13]—(NRS A 1963, 670)

NRS 645.440 Denial of application: Notice; hearing; written decision; false statement ground for denial.
1. If the Division, after an application for a license in proper form has been filed with it, accompanied by the proper fee, denies an application, the Division shall give notice of the denial to the applicant within 15 days after its ruling, order or decision.
2. Upon written request from the applicant, filed within 30 days after receipt of that notice by the applicant, the President of the Commission shall set the matter for a hearing to be conducted at the next meeting of the Commission held pursuant to NRS 645.150 after receipt of the applicant's request if the request is received at least 20 days before the meeting and contains allegations which, if true, qualify the applicant for a license.
3. The hearing must be held at such time and place as the Commission prescribes. At least 15 days before the date set for the hearing, the Division shall notify the applicant and shall accompany the notification with an exact copy of any protest filed, together with copies of all communications, reports, affidavits or depositions in the possession of the Division relevant to the matter in question. Written notice of the hearing may be served by delivery personally to the applicant, or by mailing it by certified mail to the last known address of the applicant.
4. The hearing may be held by the Commission or by a majority of its members, and a hearing must be held, if the applicant so desires. A record of the proceedings, or any part thereof, must be made available to each party upon the payment to the Division of the reasonable cost of transcription.
5. The Commission shall render a written decision on any appeal within 60 days after the final hearing and shall notify the parties to the proceedings, in writing, of its ruling, order or decision within 15 days after it is made.
6. If an applicant has made a false statement of material fact on his or her application, the false statement may in itself be sufficient ground for refusal of a license.

[Part 15:150:1947; A 1955, 80]—(NRS A 1959, 395; 1963, 670; 1969, 95; 1971, 452; 1975, 1548; 1977, 92; 1979, 1544; 1981, 1610; 1985, 1267; 1999, 181; 2007, 1540)

NRS 645.450 Time for examinations. Examination for licenses shall be held by the Real Estate Division at least bimonthly.

[Part 14:150:1947; A 1949, 433; 1943 NCL § 6396.14]—(NRS A 1963, 1074; 1973, 1102; 1975, 1549)

NRS 645.460 Examination: Subjects covered; acceptance of national examination.

1. The Division shall ascertain by written examination that the applicant has an appropriate knowledge and understanding of those subjects which commonly and customarily apply to the real estate business.

2. The Division may hire a professional testing organization to create, administer or score the written examination or perform all of those functions.

3. The Division may accept successful completion of the uniform portion of a national real estate examination in partial satisfaction of the requirements of the examination in Nevada.

[Part 14:150:1947; A 1949, 433; 1943 NCL § 6396.14]—(NRS A 1963, 1074; 1973, 1103; 1979, 1545; 1981, 1611)

NRS 645.475 Examination for license as broker may be taken before meeting requirements for experience; issuance of license as broker-salesperson upon passing examination; application and experience required for issuance of license as broker.

1. An applicant for a real estate broker's license may take the written examination before the applicant has complied with the experience requirements of subsection 4 of NRS 645.330, but the Division shall not approve the issuance of a broker's license until all the requirements of this chapter are met.

2. An applicant, pursuant to subsection 1, who passes the broker's examination must be issued a broker-salesperson's license. The applicant may be issued a broker's license upon:

(a) Making proper application to the Division; and

(b) Satisfying the experience requirements of subsection 4 of NRS 645.330.

(Added to NRS by 1975, 793; A 1979, 1545; 1981, 1611; 1995, 994)

NRS 645.490 Issuance of license; duty of Real Estate Division; renewal of license.

1. Upon satisfactorily passing the written examination and upon complying with all other provisions of law and conditions of this chapter, a license shall thereupon be granted by the Division to the successful applicant therefor as a real estate broker, broker-salesperson or salesperson, and the applicant, upon receiving the license, may conduct the business of a real estate broker, broker-salesperson or salesperson in this State.

2. The Division shall issue licenses as a real estate broker, broker-salesperson or salesperson to all applicants who qualify and comply with all provisions of law and all requirements of this chapter.

3. Except as otherwise provided in NRS 645.785:

(a) An original license as a real estate broker, broker-salesperson or salesperson must be renewed with the Division before the expiration of the initial license period of 12 consecutive months as prescribed in NRS 645.780; and

(b) Thereafter, the license must be renewed with the Division before the expiration of each subsequent license period of 24 consecutive months as prescribed in NRS 645.780.

[Part 14:150:1947; A 1949, 433; 1943 NCL § 6396.14] + [Part 15:150:1947; A 1955, 80]—(NRS A 1963, 672; 1979, 1545; 2001, 2893; 2003, 1291; 2009, 1938; 2015, 2781)

NRS 645.495 Nonresident licensee to authorize service of process upon Administrator.

1. No license may be issued pursuant to NRS 645.490 to a resident of a state other than Nevada until the applicant has appointed in writing the Administrator to be his or her agent, upon whom all process, in any action or proceeding against the applicant, may be served. In this writing the applicant must agree that any process against him or her which is served on the Administrator is of the same legal validity as if it had been served on the applicant and state that the appointment continues in force as long as any liability remains outstanding against the applicant in this State. It must contain a stipulation agreeing to venue in any judicial or administrative district in this State without regard to the location of the licensee's principal place of business. The written appointment must be acknowledged before an officer authorized to take acknowledgments of deeds and must be filed in the office of the Administrator. A copy of the appointment which is certified by the Administrator is sufficient evidence of the appointment and agreement.

2. When any process is served upon the Administrator under this section, the Administrator shall mail the process by certified mail to the last known address of the licensee. Service is complete upon such mailing. The manner of serving process described in this subsection does not affect the validity of any other service authorized by law.

(Added to NRS by 1987, 516)

NRS 645.510 Authority of license limited to person or place of business licensed. No real estate license issued under the provisions of this chapter shall give authority to do or perform any act specified in this chapter to any person other than the person to whom the license is issued, or from any place of business other than that specified therein.

[16:150:1947; 1943 NCL § 6396.16]

NRS 645.520 Form and contents; limitation on association with or employment of broker-salesperson or salesperson.

1. The Division shall issue to each licensee a license in such form and size as is prescribed by the Division.

2. Each license must:

(a) Show the name and address of the licensee, and in case of a real estate broker-salesperson's or salesperson's license show the name of the real estate broker with whom he or she will be associated.

(b) Have imprinted thereon the seal of the Division.

(c) Contain any additional matter prescribed by the Division.

3. No real estate broker-salesperson or salesperson may be associated with or employed by more than one broker or owner-developer at the same time.

[Part 17:150:1947; A 1949, 433; 1955, 77]—(NRS A 1963, 673; 1975, 1549; 1979, 1546)

NRS 645.530 Delivery; display.

1. The license of each real estate broker-salesperson or salesperson must be delivered or mailed to the real estate broker with whom the licensee is associated or to the owner-developer by whom the licensee is employed and must be kept in the custody and control of the broker or owner-developer.

2. Each real estate broker shall:

(a) Display his or her license conspicuously in the broker's place of business. If a real estate broker maintains more than one place of business within the State, an additional license must be issued to the broker for each branch office so maintained by the broker, and the additional license must be displayed conspicuously in each branch office.

(b) Prominently display in his or her place of business the licenses of all real estate broker-salespersons and salespersons associated with him or her therein or in connection therewith.

3. Each owner-developer shall prominently display in his or her place of business the license of each real estate broker-salesperson and salesperson employed by him or her.

[Part 17:150:1947; A 1949, 433; 1955, 77]—(NRS A 1975, 1549, 1641; 1979, 1546; 1981, 1034)

NRS 645.550 Broker to maintain place of business; business must be done from location designated in license; licensing of broker or owner-developer by county, city or town.

1. Every real estate broker shall have and maintain a definite place of business within the State, which must be a room or rooms used for the transaction of real estate business, or such business and any allied businesses, and which must serve as the office for the transaction of business under the authority of the license, and where the license must be prominently displayed.

2. The place of business must be specified in the application for license and designated in the license.

3. No license authorizes the licensee to transact business from any office other than that designated in the license.

4. Each city, town or county may require a license for revenue purposes for a licensed real estate broker or owner-developer who maintains an office within the city or town, or within the county outside the cities and towns of the county, respectively.

[Part 17:150:1947; A 1949, 433; 1955, 77]—(NRS A 1969, 893; 1973, 84; 1979, 1547)

NRS 645.560 Broker: Erection, maintenance, size and placement of signs.

1. Each licensed real estate broker shall erect and maintain a sign in a conspicuous place upon the premises of his or her place of business. The name of the broker or the name under which the broker conducts his or her business set forth in the license must be clearly shown thereon.

2. The size and place of the sign must conform to regulations adopted by the Commission.

3. Similar signs must also be erected and maintained in a conspicuous place at all branch offices.

[18:150:1947; 1943 NCL § 6396.18]—(NRS A 1979, 1547; 1989, 1610)

NRS 645.570 Notice of change of name, location of business or association; requirements for transfer of association; effect of failure to give notice.

1. Notice in writing must be given by the broker or a corporate officer to the Division within 10 days of any change of name or business location of any licensee or of a change of association of any broker-salesperson or salesperson

licensee. Upon the surrender of the license previously issued and the payment of the fee required by law the Division shall issue the license for the unexpired term.

2. Upon the transfer of association of any broker-salesperson or salesperson licensee, application accompanied by the fee required by law must be made to the Division for the reissuance of the license to the broker-salesperson or salesperson for the unexpired term. Such a transfer may only be into an association with a licensed broker or registered owner-developer who must certify to the honesty, truthfulness and good reputation of the transferee.

3. Failure to give notice as required by this section constitutes cause for the revocation of any outstanding license or involuntary inactivation of the license.

[Part 17:150:1947; A 1949, 433; 1955, 77]—(NRS A 1963, 673; 1975, 1550, 1641; 1979, 1547; 1983, 166)

NRS 645.575 Continuing education: Standards; renewal or reinstatement of license.

1. The Commission shall adopt regulations that prescribe the standards for the continuing education of persons licensed pursuant to this chapter.

2. The standards adopted pursuant to subsection 1 must permit alternatives of subject material, taking cognizance of specialized areas of practice and alternatives in sources of programs considering availability in area and time. The standards must include, where qualified, generally accredited educational institutions, private vocational schools, educational programs and seminars of professional societies and organizations, other organized educational programs on technical subjects, or equivalent offerings. The Commission shall qualify only those educational courses that it determines address the appropriate subject matter and are given by an accredited university or community college. Subject to the provisions of this section, the Commission has exclusive authority to determine what is an appropriate subject matter for qualification as a continuing education course.

3. In addition to any other standards for continuing education that the Commission adopts by regulation pursuant to this section, the Commission may, without limitation, adopt by regulation standards for continuing education that:

(a) Establish a postlicensing curriculum of continuing education which must be completed by a person within the first year immediately after initial licensing of the person.

(b) Require a person whose license as a real estate broker or real estate broker-salesperson has been placed on inactive status for any reason for 1 year or more or has been suspended or revoked to complete a course of instruction in broker management that is designed to fulfill the educational requirements for issuance of a license which are described in paragraph (d) of subsection 2 of NRS 645.343, before the person's license is reissued or reinstated.

4. Except as otherwise provided in this subsection, the license of a real estate broker, broker-salesperson or salesperson must not be renewed or reinstated unless the Administrator finds that the applicant for the renewal license or for reinstatement to active status has completed the continuing education required by this chapter. Any amendment or repeal of a regulation does not operate to prevent an applicant from complying with this section for the next licensing period following the amendment or repeal.

(Added to NRS by 1977, 1315; A 1979, 662; 1985, 1508; 1989, 1610; 1995, 162; 1997, 219; 2001, 2894; 2003, 1291; 2007, 1540)

NRS 645.577 Placement of license on inactive status; reinstatement.

1. The Division may place a license on inactive status for any of the following reasons:

(a) At the request of the licensee.

(b) If a broker's license or a corporate officer's license, for failure to immediately notify the Division in writing of any change in the name of the licensee's firm or its business location.

(c) If a broker-salesperson's license or a salesperson's license, for failure to notify the Division of a change in the broker or owner-developer with whom the licensee will be associated within 30 days after the licensee's previous association was terminated.

(d) For failure to apply and pay the fee for renewal before the license expired.

(e) If inactivated upon the placing of the broker under whose supervision the licensee worked in an inactive status.

(f) As a result of a formal disciplinary proceeding.

2. Any licensee whose license has been placed on inactive status may not engage in the business of a real estate broker, broker-salesperson or salesperson until the licensee has met all of the requirements for reinstatement of his or her license to active status.

(Added to NRS by 1979, 1532; A 1985, 1267)

NRS 645.580 Termination of association or employment of broker-salesperson or salesperson; duties of broker or owner-developer and broker-salesperson or salesperson; transfer of license or new license.

1. When any real estate broker-salesperson or salesperson terminates, for any reason, his or her association with the real estate broker with whom he or she was associated, or his or her employment with the owner-developer by whom he or she was employed, the real estate broker or owner-developer shall:

(a) Deliver or mail by certified mail to the Division the real estate broker-salesperson's or salesperson's license, together with a written statement of the circumstances surrounding the termination of the association or the employment, within 10 days after the termination occurs.

(b) At the time of delivering or mailing the license to the Division, address a communication to the last known residence address of the broker-salesperson or salesperson, advising him or her that the license has been delivered or mailed to the Division. A copy of the communication must accompany the license when delivered or mailed to the Division.

2. A broker-salesperson or salesperson must, within 30 days after termination of that association, become associated with or employed by another broker or owner-developer or request that the license be placed on inactive status.

3. It is unlawful for any real estate salesperson to perform any of the acts contemplated by this chapter, either directly or indirectly, under authority of the license on or after the date of receipt of the license from the broker or owner-developer by the Division and until the license is transferred or reissued or a new license is issued.

[Part 17:150:1947; A 1949, 433; 1955, 77]—(NRS A 1963, 674; 1969, 95; 1975, 1550; 1641; 1979, 1548; 1981, 1034; 1989, 1611)

NRS 645.590 Termination of association by broker with limited-liability company, partnership or corporation; new license. If any real estate broker licensed pursuant to the provisions of this chapter as a manager of a limited-liability company, member of a partnership, or as an officer of a corporation, discontinues his or her connections with the limited-liability company, partnership or corporation, and thereafter desires to act as an individual real estate broker, or become associated with any other limited-liability company, partnership or corporation, the broker must file an application and pay a transfer fee of $20 for a new license as an individual broker, as the manager of the new limited-liability company, or as a member of the new partnership or association, or as an officer of the new corporation. The payment of such a fee does not extend or otherwise alter the original license period.

[Part 17:150:1947; A 1949, 433; 1955, 77]—(NRS A 1973, 1103; 1985, 1268; 1997, 169)

NRS 645.600 Inactive status for period of military service; reinstatement.

1. Any licensee under the provisions of this chapter who shall be called into the military service of the United States shall, at his or her request, be relieved from compliance with the provisions of this chapter and placed on inactive status for the period of such military service and for a period of 6 months after discharge therefrom.

2. At any time within 6 months after termination of such service, providing the provisions of subsection 1 are complied with, the licensee may be reinstated, without examination, to active status in the appropriate classification which the licensee left upon entry into the military service, without having to meet any qualification or requirement other than the payment of the reinstatement fee, as provided in NRS 645.830, and the licensee shall not be required to make payment of the license fee for the current year.

3. Any licensee seeking to qualify for reinstatement, as provided in subsections 1 and 2, shall present a certified copy of his or her honorable discharge or certificate of satisfactory service to the Real Estate Division.

[33.5:150:1947; added 1955, 18]—(NRS A 1963, 674)

NRS 645.605 Certificate authorizing out-of-state licensed broker to cooperate with broker in Nevada: Issuance; fee; regulations. The Administrator shall have authority to issue certificates authorizing out-of-state licensed brokers to cooperate with Nevada brokers, and the Commission shall have authority to promulgate rules and regulations establishing the conditions under which such certificates shall be issued and cancelled, all subject to the provisions and penalties of this chapter. The Real Estate Division shall charge a fee for the issuance of such certificate as provided in NRS 645.830.

(Added to NRS by 1965, 1407)

NRS 645.6051 Broker to maintain record of work performed on residential property; contents of record.

1. A person licensed pursuant to this chapter as a real estate broker, real estate broker-salesperson or real estate salesperson shall maintain a record of all work performed on a residential property that the person assists a client in scheduling pursuant to subsection 11 of NRS 624.031.

2. The record required by subsection 1 must include, without limitation:
(a) The name of any person licensed pursuant to chapter 624 of NRS who performs such work;
(b) The date on which the work was performed;
(c) A copy of any written contract to perform the work; and
(d) A copy of any invoice prepared in connection with the work.
3. As used in this section, "residential property" has the meaning ascribed to it in NRS 624.031.
(Added to NRS by 2013, 580)

PROPERTY MANAGERS

NRS 645.6052 Permit to engage in property management: Persons eligible; requirements; instruction; expiration; renewal; regulations.
1. A person who is licensed pursuant to this chapter as a real estate broker, real estate broker-salesperson or real estate salesperson may apply to the Real Estate Division for a permit to engage in property management.
2. An applicant for a permit must:
(a) Furnish proof satisfactory to the Division that the applicant has successfully completed at least 24 classroom hours of instruction in property management; and
(b) Comply with all other requirements established by the Commission for the issuance of a permit.
3. A permit expires, and may be renewed, at the same time as the license of the holder of the permit.
4. An applicant for the renewal of a permit must:
(a) Furnish proof satisfactory to the Division that the applicant has successfully completed at least 3 of the hours of the continuing education required for the renewal of his or her license pursuant to the regulations adopted by the Commission pursuant to NRS 645.575 in an approved educational course, seminar or conference concerning property management; and
(b) Comply with all other requirements established by the Commission for the renewal of a permit.
5. The Commission may adopt such regulations as it determines are necessary to carry out the provisions of this section. The regulations may, without limitation:
(a) Establish additional requirements for the issuance or renewal of a permit.
(b) Establish fees for the issuance and renewal of a permit and fees to pay the costs of:
(1) Any examination for a permit, including any costs which are necessary for the administration of such an examination.
(2) Any investigation of an applicant's background.
(c) Set forth standards of education for the approval of a course of instruction to qualify an applicant for a permit.
(Added to NRS by 1997, 954; A 2003, 1292; 2007, 1542)

NRS 645.6054 Permit to engage in property management: Requirements for certain organizations.
1. To engage in the business of property management in this State:
(a) A partnership shall designate one of its members;
(b) A corporation shall designate one of its officers or employees;
(c) A limited-liability company shall designate its manager; and
(d) A broker who conducts business as a sole proprietor shall designate a person who is licensed under the broker,
☐ to submit an application for a permit to engage in property management. The partnership, corporation, limited-liability company or sole proprietor shall not engage in the business of property management unless the person so designated has been issued a permit to engage in property management by the Real Estate Division.
2. If the person designated to apply for a permit pursuant to subsection 1 meets the qualifications for a permit set forth in NRS 645.6052, the Division shall issue to that person a permit to engage in property management on behalf of the partnership, corporation, limited-liability company or sole proprietor, and thereupon the person may perform all the acts of a property manager contemplated by this chapter.
3. A person to whom a permit has been issued pursuant to this section may act as a property manager pursuant to the permit only on behalf of the partnership, corporation, limited-liability company or sole proprietor, and not on his or her own behalf. If that person ceases to be connected or associated with the partnership, corporation, limited-liability company or sole proprietor, the partnership, corporation, limited-liability company or sole proprietor shall designate another person who meets the qualifications for a permit set forth in NRS 645.6052 to hold the permit on behalf of the partnership, corporation, limited-liability company or sole proprietor.

4. Any member, officer or employee of a partnership, corporation or limited-liability company, other than the person designated as the property manager pursuant to subsection 1, who wishes to engage in the business of property management must apply in his or her own name individually for a separate permit to engage in property management. Pursuant to such a permit, the member, officer or employee of a partnership, corporation or limited-liability company may act as a property manager only as an officer or agent of the partnership, corporation or limited-liability company, and not on his or her own behalf.

NRS 645.6055 Designated property managers: Requirements; qualifications; duties.

1. If a real estate broker does not hold a permit to engage in property management but intends to have property management activities conducted at an office, the real estate broker must:

(a) Appoint a person, who has the qualifications required by this section, as the designated property manager for the office to supervise the property management activities conducted at the office; and

(b) Submit notice of the appointment to the Division.

2. The designated property manager for an office must be a natural person who:

(a) Holds a license as a real estate broker or real estate broker-salesperson;

(b) Holds a permit to engage in property management; and

(c) Has 2 years active experience, within the 4 years immediately preceding the date of the appointment, in conducting property management activities in the United States as a licensed real estate broker, real estate broker-salesperson or real estate salesperson.

3. While acting as the designated property manager for an office, the person:

(a) Must comply with the provisions of NRS 645.6052 to 645.6058, inclusive, and all other applicable provisions of this chapter; and

(b) Is subject to all the remedies and penalties provided for in this chapter.

(Added to NRS by 2003, 1287)

NRS 645.6056 Property management agreements: Requirements; contents.

1. A real estate broker who holds a permit to engage in property management shall not act as a property manager unless the broker has first obtained a property management agreement signed by the broker and the client for whom the broker will manage the property.

2. A property management agreement must include, without limitation:

(a) The term of the agreement and, if the agreement is subject to renewal, provisions clearly setting forth the circumstances under which the agreement may be renewed and the term of each such renewal;

(b) A provision for the retention and disposition of deposits of the tenants of the property during the term of the agreement and, if the agreement is subject to renewal, during the term of each such renewal;

(c) The fee or compensation to be paid to the broker;

(d) The extent to which the broker may act as the agent of the client;

(e) If the agreement is subject to cancellation, provisions clearly setting forth the circumstances under which the agreement may be cancelled. The agreement may authorize the broker or the client, or both, to cancel the agreement with cause or without cause, or both, under the circumstances set forth in the agreement; and

(f) If the broker intends to provide asset management services for the client, a provision indicating the extent to which the broker will provide those services. As used in this paragraph, "client" has the meaning ascribed to it in NRS 645H.060.

(Added to NRS by 1997, 955; A 2003, 932; 2011, 2832)

NRS 645.6058 Disposition of fees, penalties and fines received by Division; delegation of authority of Division to hearing officer or panel.

1. Except as otherwise provided in subsection 3, all fees, penalties and fines received by the Division pursuant to the provisions of NRS 645.6052 to 645.6058, inclusive, must be deposited with the State Treasurer for credit to the Division. The money must be used by the Division for the administration of the provisions of NRS 645.6052 to 645.6058, inclusive.

2. The Division may delegate to a hearing officer or panel its authority to take any disciplinary action against property managers, impose and collect fines pursuant to the disciplinary action and deposit the money with the State Treasurer for credit to the Division.

3. If a hearing officer or panel is not authorized to take disciplinary action pursuant to subsection 2, the Division shall deposit the money collected from the imposition of penalties and fines collected from property managers with the State Treasurer for credit to the State General Fund. The Division may present a claim to the State Board of Examiners for

recommendation to the Interim Finance Committee if money is needed to pay an attorney's fee or the costs of an investigation, or both.

(Added to NRS by 1997, 956; A 2003, 1293)

DISCIPLINARY AND OTHER ACTIONS

NRS 645.610 Investigation of actions of licensees and other persons. The Administrator may investigate the actions of any real estate broker, broker-salesperson, salesperson, owner-developer or any person who acts in any such capacity within this State.

[Part 20:150:1947; 1943 NCL § 6396.20]—(NRS A 1963, 675; 1975, 1551; 1979, 1548)

NRS 645.615 Duty to report certain convictions and pleas to Division.
1. A licensee, property manager or owner-developer shall notify the Division in writing if he or she is convicted of, or enters a plea of guilty, guilty but mentally ill or nolo contendere to:
(a) A felony relating to the practice of the licensee, property manager or owner-developer; or
(b) Any crime involving fraud, deceit, misrepresentation or moral turpitude.
2. A licensee, property manager or owner-developer shall submit the notification required by subsection 1:
(a) Not more than 10 days after the conviction or entry of the plea of guilty, guilty but mentally ill or nolo contendere; and
(b) When submitting an application to renew a license, permit or registration issued pursuant to this chapter.

(Added to NRS by 2007, 1539)—(Substituted in revision for NRS 645.995)

NRS 645.620 Maintenance by Division of record of complaints, investigations and denials of applications.
The Division shall maintain in each district office a public docket or other record in which it shall record from time to time as made:
1. The rulings or decisions upon all complaints filed with that district office.
2. All investigations instituted by that district office in the first instance, upon or in connection with which any hearing has been held, or in which the licensee charged has made no defense.
3. Denials of applications made to that district office for examination or licensing.

[Part 23:150:1947; 1943 NCL § 6396.23]—(NRS A 1963, 675; 1979, 1548; 1995, 163)

NRS 645.625 Certain records relating to complaint or investigation deemed confidential; certain records relating to disciplinary action deemed public records.
1. Except as otherwise provided in this section and NRS 239.0115, a complaint filed with the Division alleging a violation of this chapter, all documents and other information filed with the complaint and all documents and other information compiled as a result of an investigation conducted to determine whether to initiate disciplinary action are confidential and may be disclosed in whole or in part only as necessary in the course of administering this chapter or to a licensing board or agency or any other governmental agency, including, without limitation, a law enforcement agency, that is investigating a person who holds a license, permit or registration issued pursuant to this chapter.
2. A complaint or other document filed with the Commission to initiate disciplinary action and all documents and information considered by the Commission when determining whether to impose discipline are public records.

(Added to NRS by 2003, 3464; A 2005, 1292; 2007, 1542, 2147)

NRS 645.630 Authorized disciplinary action; grounds for disciplinary action; orders imposing discipline deemed public records.
1. The Commission may require a licensee, property manager or owner-developer to pay an administrative fine of not more than $10,000 for each violation he or she commits or suspend, revoke, deny the renewal of or place conditions upon his or her license, permit or registration, or impose any combination of those actions, at any time if the licensee, property manager or owner-developer has, by false or fraudulent representation, obtained a license, permit or registration, or the licensee, property manager or owner-developer, whether or not acting as such, is found guilty of:
(a) Making any material misrepresentation.
(b) Making any false promises of a character likely to influence, persuade or induce.
(c) Accepting a commission or valuable consideration as a real estate broker-salesperson or salesperson for the performance of any of the acts specified in this chapter or chapter 119 or 119A of NRS from any person except the licensed real estate broker with whom he or she is associated or the owner-developer by whom he or she is employed.

(d) Representing or attempting to represent a real estate broker other than the broker with whom he or she is associated, without the express knowledge and consent of the broker with whom he or she is associated.

(e) Failing to maintain, for review and audit by the Division, each brokerage agreement and property management agreement governed by the provisions of this chapter and entered into by the licensee.

(f) Failing, within a reasonable time, to account for or to remit any money which comes into his or her possession and which belongs to others.

(g) If he or she is required to maintain a trust account:
(1) Failing to balance the trust account at least monthly; and
(2) Failing to submit to the Division an annual accounting of the trust account as required in NRS 645.310.

(h) Commingling the money or other property of his or her clients with his or her own or converting the money of others to his or her own use.

(i) In the case of a broker-salesperson or salesperson, failing to place in the custody of his or her licensed broker or owner-developer, as soon as possible, any deposit or other money or consideration entrusted to him or her by any person dealing with him or her as the representative of his or her licensed broker.

(j) Accepting other than cash as earnest money unless that fact is communicated to the owner before his or her acceptance of the offer to purchase and that fact is shown in the receipt for the earnest money.

(k) Upon acceptance of an agreement, in the case of a broker, failing to deposit any check or cash received as earnest money before the end of the next banking day unless otherwise provided in the purchase agreement.

(l) Inducing any party to a brokerage agreement, property management agreement, agreement of sale or lease to break it in order to substitute a new brokerage agreement, property management agreement, agreement of sale or lease with the same or another party if the inducement to make the substitution is offered to secure personal gain to the licensee or owner-developer.

2. An order that imposes discipline and the findings of fact and conclusions of law supporting that order are public records.

[Part 20:150:1947; 1943 NCL § 6396.20]—(NRS A 1957, 338; 1963, 332; 1965, 1407; 1971, 248; 1975, 1551; 1979, 1549; 1981, 1612; 1983, 222; 1985, 1268; 1993, 890; 1995, 2076; 1997, 959; 2001, 522; 2003, 933, 3464, 3482; 2007, 1543)

NRS 645.633 Additional grounds for disciplinary action: Improper trade practices; violations of certain orders, agreements, laws and regulations; criminal offenses; other unprofessional and improper conduct; reciprocal discipline; violations relating to property management; log of complaints.

1. The Commission may take action pursuant to NRS 645.630 against any person subject to that section who is guilty of any of the following acts:

(a) Willfully using any trade name, service mark or insigne of membership in any real estate organization of which the licensee is not a member, without the legal right to do so.

(b) Violating any order of the Commission, any agreement with the Division, any of the provisions of this chapter, chapter 116, 119, 119A, 119B, 645A or 645C of NRS or any regulation adopted pursuant thereto.

(c) Paying a commission, compensation or a finder's fee to any person for performing the services of a broker, broker-salesperson or salesperson who has not secured a license pursuant to this chapter. This subsection does not apply to payments to a broker who is licensed in his or her state of residence.

(d) A conviction of, or the entry of a plea of guilty, guilty but mentally ill or nolo contendere to:
(1) A felony relating to the practice of the licensee, property manager or owner-developer; or
(2) Any crime involving fraud, deceit, misrepresentation or moral turpitude.

(e) Guaranteeing, or having authorized or permitted any person to guarantee, future profits which may result from the resale of real property.

(f) Failure to include a fixed date of expiration in any written brokerage agreement or failure to leave a copy of such a brokerage agreement or any property management agreement with the client.

(g) Accepting, giving or charging any undisclosed commission, rebate or direct profit on expenditures made for a client.

(h) Gross negligence or incompetence in performing any act for which the person is required to hold a license pursuant to this chapter, chapter 119, 119A or 119B of NRS.

(i) Any other conduct which constitutes deceitful, fraudulent or dishonest dealing.

(j) Any conduct which took place before the person became licensed which was in fact unknown to the Division and which would have been grounds for denial of a license had the Division been aware of the conduct.

Must Read.
& Memorized.

37

(k) Knowingly permitting any person whose license has been revoked or suspended to act as a real estate broker, broker-salesperson or salesperson, with or on behalf of the licensee.

(l) Recording or causing to be recorded a claim pursuant to the provisions of NRS 645.8701 to 645.8811, inclusive, that is determined by a district court to be frivolous and made without reasonable cause pursuant to NRS 645.8791.

2. The Commission may take action pursuant to NRS 645.630 against a person who is subject to that section for the suspension or revocation of a real estate broker's, broker-salesperson's or salesperson's license issued by any other jurisdiction.

3. The Commission may take action pursuant to NRS 645.630 against any person who:

(a) Holds a permit to engage in property management issued pursuant to NRS 645.6052; and

(b) In connection with any property for which the person has obtained a property management agreement pursuant to NRS 645.6056:

(1) Is convicted of violating any of the provisions of NRS 202.470;

(2) Has been notified in writing by the appropriate governmental agency of a potential violation of NRS 244.360, 244.3603 or 268.4124, and has failed to inform the owner of the property of such notification; or

(3) Has been directed in writing by the owner of the property to correct a potential violation of NRS 244.360, 244.3603 or 268.4124, and has failed to correct the potential violation, if such corrective action is within the scope of the person's duties pursuant to the property management agreement.

4. The Division shall maintain a log of any complaints that it receives relating to activities for which the Commission may take action against a person holding a permit to engage in property management pursuant to subsection 3.

(Added to NRS by 1979, 1533; A 1985, 1269, 1672; 1989, 1612; 1995, 2077, 2479; 1997, 591, 960; 1999, 1180; 2001, 1354; 2001 Special Session, 156; 2003, 934, 1502, 2718; 2007, 1475; 2015, 2778)

NRS 645.635 Additional grounds for disciplinary action: Unprofessional and improper conduct relating to real estate transactions. The Commission may take action pursuant to NRS 645.630 against any person subject to that section who is guilty of:

1. Offering real estate for sale or lease without the knowledge and consent of the owner or the owner's authorized agent or on terms other than those authorized by the owner or the owner's authorized agent.

2. Negotiating a sale, exchange or lease of real estate, or communicating after such negotiations but before closing, directly with a client if the person knows that the client has a brokerage agreement in force in connection with the property granting an exclusive agency, including, without limitation, an exclusive right to sell to another broker, unless permission in writing has been obtained from the other broker.

3. Failure to deliver within a reasonable time a completed copy of any purchase agreement or offer to buy or sell real estate to the purchaser or to the seller, except as otherwise provided in subsection 4 of NRS 645.254.

4. Failure to deliver to the seller in each real estate transaction, within 10 business days after the transaction is closed, a complete, detailed closing statement showing all of the receipts and disbursements handled by him or her for the seller, failure to deliver to the buyer a complete statement showing all money received in the transaction from the buyer and how and for what it was disbursed, or failure to retain true copies of those statements in his or her files. The furnishing of those statements by an escrow holder relieves the broker's, broker-salesperson's or salesperson's responsibility and must be deemed to be in compliance with this provision.

5. Representing to any lender, guaranteeing agency or any other interested party, verbally or through the preparation of false documents, an amount in excess of the actual sale price of the real estate or terms differing from those actually agreed upon.

6. Failure to produce any document, book or record in his or her possession or under his or her control, concerning any real estate transaction under investigation by the Division.

7. Failure to reduce a bona fide offer to writing where a proposed purchaser requests that it be submitted in writing, except as otherwise provided in subsection 4 of NRS 645.254.

8. Failure to submit all written bona fide offers to a seller when the offers are received before the seller accepts an offer in writing and until the broker has knowledge of that acceptance, except as otherwise provided in subsection 4 of NRS 645.254.

9. Refusing because of race, color, national origin, sex or ethnic group to show, sell or rent any real estate for sale or rent to qualified purchasers or renters.

10. Knowingly submitting any false or fraudulent appraisal to any financial institution or other interested person.

11. Any violation of NRS 645C.557.

(Added to NRS by 1979, 1533; A 1985, 1270; 1995, 2077; 2001, 2895; 2007, 1789; 2009, 1509)

NRS 645.645   Additional grounds for disciplinary action: Unprofessional and improper conduct relating to sale of insurance for home protection.   The Commission may take action pursuant to NRS 645.630 against any person selling insurance for home protection, as defined in NRS 690B.100, under the authority of a license issued pursuant to this chapter who:

1. Makes a misrepresentation in the sale of insurance for home protection.
2. Misrepresents the provisions of the contract of insurance for home protection.
3. Misappropriates any fees or premiums collected for the insurance for home protection.

   (Added to NRS by 1981, 1323)

NRS 645.647   Additional grounds for disciplinary action: Failure to pay money to Commission or Division.   In addition to any other remedy or penalty, the Commission or the Division, as appropriate, may:

1. Refuse to issue a license, permit, certificate or registration to a person who has failed to pay money which the person owes to the Commission or the Division.
2. Refuse to renew, or suspend or revoke, the license, permit, certificate or registration of a person who has failed to pay money which the person owes to the Commission or the Division.

   (Added to NRS by 2003, 1289)

NRS 645.648   Suspension of license for failure to pay child support or comply with certain subpoenas or warrants; reinstatement of license. [Effective until 2 years after the date of the repeal of 42 U.S.C. § 666, the federal law requiring each state to establish procedures for withholding, suspending and restricting the professional, occupational and recreational licenses for child support arrearages and for noncompliance with certain processes relating to paternity or child support proceedings.]

1. If the Division receives a copy of a court order issued pursuant to NRS 425.540 that provides for the suspension of all professional, occupational and recreational licenses, certificates and permits issued to a person who is the holder of a license as a real estate broker, broker-salesperson or salesperson, the Division shall deem the license issued to that person to be suspended at the end of the 30th day after the date on which the court order was issued unless the Division receives a letter issued to the holder of the license by the district attorney or other public agency pursuant to NRS 425.550 stating that the holder of the license has complied with the subpoena or warrant or has satisfied the arrearage pursuant to NRS 425.560.

2. The Division shall reinstate a license as a real estate broker, broker-salesperson or salesperson that has been suspended by a district court pursuant to NRS 425.540 if the Division receives a letter issued by the district attorney or other public agency pursuant to NRS 425.550 to the person whose license was suspended stating that the person whose license was suspended has complied with the subpoena or warrant or has satisfied the arrearage pursuant to NRS 425.560.

   (Added to NRS by 1997, 2164; A 2005, 2807)

NRS 645.660   Knowledge of associate or employer of violation by licensee or employee; penalties.

1. Any unlawful act or violation of any of the provisions of this chapter by any licensee is not cause to suspend, revoke or deny the renewal of the license of any person associated with the licensee, unless it appears to the satisfaction of the Commission that the associate knew or should have known thereof. A course of dealing shown to have been persistently and consistently followed by any licensee constitutes prima facie evidence of such knowledge upon the part of the associate.

2. If it appears that a registered owner-developer knew or should have known of any unlawful act or violation on the part of a real estate broker, broker-salesperson or salesperson employed by the registered owner-developer, in the course of his or her employment, the Commission may suspend, revoke or deny the renewal of the registered owner-developer's registration and may assess a civil penalty of not more than $5,000.

3. The Commission may suspend, revoke or deny the renewal of the license of a real estate broker and may assess a civil penalty of not more than $5,000 against the broker if it appears he or she has failed to maintain adequate supervision of a salesperson or broker-salesperson associated with the broker and that person commits any unlawful act or violates any of the provisions of this chapter.

NRS 645.670   Effect on limited-liability company, partnership or corporation of revocation or suspension of license of manager, partner or officer; termination of suspension or reinstatement of license.   In the event of the revocation or suspension of the license issued to a manager of a limited-liability company, a member of a partnership or to any officer of a corporation, the limited-liability company, partnership or corporation shall not conduct business unless the manager or member whose license has been revoked is severed and his or her interest in the limited-liability company or partnership and his or her share in its activities brought to an end, or if a corporation, the offending officer is discharged and has no further participation in its activities. The discharged or withdrawing manager, member or officer of such a limited-liability company, partnership or corporation may reassume his or her connection with, or be reengaged by the limited-liability company, partnership or corporation, upon termination of the suspension or upon reinstatement of his or her license.

[Part 20:150:1947; 1943 NCL § 6396.20]—(NRS A 1975, 1553; 1979, 1551; 1985, 1271; 1997, 170)

NRS 645.675 Investigations, disciplinary or other proceedings, fines and penalties not affected by expiration, revocation or voluntary surrender of license, permit or registration. The expiration or revocation of a license, permit or registration by operation of law or by order or decision of the Commission or a court of competent jurisdiction, or the voluntary surrender of a license, permit or registration by a real estate broker, real estate broker-salesperson, real estate salesperson, property manager or owner-developer does not:

1. Prohibit the Administrator, Commission or Division from initiating or continuing an investigation of, or action or disciplinary proceeding against, the real estate broker, real estate broker-salesperson, real estate salesperson, property manager or owner-developer as authorized pursuant to the provisions of this chapter or the regulations adopted pursuant thereto; or

2. Prevent the imposition or collection of any fine or penalty authorized pursuant to the provisions of this chapter or the regulations adopted pursuant thereto against the real estate broker, real estate broker-salesperson, real estate salesperson, property manager or owner-developer.

(Added to NRS by 2001, 521)

NRS 645.680 Revocation, suspension or denial of renewal of license, permit or registration: Complaint; notice of hearing.

1. The procedure set forth in this section and NRS 645.690 must be followed before the Commission revokes, suspends or denies the renewal of any license, permit or registration of an owner-developer issued pursuant to this chapter.

2. Upon the initiation of a complaint by the Administrator, the matter must be set for a hearing by the Administrator, who shall schedule a hearing before the Commission, and the licensee, permittee or owner-developer is entitled to be heard thereon in person or by counsel.

3. The Commission shall hold the hearing within 90 days after the filing of a complaint by the Administrator. The time of the hearing may be continued upon the motion of the Commission or at the discretion of the Commission, upon the written request of the licensee, permittee or owner-developer or of the Division for good cause shown.

4. The licensee, permittee or owner-developer must be given at least 30 days' notice in writing by the Division of the date, time and place of the hearing together with a copy of the complaint and copies of all communications, reports, affidavits or depositions in possession of the Division relevant to the complaint. The Division may present evidence obtained after the notice only if the Division shows that the evidence was not available after diligent investigation before the time notice was given to the licensee, permittee or owner-developer and that the evidence was given or communicated to the licensee, permittee or owner-developer immediately after it was obtained.

5. Notice is complete upon delivery personally to the licensee, permittee or owner-developer or by mailing by certified mail to the last known address of the licensee, permittee or owner-developer. If the licensee is a broker-salesperson or salesperson, the Division shall also notify the broker with whom he or she is associated, or the owner-developer by whom he or she is employed, by mailing an exact statement of the charges and the date, time and place of the hearing by certified mail to the owner-developer or broker's last known address.

[Part 21:150:1947; A 1955, 19]—(NRS A 1957, 339; 1963, 675; 1969, 95; 1971, 453; 1975, 1553; 1979, 1551; 1981, 1329; 1983, 166; 1985, 1271; 2001, 523)

NRS 645.685 Revocation, suspension or denial of renewal of license, permit or registration: Answer; limitations on time of commencing proceeding.

1. The licensee, permittee or owner-developer shall file an answer to the charges with the Commission not later than 30 days after service of the notice and other documents described in subsection 4 of NRS 645.680. The answer must contain an admission or denial of the allegations contained in the complaint and any defenses upon which the licensee, permittee or owner-developer will rely. If no answer is filed within the period described in this subsection, the Division may, after notice to the licensee, permittee or owner-developer served in the manner authorized in subsection 5 of NRS 645.680, move the Commission for the entry of a default against the licensee, permittee or owner-developer.

2. The answer may be served by delivery to the Commission, or by mailing the answer by certified mail to the principal office of the Division.

3. No proceeding to suspend, revoke or deny the renewal of any license or registration of an owner-developer may be maintained unless it is commenced by the giving of notice to the licensee, permittee or owner-developer within 5 years after the date of the act charged, whether of commission or omission, except:

(a) If the charges are based upon a misrepresentation, or failure to disclose, the period does not commence until the discovery of facts which do or should lead to the discovery of the misrepresentation or failure to disclose; and

(b) Whenever any action or proceeding is instituted to which the Division, licensee, permittee or owner-developer is a party and which involves the conduct of the licensee, permittee or owner-developer in the transaction with which the charges are related, the running of the 5-year period with respect to the institution of a proceeding pursuant to this chapter to suspend, revoke or deny the renewal of the license, permit or registration is suspended during the pendency of the action or proceeding.

(Added to NRS by 1979, 1534; A 1985, 1272; 1987, 517; 1989, 1613; 2001, 524; 2007, 1543)

NRS 645.690 Revocation, suspension or denial of renewal of license, permit or registration: Hearing; transcript.

1. The hearing on the charges must be held at such time and place as the Commission prescribes. The hearing may be held by the Commission or a majority thereof, and the hearing must be held, if the licensee, permittee or owner-developer so requests in writing, within the northern or southern district, as set forth in NRS 645.100, within which the principal place of business of the licensee, permittee or owner-developer is situated.

2. At the hearing, a stenographic transcript of the proceedings must be made if requested or required for judicial review. Any party to the proceedings desiring a transcript must be furnished with a copy upon payment to the Division of the reasonable cost of transcription.

[Part 21:150:1947; A 1955, 19]—(NRS A 1963, 1075; 1979, 1552; 1981, 1613; 1985, 1273; 2001, 524)

NRS 645.700 Power of Commission to administer oaths, certify acts and issue subpoenas; service of process.

1. The Commission, or any member thereof, shall have power to administer oaths, certify to all official acts, and to issue subpoenas for attendance of witnesses and the production of books and papers.

2. In any hearing or investigation in any part of the State the process issued by the Commission shall extend to all parts of the State and may be served by any person authorized to serve process of courts of record. The person serving any such process shall receive such compensation as may be allowed by the Commission, not to exceed the fees prescribed by law for similar service, and such fees shall be paid in the same manner as provided in NRS 645.710 for the payment of the fees of witnesses.

[Part 22:150:1947; 1943 NCL § 6396.22]—(NRS A 1973, 1103)

NRS 645.710 Fees and mileage for witness.

1. Each witness who appears by order of the Commission is entitled to receive for his or her attendance the same fees and mileage allowed by law to a witness in civil cases, which amount must be paid by the party at whose request the witness is subpoenaed.

2. When any witness not otherwise required to attend, is subpoenaed by the Commission, his or her fees and mileage must be paid by the Division.

[Part 22:150:1947; 1943 NCL § 6396.22]—(NRS A 1979, 1553)

NRS 645.720 Enforcement of subpoenas.

1. The district court in and for the county in which any hearing may be held shall have the power to compel the attendance of witnesses, the giving of testimony and the production of books and papers as required by any subpoena issued by the Commission.

2. In case of the refusal of any witness to attend or testify or produce any papers required by such subpoena the Commission may report to the district court in and for the county in which the hearing is pending by petition, setting forth:

(a) That due notice has been given of the time and place of attendance of the witness or the production of the books and papers;

(b) That the witness has been subpoenaed in the manner prescribed in this chapter; and

(c) That the witness has failed and refused to attend or produce the papers required by subpoena before the Commission in the cause or proceeding named in the subpoena, or has refused to answer questions propounded to him or her in the course of such hearing, and asking an order of the court compelling the witness to attend and testify or produce the books or papers before the Commission.

3. The court, upon petition of the Commission, shall enter an order directing the witness to appear before the court at a time and place to be fixed by the court in such order, the time to be not more than 10 days from the date of the order, and then and there show cause why the witness has not attended or testified or produced the books or papers before the Commission. A certified copy of the order shall be served upon the witness. If it shall appear to the court that the subpoena was regularly issued by the Commission, the court shall thereupon enter an order that the witness appear before the Commission at the time and place fixed in the order and testify or produce the required books or papers, and upon failure to obey the order the witness shall be dealt with as for contempt of court.

[Part 22:150:1947; 1943 NCL § 6396.22]

NRS 645.730 Depositions; taking of evidence in another state; rights of party to hearing.

1. The Commission may, in any hearing before it, cause the depositions of witnesses residing within or without the State to be taken in the manner prescribed by the Nevada Rules of Civil Procedure for like depositions in civil actions in the district courts of this State, and to that end may compel the attendance of witnesses and the production of books and papers.

2. The clerk of the district court in and for the county in which any hearing may be held by the Commission shall, upon the application of the Commission, issue commissions or letters rogatory to other states for the taking of evidence therein for use in any proceedings before the Commission.

3. Any party to any hearing before the Commission shall have the right to the attendance of witnesses in the party's behalf at such hearing or upon deposition as set forth in this section upon making request therefor to the Commission and designating the name and address of the person or persons sought to be subpoenaed.

[Part 22:150:1947; 1943 NCL § 6396.22]

NRS 645.740 Decision of Commission: Rendition; notice; effective date; stay of decision.

1. The Commission shall render an informal decision on any complaint within 15 days after the final hearing thereon and shall give notice in writing of the ruling or decision to the applicant or licensee affected thereby within 60 days after the final hearing thereon by certified mail to the last known address of the person to whom the notice is sent.

2. If the ruling is adverse to the licensee, the Commission shall also state in the notice the date upon which the ruling or decision becomes effective, which date must not be less than 30 days after the date of the notice.

3. The decision of the Commission may not be stayed by any appeal in accordance with the provisions of NRS 645.760, unless the district court so orders upon motion of the licensee, notice to the Division of the motion and opportunity for the Division to be heard.

4. An appeal from a decision of the district court affirming the revocation or suspension of a license does not stay the order of the Commission unless the district or appellate court, in its discretion and upon petition of the licensee, after notice and hearing orders such stay, and upon the filing of a bond for costs in the amount of $1,000.

[Part 23:150:1947; 1943 NCL § 6396.23]—(NRS A 1965, 1409; 1969, 95; 1971, 454; 1973, 1103; 1979, 1553; 1985, 1273)

NRS 645.760 Decision final when in favor of licensee; judicial review of decision against licensee.

1. A ruling or decision of the Commission in any disciplinary action is final when in favor of the licensee.

2. If a ruling or decision is against the licensee, the licensee is entitled to judicial review of the ruling or decision in the manner provided by chapter 233B of NRS.

[Part 23:150:1947; 1943 NCL § 6396.23]—(NRS A 1963, 676; 1979, 1553; 1981, 1613; 1985, 1273; 1989, 1659)

NRS 645.770 Restrictions on issuance of new license, permit or registration after revocation. After the revocation of any license, permit or registration by the Commission as provided in this chapter, no new license, permit or registration may be issued to the same licensee, permittee or registrant, as appropriate, within 1 year after the date of the revocation, nor at any time thereafter except in the sole discretion of the Real Estate Division, and then only provided that the licensee, permittee or registrant satisfies all the requirements for an original license, permit or registration.

[Part 14:150:1947; A 1949, 433; 1943 NCL § 6396.14] + [24:150:1947; 1943 NCL § 6396.24]—(NRS A 1963, 677; 2005, 1292)

NRS 645.780   Expiration of licenses; length of license periods; additional fees for electronic renewal.

1.   Each license issued under the provisions of this chapter expires at midnight on the last day of the last month of the applicable license period for the license.

2.   The initial license period for an original license as a real estate broker, broker-salesperson or salesperson is a period of 12 consecutive months beginning on the first day of the first calendar month after the original license is issued by the Division. Thereafter, each subsequent license period is a period of 24 consecutive months beginning on the first day of the first calendar month after a renewal of the license is issued by the Division for the subsequent license period.

3.   For all other licenses, the license period is a period of 24 consecutive months beginning on the first day of the first calendar month after the license or any renewal of the license is issued by the Division, unless a specific statute:

(a)   Provides for a different license period; or

(b)   Expressly authorizes a different license period to be provided for by regulation.

4.   The Division may:

(a)   Create and maintain a secure website on the Internet through which each license, permit, certificate or registration issued pursuant to the provisions of this chapter may be renewed; and

(b)   For each license, permit, certificate or registration renewed through the use of a website created and maintained pursuant to paragraph (a), charge a fee in addition to any other fee provided for pursuant to this chapter which must not exceed the actual cost to the Division for providing that service.

[Part 19:150:1947; A 1949, 433; 1955, 77]—(NRS A 1963, 334; 1969, 565; 1973, 1104; 1975, 1554; 1977, 1316; 2003, 1294; 2007, 584; 2009, 1939; 2015, 2781)

NRS 645.785   Effect of failure to renew license or permit; increased fee for late renewal.

1.   If a licensee fails to apply for a renewal of his or her license before the date of the expiration thereof, no license may be issued to the licensee except upon another application for an original license, except that within 1 year of such expiration a renewal may be issued upon payment of a fee in the amount of $100, in addition to the amount otherwise required for renewal.

2.   If a licensee fails to apply for a renewal of his or her permit before the date of the expiration thereof, no permit may be issued to the licensee except upon another application for an original permit, except that within 1 year of such expiration a renewal may be issued upon payment of a fee in the amount of $20, in addition to the amount otherwise required for renewal and compliance with any other requirement for renewal pursuant to NRS 645.6052 or 645.863.

[Part 19:150:1947; A 1949, 433; 1955, 77]—(NRS A 1975, 1555; 2013, 1025)

FEES

NRS 645.830   Fees; regulations.

1.   The following fees must be charged by and paid to the Division:

For each original real estate broker's, broker-salesperson's or corporate broker's license $105
For each original real estate salesperson's license... 85
For each original branch office license.. 120
For real estate education, research and recovery to be paid at the time an application for an original license is filed   40
For real estate education, research and recovery to be paid at the time an application for renewal of a license is filed   40
For each renewal of a real estate broker's, broker-salesperson's or corporate broker's license   180
For each renewal of a real estate salesperson's license.................................. 140
For each renewal of a real estate branch office license.................................. 110
For each penalty for late filing of a renewal for a broker's, broker-salesperson's or corporate broker's license   95
For each penalty for late filing of a renewal for a salesperson's license......... 75
For each change of name or address.. 20
For each transfer of a real estate salesperson's or broker-salesperson's license and change of association or employment... 20
For each duplicate license where the original license is lost or destroyed, and an affidavit is made thereof   20

For each change of broker status from broker to broker-salesperson............. 20

For each change of broker status from broker-salesperson to broker............. 40

For each reinstatement to active status of an inactive real estate broker's, broker-salesperson's or salesperson's license... 20

For each reinstatement of a real estate broker's license when the licensee fails to give immediate written notice to the Division of a change of name or business location................................... 30

For each reinstatement of a real estate salesperson's or broker-salesperson's license when he or she fails to notify the Division of a change of broker within 30 days of termination by previous broker 30

For each original registration of an owner-developer.................................... 125

For each annual renewal of a registration of an owner-developer............... 125

For each enlargement of the area of an owner-developer's registration........ 50

For each cooperative certificate issued to an out-of-state broker licensee for 1 year or fraction thereof   150

For each original accreditation of a course of continuing education............ 100

For each renewal of accreditation of a course of continuing education........ 50

For each annual approval of a course of instruction offered in preparation for an original license or permit   100

2.   The fees prescribed by this section for courses of instruction offered in preparation for an original license or permit or for courses of continuing education do not apply to:

(a) Any university, state college or community college of the Nevada System of Higher Education.

(b) Any agency of the State.

(c) Any regulatory agency of the Federal Government.

3.   The Commission shall adopt regulations which establish the fees to be charged and collected by the Division to pay the costs of any investigation of a person's background.

[Part 19:150:1947; A 1949, 433; 1955, 77]—(NRS A 1957, 340; 1959, 396; 1963, 1075; 1965, 1409; 1967, 1046; 1975, 1554, 1642; 1977, 1316; 1979, 1080, 1554; 1981, 1035, 1614; 1985, 1274; 1989, 1613; 1993, 420, 941, 2292; 1995, 163; 2001, 2895; 2003, 1295; 2005, 372; 2009, 1939; 2015, 2782)

REAL ESTATE EDUCATION, RESEARCH AND RECOVERY FUND

NRS 645.841 "Fund" defined.   As used in NRS 645.841 to 645.8494, inclusive, "Fund" means the Real Estate Education, Research and Recovery Fund.

(Added to NRS by 1967, 1043)

NRS 645.842 Creation; use; balances; interest and income.

1.   The Real Estate Education, Research and Recovery Fund is hereby created as a special revenue fund.

2.   A balance of not less than $300,000 must be maintained in the Fund, to be used for satisfying claims against persons licensed under this chapter, as provided in NRS 645.841 to 645.8494, inclusive. Any balance over $300,000 remaining in the Fund at the end of any fiscal year must be set aside and used:

(a) By the Administrator, after approval of the Commission, for real estate education and research; or

(b) For any other purpose authorized by the Legislature.

3.   The interest and income earned on the money in the Fund, after deducting any applicable charges, must be credited to the Fund.

(Added to NRS by 1967, 1043; A 1973, 1763; 1979, 119; 1981, 1615; 2003, 1296; 2005, 665; 2010, 26th Special Session, 24)

NRS 645.843 Payment of additional fee by licensee for augmentation of Fund.

1.   Upon application for or renewal of every real estate broker's, broker-salesperson's and salesperson's license, every licensed broker, broker-salesperson and salesperson shall pay in addition to the original or renewal fee, a fee for real estate education, research and recovery. The additional fee must be deposited in the State Treasury for credit to the Real Estate Education, Research and Recovery Fund, and must be used solely for the purposes provided in NRS 645.841 to 645.8494, inclusive.

2.   Owner-developers need not contribute to the Fund.

(Added to NRS by 1967, 1044; A 1969, 566; 1973, 1105, 1764; 1975, 1643; 1977, 1318; 1979, 119, 1555; 1981, 1615; 1985, 1275)

NRS 645.844   Recovery from Fund: Procedure; grounds; amount; hearing.

1.   Except as otherwise provided in subsection 2, when any person obtains a final judgment in any court of competent jurisdiction against any licensee or licensees pursuant to this chapter, upon grounds of fraud, misrepresentation or deceit with reference to any transaction for which a license is required pursuant to this chapter, that person, upon termination of all proceedings, including appeals in connection with any judgment, may file a verified petition in the court in which the judgment was entered for an order directing payment out of the Fund in the amount of the unpaid actual damages included in the judgment, but not more than $25,000 per judgment. The liability of the Fund does not exceed $100,000 for any person licensed pursuant to this chapter, whether the person is licensed as a limited-liability company, partnership, association or corporation or as a natural person, or both. The petition must state the grounds which entitle the person to recover from the Fund.

2.   A person who is licensed pursuant to this chapter may not recover from the Fund for damages which are related to a transaction in which the person acted in his or her capacity as a licensee.

3.   A copy of the:

(a) Petition;

(b) Judgment;

(c) Complaint upon which the judgment was entered; and

(d) Writ of execution which was returned unsatisfied,

☐ must be served upon the Administrator and the judgment debtor and affidavits of service must be filed with the court.

4.   Upon the hearing on the petition, the petitioner must show that:

(a) The petitioner is not the spouse of the debtor, or the personal representative of that spouse.

(b) The petitioner has complied with all the requirements of NRS 645.841 to 645.8494, inclusive.

(c) The petitioner has obtained a judgment of the kind described in subsection 1, stating the amount thereof, the amount owing thereon at the date of the petition, and that the action in which the judgment was obtained was based on fraud, misrepresentation or deceit of the licensee in a transaction for which a license is required pursuant to this chapter.

(d) A writ of execution has been issued upon the judgment and that no assets of the judgment debtor liable to be levied upon in satisfaction of the judgment could be found, or that the amount realized on the sale of assets was insufficient to satisfy the judgment, stating the amount so realized and the balance remaining due.

(e) The petitioner has made reasonable searches and inquiries to ascertain whether the judgment debtor possesses real or personal property or other assets, liable to be sold or applied in satisfaction of the judgment, and after reasonable efforts that no property or assets could be found or levied upon in satisfaction of the judgment.

(f) The petitioner has made reasonable efforts to recover damages from each and every judgment debtor.

(g) The petition has been filed no more than 1 year after the termination of all proceedings, including reviews and appeals, in connection with the judgment.

5.   The provisions of this section do not apply to owner-developers.

(Added to NRS by 1967, 1044; A 1973, 1764; 1975, 1555; 1979, 1555; 1981, 1615; 1985, 1276; 1987, 1048; 1997, 170; 2005, 666)

NRS 645.845   Administrator may answer petition for recovery; effect of judgment; compromise of claim.

1.   Whenever the court proceeds upon a petition as provided in NRS 645.844, the Administrator may answer and defend any such action against the Fund on behalf of the Fund and may use any appropriate method of review on behalf of the Fund. The judgment debtor may answer and defend any such action on his or her own behalf.

2.   Unless the judgment was entered by default, consent or stipulation or the case was uncontested, the judgment set forth in the petition is prima facie evidence but the findings of fact therein are not conclusive for the purposes of NRS 645.841 to 645.8494, inclusive.

3.   The Administrator may, subject to court approval, compromise a claim based upon the application of a petitioner. The Administrator shall not be bound by any prior compromise of the judgment debtor.

(Added to NRS by 1967, 1044; A 1985, 1277)

NRS 645.846   Court order requiring payment from Fund.   If the court finds after the hearing that the claim should be levied against the portion of the Fund allocated for the purpose of carrying out the provisions of NRS 645.841 to 645.8494, inclusive, the court shall enter an order directed to the Administrator requiring payment from the Fund of whatever sum it finds to be payable upon the claim pursuant to the provisions of and in accordance with the limitations contained in NRS 645.841 to 645.8494, inclusive.

(Added to NRS by 1967, 1045)

NRS 645.847 Automatic suspension of license upon payment from Fund; conditions for reinstatement of license. If the Administrator pays from the Fund any amount in settlement of a claim or towards satisfaction of a judgment against a licensee, the licensee's license issued pursuant to this chapter and chapter 119 of NRS must be automatically suspended upon the effective date of an order by the court authorizing payment from the Fund. The license of the broker, broker-salesperson or salesperson may not be reinstated and no other license may be granted to him or her pursuant to this chapter until he or she has repaid in full, plus interest at a rate equal to the prime rate at the largest bank in Nevada, as ascertained by the Commissioner of Financial Institutions, on January 1 or July 1, as the case may be, immediately preceding the date of judgment, plus 2 percent, the amount paid from the Fund on his or her account. Interest is computed from the date payment from the Fund was made by the Administrator and the rate must be adjusted accordingly on each January 1 and July 1 thereafter until the judgment is satisfied.

(Added to NRS by 1967, 1045; A 1973, 1765; 1979, 1556; 1981, 1616; 1985, 1277; 1987, 942)

NRS 645.848 Distribution of payment from Fund if claims exceed maximum liability of Fund; order of payment of claims if balance of Fund insufficient; interest; use of certain money deposited in Fund.

1. Whenever claims are filed against the Fund which total more than the maximum liability for the acts of one licensee, the maximum liability of the Fund for each licensee must be distributed among the claimants in a ratio that their respective claims bear to the total of all claims, or in any other manner that the court may find equitable.

2. The distribution must be made without regard to the order of priority in which claims were filed or judgments entered.

3. Upon petition of the Administrator, the court may require all claimants and prospective claimants to be joined in one action so that the respective rights of all claimants may be equitably determined.

4. If, at any time, the money deposited in the Fund and allotted for satisfying claims against licensees is insufficient to satisfy any authorized claim or portion thereof, the Administrator shall, when sufficient money has been deposited in the Fund, satisfy the unpaid claims or portions thereof, in the order that the claims or portions thereof were originally filed, plus accumulated interest at the rate of 6 percent per annum. Any sums received by the Division pursuant to NRS 645.847 and 645.8491 must be deposited in the State Treasury for credit to the account for education and research in the Fund.

(Added to NRS by 1967, 1045; A 1973, 1765; 1975, 1556; 1979, 1556; 1985, 1277)

NRS 645.8491 Administrator subrogated to rights of judgment creditor; deposit of money recovered. When the Administrator has paid from the Fund any money to the judgment creditor, the Administrator is subrogated to all other rights of the judgment creditor to the extent of the amount paid and any amount and interest so recovered by the Administrator on the judgment must be deposited in the State Treasury for credit to the Fund.

(Added to NRS by 1967, 1045; A 1985, 1278)

NRS 645.8492 Waiver of rights. The failure of a person to comply with any of the provisions of NRS 645.841 to 645.8494, inclusive, shall constitute a waiver of any rights hereunder.

(Added to NRS by 1967, 1045; A 1973, 1765)

NRS 645.8494 Disciplinary action against licensee not restricted. Nothing contained in NRS 645.841 to 645.8494, inclusive, limits the authority of the Commission to take disciplinary action against a licensee for a violation for any of the provisions of this chapter, or of the rules and regulations of the Commission, nor shall the repayment in full of all obligations to the Fund by any licensee nullify or modify the effect of any other disciplinary proceeding brought pursuant to the provisions of this chapter or the rules and regulations promulgated thereunder.

(Added to NRS by 1967, 1046)

BUSINESS BROKERS

NRS 645.863 Permit to engage in business as business broker: Persons eligible; requirements; continuing education; expiration; renewal; regulations.

1. A person who is licensed as a real estate broker, real estate broker-salesperson or real estate salesperson pursuant to this chapter may apply to the Real Estate Division for a permit to engage in business as a business broker.

2. An applicant for a permit must:

(a) Provide proof satisfactory to the Real Estate Division that the applicant has successfully completed at least 24 hours of instruction relating to business brokerage; and

(b) Comply with any other requirements for the issuance of a permit established by the Commission.

3. A permit expires on the same date as the license of the holder of the permit expires. A permit may be renewed at the time that a person licensed pursuant to this chapter applies for renewal of his or her license.

4. An applicant for the renewal of a permit must:

(a) Provide proof satisfactory to the Real Estate Division that the applicant has successfully completed at least 3 hours of continuing education required for the renewal of his or her license pursuant to the regulations adopted by the Commission pursuant to NRS 645.575 in an approved educational course, seminar or conference relating to business brokerage.

(b) Comply with any other requirements for renewal of a permit established by the Commission.

5. The Commission shall adopt such regulations as are necessary to carry out the provisions of this section. The regulations must include, without limitation, provisions that establish:

(a) Requirements for the issuance or renewal of a permit.

(b) Fees for:

(1) The issuance or renewal of a permit;

(2) The cost of any examination required of an applicant for a permit, including, without limitation, any costs which are necessary for the administration of an examination; and

(3) The cost of any investigation of an applicant for a permit.

(c) Standards of education for the approval of a course of instruction to qualify an applicant for the issuance or renewal of a permit.

(Added to NRS by 2005, 646; A 2007, 1544)

NRS 645.865 Permit to engage in business as business broker: Requirements for certain organizations.

1. To engage in business as a business broker in this State:

(a) A partnership shall designate one of its members;

(b) A corporation shall designate one of its officers or employees;

(c) A limited-liability company shall designate its manager; and

(d) A real estate broker who conducts business as a sole proprietor shall designate himself or herself or a person who is licensed under the real estate broker,

☐ to submit an application for a permit pursuant to NRS 645.863. The partnership, corporation, limited-liability company or sole proprietor shall not engage in business as a business broker unless the person so designated has been issued such a permit.

2. If the person designated to apply for a permit meets the qualifications for a permit set forth in NRS 645.863, the Real Estate Division shall issue to that person a permit to engage in business as a business broker on behalf of the partnership, corporation, limited-liability company or sole proprietor.

3. A person to whom such a permit has been issued may act as a business broker pursuant to the permit only on behalf of the partnership, corporation, limited-liability company or sole proprietor, and not on his or her own behalf. If that person ceases to be connected or associated with the partnership, corporation, limited-liability company or sole proprietor, the partnership, corporation, limited-liability company or sole proprietor shall designate another person who meets the qualifications for a permit set forth in NRS 645.863 to hold the permit on behalf of the partnership, corporation, limited-liability company or sole proprietor.

4. Any member, officer or employee of a partnership, corporation, limited-liability company or sole proprietor, other than the person designated as the business broker pursuant to subsection 1, who wishes to engage in business as a business broker must apply in his or her own name for a permit. Pursuant to such a permit, the member, officer or employee of a partnership, corporation, limited-liability company or sole proprietor may act as a business broker only as an officer, agent or employee of the partnership, corporation, limited-liability company or sole proprietor, and not on his or her own behalf.

(Added to NRS by 2005, 647)

NRS 645.867 Designated business brokers: Requirements; qualifications; duties.

1. If a real estate broker does not hold a permit to engage in business as a business broker but intends to have the activities of a business broker conducted at an office, the real estate broker must:

(a) Appoint a person, who has the qualifications required by this section, as the designated business broker for the office to supervise the activities of a business broker conducted at the office; and

(b) Submit notice of the appointment to the Division.

2. The designated business broker for an office must be a natural person who:

(a) Holds a license as a real estate broker or real estate broker-salesperson;

(b) Holds a permit to engage in business as a business broker; and

(c) Has 2 years active experience, within the 4 years immediately preceding the date of the appointment, in conducting the activities of a business broker in the United States as a licensed real estate broker, real estate broker-salesperson or real estate salesperson.

3. While acting as the designated business broker for an office, the person:

(a) Must comply with all applicable provisions of this chapter; and

(b) Is subject to all the remedies and penalties provided for in this chapter.

(Added to NRS by 2005, 647)

BROKERAGE AGREEMENTS INVOLVING COMMERCIAL REAL ESTATE

General Provisions

NRS 645.8701 Definitions. As used in NRS 645.8701 to 645.8811, inclusive, unless the context otherwise requires, the words and terms defined in NRS 645.8705 to 645.8741, inclusive, have the meanings ascribed to them in those sections.

(Added to NRS by 1999, 1174)

NRS 645.8705 "Brokerage agreement" defined. "Brokerage agreement" means a written contract between an owner and a real estate broker in which the owner agrees to pay a commission to the real estate broker for services provided by the broker relating to the disposition of commercial real estate as specified in the agreement.

(Added to NRS by 1999, 1174)

NRS 645.8711 "Commercial real estate" defined. "Commercial real estate" means any real estate located in this State. The term does not include:

1. Improved real estate that consists of not more than four residential units;

2. Unimproved real estate for which not more than four residential units may be developed or constructed pursuant to any zoning regulations or any development plan applicable to the real estate; or

3. A single-family residential unit, including a condominium, townhouse or home within a subdivision, if the unit is sold, leased or otherwise conveyed unit by unit, regardless of whether the unit is part of a larger building or parcel that consists of more than four units.

(Added to NRS by 1999, 1174)

NRS 645.8715 "Commission" defined. "Commission" means any fee or other compensation agreed upon by a real estate broker and an owner specified in a brokerage agreement.

(Added to NRS by 1999, 1175)

NRS 645.8721 "Disposition" defined. "Disposition" means a voluntary conveyance or other transfer of title or any interest of an owner in any commercial real estate specified in a brokerage agreement.

(Added to NRS by 1999, 1175)

NRS 645.8725 "Escrow" defined. "Escrow" has the meaning ascribed to it in NRS 645A.010.
(Added to NRS by 1999, 1175; A 2011, 3595; 2015, 2790)

NRS 645.8731 "Escrow agent" defined. "Escrow agent" has the meaning ascribed to it in NRS 645A.010.
(Added to NRS by 1999, 1175; A 2011, 3595; 2015, 2790)

NRS 645.8735 "Owner" defined. "Owner" means a person who holds legal title to or any interest in any commercial real estate that is described in a brokerage agreement, including, without limitation, any assignee in interest and any agent of a person. The term does not include a mortgagee, trustee under or beneficiary of a deed of trust or an owner or holder of a claim that encumbers any real estate or any improvement on that real estate.

(Added to NRS by 1999, 1175)

NRS 645.8741 "Owner's net proceeds" defined. "Owner's net proceeds" means the gross receipts to which an owner is entitled upon the disposition of any commercial real estate specified in a brokerage agreement. The term does not include:

1. Any money that is required to pay an encumbrance, claim or lien that has priority over a claim recorded pursuant to the provisions of NRS 645.8775 other than an encumbrance, claim or lien that the person to whom the commercial real estate is conveyed or otherwise transferred authorizes to remain after the disposition of the real estate; or

2. Any costs incurred by the owner to close escrow for that commercial real estate.

(Added to NRS by 1999, 1175)

Rights, Duties and Liabilities Relating to Commissions

NRS 645.8761 **Broker has claim upon owner's net proceeds for earned commissions; conditions and limitations on enforcement of claim; waiver; inapplicability to third-party claims; obligation to close escrow unaffected by claim.**

1. A real estate broker has a claim upon the owner's net proceeds from the disposition of commercial real estate for any commission earned by the real estate broker pursuant to a brokerage agreement. For the purposes of this subsection, a commission shall be deemed to be earned when the real estate broker has performed his or her duties pursuant to the brokerage agreement.

2. The claim belongs to the real estate broker named in the brokerage agreement and not to an employee or independent contractor of the real estate broker.

3. A claim that is recorded pursuant to the provisions of NRS 645.8775:

(a) Is a claim upon personal property and does not attach to the title of any real property.

(b) May be waived if, on or before the date the brokerage agreement is executed, the real estate broker signs a written waiver of the real estate broker's right to enforce the claim. The waiver must be printed in uppercase letters and must be limited to one transaction. A person other than the real estate broker may not waive the rights of the real estate broker pursuant to this section, regardless of whether that person may execute and bind the real estate broker to a brokerage agreement.

(c) May not be enforced by a person other than the real estate broker and the owner.

4. A claim of a third party may not be brought or otherwise adjudicated pursuant to the provisions of NRS 645.8701 to 645.8811, inclusive.

5. The recording or enforcement of a claim by a real estate broker pursuant to the provisions of NRS 645.8701 to 645.8811, inclusive, does not relieve the owner of his or her obligation to close escrow for any commercial real estate.

(Added to NRS by 1999, 1175)

NRS 645.8765 **Requirements for broker to enforce claim: Written notice to owner and escrow agent; effect of failure to provide notice; exceptions.**

1. Except as otherwise provided in subsection 3, if a real estate broker wishes to enforce a claim pursuant to the provisions of NRS 645.8701 to 645.8811, inclusive, the real estate broker shall, within 7 days after a commission is earned by the real estate broker pursuant to a brokerage agreement, provide a written notice of the claim to:

(a) The owner of the commercial real estate specified in the brokerage agreement; and

(b) The escrow agent closing the transaction for the commercial real estate.

2. A real estate broker who fails to provide a notice of a claim within the period specified in subsection 1 may not enforce the claim pursuant to the provisions of NRS 645.8701 to 645.8811, inclusive.

3. A real estate broker is not required to provide a written notice of a claim to an escrow agent pursuant to this section if the identity of the escrow agent is unknown to the real estate agent at the time the notice is provided by the real estate broker to the owner pursuant to paragraph (a) of subsection 1.

(Added to NRS by 1999, 1176)

NRS 645.8771 **Requirements for broker to enforce claim: Information required in notice; verification by oath; acknowledgment.**

1. A notice of claim specified in NRS 645.8765 must include:

(a) The name of the owner of the commercial real estate;

(b) The name of the person who executed the brokerage agreement, if other than the owner;

(c) The name, business name, if any, and the license number of the real estate broker;

(d) The amount claimed by the real estate broker;

(e) A detailed description of the commercial real estate; and

(f) A copy of the brokerage agreement pursuant to which the real estate broker claims a commission.

2. The notice must:

(a) Be verified by the oath of the real estate broker who provides the notice; and

49

(b) Include an acknowledgment by the real estate broker.

(Added to NRS by 1999, 1176)

NRS 645.8775 Duty of owner to confirm or deny claim; effect of confirming claim; effect of denying claim or failing to respond; recording of claim by broker.

1. If an owner is served with a notice of a claim pursuant to NRS 645.8765, the owner shall, within 5 days after service of the notice but not later than 7 days before the disposition of the commercial real estate:

(a) Confirm or deny the claim set forth in the notice; and

(b) Notify, in writing, the real estate broker who provided the notice to the owner.

2. If the owner confirms the claim and notifies the real estate broker of that fact pursuant to subsection 1, the owner may instruct the escrow agent for the commercial real estate to pay to the real estate broker the amount claimed by the real estate broker in the notice of the claim.

3. If the owner fails to notify the real estate broker within the period specified in subsection 1 or notifies the real estate broker that the owner denies the claim, the real estate broker may record the notice of the claim in the office of the county recorder where the commercial real estate or any portion of the commercial real estate is located.

(Added to NRS by 1999, 1176)

NRS 645.8781 Duties of escrow agent upon notice of claim.

1. Except as otherwise provided in this subsection, if:

(a) An escrow agent receives a notice of a claim pursuant to NRS 645.8765;

(b) A notice of claim is recorded pursuant to NRS 645.8775; or

(c) An escrow agent has actual notice of a claim specified in paragraph (b),

□ the escrow agent shall reserve from the owner's net proceeds an amount that is equal to the amount claimed by the real estate broker in his or her recorded claim. If the amount of the owner's net proceeds is insufficient to satisfy the amount of the claim, the escrow agent shall reserve the entire amount of the owner's net proceeds. In determining whether the amount of the owner's net proceeds is insufficient to satisfy the amount of the claim, the escrow agent may consider any encumbrance, claim or lien that has priority over the claim of the real estate broker pursuant to NRS 645.8795.

2. If the escrow agent determines that the amount of the owner's net proceeds is insufficient to satisfy the amount of the claim, the escrow agent:

(a) Shall, within 3 days after making that determination but not later than the close of escrow, notify the real estate broker of that fact in writing; and

(b) Shall not release to the owner any portion of the owner's net proceeds unless the escrow agent receives a copy of the written agreement executed by the owner and the real estate broker authorizing the escrow agent to release those proceeds to the owner.

3. Except as otherwise provided in paragraph (b) of subsection 2 and NRS 645.8791, if an owner's net proceeds or any portion of an owner's net proceeds are reserved pursuant to this section, the escrow agent who reserves those proceeds shall not release the proceeds to any person until the rights of the owner and the real estate broker are determined pursuant to NRS 645.8791.

4. A reservation of an owner's net proceeds or any portion of an owner's net proceeds pursuant to this section does not relieve the owner of the obligation to close escrow for the commercial real estate.

(Added to NRS by 1999, 1177)

NRS 645.8785 Deposit of proceeds with district court; discharge of escrow agent from further liability concerning proceeds.

1. If:

(a) A notice of a claim is recorded pursuant to NRS 645.8775;

(b) An escrow agent has reserved an owner's net proceeds or any portion of an owner's net proceeds pursuant to NRS 645.8781; and

(c) Escrow for the disposition of the commercial real estate has closed,

□ the escrow agent may, in accordance with the provisions of NRS 645A.177, deposit with the district court of the county where the claim is recorded the amount of the owner's net proceeds reserved by him or her pursuant to NRS 645.8781.

2. If an escrow agent deposits an owner's net proceeds with a district court pursuant to subsection 1, the escrow agent is discharged from any further liability concerning those proceeds.

NRS 645.8791   Civil action concerning claim: Issuance of order to broker to appear and show cause; effect of failure to appear; hearings; release of proceeds; frivolous claims; compensatory damages; award of costs and attorney's fees to prevailing party.

1.   If a claim is recorded pursuant to NRS 645.8775, the owner against whom the claim is recorded may:

(a) File a civil action concerning the claim in the district court of the county where the commercial real estate or a portion of the commercial real estate is located; and

(b) At the time the summons is issued or at any time before the complaint is answered by the real estate broker, apply to the district court for an order directing the real estate broker to appear before the court to show cause why the claim should not be dismissed.

2.   If the court issues an order directing the real estate broker to appear before the court, the order must:

(a) State that, if the real estate broker fails to appear at the time and place specified in the order, the claim will be dismissed with prejudice pursuant to subsection 3;

(b) Specify a time and date on which the court will conduct a hearing on the matter; and

(c) Establish a period within which the owner must serve a notice of the order on the real estate broker and the escrow agent.

3.   If the real estate broker fails to appear at the time and place specified in the order issued pursuant to subsection 2, the court shall issue an order:

(a) Dismissing the claim with prejudice;

(b) Cancelling the notice of the claim recorded pursuant to NRS 645.8775; and

(c) Requiring the real estate broker to record in the office of the county recorder of the county where the notice of the claim is recorded a copy of the order of cancellation issued pursuant to paragraph (b).

☐ An order issued pursuant to this subsection must state that the cancellation of the notice of the claim has the same effect as an expungement of that notice.

4.   If a hearing is conducted pursuant to this section, the court shall consider the showing made by the parties at the hearing and shall make a preliminary determination of which party, with reasonable probability, is entitled to the amount of the owner's net proceeds claimed by the broker pending final adjudication of the claims of the parties.

5.   If, after the hearing, the district court determines there is a reasonable probability that:

(a) The real estate broker is entitled to the amount of the owner's net proceeds claimed by him or her, the court shall, if those proceeds:

(1) Have been deposited with the court by the escrow agent pursuant to NRS 645.8785, release the proceeds to the real estate broker; or

(2) Have not been deposited with the court by the escrow agent pursuant to that section, order the escrow agent to release the proceeds to the real estate broker; or

(b) The owner is entitled to the amount of the owner's net proceeds claimed by the real estate broker, the court shall, if those proceeds:

(1) Have been deposited with the court by the escrow agent pursuant to NRS 645.8785, release the proceeds to the owner; or

(2) Have not been deposited with the court by the escrow agent, order the escrow agent to release the proceeds to the owner.

6.   If the owner believes the claim is frivolous and is made without reasonable cause, the owner may include in the application submitted pursuant to subsection 1 a request for an order directing the real estate broker to appear and show cause why the claim should not be dismissed on those grounds. If the court issues such an order, any hearing conducted pursuant to that order must be conducted in the manner provided in NRS 108.2275. In addition to any remedy set forth in that section, the court may award compensatory damages to the owner.

7.   The prevailing party in any civil action filed or hearing conducted pursuant to this section is entitled to receive:

(a) Any costs incurred by that party for the civil action or hearing; and

(b) A reasonable attorney's fee.

8.   Proceedings conducted pursuant to this section do not affect any rights or remedies otherwise available to the owner or the real estate broker.

(Added to NRS by 1999, 1178)

NRS 645.8795   Priority of recorded claim.

1. Except as otherwise provided in subsection 2, a claim that is recorded pursuant to the provisions of NRS 645.8775 has priority over any other encumbrance, claim or lien, if the claim of the real estate broker is recorded before the encumbrance, claim or lien.

2. The provisions of subsection 1 do not apply to a lien recorded pursuant to the provisions of NRS 108.221 to 108.246, inclusive.

(Added to NRS by 1999, 1179)

NRS 645.8801   Release of recorded claim.   If a real estate broker records a claim pursuant to the provisions of NRS 645.8775 and that claim is paid or otherwise satisfied pursuant to that section, the real estate broker shall, within 3 days after the claim is paid or otherwise satisfied, record a written release of that claim. The release must be recorded in the office of the county recorder where the claim was recorded.

(Added to NRS by 1999, 1179)

NRS 645.8805   Service of notice.   Any notice that is required to be served pursuant to the provisions of NRS 645.8701 to 645.8811, inclusive, must be served in the manner provided in NRS 108.227.

(Added to NRS by 1999, 1179)

NRS 645.8811   Escrow agents: Immunity; collection of fees for services.   An escrow agent:

1. Is not liable in any civil action for any action taken to comply with the provisions of NRS 645.8701 to 645.8811, inclusive.

2. May charge and collect a fee from an owner or real estate broker for any services provided by the escrow agent to the owner or real estate broker pursuant to NRS 645.8701 to 645.8811, inclusive.

(Added to NRS by 1999, 1179)

PROHIBITED ACTS; PENALTIES; ENFORCEMENT

NRS 645.990   Unlawful acts; penalties.

1. A person who:

(a) Obtains or attempts to obtain a license pursuant to this chapter by means of intentional misrepresentation, deceit or fraud; or

(b) Sells or attempts to sell in this State any interest in real property by means of intentional misrepresentation, deceit or fraud,

☐ is guilty of a category D felony and shall be punished as provided in NRS 193.130. In addition to any other penalty, the court shall order the person to pay restitution.

2. Any licensee, permittee or owner-developer who commits an act described in NRS 645.630, 645.633 or 645.635 shall be punished by a fine of not more than $5,000 $10,000 for each offense.

3. A person who violates any other provision of this chapter, if a natural person, is guilty of a gross misdemeanor, and if a limited-liability company, partnership, association or corporation, shall be punished by a fine of not more than $2,500.

4. Any officer or agent of a corporation, or member or agent of a limited-liability company, partnership or association, who personally participates in or is an accessory to any violation of this chapter by the limited-liability company, partnership, association or corporation, is subject to the penalties prescribed in this section for natural persons.

5. The provisions of this section do not release a person from civil liability or criminal prosecution pursuant to the general laws of this State.

6. The Administrator may prefer a complaint for violation of NRS 645.230 before any court of competent jurisdiction and may take the necessary legal steps through the proper legal officers of this State to enforce the provisions thereof.

7. Any court of competent jurisdiction may try any violation of this chapter, and upon conviction, the court may revoke or suspend the license of the person so convicted, in addition to imposing the other penalties provided in this section.

NRS 645.993   Unlawful to file documents that are false or contain willful, material misstatement of fact; penalty.

1. It is unlawful for any person to file with the Administrator, the Division or the Commission any notice, statement, complaint or other document required under the provisions of this chapter which is false or which contains any willful, material misstatement of fact.

2. A person who violates any provision of this section is guilty of a gross misdemeanor.
(Added to NRS by 2003, 1289)

NRS 645.995   Duty to report conviction to Division.   [Replaced in revision by NRS 645.615.]

NAC 645

CHAPTER 645 - REAL ESTATE BROKERS AND SALESPERSONS

PROCEEDINGS BEFORE COMMISSION

PERMIT TO ENGAGE IN BUSINESS AS BUSINESS BROKER

GENERAL PROVISIONS

NAC 645.005 Definitions. (NRS 645.190) As used in this chapter, unless the context otherwise requires, the words and terms defined in NAC 645.007 to 645.055, inclusive, have the meanings ascribed to them in those sections.

[Real Estate Adv. Comm'n, part § I, eff. 10-31-75] — (NAC A by Real Estate Comm'n by R146-99, 1-21-2000; R031-04, 11-30-2004; R123-06, 6-1-2006; R165-07, 4-17-2008)

NAC 645.007 "Active experience" defined. (NRS 645.190, 645.343) "Active experience" for the purposes of NRS 645.343 means experience gained while engaged in those activities described in subsections 1 and 2 of NRS 645.030 and NRS 645.035 and 645.040 for at least 30 hours a week during at least 48 weeks of any 12-month period.

(Added to NAC by Real Estate Comm'n, eff. 8-21-81; A by R146-99, 1-21-2000)

NAC 645.010 "Active status" defined. (NRS 645.190) "Active status" means that a person holds a current license, is otherwise in good standing with the Division and may engage in the real estate business.

[Real Estate Adv. Comm'n, § I subsec. 1, eff. 10-31-75]

NAC 645.011 "Administrator" defined. (NRS 645.190) "Administrator" means the Real Estate Administrator.

(Added to NAC by Real Estate Comm'n by R146-99, eff. 1-21-2000)

NAC 645.0115 "Advisory committee" defined. (NRS 645.190) "Advisory committee" means a committee established pursuant to NAC 645.490.

(Added to NAC by Real Estate Comm'n by R146-99, eff. 1-21-2000)

NAC 645.013 "Approved course" defined. (NRS 645.190) "Approved course" means a course of education that has been approved as a course for continuing education pursuant to NAC 645.455 or as a course for postlicensing education pursuant to NAC 645.4444.

(Added to NAC by Real Estate Comm'n by R031-04, eff. 11-30-2004)

NAC 645.017 "Branch office" defined. (NRS 645.190) "Branch office" means an office operated by a licensed real estate broker or corporation, separate from the principal location of the broker, for the purpose of engaging in a general real estate business. It does not include a sales office within the same or a nearby community which is used only for sales activities pertaining to the development.

[Real Estate Adv. Comm'n, § I subsec. 12 + § VI subsec. 17, eff. 12-20-75]

NAC 645.020 "Commission" defined. "Commission" means the Real Estate Commission.

(Supplied in codification)

NAC 645.021 "Distance education" defined. (NRS 645.190) "Distance education" means instruction that is delivered by video, computer, television, correspondence, the Internet or other electronic means of communication, or any combination thereof, in such a manner that the person supervising or providing the instruction and the student receiving the instruction are separated by distance or by time, or by both distance and time.

(Added to NAC by Real Estate Comm'n by R031-04, eff. 11-30-2004)

NAC 645.022 "Division" defined. "Division" means the Real Estate Division of the Department of Business and Industry.

(Supplied in codification)

NAC 645.025 "Employment" defined. (NRS 645.190) "Employment" means the relationship between a salesperson and the broker with whom the salesperson is associated. It includes any employee-employer relationship as well as any independent contractor relationship.

[Real Estate Adv. Comm'n, § I subsec. 4, eff. 10-31-75]

NAC 645.0255 "Exclusive agency listing agreement" defined. (NRS 645.190) "Exclusive agency listing agreement" means an agreement between a broker and a seller or lessor that:
1.   Meets the requirements of NRS 645.320;
2.   Grants the broker the exclusive right to represent the seller or lessor in the sale or lease of any property; and
3.   Provides the broker with the expectation of receiving compensation if the broker or any other person produces a purchaser or tenant in accordance with the terms of the exclusive agency listing agreement or if the property is sold or leased during the term of the exclusive agency listing agreement, unless the property is sold or leased solely through the efforts of the seller or lessor or to a person who is specifically exempted under the exclusive agency listing agreement.

(Added to NAC by Real Estate Comm'n by R165-07, eff. 4-17-2008)

NAC 645.026 "Exclusive buyer's brokerage agreement" defined. (NRS 645.190) "Exclusive buyer's brokerage agreement" means an agreement between a broker and a purchaser or tenant that:
1.   Meets the requirements of NRS 645.320;
2.   Grants the broker the exclusive right to represent the purchaser or tenant in the purchase or lease of any property; and
3.   Provides the broker with the expectation of receiving compensation in accordance with the terms specified in the exclusive buyer's brokerage agreement or if any property is purchased or leased by the purchaser or tenant during the term of the exclusive buyer's brokerage agreement, unless the property is specifically exempted in the exclusive buyer's brokerage agreement.

(Added to NAC by Real Estate Comm'n by R165-07, eff. 4-17-2008)

NAC 645.0265 "Exclusive right to sell or lease listing agreement" defined. (NRS 645.190) "Exclusive right to sell or lease listing agreement" means an agreement that:

1. Meets the requirements of NRS 645.320;
2. Grants the broker the exclusive right to represent the seller or lessor in the sale or lease of any property; and
3. Provides the broker with the expectation of receiving compensation if the broker, the seller or any other person produces a purchaser or tenant in accordance with the terms specified in the exclusive right to sell or lease listing agreement or if the property is sold or leased during the term of the exclusive right to sell or lease listing agreement to any person other than a person who is specifically exempted under the exclusive right to sell or lease listing agreement.

(Added to NAC by Real Estate Comm'n by R165-07, eff. 4-17-2008)

NAC 645.027 "Franchise" defined. (NRS 645.190) "Franchise" means an agreement, whether expressed or implied, oral or written, between two or more persons by which:

1. The holder is granted the right to engage in the business of offering, selling or distributing goods or services under a marketing plan or system prescribed in substantial part by the grantor;
2. The operation of the holder's business pursuant to such a plan or system is substantially associated with the grantor's trademark, service mark, trade name, logotype, advertising or other commercial symbol which identifies the grantor or its affiliate; and
3. The holder is required to pay, directly or indirectly, a fee for this right.

[Real Estate Adv. Comm'n, § I subsec. 13, eff. 12-30-76] — (NAC A by Real Estate Comm'n, 8-21-81; 8-26-83)

NAC 645.040 "Inactive renewed status" defined. (NRS 645.190) "Inactive renewed status" means that a licensee holds a current unsuspended or unrevoked license, but has cancelled the license and may not transact any real estate business until the licensee reinstates the license to active status. When a licensee is on inactive renewed status, the Division shall keep his or her license.

[Real Estate Adv. Comm'n, § I subsec. 6, eff. 10-31-75]

NAC 645.042 "Involuntarily inactivate" defined. (NRS 645.190) "Involuntarily inactivate" means to transfer a license from active status to inactive renewed status at the initiative of the Division and not at the request of the licensee.

[Real Estate Adv. Comm'n, § I subsec. 7, eff. 10-31-75] — (NAC A by Real Estate Comm'n by R031-04, 11-30-2004)

NAC 645.043 "Licensee" defined. (NRS 645.190) "Licensee" means any person who holds a license as a real estate broker, broker-salesperson or salesperson pursuant to chapter 645 of NRS.

(Added to NAC by Real Estate Comm'n, eff. 12-16-82)

NAC 645.045 "Owner-developer" defined. (NRS 645.190) "Owner-developer" has the meaning ascribed to it by NRS 645.018.

[Real Estate Adv. Comm'n, § I subsec. 8, eff. 10-31-75]

NAC 645.046 "Postlicensing education" defined. (NRS 645.190) "Postlicensing education" means the postlicensing curriculum of continuing education that, pursuant to NRS 645.575, a person is required to complete within the first year after his or her initial licensing.

(Added to NAC by Real Estate Comm'n by R031-04, eff. 11-30-2004)

NAC 645.047 "Principal place of business" defined. (NRS 645.190) "Principal place of business" means the principal office of a licensed real estate broker which he or she uses to conduct a general real estate business.

[Real Estate Adv. Comm'n, § I subsec. 11, eff. 12-20-75]

NAC 645.050 "Reinstatement" defined. (NRS 645.190) "Reinstatement" means the return to active status.

[Real Estate Adv. Comm'n, § I subsec. 9, eff. 10-31-75]

NAC 645.051 "Sign" defined. (NRS 645.190) "Sign" means to affix a signature to a record.

(Added to NAC by Real Estate Comm'n by R123-06, eff. 6-1-2006)

NAC 645.0515 "Signature" defined. (NRS 645.190) "Signature" means a name, word, symbol or mark executed or otherwise adopted, or a record encrypted or similarly processed in whole or in part, by a person with the present intent to identify himself or herself and adopt or accept a record. The term includes, without limitation, an electronic signature as defined in NRS 719.100.

(Added to NAC by Real Estate Comm'n by R123-06, eff. 6-1-2006)

NAC 645.052 "Single-family residence" defined. (NRS 645.018, 645.190) "Single-family residence," for the purposes of NRS 645.018, includes, without limitation, an attached residential dwelling, a condominium, a cooperative apartment, a manufactured home and a townhouse unit.

(Added to NAC by Real Estate Comm'n, eff. 8-21-81; A by R031-04, 11-30-2004)

NAC 645.055 "Voluntary cancellation" defined. (NRS 645.190) "Voluntary cancellation" means the transferring of a license from active status to inactive renewed status by a licensee.

[Real Estate Adv. Comm'n, § I subsec. 10, eff. 10-31-75]

NAC 645.070 Severability of provisions. (NRS 645.190) If any provision of these regulations, or the application thereof to any person, thing, or circumstance is held invalid, such invalidity does not affect the provisions or application of these regulations which can be given effect without the invalid provision or application, and to this end the provisions of these regulations are declared to be severable.

[Real Estate Adv. Comm'n, § II subsec. 2, eff. 10-31-75] — (Substituted in revision for NAC 645.920)

ADMINISTRATION

NAC 645.075 Distribution of booklet concerning certain disclosures required in sale of residential property. (NRS 645.190, 645.194)

1. The Division shall make copies of the booklet prepared pursuant to NRS 645.194 available to licensees using one or more of the following methods of distribution:

(a) Making a printable version of the booklet available on the Internet website maintained by the Division.

(b) Providing an electronic copy of the booklet to each approved sponsor of real estate education courses.

(c) Authorizing any person to reproduce the most recent version of the booklet without obtaining the approval of the Division.

(d) Providing to schools or instructors approved by the Commission printed copies of the booklet for use in courses to fulfill the educational requirements for issuance of an original license pursuant to chapter 645 of NRS, courses for postlicensing education and courses for continuing education which are devoted to the legal aspects of real estate.

(e) Providing at no cost not more than 10 printed copies of the booklet upon request at an office of the Division, if a sufficient supply of booklets is available at the office.

(f) Mailing a printed copy of the booklet to any licensee upon the request of the licensee.

(g) Any other method of distribution deemed appropriate by the Division.

2. Upon the request of any person at an office of the Division, the Division shall provide the person a printed copy of the booklet prepared pursuant to NRS 645.194.

(Added to NAC by Real Estate Comm'n by R090-09, eff. 4-20-2010)

NAC 645.080 Investigations of background: Fee. (NRS 645.190, 645.6052, 645.830) The fee for the investigation of the background of an applicant, licensee, certificate holder, registrant or permit holder will not exceed the actual cost to conduct the investigation.

(Added to NAC by Real Estate Comm'n by R050-04, eff. 8-25-2004)

NAC 645.085 Check or draft returned to Division for lack of payment: Sanctions; fee. (NRS 645.190)

1. If a person submits a check or draft to the Division to obtain a certificate, approval, accreditation or other type of authorization to engage in an activity for which authorization is required pursuant to this chapter, or chapter 645 of NRS, and the check or draft is returned to the Division because the person had insufficient money or credit with the drawee to pay the check or draft or because the person stopped payment on the check or draft:

(a) The certificate, approval, accreditation or other type of authorization obtained by the person from the Division is involuntarily inactivated; or

(b) If the person has not obtained the certificate, approval, accreditation or other type of authorization from the Division, the Division may refuse to issue or reinstate the authorization.

2. In accordance with NRS 353C.115 and NAC 353C.400, the Division shall charge a person, for each check or draft returned to the Division because the person had insufficient money or credit with the drawee to pay the check or draft or because the person stopped payment on the check or draft, a fee of $25 or such other amount as may subsequently be required by NRS 353C.115 and NAC 353C.400.

(Added to NAC by Real Estate Comm'n by R031-04, eff. 11-30-2004)

NAC 645.095 Denial of application, license or permit; proof of moral character; appeal. (NRS 645.190, 645.285, 645.330, 645.400, 645.6052)

1. The Division may deny any application for registration as an owner-developer, a license or a permit issued by the Division pursuant to this chapter or chapter 645 of NRS for any reason which is sufficient to deny a license pursuant to NRS 645.330 or when one or more of the following conditions exist:

(a) The application is not in proper form;

(b) The application is not accompanied by the required fees;

(c) The accompanying forms are incomplete or otherwise unsatisfactory;

(d) The application contains a false statement;

(e) Other deficiencies appear in the application;

(f) An investigation fails to show affirmatively that the applicant possesses the necessary qualifications, including, without limitation, good moral character and financial responsibility;

(g) The applicant has willfully acted or attempted to act in violation of chapter 113, 116, 119, 119A, 645, 645A, 645C or 645D of NRS or the regulations adopted pursuant thereto, or has willfully aided and abetted another to act or attempt to act in violation of those chapters or regulations;

(h) The check used in paying the required fees for the registration, license or permit is not honored by the financial institution upon which it is drawn; or

(i) If the application is for registration as an owner-developer, the applicant fails to verify that he or she is a licensed contractor in this State.

2. The Administrator may require proof of the applicant's moral character. In determining that character, the Administrator shall consider:

(a) The results of the Division's investigation of matters stated in the application and other matters that have come to the attention of the Division as a result of the investigation of the Division;

(b) Any history of arrest and conviction of the applicant;

(c) The nature and history of the business of the applicant; and

(d) Any past failure of the applicant to comply with any applicable requirements of chapter 113, 116, 119, 119A, 645, 645A, 645C or 645D of NRS.

3. An applicant whose application is denied by the Division may appeal the denial to the Commission in the manner set forth in NRS 645.440. If the Commission reverses the original decision and determines that the petitioner qualifies for registration, a license or a permit, the application may be accepted as of the date the application was originally submitted or the date on which the fee for the registration, license or permit was paid, whichever is later. The Division shall not charge an additional fee.

4. If the Division denies an application pursuant to this section, the Division will not refund any fees paid pursuant to that application.

(Added to NAC by Real Estate Comm'n by R111-01, eff. 12-17-2001)

LICENSES, CERTIFICATES AND EXAMINATIONS

NAC 645.100 Applicant for license as real estate salesperson: Minimum age; requirements. (NRS 645.190, 645.330, 645.400) An applicant for a license as a real estate salesperson must:

1. Be at least 18 years of age; and

2. Include with an application submitted to the Division pursuant to NRS 645.350:

(a) His or her fingerprint card as required pursuant to NRS 645.355;

(b) Proof that the applicant has satisfied the educational requirements for a license as a real estate salesperson as set forth in NRS 645.343;

(c) In accordance with NRS 645.358, the statement prescribed by the Division of Welfare and Supportive Services of the Department of Health and Human Services pursuant to NRS 425.520;

(d) Proof that the applicant has received a passing grade as described in NAC 645.220 on the examination for the license;

(e) The verified statement required by NRS 645.350;

(f) Any information required pursuant to NAC 645.150, including, without limitation, proof of honesty, truthfulness and good reputation; and

(g) The required fees.

(Added to NAC by Real Estate Comm'n by R111-01, eff. 12-17-2001)

NAC 645.101 Applicant for license as real estate broker-salesperson: Requirements. (NRS 645.190, 645.400) An applicant for a license as a real estate broker-salesperson must satisfy the requirements for a license as a real estate salesperson as set forth in NAC 645.100 except the educational requirements set forth in paragraph (b) of subsection 2 of NAC 645.100. In lieu of providing proof that he or she has satisfied the educational requirements for a license as a real estate salesperson, the applicant must include with an application submitted to the Division pursuant to NRS 645.350 proof that he or she has satisfied the educational requirements for a license as a real estate broker-salesperson as set forth in NRS 645.343.

(Added to NAC by Real Estate Comm'n by R111-01, eff. 12-17-2001)

NAC 645.102 Applicant for license as real estate broker: Requirements. (NRS 645.190, 645.400)

1. Before a person who wishes to apply for a license as a real estate broker submits an application for the license pursuant to NRS 645.350, the person must obtain approval of his or her financial condition from the Division pursuant to NAC 645.120.

2. An applicant for a license as a real estate broker must satisfy the requirements for a license as a real estate salesperson as set forth in NAC 645.100 except the educational requirements set forth in paragraph (b) of subsection 2 of NAC 645.100. In lieu of providing proof that he or she has satisfied the educational requirements for a license as a real estate salesperson, the applicant must include with an application submitted to the Division pursuant to NRS 645.350 proof that he or she has satisfied the educational requirements for a license as a real estate broker as set forth in NRS 645.343.

3. In addition to satisfying the requirements set forth in subsection 2, an applicant for a license as a real estate broker must include with the application he or she submits to the Division pursuant to NRS 645.350 proof that the applicant has satisfied the experience requirements for a license as a real estate broker as set forth in subsection 4 of NRS 645.330.

(Added to NAC by Real Estate Comm'n by R111-01, eff. 12-17-2001; A by R025-10, 12-16-2010)

NAC 645.105 Preparation of application. (NRS 645.190, 645.400) Each application must be completed personally by the applicant. Members of the Commission or employees of the Division are expressly prohibited from helping a person prepare his or her license application.

[Real Estate Adv. Comm'n, § III part subsec. 1 § subsec. 2, eff. 10-31-75] — (NAC A by Real Estate Comm'n, 8-26-83)

NAC 645.115 Application by partnership, limited-liability company or corporation. (NRS 645.190, 645.400) If an applicant for a license is a partnership, limited-liability company or corporation, the applicant must file with the Division a certified or verified copy of the partnership agreement, articles of organization or articles of incorporation, as appropriate.

[Real Estate Adv. Comm'n, § III subsec. 5, eff. 10-31-75] — (NAC A by Real Estate Comm'n, 8-21-81; 6-3-86; R031-04, 11-30-2004)

NAC 645.120 Financial condition of applicant for license as real estate broker. (NRS 645.190, 645.400)

1. Before a person who wishes to apply for a license as a real estate broker submits an application for the license pursuant to NRS 645.350, the Division shall consider the financial condition of the person and require the person to submit to the Division the following financial information:

(a) The person's current employer and the employer's address;

(b) The person's checking accounts with amounts;

(c) The person's savings accounts with amounts; and

(d) Such other information concerning the person's finances as the Division deems pertinent.

2. A person may not apply for a license as a real estate broker unless the person has submitted to the Division the information required by this section and the Division has approved the financial condition of the person.

[Real Estate Adv. Comm'n, § III subsec. 1 par. a, eff. 10-31-75] — (NAC A by Real Estate Comm'n, 8-21-81; R031-04, 11-30-2004; R025-10, 12-16-2010)

NAC 645.140 Requirement of instruction. (NRS 645.190, 645.343, 645.345, 645.400)

1. An applicant for an original license must submit a certificate from an accredited educational institution or an institution approved by the Commission as proof that the applicant has successfully completed the course or courses of instruction required in NRS 645.343. If the applicant states in his or her application that he or she has completed any of the courses at a university or community college the applicant must have the college or university furnish the Division with a transcript of his or her record. The Division may allow substitution of those courses already completed and may require additional instruction as is necessary to complete the course of instruction required in NRS 645.343.

2. Mere attendance in a classroom does not constitute successful completion of a course.

3. Proof of active experience as a real estate salesperson must be made on a form provided by the Division and attested by the applicant's broker or brokers.

4. For the purposes of subsection 4 of NRS 645.343, the substitution of each 2 years' active experience for 16 semester units of college level courses applies to experience as a real estate salesperson or broker in this State, any other state or the District of Columbia. No substitution may be made for any period which is less than 2 years.

[Real Estate Adv. Comm'n, § III subsecs. 21-23, eff. 1-4-78; A 4-20-78] — (NAC A by Real Estate Comm'n, 8-21-81; 12-16-82; 8-26-83; 4-27-84)

NAC 645.141 Requirement of active experience. (NRS 645.190, 645.400)

1. The Division will require a verified statement from an employing broker indicating extended experience of any licensee associated with the employing broker in order to determine the extent of experience the licensee has gained while associated with the broker.

2. This information must be reported on a form provided by the Division which must request the following information:

(a) The period of association with the broker.

(b) The average number of hours worked per week for the broker.

(c) Any other information concerning the activities of the licensee which should be considered as contributing towards the licensee's experience while associated with the broker.

(Added to NAC by Real Estate Comm'n, eff. 8-21-81)

NAC 645.150 Investigation of financial responsibility of applicant for license as real estate broker; proof of good character of any applicant. (NRS 645.190, 645.400)

1. The Division may investigate the financial responsibility of each applicant for a license as a real estate broker. If the Division determines that an applicant is not financially responsible, it may require that the applicant be licensed as a real estate broker-salesperson until he or she meets the requirements of financial responsibility as determined by the Commission. The Division may require an applicant for a license as a real estate broker to submit a credit report to the Division at his or her own expense.

2. An applicant for a license as a real estate broker shall be deemed financially responsible if the applicant can show liquid assets sufficient to maintain an office for at least 180 days. The applicant's cash on hand must be on deposit at least 90 days before the date of the application. Anyone denied a license for lack of financial responsibility does not waive his or her right to appeal pursuant to NRS 645.440 by acceptance of a license as a real estate broker-salesperson.

3. The Administrator may require other proof of the honesty, truthfulness and good reputation of any applicant, including the officers and directors of any corporation, or the members of any partnership or association making an application, before accepting an application for a license.

4. As used in this section, "liquid assets" means assets that are the equivalent of cash or easily converted into cash. The term:

(a) Includes, without limitation, money in a checking, savings or money market account and certificates of deposit.

(b) Does not include a line of credit.

[Real Estate Adv. Comm'n, § III subsecs. 12 & 13, eff. 10-31-75] — (NAC A by Real Estate Comm'n, 8-21-81; A by Real Estate Div., 3-1-96; A by Real Estate Comm'n by R111-01, 12-17-2001; R031-04, 11-30-2004; R025-10, 12-16-2010)

NAC 645.175 Licensing of branch offices. (NRS 645.050, 645.190, 645.530)

1. The real estate broker to whom the license is issued is responsible for all branch offices operated by the real estate broker.

2. A license for a branch office may only be issued in the name in which the real estate broker is licensed to conduct business at his or her main office.

3. A supervisor of a branch office may not manage more than one branch office.

4. A branch office is not required to establish a trust account, but if one is established, one of the signatures required on the account must be that of the supervisor of the branch office.

[Real Estate Adv. Comm'n, § VI subsecs. 9-12 & 14, eff. 12-20-75] — (NAC A by Real Estate Comm'n by R111-01, 12-17-2001)

NAC 645.177 Supervision of branch office. (NRS 645.050, 645.190)

1. Every branch office of a real estate broker must be under the supervision of a broker or a broker-salesperson who, within the preceding 4 years, has had 2 years of active experience as a broker, broker-salesperson, or salesperson in the United States.

2. While supervising a branch office, a broker-salesperson has all the duties of and is subject to the penalties applicable to a broker under chapter 645 of NRS and this chapter.

[Real Estate Adv. Comm'n, § VI subsec. 7, eff. 12-20-75] — (NAC A 12-16-82; A by Real Estate Div., 3-1-96)

NAC 645.178 Management of principal and branch offices. (NRS 645.050, 645.190)

1. A real estate broker-salesperson with at least 2 years of active experience within the immediately preceding 4 years of having a licensed status may act as an office manager for the principal office or a branch office operated by a real estate broker.

2. A real estate broker-salesperson who is acting as manager of a principal or branch office must notify the Division that he or she is acting in that capacity.

(Added to NAC by Real Estate Comm'n, eff. 8-21-81; A by Real Estate Div., 3-1-96; A by Real Estate Comm'n by R111-01, 12-17-2001)

NAC 645.180 Cooperative certificate: Application. (NRS 645.190, 645.605)

1. A real estate broker who is licensed in another state and wishes to work in cooperation with a Nevada real estate broker must apply to do so on a form provided by the Division. The application must be accompanied by:

(a) A copy of his or her current license issued in the other state;

(b) A history of his or her employment for the past 10 years;

(c) Information identifying him or her and the Nevada broker with whom the applicant wishes to cooperate;

(d) A history of any disciplinary, criminal or other legal proceeding involving the real estate salesperson or broker-salesperson who will be working for the applicant under the cooperative certificate;

(e) A list of other cooperative agreements currently in effect with the Nevada broker;

(f) A photograph of the applicant;

(g) A copy of the license of the real estate salesperson or broker-salesperson who will be working for the applicant; and

(h) A statement of consent by the Nevada broker to the cooperative agreement.

2. The Nevada broker and out-of-state broker must verify the truth of the contents of the application.

3. The application must be completed personally by the out-of-state broker, and no licensed Nevada broker or employee of the Division may assist in the preparation of any part of the application.

4. The required fee must be paid at the time of filing. If the Administrator does not issue the certificate as applied for, the fee will not be refunded.

5. The applicant must furnish proof satisfactory to the Administrator that the applicant has a current active real estate broker's license issued by the state in which his or her principal place of business is located.

6. A person who resides in this State and holds a real estate license issued by another state is not eligible to hold a cooperative certificate or act on behalf of a holder of a certificate.

7. The Administrator may require proof of the applicant's moral character. In determining that character, the Administrator may consider:

(a) The results of the Division's investigation of matters stated in the application and other matters that have come to the attention of the Division as a result of the investigation;

(b) Any history of arrest and conviction of the applicant;

(c) The nature and history of the business of the applicant; and

(d) Any past failure of the applicant to comply with:

(1) Any requirement of chapter 113, 116, 119, 119A, 645, 645A, 645C or 645D of NRS or any other specific statute that is applicable to real estate transactions; or

(2) Any similar statutory or regulatory requirement of another jurisdiction that is applicable to real estate transactions.

[Real Estate Adv. Comm'n, § XI, eff. 10-31-75] — (NAC A by Real Estate Comm'n, 8-21-81; 12-16-82; 4-27-84; R111-01, 12-17-2001; R031-04, 11-30-2004)

NAC 645.183 Cooperative certificate: Denial, cancellation, suspension or revocation; appeal. (NRS 645.190, 645.605)

1. The Administrator may deny an application for a cooperative certificate for any reason which is sufficient to deny an application for a license, permit or registration pursuant to NAC 645.095 or to initiate disciplinary proceedings pursuant to NRS 645.630 to 645.645, inclusive.

2. An applicant whose application for a cooperative certificate has been denied by the Administrator or an out-of-state real estate broker whose cooperative certificate has been cancelled, suspended or revoked by the Administrator may appeal the denial, cancellation, suspension or revocation to the Commission in the manner set forth in NRS 645.440. The Commission will review the decision by the Administrator in the manner set forth in NRS 645.440, except that the hearing need not be held at a time or place other than that set for the next regular meeting of the Commission.

3. If the Commission reverses a decision by the Administrator to deny an application for a cooperative certificate and determines that the petitioner qualifies for a certificate, the application may be accepted as of the date the application was originally submitted or the date on which the fee for the certificate was paid, whichever is later. The Division shall not charge an additional fee.

[Real Estate Adv. Comm'n, § XIII, eff. 10-31-75] — (NAC A by Real Estate Comm'n, 8-21-81; 4-27-84; R111-01, 12-17-2001)

NAC 645.185 Cooperative certificate: Use of certificate. (NRS 645.050, 645.190, 645.605)

1. A certificate authorizing an out-of-state broker to cooperate with a Nevada broker is valid for 12 months after the date of issuance. The fee paid for the issuance covers that period. The certificate is not transferable.

2. An out-of-state broker holding such a certificate shall immediately report any change in his or her address to the Administrator.

3. If, at any time during which a cooperative certificate is in effect, the out-of-state broker or the Nevada broker wishes to terminate the relationship, he or she must give written notice of the termination to the Division and the broker with whom he or she has been cooperating and the out-of-state broker shall immediately surrender his or her certificate to the Division.

4. If the license of the out-of-state broker expires or is inactivated, suspended, revoked or cancelled, the out-of-state broker shall immediately give written notice to the Division of each Nevada broker with whom he or she is cooperating and surrender his or her cooperative certificate to the Division.

5. The Administrator may not issue a cooperative certificate to an out-of-state association, partnership or corporation which is licensed as a broker. Only a natural person who is a broker may be issued such a certificate.

6. When acting under a cooperative certificate, an out-of-state broker shall work through the cooperating Nevada broker or a licensee associated with a Nevada broker. The Nevada broker is in charge of the transaction from beginning to end.

7. Any money received in a cooperative transaction may be handled only by the cooperating Nevada broker in accordance with NRS 645.310.

8. Each out-of-state broker, while cooperating with a Nevada broker, is governed by the provisions of this chapter and chapter 645 of NRS. Any violation of such a provision by the out-of-state broker subjects his or her cooperative certificate and the Nevada broker's license to fine or suspension, or both, or revocation. By accepting a cooperative certificate, the out-of-state broker shall be deemed to have appointed the Nevada broker as his or her agent for service of all notices and process in any proceeding initiated by the Division pursuant to chapter 645 of NRS.

9. A cooperating out-of-state broker may authorize only one broker-salesperson or one salesperson employed by him or her to act in his or her behalf. The authorization must be on a form supplied by the Division, and a copy must be sent to the Division before the authorized representative of the out-of-state broker may conduct any transaction. The authorized representative shall carry the completed form with him or her whenever the authorized representative is in Nevada for the purpose of conducting his or her real estate business. The Division shall establish the time during which the authorization is valid. Such an authorization is renewable.

10. An out-of-state broker may cooperate with more than one Nevada broker and a Nevada broker may cooperate with more than one out-of-state broker. Each arrangement is considered a separate agreement for which the appropriate form must be completed and submitted, the appropriate fee paid and a separate cooperative certificate obtained.

11. An out-of-state broker may not use a cooperating broker's certificate as authority to sell or attempt to sell real estate in Nevada to a resident of Nevada. Such a certificate may be used only for the purpose of allowing the out-of-state broker or salesperson to offer real estate in Nevada for sale to a person other than a resident of Nevada.

[Real Estate Adv. Comm'n, § XII, eff. 10-31-75] — (NAC A by Real Estate Comm'n, 8-21-81; 12-16-82; 4-27-84; R031-04, 11-30-2004)

NAC 645.205 Availability of handbook on examinations. (NRS 645.190) An applicant may obtain the handbook on candidate examinations that is currently approved by the Division at an office of the Division at no cost.

[Real Estate Adv. Comm'n, § IV subsecs. 1, 3 & 4, eff. 10-31-75] — (NAC A by Real Estate Comm'n, 8-21-81; R146-99, 1-21-2000; R031-04, 11-30-2004)

NAC 645.207 Fee for examination. (NRS 645.190, 645.410) The fee for an examination for an original license or the reinstatement of a license as a real estate broker, broker-salesperson or salesperson is $100.

(Added to NAC by Real Estate Comm'n by R111-01, eff. 12-17-2001; A by R031-04, 11-30-2004)

NAC 645.210 Scope of examination. (NRS 645.190, 645.460) The examination for salespersons may be a different examination from the examination for brokers. Each of the examinations will consist of questions covering any or all of the following subjects:
1. Principles:
(a) Contract law;
(b) Real estate law and conveyancing;
(c) Listing property and services to the seller;
(d) Selling property and services to the buyer; and
(e) Deposits.
2. Practices:
(a) Land economics and appraising;
(b) Land descriptions;
(c) Financing and insurance;
(d) Mathematics;
(e) Escrows and closings;
(f) Subdivisions and developments;
(g) Property management;
(h) Environmental issues; and
(i) Tax issues that affect real estate ownership.
3. Procedures and ethics:
(a) NRS 113.060 to 113.150, inclusive, 116.4109 and 116.41095, and chapters 119, 119A, 119B and 645 of NRS and the regulations adopted pursuant to them;
(b) Federal laws, including, without limitation:
    (1) Fair Housing Act, 42 U.S.C. §§ 3601 et seq.;
    (2) Interstate Land Sales Full Disclosure Act, 15 U.S.C. §§ 1701 et seq.;
    (3) Truth in Lending Act, 15 U.S.C. §§ 1601 et seq.;
    (4) Americans with Disabilities Act of 1990, 42 U.S.C. §§ 12101 et seq.;
    (5) Real Estate Settlement Procedures Act, 12 U.S.C. §§ 2601 et seq.;
    (6) Equal Credit Opportunity Act, 15 U.S.C. §§ 1691 et seq.; and
    (7) The Residential Lead-Based Paint Exposure Reduction Act of 1992, 42 U.S.C. §§ 4851 et seq.; and

(c) Real estate brokerage and ethics, professional responsibility, fair practice and the duties listed in any form prepared by the Division pursuant to NRS 645.193. A copy of a form prepared by the Division pursuant to NRS 645.193 may be obtained from the Division.

[Real Estate Adv. Comm'n, § IV subsec. 2, eff. 10-31-75] — (NAC A by Real Estate Comm'n by R146-99, 1-21-2000)

NAC 645.215 Length and confidentiality of examination. (NRS 645.190) The examination period must not exceed 4 hours without prior written consent of the Division. An applicant may not retain any examination materials. Examinations must not be made public except as provided in NRS 645.180.

[Real Estate Adv. Comm'n, § IV subsec. 5, eff. 10-31-75] — (NAC A by Real Estate Comm'n by R146-99, 1-21-2000; R031-04, 11-30-2004)

NAC 645.220 Passing grade on examination. (NRS 645.190) To pass an examination, an applicant must achieve a grade of at least 75 percent on each section of the examination.

[Real Estate Adv. Comm'n, § IV subsec. 6, eff. 10-31-75; A 2-20-76] — (NAC A by Real Estate Comm'n by R031-04, 11-30-2004)

NAC 645.225 Period for acceptance of results of examination. (NRS 645.190) The Division shall only accept results of an examination taken during the 12 months, to the day, immediately preceding the date of application for a license.

[Real Estate Adv. Comm'n, § IV subsecs. 7 & 10 eff. 10-31-75] — (NAC A by Real Estate Comm'n, 8-21-81; 6-3-86; R031-04, 11-30-2004)

NAC 645.230 Examination aids. (NRS 645.190)
1. The use or possession of any unfair methods or notes, the giving or receiving of aid of any kind, or the failure to obey instructions during the examination will result in a denial of the application and license.
2. A silent, cordless, electronic calculator may be used by an applicant during the examination if the calculator:
(a) Is not programmable;
(b) Does not have the capability to print on paper tape; and
(c) Does not have a keyboard containing the alphabet.

NAC 645.305 Change in license. (NRS 645.190, 645.570)
1. Within 10 days after a change of his or her association with a real estate broker, other than termination, or a change of his or her name, business location or status, the licensee shall:
(a) Submit a request to the Division to change his or her license on a form provided by the Division; and
(b) Pay the required fees.
2. If a licensee requests a change and pays the required fee, the receipt issued by the Division constitutes a temporary working permit pending receipt of the requested license.
3. A real estate broker may change his or her status to that of a real estate broker-salesperson by filing an application on a form supplied by the Division.
4. Licensees associated with a real estate broker licensed pursuant to chapter 645 of NRS as a manager of a limited-liability company, member of a partnership or officer of a corporation are not considered to have changed their association with the real estate broker if the corporation, limited-liability company or partnership designates a new real estate broker to act in the capacity of a manager of the limited-liability company, member of the partnership or officer of the corporation on or before the last date that the former real estate broker works in that capacity.

[Real Estate Adv. Comm'n, § V subsecs. 1, 2 & 8, eff. 10-31-75] — (NAC A by Real Estate Comm'n, 8-21-81; R111-01, 12-17-2001; R031-04, 11-30-2004)

NAC 645.310 Real estate broker-salesperson or salesperson: Termination of association or employment with real estate broker or owner-developer. (NRS 645.190, 645.580)
1. If a real estate broker-salesperson or salesperson terminates, for any reason, his or her association with the real estate broker with whom he or she is associated, or his or her employment with the owner-developer by whom he or she is employed, the real estate broker or owner-developer shall, in addition to complying with the requirements of NRS 645.580, file with the Division:

(a) A notice of termination on a form provided by the Division; and

(b) Any other pertinent information the Division requests.

2. A real estate broker-salesperson or salesperson whose association or employment with a real estate broker or owner-developer is terminated may personally deliver his or her broker-salesperson or salesperson license to the Division on behalf of the real estate broker or owner-developer if the real estate broker-salesperson or salesperson, at the time he or she submits the license, also submits to the Division the original notice of termination that has been completed and signed by the real estate broker or owner-developer. The original notice of termination must include the signature of the broker or owner-developer, as appropriate, in any designated area on the notice which is required to be completed for the personal delivery of the license.

3. If a real estate broker or owner-developer does not comply with subsections 1 and 2 and NRS 645.580 in a timely manner, the licensee may apply for an administrative termination on a form provided by the Division.

[Real Estate Adv. Comm'n, § V subsec. 5, eff. 10-31-75] — (NAC A by Real Estate Comm'n, 8-21-81; R111-01, 12-17-2001; R031-04, 11-30-2004)

NAC 645.313 Proof of compliance with requirements for continuing education requisite to renewal of license. (NRS 645.190, 645.575) The Division shall not renew the license of an active broker, broker-salesperson or salesperson unless he or she submits to the Division proof of compliance with the requirements for continuing education set forth in NRS 645.575 and the regulations adopted pursuant thereto.

[Real Estate Adv. Comm'n, § V subsec. 27, eff. 4-20-78] — (NAC A by Real Estate Comm'n, 5-14-96) — (Substituted in revision for NAC 645.390)

NAC 645.315 Renewal of license: Failure to file application before license expires. (NRS 645.190, 645.577, 645.785) If a licensee fails to file an application for the renewal of his or her license before it expires, the licensee shall not engage in the business of real estate until the license is reinstated. To have his or her license reinstated, the licensee must:

1. Apply on the appropriate form;
2. Pay the required fees;
3. If required, pass the examination; and
4. Submit any other information required by the Administrator, including, without limitation, current fingerprint cards.

[Real Estate Adv. Comm'n, § V subsec. 11, eff. 10-31-75; A and renumbered as subsec. 9, 2-20-76] — (NAC A by Real Estate Comm'n by R111-01, 12-17-2001; R031-04, 11-30-2004)

NAC 645.320 Inactive renewed status: Placement; renewal of license required. (NRS 645.190, 645.577)

1. A licensee may be placed on inactive renewed status by applying to the Division on the appropriate form. The licensee is not entitled to a refund of any part of the fees paid for the unexpired term of his or her license.

2. A licensee who is on inactive renewed status must apply for renewal of his or her license on or before each anniversary of the license.

[Real Estate Adv. Comm'n, § V part subsecs. 9 & 10, eff. 10-31-75; A and renumbered as subsecs. 10 & 11, 2-20-76]

NAC 645.325 Inactive renewed status: Requirements for reinstatement. (NRS 645.190) Except as otherwise provided in NAC 645.345:

1. A licensee who is in good standing with the Division and whose license is on inactive renewed status may apply to the Division to have his or her license reinstated to active status. The application must:

(a) Be on a form supplied by the Division;

(b) Be accompanied by the required fees;

(c) Contain evidence that the licensee has paid the required fee for the Real Estate Education, Research and Recovery Fund;

(d) If the application is for reinstatement of a real estate broker's license, be accompanied by a completed financial statement that is prepared on the form prescribed by the Division;

(e) Contain evidence that requirements for continuing education have been met; and

(f) Include any other information required by the Administrator, including, without limitation, current fingerprint cards.

2. If a license has been on inactive renewed status for more than 2 years, the licensee must, in addition to fulfilling the requirements of subsection 1:

(a) Show, to the Administrator's satisfaction, that he or she has the competency to engage in the business of real estate; and

(b) Complete an examination, including payment of the appropriate examination fees, and attain a score of at least 75 percent.

3. If the licensee fails the examination, he or she may retake the examination after paying the appropriate examination fee.

4. A license placed on inactive status for the holder's failure to comply with NRS 645.570 or for any of the reasons listed in NRS 645.577 remains inactive until an application for reinstatement has been approved by the Division.

[Real Estate Adv. Comm'n, § V part subsecs. 9 & 12, eff. 10-31-74; A and renumbered as subsecs. 12 & 13, 2-20-76] — (NAC A by Real Estate Comm'n, 8-21-81; 12-16-82; 4-27-84; 6-3-86; R111-01, 12-17-2001; R031-04, 11-30-2004)

NAC 645.330 Review of application for reinstatement. (NRS 645.190) In reviewing the application for reinstatement, the Division shall apply the same standards as are applied for original applicants. The Division shall determine whether the application is accepted or denied within 10 days after the later of:

1. The determination by the Division that the applicant has passed the examination, if required; and

2. The receipt by the Division of the following, if required:

(a) The FBI report;

(b) A completed financial statement that is prepared on a form prescribed by the Division;

(c) The required fees and forms; and

(d) Such other information as may be requested by the Division.

[Real Estate Adv. Comm'n, § V subsec. 14, eff. 2-20-76] — (NAC A by Real Estate Comm'n by R111-01, 12-17-2001; R031-04, 11-30-2004)

NAC 645.335 Appeal from a denial of a request for reinstatement. (NRS 645.190) If the Division denies an application for any reason, the licensee may appeal the denial pursuant to the provisions of NRS 645.440.

[Real Estate Adv. Comm'n, § V subsec. 15, eff. 2-20-76] — (NAC A by Real Estate Comm'n, 8-21-81)

NAC 645.340 Activation of license after approval of reinstatement. (NRS 645.190) The licensee must activate his or her license within 30 days after receiving notice from the Division that his or her application for reinstatement has been approved.

[Real Estate Adv. Comm'n, § V subsec. 9 par. c, eff. 10-31-75]

NAC 645.345 Failure of broker to renew license. (NRS 645.190)

1. If a real estate broker fails to renew his or her license, the license of a licensee with whom he or she is associated who has renewed that license will immediately be placed on inactive renewed status. A licensee associated with the real estate broker may:

(a) Within 30 calendar days, apply for a transfer to the association of another real estate broker, and pay any required fees; or

(b) If the real estate broker with whom the licensee was associated reinstates and renews his or her license within 30 calendar days, reactivate his or her license with that real estate broker.

2. If the licensee fails to reassociate with a broker within 30 days after the license of the broker with whom the licensee was associated became inactive, the licensee may only reinstate his or her license pursuant to NAC 645.325.

[Real Estate Adv. Comm'n, § V subsec. 13, eff. 10-31-75] — (NAC A by Real Estate Comm'n by R111-01, 12-17-2001; R031-04, 11-30-2004)

NAC 645.350 Involuntary inactivation, suspension or revocation of broker's license; expiration of license upon death of licensee; death of person acting as broker of brokerage. (NRS 645.050, 645.190)

1. If the license of a real estate broker is involuntarily inactivated, suspended or revoked, the real estate broker shall deliver his or her license to the Division with the license of each licensee with whom he or she is associated. A licensee who is associated with the real estate broker may, upon proper application and payment of the required fee, transfer to the

association of another real estate broker. No refund will be made when a license is involuntarily inactivated, suspended or revoked.

2. Upon the death of a licensee, the license held by that licensee automatically expires.

3. Upon the death of a person who was licensed as a real estate broker and who was acting as the broker of a brokerage, a person who is licensed as a real estate broker in the State of Nevada may submit to the Division an affidavit stating that he or she will act as the broker of that brokerage for not more than 60 days after the death of the person who was acting as the broker of the brokerage. Notice of such an appointment must be submitted to the Division, in writing, within 7 business days after the death of the person who was acting as the broker of the brokerage.

[Real Estate Adv. Comm'n, § V subsec. 14, eff. 10-31-75] — (NAC A by Real Estate Comm'n by R111-01, 12-17-2001; R031-04, 11-30-2004; R123-06, 6-1-2006)

NAC 645.355 Loss of license. (NRS 645.190) If a license must be surrendered and it is not, the licensee shall file an affidavit with the Division showing that the license has been lost, destroyed or stolen. The affidavit must contain the licensee's promise to return the license if it is recovered.

[Real Estate Adv. Comm'n, § V subsec. 15, eff. 10-31-75] — (NAC A by Real Estate Comm'n, 8-21-81)

NAC 645.360 Involuntary inactivation of license: Grounds; reinstatement of license. (NRS 645.190)

1. The Division may involuntarily inactivate a license if:

(a) A real estate broker has discontinued business at the address at which he or she is registered;

(b) A licensee is no longer associated with a real estate broker under whom he or she is shown to be licensed;

(c) A licensee, whether active or inactive, fails to inform the Division within 10 days after a change in the address of his or her business;

(d) A licensee has not paid the renewal fee;

(e) A licensee fails to comply with subsection 2 of NRS 645.580 in a timely manner; or

(f) A licensee fails to submit a request to the Division as required by NAC 645.305 to change his or her license within 10 days after the licensee changes his or her name, business location or status.

2. A licensee whose license is involuntarily inactivated pursuant to this section must satisfy the applicable requirements for reinstatement as set forth in NAC 645.325 to have his or her license reinstated.

[Real Estate Adv. Comm'n, § V subsec. 16, eff. 10-31-75] — (NAC A by Real Estate Comm'n, 4-27-84; R111-01, 12-17-2001; R031-04, 11-30-2004)

NAC 645.380 Brokers designated by certain business organizations; members or officers of certain business organizations acting as brokers; service of certain business organizations as salespersons or broker-salespersons. (NRS 645.050, 645.190, 645.385, 645.400)

1. A broker designated by a partnership, limited-liability company or corporation pursuant to NRS 645.370 or a broker who has obtained a license pursuant to NRS 645.380 may also obtain an individual license to act on his or her own behalf. To obtain an individual license, a broker must complete and submit forms as supplied by the Division and must pay an original license fee and any other required fees.

2. The Division will issue an additional license to such a broker and subject him or her to the same rights and duties as any other licensed Nevada broker. He or she may maintain an office separate from the offices of the partnership, limited-liability company or corporation and shall maintain separate records and a separate trust account so that the business of the partnership, limited-liability company or corporation remains separate from his or her independent business.

3. The partnership, limited-liability company or corporation must submit a statement, on a form supplied by the Division, indicating that it is fully aware of the intention of the broker to maintain an independent business.

4. Revocation, suspension, or any other penalty of the Commission or the Division applies to both licenses of a broker who is licensed pursuant to this section.

5. A partnership, limited-liability company or corporation may not serve as a salesperson or broker-salesperson except as otherwise provided by a specific statute.

6. A broker who is licensed individually and as a partnership, limited-liability company or corporation, even though he or she has been issued two licenses by the Division, is considered to be only one licensee for the purposes of disciplinary action or claims against the Real Estate Education, Research and Recovery Fund.

[Real Estate Adv. Comm'n, § V subsec. 20, eff. 10-31-75] — (NAC A by Real Estate Comm'n, 8-21-81; 4-27-84; A by Real Estate Div., 3-31-94; R126-04, 10-31-2005)

EDUCATION IN REAL ESTATE

General Provisions

NAC 645.400 "School" defined. (NRS 645.190, 645.343, 645.575)   For the purposes of NAC 645.400 to 645.467, inclusive, "school" includes:

1. Any university, school or community college which is a part of the Nevada System of Higher Education, or any other university or college bearing the same or an equivalent accreditation.

2. Any professional school or college licensed by the Nevada Commission on Postsecondary Education.

3. Any out-of-state professional school or college licensed or accredited by a real estate commission, a department of education or an equivalent agency of any other state.

[Real Estate Adv. Comm'n, § X subsec. 3, eff. 10-31-75; A and renumbered as subsec. A par. 3, 1-4-78] — (NAC A by Real Estate Comm'n by R031-04, 11-30-2004)

NAC 645.403 Approval of school: Application. (NRS 645.190, 645.343)   A school that wishes to offer courses to meet the educational requirements for licensure under chapter 645 of NRS must apply to the Commission annually for approval on a form prescribed by the Division and pay the appropriate fees. The application must include, without limitation:

1. The name and address of the school;

2. The type of school and a description of its facilities;

3. Information concerning the ownership of the school, including the business organization and the names and addresses of all directors, principals, officers and others having interests as owners;

4. A list of the instructors;

5. A list of the courses to be offered and a topical syllabus for each;

6. The allotment of time for each subject;

7. A proposed schedule of courses for 1 year;

8. The titles, authors and publishers of all required textbooks;

9. A copy of each examination to be used and the correct answer for each question;

10. A statement of:

(a) The purpose of the school;

(b) The fees to be charged;

(c) The days, times and locations of classes;

(d) The number of quizzes and examinations;

(e) The grading systems, including the methods of testing and standards of grading;

(f) The requirements for attendance; and

(g) The location of the students' records;

11. A statement as to whether the school or any instructor employed by the school has been disciplined by any governmental agency in this or any other state; and

12. A statement that to pass a course, a student must earn at least 75 percent of the points possible for the entire course.

(Added to NAC by Real Estate Comm'n, eff. 12-16-82; A by R031-04, 11-30-2004; R123-06, 6-1-2006)

NAC 645.404 Approval of school: Conditions of approval; evidence of licensure required from certain schools. (NRS 645.190, 645.343)

1. If a school has applied for and received the Commission's approval to offer courses to meet requirements for licensure under chapter 645 of NRS, the school shall, as a condition of the approval:

(a) Maintain a record of each student's attendance and certification in any of those courses for 7 years after the student's enrollment and shall have such records open to inspection by the Division, upon its request, during the school's business hours.

(b) Upon a transferring student's request, furnish the school to which the student is transferring a copy of his or her attendance record and certification for each of those courses which he or she has completed.

(c) Upon a student's request, furnish the Division a transcript of the record of his or her grades and attendance.

2. A school that does not meet the definition of a "school" set forth in either subsection 1 or 3 of NAC 645.400 must provide evidence to the Division that the school is licensed to operate by the Commission on Postsecondary Education.

(Added to NAC by Real Estate Comm'n, eff. 12-16-82; A 12-27-91)

NAC 645.407 Approval of school: Notice of material change in information provided in application; annual renewal of approval; denial of renewal. (NRS 645.190, 645.343)

1. Within 15 days after the occurrence of any material change in the information provided by the school in its application pursuant to NAC 645.403 which would affect its approval by the Commission, the school shall give the Division written notice of that change.

2. To qualify for annual renewal of approval by the Commission, a school must submit to the Commission before July 1:

(a) A written certification, in a form prescribed by the Division, declaring that the school has met all applicable requirements of this chapter;

(b) A sworn statement, in a form prescribed by the Division, declaring that the information contained in the original application is current or, if it is not current, a list of all material changes; and

(c) Payment of the appropriate fee for each course for which renewal is being sought.

3. The Commission may deny renewal of approval to any school that does not meet the standards required by this chapter.

4. Within 60 days after a decision is made to deny renewal of approval, the Commission must give written notice of the decision and the basis for that decision by certified mail to the last known address of the school.

(Added to NAC by Real Estate Comm'n, eff. 12-16-82; A 4-27-84; A by R031-04, 11-30-2004) — (Substituted in revision for NAC 645.446)

NAC 645.410 Approved schools: General requirements for certification of students. (NRS 645.190, 645.343)

1. Except as otherwise provided in NAC 645.412, a school which the Commission has approved to give a course fulfilling the educational requirements for original licensing shall require each student to attend the required number of hours of instruction and take at least two examinations in the course as a condition of receiving certification for the course.

2. The school may certify only the number of hours for which the course has been approved by the Commission.

3. The entire course must be completed by the applicant or licensee to satisfy the licensing requirements.

4. For the purposes of this section:

(a) An "hour of instruction" means 50 minutes or more; and

(b) One semester credit is equal to 15 hours of instruction.

[Real Estate Adv. Comm'n, § X part subsec. 8, eff. 10-31-75; A and renumbered as subsec. C pars. 5 & 6, 1-4-78; § X subsec. C par. 10, eff. 4-20-78] — (NAC A by Real Estate Comm'n, 8-21-81; 12-16-82; 12-27-89; R031-04, 11-30-2004)

NAC 645.412 Approved schools: Certification of students taking courses by correspondence. (NRS 645.190, 645.343) If the Commission approves a school to give a course of study which fulfills the educational requirements for an original license and the school offers the course by correspondence, the school shall:

1. Require each student to:

(a) Take a closed-book final examination with a proctor present at a location designated by the school in its application for approval filed with the Commission;

(b) Take two progress examinations or quizzes in addition to the final examination;

(c) Prove his or her identity before the student is allowed to take any examination; and

(d) Complete each course within an established minimum and maximum time.

2. Certify the completion of only the number of hours for which the course has been approved by the Commission. A portion of a course does not satisfy the requirements for a license.

(Added to NAC by Real Estate Comm'n, eff. 12-27-89)

NAC 645.420 Approved schools: Misrepresentation in advertising prohibited. (NRS 645.190, 645.343) A school approved by the Commission shall not make any misrepresentation in its advertising about any course of instruction which it offers to fulfill requirements for licensing under this chapter.

[Real Estate Adv. Comm'n, § X subsec. C par. 9, eff. 1-4-78] — (NAC A by Real Estate Comm'n, 12-16-82)

NAC 645.425 Approved schools: Instructors; guest lecturers; statement required in advertisements. (NRS 645.190, 645.343) A school which conducts courses approved by the Commission:

1. May employ as instructors of those courses only persons who meet the qualifications set forth in NAC 645.426.

2. Shall limit noncertificated guest lecturers who are experts in the related fields to a total of 9 instructional hours per approved course.

3. Shall include a statement that the school is approved by the Commission on all advertisements of the school.

[Real Estate Adv. Comm'n, § X subsec. C par. 7, eff. 1-4-78] — (NAC A by Real Estate Comm'n, 8-21-81; 12-16-82; 12-27-89; R146-99, 1-21-2000; R031-04, 11-30-2004)

NAC 645.426 Instructors: Requirements for and restrictions on approval; appeal of denial of approval; periodic review and evaluation. (NRS 645.190, 645.343, 645.575)

1. An instructor must have written approval from the Division before teaching an approved course.

2. An applicant for approval as an instructor must apply on a form prescribed by the Division.

3. The Division shall not, without the approval of the Commission, approve a person as an instructor if the person:

(a) Has been disciplined by the Commission or the Division acting on behalf of the Commission:

   (1) Within the immediately preceding 5 years; or

   (2) More than one time; or

(b) Has been determined in an administrative or judicial proceeding to have violated any statute, rule, regulation or order pertaining to real estate in this or any other state.

4. A person may be approved as an instructor to teach an approved course relating to his or her principal occupation if:

(a) The person has:

   (1) A bachelor's degree or a more advanced degree, plus at least 2 years of full-time experience, in the field in which he or she will be providing instruction;

   (2) Teaching experience of at least 75 hours in the field in which he or she will be providing instruction within the 3 years immediately preceding the date of the person's application for approval plus at least 3 years of full-time experience in that field;

   (3) At least 6 years of full-time experience in the field in which the person will be providing instruction; or

   (4) Any combination of at least 6 years of college-level course work and full-time experience in the field in which the person will be providing instruction;

(b) The person has a good reputation for honesty, integrity and trustworthiness; and

(c) The person submits to the Division satisfactory documentation of his or her qualifications and a resume outlining his or her experience, education and teaching experience in the field in which the person will be providing instruction.

5. If the Division denies an application for approval as an instructor, the applicant may appeal the decision of the Division by filing an appeal with the Commission not later than 30 days after the date on which the applicant received notification of the denial of the application for approval as an instructor.

6. If the applicant files a timely appeal, the Commission will, as soon as practicable, hold a hearing concerning the denial of the application for approval as an instructor at a regularly scheduled meeting of the Commission and will:

(a) Affirm the decision of the Division to deny the application for approval as an instructor;

(b) Approve the instructor for a limited period and under such conditions as the Commission deems appropriate; or

(c) Reverse the decision of the Division to deny the application for approval as an instructor.

7. The Division shall periodically review and evaluate each approved instructor.

(Added to NAC by Real Estate Comm'n by R031-04, eff. 11-30-2004; A by R123-06, 6-1-2006)

NAC 645.427 Instructors: Withdrawal of approval. (NRS 645.190, 645.343, 645.575)

1. The Administrator may withdraw the approval of an instructor who:

(a) Does an inadequate job of teaching the subject matter of a course as evidenced by student evaluations or an audit conducted by the Division.

(b) Has been determined in any administrative or judicial proceeding to have violated any statute, rule, regulation or order pertaining to real estate.

(c) Has been convicted of, or entered a plea of guilty or nolo contendere to, any crime involving fraud, deceit, misrepresentation or moral turpitude; or

(d) Engages in inappropriate behavior in the classroom as evidenced by an audit conducted by the Division.

2. Before withdrawing approval of the instructor of a course, the Administrator must notify the sponsor of the course of his or her intent to withdraw approval of the instructor. The notice must include the specific reasons upon which the Administrator is basing the decision to withdraw the approval of the instructor. Not later than 30 days after the date on

which he or she receives the notice, a sponsor may provide a written response to the Administrator that clearly sets forth the reasons why the approval of the instructor should not be withdrawn and outlining any corrective measures that the sponsor will undertake. After the 30-day period has elapsed, the Administrator shall review the notice and any response submitted by the sponsor and shall:

(a) Withdraw approval of the instructor;

(b) Allow the instructor to remain approved if certain specific enumerated conditions are met; or

(c) Allow the continued approval of the instructor.

☐ If the Administrator decides to withdraw approval of the instructor, the withdrawal of approval of the instructor becomes effective upon the mailing of the Administrator's decision to the sponsor of the course taught by the instructor by certified mail, return receipt requested, to the sponsor's last known business address.

3. If the Administrator withdraws approval of an instructor, the Division shall give credit to a student for completing the course if the student began the course before the sponsor received written notice of the withdrawal of approval of the instructor.

4. The sponsor may appeal the decision of the Administrator to withdraw approval of an instructor by filing an appeal with the Commission not later than 30 days after the date on which the withdrawal of the approval of the instructor becomes effective.

5. If the sponsor files a timely appeal, the Commission will, as soon as practicable, hold a hearing concerning the withdrawal of approval of the instructor at a regularly scheduled meeting and will:

(a) Affirm the decision of the Administrator to withdraw approval of the instructor;

(b) Suspend approval of the instructor for a limited period and under such conditions as the Commission deems appropriate; or

(c) Reverse the decision of the Administrator to withdraw approval of the instructor.

(Added to NAC by Real Estate Comm'n by R031-04, eff. 11-30-2004)

NAC 645.428 Instructors: Duties. (NRS 645.190, 645.343, 645.575)

1. An instructor shall ensure that:

(a) Class sessions are commenced in a timely manner and are conducted for the full amount of time that is approved; and

(b) Each course is taught according to the course plan and instructor guide that was approved by the Commission, including the furnishing to students of appropriate student materials.

2. An instructor shall conduct himself or herself in a professional and courteous manner when performing his or her instructional duties and shall conduct classes in a manner that demonstrates the following basic teaching skills:

(a) The ability to present instruction in a thorough, accurate, logical, orderly and understandable manner, to utilize illustrative examples as appropriate and to respond appropriately to questions from students;

(b) The ability effectively to utilize varied instructional techniques in addition to lectures, including, without limitation, class discussion, role-playing and other techniques;

(c) The ability to utilize varied instructional aids effectively to enhance learning;

(d) The ability to maintain an appropriate learning environment and effective control of a class; and

(e) The ability to interact with adult students in a positive manner that:

(1) Encourages students to learn;

(2) Demonstrates an understanding of varied student backgrounds;

(3) Avoids offending the sensibilities of students; and

(4) Avoids personal criticism of any other person, agency or organization.

(Added to NAC by Real Estate Comm'n by R031-04, eff. 11-30-2004)

NAC 645.430 Satisfaction of requirement for course in principles of real estate to obtain original license as broker or broker-salesperson. (NRS 645.190, 645.343) The course in principles, practices, ethics, law and procedures which is required for a salesperson's license under subsection 1 of NRS 645.343 and was approved by the Commission before November 1, 1977, fulfills the requirement under subsection 2 of NRS 645.343 for a course of 3 semester units in the principles of real estate for an original broker's or broker-salesperson's license.

[Real Estate Adv. Comm'n, § X subsec. C par. 8, eff. 1-4-78] — (NAC A by Real Estate Comm'n, 12-16-82)

NAC 645.435 Course required to obtain original license as salesperson. (NRS 645.190, 645.343)

1. A course of instruction in real estate principles, practices, procedures, law and ethics which is designed to meet the educational requirements of an applicant for an original license as a salesperson must consist of:

(a) At least 90 hours of classroom lectures; or

(b) The equivalent in a correspondence or extension course.

2. The content of the course must be divided among subjects listed in NAC 645.210, including:

(a) At least 45 hours on the principles and practices of real estate, which must include:

   (1) Brokerage and laws of agency, 21 hours.

   (2) Valuation and economics, 12 hours.

   (3) Finance, 12 hours.

(b) At least 45 hours on the law of property and the regulation of brokers and salespersons and the ethics of selling real estate, which must include:

   (1) Ownership, transfer and use of property, 25 hours.

   (2) Chapters 113, 116, 119, 119A, 645, 645C and 645D of NRS and the regulations adopted pursuant thereto, 18 hours.

   (3) Applied practice and statutory disclosures, 2 hours.

[Real Estate Adv. Comm'n, § X subsecs. 1 & 2, eff. 10-31-75; A and renumbered subsec. A pars. 1 & 2, 1-4-78] — (NAC A by Real Estate Comm'n, 8-21-81; 12-16-82; 6-3-86; R031-04, 11-30-2004)

NAC 645.437 Approval of course in broker management required to obtain original license as broker or broker-salesperson. (NRS 645.190, 645.343)

1. A course of instruction in broker management that is designed to fulfill the educational requirements for issuance of an original license which are described in paragraph (d) of subsection 2 of NRS 645.343 must be approved by the Commission.

2. To be approved by the Commission, a course in broker management must include, without limitation:

(a) Six hours of instruction relating to office policy and procedure, risk management, errors and omissions, controlled business arrangements, compensation, employee-employer relationships and the status of independent contractors;

(b) Three hours of instruction relating to creating business plans;

(c) Three hours of instruction on forms used by real estate brokerages for real estate transactions;

(d) Six hours of instruction that provides an overview of programs for financing real estate transactions, including, without limitation, terminology relating to such programs, the cost of transactions, customary transaction closing costs, and transaction cost and net sheets;

(e) Six hours of instruction in state and local laws;

(f) Six hours of instruction on federal laws governing real estate transactions;

(g) Six hours of instruction on professional relationships between agents and their clients;

(h) Three hours of instruction on valuation of real estate and general principles of economics; and

(i) Six hours of instruction on emerging trends and practices.

(Added to NAC by Real Estate Comm'n by R092-00, 8-29-2000, eff. 1-1-2001; A by R031-04, 11-30-2004)

NAC 645.440 Courses required for original licensing: Approval of school; acceptance without prior approval of school. (NRS 645.190, 645.343)

1. Except as otherwise provided in subsection 2, before any school offers or conducts a course of instruction designed to fulfill the educational requirements for issuance of an original license under chapter 645 of NRS, the school must be approved by the Commission.

2. Unless the course is a course in broker management, the Commission may accept such a course from any of the following schools without prior approval of the school:

(a) Any university, school or community college of the Nevada System of Higher Education, or other university or college bearing the same or equivalent accreditation.

(b) Any other school offering a course in real estate, business or economics if the course is:

   (1) Approved by any real estate commission or division in any state of the United States or province of Canada; or

   (2) In the judgment of the Commission, equivalent in quality to the courses of colleges or universities accredited by any regional accrediting agency recognized by the United States Department of Education.

(c) The American Institute of Real Estate Appraisers, the American Society of Appraisers, the Appraisal Institute, the International Association of Assessing Officers or the Society of Real Estate Appraisers for courses in real estate appraisal consisting of not less than 45 hours of instruction. Forty-five hours of instruction shall be deemed to be the equivalent of 3 semester credits in appraisal.

NAC 645.441 Courses required for original licensing: Unacceptable courses. (NRS 645.190, 645.343)

1. The Division shall not accept an applicant's completion of any course which is designed to prepare students for examination, commonly known as a "cram course," as fulfillment of the educational requirements for the applicant's original licensing.

2. None of the following kinds of courses will be accepted from an applicant as fulfillment of the education which is required by subsections 1 to 4, inclusive, of NRS 645.343 for original licensing:

(a) Courses designed to develop or improve clerical, office or business skills that are not related to the activities described in NRS 645.030, 645.035 and 645.040, such as typing, shorthand, operation of business machines, the use of computers, the use of computer software, improvement of memory, or writing of letters and reports; or

(b) Business courses in advertising or psychology.

3. The Division shall not accept a course in broker management required pursuant to paragraph (d) of subsection 2 of NRS 645.343 unless the course and the school that offers the course have been approved by the Commission.

(Added to NAC by Real Estate Comm'n, eff. 12-16-82; A by R092-00, 8-29-2000, eff. 1-1-2001; R031-04, 11-30-2004)

NAC 645.442 Real estate examination: Restrictions on persons associated with school. (NRS 645.190, 645.343)

1. An owner, instructor, or affiliate of a school approved by the Commission or other person associated with the school shall not take a real estate examination conducted by the Division or its agent unless he or she first submits to the Division:

(a) A written statement that his or her purpose in taking the examination is to fulfill one of the requirements for obtaining a license; and

(b) A written agreement to apply for a license upon passing the examination.

2. Such a school or anyone associated with its operation shall not:

(a) Solicit information from any person for the purpose of discovering past questions asked on any such examination; or

(b) Distribute to any person a copy of the questions or otherwise communicate to the person the questions without the prior written approval of the owner of the copyright to the questions.

(Added to NAC by Real Estate Comm'n, eff. 12-16-82)

NAC 645.443 Approval of distance education course. (NRS 645.190, 645.575)

1. A person who requests approval of a distance education course must demonstrate to the satisfaction of the Commission that the proposed distance education course satisfies the following requirements:

(a) The course must be designed to ensure that students actively participate in the instructional process by utilizing techniques that require substantial interaction with the instructor, other students or a computer program. If the subject matter of the course is such that the learning objectives for the course cannot be reasonably accomplished without direct interaction between the instructor and the students, the course design must provide for such interaction.

(b) If the course does not provide students with the opportunity for continuous audio and visual communication with the instructor during the presentation of the course, the course must utilize testing and remedial processes appropriate to ensure mastery of the subject matter of the course by the students.

(c) If the course involves self-paced study, the course must be designed so that the time required for a student of average ability to complete the course is within the number of hours for which the course is approved, and the sponsor of the course shall utilize a system which ensures that students have actually performed all tasks designed to ensure participation and mastery of the subject matter of the course by the students.

(d) The proposed methods of instruction used in the course must be appropriate to the proposed learning objectives of the course, and the scope and depth of the instructional materials must be consistent with the proposed learning objectives.

(e) The sponsor of the course shall provide appropriate technical support to enable students to complete the course satisfactorily.

(f) An approved instructor must be reasonably available to respond timely to questions asked by students concerning the subject matter of the course and to direct students to additional sources of information. For the purposes of this paragraph, a response by an approved instructor shall be deemed timely if the response is made within 2 business days after the question is submitted.

(g) The sponsor of the course shall provide students with an orientation or information package which contains all information that the Division requires to be provided to students and all necessary information about the course, including, without limitation, information concerning fees and refund policies, subject matter and learning objectives, procedures and requirements for satisfactory completion, any special requirements with regard to computer hardware and software or other equipment, and instructor and technical support. The sponsor shall make available to students technical support relating to the use of any computer hardware or software, or other equipment or technology needed to complete the course.

(h) The sponsor of the course shall utilize procedures which reasonably ensure that a student who receives continuing education credit for completing the course actually performed all the work required to complete the course. If the course involves independent study by students, such procedures must include, without limitation, the opportunity for direct contact by the sponsor with the student at the student's home or business via the telephone or electronic mail and a signed statement by the student certifying that he or she personally completed all course work. The sponsor shall retain such signed statements and records of student contact together with all other course records the sponsor must maintain.

2. A sponsor seeking approval of a computer-based distance education course must submit a complete copy of the course to the Division in the medium to be used and, if requested, must make available, at a date and time satisfactory to the Division and at the sponsor's expense, all equipment and software necessary to enable the Division to review the course. In the case of an Internet-based course, the sponsor shall provide the Division with access to the course via the Internet at no charge at a date and time satisfactory to the Division.

3. In determining whether to approve a distance education course pursuant to this section, the Commission will consider whether:

(a) The course consists of at least 3 hours of instruction;

(b) Students are required to complete a written examination proctored by a person acceptable to the Division or using a secure electronic method acceptable to the Division; and

(c) The course is presented by an accredited college or university that offers distance education in other disciplines, or whether the course design and method of delivery has been accredited by an accrediting agency which accredits distance education and which is approved by the Commission. For an accrediting agency to be approved by the Commission for the purposes of this paragraph, the accrediting agency must use the following considerations when making its determination on whether to accredit a distance education course:

(1) The mission statement of the sponsor of the course;

(2) The minimum design of the course and the procedures for updating the course;

(3) The interactivity of the instruction with the students;

(4) Whether the instruction provided in the course teaches mastery of the course material;

(5) The support services that are available to students;

(6) The medium through which the course is delivered to students;

(7) A time study of the range of instructional hours for which a course should be approved or accredited;

(8) For each module of instruction, whether there is:

(I) At least one learning objective for the module of instruction;

(II) A structured learning method to enable the student to achieve each such learning objective;

(III) A method of assessment of the student's performance during the module of instruction; and

(IV) A method of remediation pursuant to which a student who, based on the assessment of his or her performance, is determined to be deficient in his or her mastery of the course material may repeat the module until the student understands the course material; and

(9) Whether a complete syllabus or student manual, or both, for all courses or programs is provided in written form and includes accurate and clearly stated information about admissions, progression, completion, criteria, dismissal and any applicable licensing requirements.

(Added to NAC by Real Estate Comm'n by R031-04, eff. 11-30-2004)

NAC 645.4432 Duties of sponsor of approved course; period and renewal of approval of course; review and audit by Division; grounds for withdrawal of or refusal to renew approval of course; disciplinary action against licensee who sponsors approved course. (NRS 645.190, 645.575)

1. The sponsor of an approved course:

(a) Shall not allow a licensee to pass the course by taking an examination without having the required attendance;

(b) Shall admit authorized personnel of the Division to audit and evaluate the presentation of the course;

(c) Shall notify the Division within 15 days after making any material change in the course; and

(d) Shall not present a course for the main purpose of selling products and shall limit the announcement of products during the course to not more than 1 minute for each credit hour.

2. The Commission's approval of:

(a) A course to meet the educational requirements for an original license;

(b) A course for postlicensing education; and

(c) A course for continuing education,

☐ is effective for 1 year after the original approval or a renewal.

3. The school or sponsor must apply for renewal on a form provided by the Division and describe on that form any changes in the course. An application for renewal must be filed at least 2 weeks before the previous approval expires. If the school or sponsor does not timely file the application for renewal, the school or sponsor must apply for an original approval.

4. Each approved course and instructor is subject to review and audit by the Division. If the Division conducts such a review or audit, the sponsor shall make available to the Division all records requested which are necessary to the review.

5. The Division shall renew the approval of a course if the information concerning the course has been updated and there is no material change in the content of the course.

6. Each of the following acts and conditions is a ground for the Commission to withdraw or refuse to renew its approval of a course:

(a) The curriculum or instruction, as shown by evaluations or audits, is of poor quality.

(b) The violation of any provision of this chapter relating to continuing education.

(c) The course is not taught within the last period for which the course is approved.

(d) The sponsor of the course has made a false statement or has presented any false information in connection with an application for the approval of the course, the renewal of such approval or the approval of the sponsor.

(e) The sponsor of the course or any official or instructor employed by the sponsor has refused or failed to comply with any provision of this chapter or chapter 645 of NRS.

(f) The sponsor of the course or any official or instructor employed by the sponsor has provided false or incorrect information in connection with any report the sponsor is required to submit to the Commission.

(g) The sponsor of the course has engaged in a pattern of consistently cancelling scheduled courses.

(h) The sponsor of the course has remitted to the Commission in payment for required fees a check which was dishonored by a bank.

(i) An instructor employed by the sponsor of an approved course fails to conduct approved courses in a manner that demonstrates possession of the teaching skills described in this chapter.

(j) A court of competent jurisdiction has found the sponsor of the approved course or any official or instructor employed by the sponsor to have violated, in connection with the offering of education courses, any applicable federal or state law or regulation:

(1) Prohibiting discrimination on the basis of disability;

(2) Requiring places of public accommodation to be in compliance with prescribed standards relating to accessibility; or

(3) Requiring that courses related to licensing or certification for professional or trade purposes be offered in a place and manner accessible to persons with disabilities.

(k) The sponsor of the course or any official or instructor employed by the sponsor has been disciplined by the Commission or any other occupational licensing agency in this State or any other jurisdiction.

(l) The sponsor of the course or any official or instructor employed by the sponsor has collected money for an educational course but has refused or failed to provide the promised instruction.

7. A licensee who is the sponsor of an approved course is subject to disciplinary action pursuant to this chapter for any dishonest, fraudulent or improper conduct by the licensee, or an instructor of the approved course employed by the licensee, in connection with activities related to the approved course.

NAC 645.4434 Approved courses: Withdrawal of approval. (NRS 645.190, 645.575)

1. If the Administrator determines, whether pursuant to an audit or otherwise, that an approved course does not meet the standards for such a course set forth in this chapter, the Administrator shall notify the sponsor of the course of his or her intent to withdraw approval of the course. The notice must include the specific reasons upon which the Administrator is basing the decision to withdraw approval of the course. Not later than 30 days after the date on which he or she receives the notice, the sponsor may provide a written response to the Administrator that clearly sets forth the reasons why approval of the course should not be withdrawn and outlining any corrective measures that the sponsor will undertake.

After the 30-day period has elapsed, the Administrator shall review the notice and any response submitted by the sponsor and:

(a) Withdraw approval of the course;

(b) Allow the course to remain approved if certain specific enumerated conditions are met; or

(c) Allow the continued approval of the course.

If the Administrator decides to withdraw approval of the course, the withdrawal of approval of the course becomes effective upon the mailing of the Administrator's decision to withdraw approval to the sponsor by certified mail, return receipt requested to the sponsor's last known business address.

2. If the Administrator withdraws approval of a course, the Division shall give credit to a student for completing the course if the student began the course before the sponsor received written notice of the withdrawal of approval of the course.

3. The sponsor may appeal the decision of the Administrator to withdraw approval of a course by filing an appeal with the Commission not later than 30 days after the date on which the withdrawal of the approval of the course becomes effective.

4. If the sponsor files a timely appeal, the Commission will, as soon as practicable, hold a hearing concerning the withdrawal of approval of the course at a regularly scheduled meeting and will:

(a) Affirm the decision of the Administrator to withdraw approval of the course;

(b) Suspend approval of the course for a limited period and under such conditions as the Commission deems appropriate; or

(c) Reverse the decision of the Administrator to withdraw approval of the course.

(Added to NAC by Real Estate Comm'n by R031-04, eff. 11-30-2004)

NAC 645.4436 Approved courses: Reapproval. (NRS 645.190, 645.575) The Division shall, on behalf of the Commission, reapprove an approved course if no changes in the course have occurred since the course was last approved or reapproved.

(Added to NAC by Real Estate Comm'n by R031-04, eff. 11-30-2004)

NAC 645.4438 Approved courses: Award of certificate of completion. (NRS 645.190, 645.575)

1. To receive a certificate of completion for an approved course a student must:

(a) Direct his or her attention to the instruction being provided and refrain from engaging in activities unrelated to the instruction; and

(b) Refrain from engaging in activities which are distracting to other students or the instructor, or which otherwise disrupt the orderly conduct of a class, including, without limitation, the use of voice pagers, beepers and telephones.

2. An instructor shall deny the award of a certificate of completion to a student who fails to satisfy the conditions set forth in subsection 1.

3. If an instructor denies the award of a certificate of completion to a student, the student may, within 30 days after that denial, file a written request with the Administrator to review the matter. If the written request contains allegations which, if true, would qualify the applicant to receive a certificate of completion, the Administrator shall set the matter for an informal hearing before him or her to be conducted as soon as practicable.

(Added to NAC by Real Estate Comm'n by R031-04, eff. 11-30-2004)

NAC 645.444 Approved courses: Evaluation by students. (NRS 645.190, 645.575)

1. Each approved course and each instructor of an approved course must be evaluated by students on a form prescribed by the Division and provided by the sponsor during every course offering.

2. The sponsor shall:

(a) Arrange for the collection of the completed evaluations by a person other than the instructor of the approved course; and

(b) Mail or deliver copies of the completed evaluations to the Division within 10 working days after the last day of class for the course.

(Added to NAC by Real Estate Comm'n by R031-04, 11-30-2004, eff. 10-1-2005)

Postlicensing Education

NAC 645.4442 Courses required for first-time licensees; exempt licensees; standards for courses; effect of noncompliance. (NRS 645.190, 645.343, 645.575, 645.630, 645.633)

1. Except as otherwise provided in subsection 2, each first-time licensee shall take a prescribed postlicensing course of education that focuses on practical applications of real estate transactions. The postlicensing course:

(a) Must not repeat the content of the course work required to meet the educational requirements for an original license;

(b) Must constitute the education required to be completed by a licensee within the first year immediately after initial licensing pursuant to NRS 645.575;

(c) Must be offered in modules;

(d) Must be provided through live instruction in which the licensee and the instructor are in the same room, except that first-time licensees who live in a rural area may, with the prior written approval of the Division, take the postlicensing course as an interactive or televideo course that involves interaction with the instructor and other students; and

(e) Must provide the Division with proof of completion within the first year immediately after initial licensing.

2. The requirement for postlicensing education set forth in subsection 1 does not apply to a first-time licensee who:

(a) Holds a real estate license issued by another state or territory of the United States, or the District of Columbia, on the date on which the first-time licensee obtains a real estate license issued by the State of Nevada;

(b) Held a license as a real estate broker, real estate broker-salesperson or real estate salesperson issued by the State of Nevada within the 5 years immediately preceding the date on which the first-time licensee obtained a license as a real estate salesperson; or

(c) Is licensed as a real estate broker-salesperson and obtained the qualifications for licensure as a real estate broker-salesperson pursuant to the provisions of subsection 4 of NRS 645.343.

3. The postlicensing course may include material that has not previously been approved or allowed for continuing education credit. Courses approved for postlicensing education will not be accepted or approved as a course for continuing education.

4. The curriculum for postlicensing education must contain at least 15 modules that include, without limitation:

(a) Real estate contracts, including the writing and presenting of a purchase agreement and qualifying prospects;

(b) The listing process, market analysis and inspections;

(c) Communication, technology and records management, including time management, goal setting and devising a plan of action;

(d) Buyer representation, including the buyer's brokerage contract, fiduciary duties, disclosures, cooperation between agents and new-home tracts;

(e) Professional conduct, etiquette and ethics;

(f) Advertising, including Regulation Z of the Truth in Lending Act of the Federal Trade Commission issued by the Board of Governors of the Federal Reserve System, 12 C.F.R. Part 226, fair housing, the multiple-listing service, Internet websites and electronic mail;

(g) Proceeds of sale, costs of sale and cost sheets;

(h) Agency relationships;

(i) Land;

(j) Regulatory disclosures, including disclosures required by federal, state and local governments;

(k) Property management and the management of common-interest communities;

(l) Escrow, title and closing processes;

(m) Financing;

(n) Negotiation; and

(o) Tax opportunities and liabilities related to the client.

5. Each first-time licensee must complete an additional 12 hours of continuing education within the first 2 years immediately after initial licensing. The additional 12 hours of continuing education:

(a) Must include 3 hours in each of the following areas:

(1) Agency relationships;

(2) Nevada law, with an emphasis on recent statutory and regulatory changes;

(3) Contracts; and

(4) Ethics.

(b) Must be provided through live instruction in which the licensee and the instructor are in the same room, except that first-time licensees who live in a rural area may, with the prior written approval of the Division, take the additional continuing education course as an interactive or televideo course that involves interaction with the instructor and other students.

6. A first-time licensee who fails to comply with the requirements for postlicensing education set forth in this section is subject to immediate involuntary inactivation of the license by the Division and an administrative fine in the amount set forth in subsection 1 of NAC 645.695.

7. As used in this section, "rural area" means any area which is more than 100 miles from a city in this State whose population is 40,000 or more.

(Added to NAC by Real Estate Comm'n by R031-04, 11-30-2004, eff. 1-1-2006; A by R123-06, 6-1-2006; R093-10, 5-30-2012)

REVISER'S NOTE.
   The regulation of the Real Estate Commission filed with the Secretary of State on May 30, 2012 (LCB File No. R093-10), which amended this section, contains the following provisions not included in NAC:
   "1. The amendatory provisions of section 1 of this regulation [NAC 645.4442] apply only to first-time licensees whose licenses expire on or after July 1, 2012.
   2. The amendatory provisions of section 3 of this regulation [NAC 645.448] apply only to licensees whose licenses expire on or after July 1, 2013.
   3. The amendatory provisions of section 4 of this regulation [NAC 645.695] apply only to:
   (a) A first-time licensee whose license expires on or after July 1, 2012.
   (b) A licensee whose license expires on or after July 1, 2013."

NAC 645.4444 Approval and accreditation of courses; certificate of completion. (NRS 645.190, 645.575)
   1. An application for the approval of a course for postlicensing education must be submitted to the Division on a form provided by the Division for review and presentation to the Commission.
   2. The Commission will not grant retroactive approval for a course in postlicensing education.
   3. The Commission will grant credit for a course for postlicensing education only if the sponsor of the course:
   (a) Certifies the attendance of the licensees who take the course for credit.
   (b) Maintains for at least 4 years a record of attendance which contains the following information with respect to each licensee who has taken the course for credit:
      (1) The name of the licensee in attendance and the number of his or her license;
      (2) The title and number of the course;
      (3) The hours of instruction attended and the dates of attendance by the licensee; and
      (4) A statement that the licensee has successfully completed the course.
   (c) Assures the Commission that an approved instructor will preside throughout the course.
   (d) Requires each licensee who takes the course to:
      (1) Take a closed-book final examination with a proctor present at a location designated by the sponsor in its application for approval filed with the Division and to receive a score of at least 75 percent to pass the course;
      (2) Prove his or her identity before the licensee is allowed to take any examination; and
      (3) Complete the entire course to receive credit for taking the course.
   (e) Gives credit for only the number of hours for which the course has been approved by the Division to a licensee who completes the course.
   (f) Publishes a policy for retaking an examination which a licensee has failed.
   4. If a course for postlicensing education has been approved, the sponsor of the course shall provide a certified copy of the record of completion to the licensee upon his or her completion of the course. The Division shall accept the certificate as proof of completion of the course by the licensee. The certificate of a sponsor must contain:
   (a) The name of the sponsor;
   (b) The name of the licensee and his or her license number;
   (c) The title of the course and the number of hours for which the course has been approved;
   (d) The dates of instruction;
   (e) The number of the sponsor assigned by the Division and a statement that the course was approved by the Commission;
   (f) The signature of the person who is authorized to sign for the sponsor; and
   (g) A statement indicating that the licensee fulfilled the requirements to pass the course.

(Added to NAC by Real Estate Comm'n by R031-04, 11-30-2004, eff. 7-1-2005)

NAC 645.4446 Information required on course materials; restriction on attendance. (NRS 645.190, 645.575)

1. If a course has been approved and is being offered for postlicensing education, the sponsor must state on all the course materials:

(a) That the course is approved for postlicensing education in Nevada;

(b) The number of hours of credit for postlicensing education for which the course is approved; and

(c) The number of the sponsor assigned by the Division.

2. If a course offered by a sponsor that is a professional organization has been approved for postlicensing education, the sponsor shall not restrict attendance at the course to members of that organization.

(Added to NAC by Real Estate Comm'n by R031-04, 11-30-2004, eff. 7-1-2005)

NAC 645.4448 Notice of policy of sponsor concerning cancellations and refunds. (NRS 645.190, 645.575) Any advertising, promotional brochure or form for registration for a course for postlicensing education must contain, in writing, the policy of the sponsor concerning cancellations and refunds.

(Added to NAC by Real Estate Comm'n by R031-04, 11-30-2004, eff. 7-1-2005)

Continuing Education

NAC 645.445 General requirements for renewal or reinstatement of license. (NRS 645.190, 645.575)

1. To renew an active license, the licensee must provide the Division with proof that he or she has met the requirements set forth in NAC 645.448.

2. To reinstate a license which has been placed on inactive status, a person must provide the Division with proof that he or she has met the requirements set forth in NAC 645.448.

3. For the purpose of compliance with this section, 50 or more minutes of actual instruction constitutes a clock hour and initial licensing refers to the first issuance of a real estate license of any kind in Nevada.

[Real Estate Adv. Comm'n, § X subsec. F pars. 1-4 & 8, eff. 4-20-78] — (NAC A by Real Estate Comm'n, 8-21-81; 12-16-82; 4-27-84; 12-27-89; R093-10, 5-30-2012)

NAC 645.448 Specific requirements for renewal of license other than initial license and for reinstatement of license. (NRS 645.190, 645.575, 645.630, 645.633) *This regulation has not been updated by the Division.*

1. Except as otherwise provided in subsection 3, a real estate salesperson who wishes to renew his or her license must complete at least 48 24 hours of continuing education at approved educational courses, seminars or conferences during the license renewal period. Twenty-four of the hours must be completed before the end of each 2-year period. Each licensee must provide the Division with proof of completion before the end of each 2-year period. Not less than 12 of the hours in each 2-year period must be devoted to ethics, professional conduct or the legal aspects of real estate, including:

(a) Three hours in the area of agency relationships;

(b) Three hours in the area of Nevada law with an emphasis on recent statutory and regulatory changes;

(c) Three hours in the area of contracts; and

(d) Three hours in the area of ethics.

2. Except as otherwise provided in subsection 3, a real estate broker or real estate broker-salesperson who wishes to renew his or her license must complete at least 48 24 hours of continuing education at approved educational courses, seminars or conferences during the license renewal period. Twenty-four of the hours must be completed before the end of each 2-year period. Each licensee must provide the Division with proof of completion before the end of each 2-year period. Not less than 15 of the hours in each 2-year period must be devoted to ethics, professional conduct or the legal aspects of real estate, including:

(a) Three hours in the area of agency relationships;

(b) Three hours in the area of Nevada law with an emphasis on recent statutory and regulatory changes;

(c) Three hours in the area of contracts;

(d) Three hours in the area of ethics; and

(e) Three hours in the area of broker management.

3. The requirements for continuing education set forth in subsections 1 and 2 do not apply to the renewal of a license upon the expiration of the initial license.

4. If a license has been placed on inactive status and the licensee wishes to have the license reinstated, the licensee must comply with the following requirements:

(a) If the license was on inactive status for 1 year or less, all of which was during the period of the initial license, the licensee must complete the postlicensing course described in NAC 645.4442.

(b) If the license was on inactive status for more than 1 year but less than 2 years, any part of which was during the period of the initial license, the licensee must complete at approved educational courses, seminars or conferences:

    (1) The postlicensing course described in NAC 645.4442; and

    (2) At least 18 hours of continuing education. Not less than 12 of the hours must be devoted to ethics, professional conduct or the legal aspects of real estate, including:

        (I) Three hours in the area of agency relationships;

        (II) Three hours in the area of Nevada law with an emphasis on recent statutory and regulatory changes;

        (III) Three hours in the area of contracts; and

        (IV) Three hours in the area of ethics.

(c) If the license was on inactive status for 2 years or less, no part of which was during the period of the initial license, the licensee must complete at least 24 hours of continuing education at approved educational courses, seminars or conferences. Not less than 12 of the hours must be devoted to ethics, professional conduct or the legal aspects of real estate, including:

    (1) Three hours in the area of agency relationships;

    (2) Three hours in the area of current Nevada law with an emphasis on recent statutory and regulatory changes;

    (3) Three hours in the area of contracts; and

    (4) Three hours in the area of ethics.

(d) If the license was on inactive status for more than 2 years, any part of which was during the period of the initial license, the licensee must complete at approved educational courses, seminars or conferences:

    (1) The postlicensing course described in NAC 645.4442; and

    (2) At least 24 hours of continuing education. Not less than 12 of the hours must be devoted to ethics, professional conduct or the legal aspects of real estate, including:

        (I) Three hours in the area of agency relationships;

        (II) Three hours in the area of current Nevada law with an emphasis on recent statutory and regulatory changes;

        (III) Three hours in the area of contracts; and

        (IV) Three hours in the area of ethics.

(e) If the license was on inactive status for more than 2 years, no part of which was during the period of the initial license, the licensee must complete at least 48 hours of continuing education at approved educational courses, seminars or conferences. Not less than 24 of the hours must be devoted to ethics, professional conduct or the legal aspects of real estate, including:

    (1) Six hours in the area of agency relationships;

    (2) Six hours in the area of current Nevada law with an emphasis on recent statutory and regulatory changes;

    (3) Six hours in the area of contracts; and

    (4) Six hours in the area of ethics.

5. Not more than 3 hours of any of the required hours in each 2-year period set forth in this section for continuing education may be taken in courses for personal development.

6. At least 50 percent of the total hours of required continuing education set forth in this section must be taken through live instruction by a licensee.

7. A licensee who fails to comply with the requirements for continuing education set forth in this section is subject to immediate involuntary inactivation of the license by the Division and an administrative fine in the amount set forth in subsection 1 of NAC 645.695.

8. As used in this section, "initial license" means the license of a licensee who:

(a) Did not hold a real estate license issued by another state or territory of the United States, or the District of Columbia, on the date on which the licensee obtained a real estate license issued by the State of Nevada;

(b) Had not held a license as a real estate broker, real estate broker-salesperson or real estate salesperson issued by the State of Nevada within the 5 years immediately preceding the date on which the licensee obtained a license as a real estate salesperson; or

(c) Is licensed as a real estate broker-salesperson and obtained the qualifications for licensure as a real estate broker-salesperson pursuant to the provisions of subsection 2 of NRS 645.343.

(Added to NAC by Real Estate Comm'n by R031-04, 11-30-2004, eff. 1-1-2006; A by R123-06, 6-1-2006; R093-10, 5-30-2012)

REVISER'S NOTE.

The regulation of the Real Estate Commission filed with the Secretary of State on May 30, 2012 (LCB File No. R093-10), which amended this section, contains the following provisions not included in NAC:

"1.   The amendatory provisions of section 1 of this regulation [NAC 645.4442] apply only to first-time licensees whose licenses expire on or after July 1, 2012.

2.   The amendatory provisions of section 3 of this regulation [NAC 645.448] apply only to licensees whose licenses expire on or after July 1, 2013.

3.   The amendatory provisions of section 4 of this regulation [NAC 645.695] apply only to:

(a) A first-time licensee whose license expires on or after July 1, 2012.

(b) A licensee whose license expires on or after July 1, 2013."

NAC 645.450   Standards for courses. (NRS 645.190, 645.575)

1.   A course for continuing education must contain:

(a) Current information on real estate which will improve the professional knowledge of the licensee and enable him or her to give better service to the public.

(b) Information that relates to pertinent Nevada laws and regulations.

2.   The Commission considers courses in the following areas to be acceptable for continuing education:

(a) Ethics of selling real estate;

(b) Legislative issues which concern the practice of real estate or licensees, including pending and recent legislation;

(c) The administration of real estate law and regulations, including licensing and enforcement;

(d) Real estate financing, including mortgages and other techniques;

(e) The measurement and evaluation of the market for real estate, including evaluations of sites, market data and studies of feasibility;

(f) The administration of real estate brokerage, including the management of the office, trust accounts and employees' contracts;

(g) Real estate mathematics;

(h) The management of real property, including leasing agreements, procedures for accounting and contracts for management;

(i) The exchange of real property;

(j) Planning and zoning for land use;

(k) Real estate securities and syndications;

(l) Accounting and taxation as applied to real property;

(m) The development of land;

(n) Agency and subjects related to agency;

(o) The use of calculators and other technologies as applied to the practice of real estate;

(p) The preparation of real estate contracts; and

(q) Personal development courses.

3.   If the sponsor agrees to comply with the provisions of subsections 3 and 4 of NAC 645.455, NAC 645.457 and 645.463 and subsection 1 of NAC 645.4432, the Administrator may accept the following courses as meeting standards for continuing education without application or specific approval:

(a) Any course in real estate or a directly related subject if the course has been previously approved by the Commission.

(b) Any course in real estate or a directly related subject if the course is offered by an accredited university or community college for college credit.

4.   The Commission may, upon application, approve a course conducted by any other school, professional society or organization if the Commission finds that the course meets the standards for continuing education.

5.   The following kinds of courses and activities do not meet the standards for continuing education:

(a) A course designed to prepare students for examination.

(b) A course designed to develop or improve clerical, office or business skills that are not related to the activities described in NRS 645.030, 645.035 and 645.040, such as typing, shorthand, the operation of business machines, the use of computers, the use of computer software, speed-reading, the improvement of memory, and writing letters and reports.

(c) A meeting for the promotion of sales, a program of office training, or other activity which is held as part of the general business of the licensee.

(d) A course for the orientation of licensees, such as a course offered for that purpose through local real estate boards.

(e) A course for the development of instructors.

6.   The Commission will not approve more than:

(a) Seven full hours of credit per day of instruction in a course for continuing education if a final examination is not given; or

(b) Eight full hours of credit per day of instruction in a course for continuing education if a final examination is given.

NAC 645.455 Approval and accreditation of courses; certificate of attendance or completion. (NRS 645.190, 645.575)

1. An application for the approval of a course for continuing education must be submitted to the Division on a form provided by the Division for review and presentation to the Commission.

2. The Commission may grant retroactive approval for a course for continuing education.

3. The Commission will grant credit for a course for continuing education only if:

(a) The course consists of at least 3 hours of distance education or instruction in a classroom.

(b) For a course of instruction in a classroom, the sponsor of the course:

(1) Certifies the attendance of licensees who take the course for credit.

(2) Maintains for at least 4 years a record of attendance which contains the following information with respect to each licensee who has taken the course for credit:

(I) The name of the licensee in attendance and the number of his or her license.

(II) The title and number of the course.

(III) The hours of instruction attended and dates of attendance by the licensee.

(IV) A statement that the licensee has successfully completed the course, if applicable.

(3) Assures the Commission that an approved instructor will preside throughout the course.

(c) For a course of distance education, the sponsor of the course:

(1) Requires each student to:

(I) Take a closed-book final examination with a proctor present at a location designated by the sponsor in its application for approval filed with the Division and receive a score of at least 75 percent to pass the course;

(II) Prove his or her identity before the student is allowed to take any examination;

(III) Complete an entire course to receive credit for taking the course; and

(IV) Complete each course within an established minimum and maximum time.

(2) Gives credit for only the number of hours for which the course has been approved by the Division to a licensee who has completed the course.

(3) Publishes a policy for retaking an examination which a licensee failed.

(4) Maintains for at least 4 years a record of completion of the course which contains the following information with respect to each licensee who has taken the course for credit:

(I) The name of the licensee who completes the course and the number of his or her license.

(II) The title and number of the course.

(III) A statement that the licensee has successfully completed the course which includes, without limitation, the date that the course was completed and the number of hours completed.

4. If a course is approved, the sponsor shall provide a certified copy of the record of attendance or record of completion to the licensee upon his or her completion of the course. The Division shall accept the certificate as proof of the attendance of the licensee or completion of the course by the licensee for the purpose of renewal or reinstatement of his or her license. If the course is taken at a university or community college, the proof of attendance must be a certified transcript. The certificate of a sponsor must contain the:

(a) Name of the sponsor;

(b) Name of the licensee and his or her license number;

(c) Number of hours of credit for continuing education for which the course is approved;

(d) Dates of instruction for a course of instruction in a classroom;

(e) Date of completion of the course for a course of distance education;

(f) Title of the course or seminar;

(g) Number of the sponsor assigned by the Division and a statement that the course was approved by the Commission;

(h) Signature of the person authorized to sign for the sponsor;

(i) Grade received by the licensee or a statement of whether the licensee passed the class if an examination was given; and

(j) Manner in which instruction for the course was delivered.

[Real Estate Adv. Comm'n, § X subsec. F par. 10, eff. 4-20-78] — (NAC A by Real Estate Comm'n, 8-21-81; 12-16-82; 8-26-83; 12-27-89; 5-14-96; R146-99& R186-99, 1-21-2000; R092-00, 8-29-2000; R031-04, 11-30-2004)

NAC 645.457 **Information required on course materials; restriction of attendance.** (NRS 645.190, 645.575)

1. If a course has been approved and is being offered for continuing education, the sponsor must state on all the course materials:

(a) That the course is approved for continuing education in Nevada;

(b) The number of hours of credit for continuing education for which the course is approved;

(c) The number of the sponsor assigned by the Division; and

(d) The manner in which instruction for the course will be delivered.

2. If a course offered by a sponsor that is a professional organization has been approved for continuing education, the sponsor shall not restrict attendance at the course to members of that organization.

(Added to NAC by Real Estate Comm'n, eff. 8-21-81; A 12-16-82; R031-04, 11-30-2004)

NAC 645.458 **Notice of policy of sponsor concerning cancellations and refunds.** (NRS 645.190, 645.575) Any advertising, promotional brochure or form for registration for a course for continuing education must contain, in writing, the policy of the sponsor concerning cancellations and refunds.

(Added to NAC by Real Estate Comm'n, eff. 6-3-86; A by R031-04, 11-30-2004)

NAC 645.463 **Restrictions on receipt of credit for course.** (NRS 645.190, 645.575)

1. A course may not be taken for credit to meet the requirements for continuing education more than once during any two consecutive periods for renewal of a license.

2. Courses taken to satisfy requirements for renewal or reinstatement of a license must be completed within 2 years immediately before the latest date for renewing or reinstating the license.

3. A licensee may receive credit for continuing education only upon certification by the sponsor that the licensee has attended and completed at least 90 percent of the course.

4. The sponsor shall determine whether a final examination is required for the completion of a course.

(Added to NAC by Real Estate Comm'n, eff. 8-21-81; A 12-16-82; 8-26-83; 6-3-86; 12-27-89; R092-00, 8-29-2000; R031-04, 11-30-2004)

NAC 645.467 **Credit for attendance at meeting of Commission.** (NRS 645.190, 645.575)

1. The Commission will grant credit for continuing education, not to exceed 6 hours during a licensing period, to a licensee for attending a meeting of the Commission if:

(a) The meeting of the Commission for which credit for continuing education is being sought is not a hearing in which the licensee is participating as the result of a disciplinary action;

(b) The meeting of the Commission for which credit for continuing education is being sought lasts at least 3 hours; and

(c) The Commission certifies, for the purposes of providing credit for continuing education, the attendance of the licensee at the meeting.

2. If a licensee attends only part of a meeting of the Commission, the Division may determine the number of hours of credit, if any, that the licensee may receive for credit for continuing education pursuant to this section.

(Added to NAC by Real Estate Comm'n, eff. 4-27-84; A by Real Estate Div., 3-31-94; A by Real Estate Comm'n by R031-04, 11-30-2004; R123-06, 6-1-2006)

REAL ESTATE EDUCATION, RESEARCH AND RECOVERY FUND

NAC 645.470 **Annual financial statement and budget.** (NRS 645.190, 645.842)

1. Within 60 days after the close of the fiscal year, the Administrator shall deliver to the Commission a financial statement showing beginning balances, receipts, expenditures and ending balances of the Real Estate Education, Research and Recovery Fund in such detail as the Commission requires.

2. Before the first meeting of each fiscal year, the Commission will have a budget prepared for the yearly allocation of expenditures of the Fund from money available for research and education. The budget so prepared will be presented at the first meeting of the Commission in the fiscal year.

[Real Estate Adv. Comm'n, § XV, eff. 10-31-75] — (NAC A by Real Estate Comm'n, 6-3-86; R111-01, 12-17-2001; R031-04, 11-30-2004)

NAC 645.475 Request for showing that judgment debtor has been examined by person who files petition against Fund. (NRS 645.190, 645.844) For purposes of determining whether a person who has filed a petition against the Real Estate Education, Research and Recovery Fund has made reasonable searches and inquiries to ascertain whether the judgment debtor possesses real or personal property or other assets, liable to be sold or applied in satisfaction of the judgment, the Administrator shall request that the court require the petitioner to show that he or she has conducted an examination of the judgment debtor pursuant to NRS 21.270 to 21.340, inclusive, unless:

1. The judgment debtor cannot, with the exercise of due diligence, be found within the jurisdiction;
2. The judgment debtor has filed a petition in bankruptcy; or
3. There is good cause for not requiring the examination.

(Added to NAC by Real Estate Comm'n, eff. 6-3-86)

NAC 645.480 "Unpaid actual damages" interpreted. (NRS 645.190, 645.844) The Administrator shall interpret the phrase "unpaid actual damages" as it is used in NRS 645.844 to exclude any attorney's fees, prejudgment interest, or court costs related to the judgment upon which the petition is based.

(Added to NAC by Real Estate Div., eff. 3-31-94)

NAC 645.485 Compromise of claim. (NRS 645.190, 645.845)

1. In compromising a claim pursuant to NRS 645.845, the Administrator may prepare and enter into a stipulation with the petitioner and file a joint petition with the court.

2. Before the Administrator and the petitioner file such a joint petition, the Administrator shall advise the petitioner in writing that:

(a) The Division does not represent the interests of the petitioner; and

(b) The petitioner should seek the advice of independent legal counsel regarding the proposed compromise.

3. The Administrator shall compromise any claim and defend any action against the Real Estate Education, Research and Recovery Fund on behalf of the Fund in which a settlement has been agreed upon by the petitioner or paid to the petitioner, including, without limitation, any settlement by a third party that has been agreed upon by the petitioner or paid to the petitioner.

(Added to NAC by Real Estate Div., eff. 3-31-94; A by Real Estate Comm'n by R111-01, 12-17-2001)

ADVISORY COMMITTEE

NAC 645.490 Establishment and purpose; list of persons approved to serve; appointment of members; restrictions on service; allowance and expenses. (NRS 645.190)

1. The Commission may establish an advisory committee to assist the Commission with any matter that the Commission determines to be appropriate for submission to an advisory committee.

2. The Administrator may establish an advisory committee to assist the Administrator in:

(a) The evaluation of any educational course, seminar or conference; or

(b) The review of a matter that is the subject of an investigation conducted pursuant to NAC 645.680, if the licensee who is the subject of the investigation agrees to participate in an informal review of the matter with an advisory committee.

3. The Commission will create and maintain a list of persons who are approved by the Commission to serve on an advisory committee. The Commission will not include any person on the list unless that person meets the qualifications for appointment to the Commission set forth in subsection 3 of NRS 645.090.

4. If the Administrator or the Commission determines that an advisory committee should be formed, the Administrator shall appoint three persons to serve on the advisory committee from the list of persons approved by the Commission to serve on the advisory committee. At least one person so appointed must be a current or former member of the Commission. The Administrator shall appoint one member of the advisory committee, who must be a current or former member of the Commission, to serve as chair of the advisory committee.

5. A member of an advisory committee:

(a) Serves at the pleasure of the Commission and without compensation; and

(b) Shall abstain from participating in any proceeding in which he or she would be prohibited from participating if he or she were a member of the Commission.

6. Each member of an advisory committee is entitled to receive a per diem allowance and travel expenses as provided for state officers and employees generally for the period during which the member was engaged in the discharge of his or her official duties.

(Added to NAC by Real Estate Comm'n by R146-99, eff. 1-21-2000; A by R111-01, 12-17-2001; R031-04, 11-30-2004)

NAC 645.493 Review of matter investigated as result of complaint or upon request of Division: Duties of advisory committee and Administrator. (NRS 645.190)

1. An advisory committee which is established to assist the Administrator with the review of a matter that is the subject of an investigation conducted pursuant to NAC 645.680 shall:

(a) Review the written report submitted by an investigator pursuant to NAC 645.680 and any other information that is relevant to the matter to determine whether there is probable cause to show that the licensee who is the subject of the investigation has violated a provision of chapter 113, 116, 119, 119A, 119B, 645, 645C or 645D of NRS or the regulations adopted pursuant to those chapters;

(b) Hold an informal conference in accordance with NAC 645.497;

(c) Work with the licensee who is the subject of the investigation to attempt to arrive at a recommendation for resolution of the matter; and

(d) Submit a recommendation for resolution of the matter to the Administrator or recommend that the matter be submitted to the Commission.

2. If the Administrator and the licensee who is the subject of the investigation accept the advisory committee's recommendation for resolution of the matter, the Administrator shall enter into a written agreement with the licensee who is the subject of the investigation which must contain the terms of the resolution recommended by the advisory committee. If the agreement provides for disciplinary action that is authorized pursuant to NRS 645.630, the Administrator may impose the discipline on behalf of the Commission.

3. If disciplinary action is taken pursuant to this section against a licensee who is the subject of an investigation, the Administrator shall file with the Commission a written summary of the facts and disciplinary actions taken against the licensee.

4. If the Administrator or the licensee who is the subject of the investigation does not accept the advisory committee's recommendation for resolution of the matter, the Administrator shall:

(a) Schedule a hearing which must be conducted pursuant to NAC 645.810; or

(b) Negotiate a resolution of the matter with the licensee who is the subject of the investigation, which may include, without limitation, assessing administrative sanctions pursuant to NAC 645.695. A resolution negotiated pursuant to this paragraph is contingent upon the approval of the Commission at a hearing in which the licensee who is the subject of the investigation is in attendance.

(Added to NAC by Real Estate Comm'n by R146-99, eff. 1-21-2000; A by R111-01, 12-17-2001; R031-04, 11-30-2004)

NAC 645.497 Review of matter investigated as result of complaint or upon request of Division: Informal conference; report to Administrator. (NRS 645.190)

1. If an advisory committee is established to assist the Administrator with the review of an investigation conducted pursuant to NAC 645.680, the Administrator shall schedule an informal conference between the advisory committee and the licensee who is the subject of the investigation. The Administrator shall provide written notice of the time and place of the conference to:

(a) Each member of the advisory committee;

(b) The licensee who is the subject of the investigation; and

(c) Each witness who has been requested to appear at the informal conference.

2. The advisory committee may request the attendance at an informal conference of any person whom the advisory committee believes to have information that is relevant to the matter.

3. When conducting an informal conference, an advisory committee:

(a) May consider all evidence that it deems relevant to the investigation;

(b) Shall rule on the admissibility of evidence;

(c) Shall be the controlling authority with regard to the admissibility of evidence; and

(d) Need not follow the rules of admissibility of evidence that a court must follow.

4. The chair of an advisory committee shall file a written report with the Administrator that explains the results of the informal conference within 30 days after the conclusion of the informal conference. Except as otherwise provided in NRS 645.180, the report is and must remain confidential.

(Added to NAC by Real Estate Comm'n by R146-99, eff. 1-21-2000; A by R111-01, 12-17-2001)

NAC 645.500 Informal conference upon review of matter investigated by Administrator; report to Administrator; confidentiality. (NRS 645.190)

1. If an advisory committee is established to assist the Administrator with the review of an investigation conducted pursuant to NRS 645.610, the Administrator shall schedule an informal conference between the advisory committee and the licensee who is the subject of the investigation. The Administrator shall provide written notice of the time and place of the informal conference to:

(a) Each member of the advisory committee;

(b) The licensee who is the subject of the investigation; and

(c) Each witness who has been requested to appear at the informal conference.

2. An advisory committee may request the attendance at an informal conference of any person whom the advisory committee believes to have information that is relevant to the matter.

3. When conducting an informal conference, an advisory committee:

(a) May consider all evidence that it deems relevant to the investigation;

(b) Shall rule on the admissibility of evidence;

(c) Is the controlling authority with regard to the admissibility of evidence; and

(d) Need not follow the rules of admissibility of evidence that a court must follow.

4. The chair of an advisory committee shall file a written report with the Administrator that explains the results of the informal conference within 30 days after the conclusion of the informal conference.

5. A written report reviewed pursuant to subsection 1 of NAC 645.493, a written report filed pursuant to subsection 4 and all proceedings before an advisory committee are confidential.

(Added to NAC by Real Estate Comm'n by R031-04, eff. 11-30-2004)

STANDARDS OF PRACTICE

NAC 645.525 Naming of false consideration in document. (NRS 645.050, 645.190) Regardless of disclosure or any agreement on the part of the seller, a licensee shall not participate in the naming of a false consideration in any document, unless it is an obviously nominal consideration.

[Real Estate Adv. Comm'n, § VII Code of Ethics Part I subsec. 4, eff. 10-31-75] — (NAC A by Real Estate Comm'n by R031-04, 11-30-2004)

NAC 645.535 Exclusive agency agreements; placement of signs. (NRS 645.050, 645.190)

1. A licensee cooperating with a broker who holds an exclusive listing or other exclusive agency agreement shall not invite the cooperation of another licensee without the consent of the listing broker or the agent.

2. Signs giving notice of property for sale, rent, lease, or exchange must not be placed on any property by more than one licensee unless authorized by the owner in writing.

3. A person must obtain the consent of the broker who holds an exclusive listing or other exclusive agency agreement before negotiating a lease or sale with the owner of that property or the principal.

4. A broker who holds an exclusive listing or other exclusive agency agreement shall cooperate with other brokers whenever it is in the interest of his or her client and may share commissions on a previously agreed basis.

[Real Estate Adv. Comm'n, § VII Code of Ethics Part II subsecs. 7 & 10-12, eff. 10-31-75] — (NAC A by Real Estate Comm'n, 12-27-91; A by Real Estate Div., 3-1-96)

NAC 645.541 Authorization of licensee to negotiate directly with client of broker with exclusive authority to represent client. (NRS 645.050, 645.190)

1. A broker who has the exclusive authority to represent a client under an exclusive agency listing agreement, exclusive buyer's brokerage agreement or exclusive right to sell or lease listing agreement may authorize another licensee to negotiate directly with that client if written authorization is obtained from the broker pursuant to subsection 2 of NRS 645.635. The authorization must be prepared on a form prescribed by the Division. The broker shall, upon request, provide a copy of the authorization to any licensee cooperating with the broker.

2. Any negotiation conducted by a licensee with a seller, purchaser, lessor or tenant pursuant to the authorization described in subsection 1 does not create an express or implied agency relationship between the licensee and the client of the authorizing broker.

3. A licensee who cooperates with a broker and who negotiates an agreement pursuant to this section may communicate with the authorizing broker's client to assist in closing the agreement. Any communication engaged in

pursuant to this subsection does not create an express or implied agency relationship between the licensee and the client or the authorizing broker.

4. As used in this section, "negotiate" means:

(a) To communicate, deliver, discuss or review the terms of an offer, counteroffer or proposal; or

(b) To communicate or assist in communication regarding an offer, counteroffer or proposal and preparing any response as directed.

(Added to NAC by Real Estate Comm'n by R165-07, eff. 4-17-2008)

NAC 645.546 Representation of clients under brokerage agreements: "Present all offers" and "exclusive agency representation" interpreted. (NRS 645.050, 645.190, 645.254, 645.320)

1. As used in NRS 645.254, the Commission will interpret the term "present all offers" to include, without limitation:

(a) Accepting delivery of or conveying an offer or counteroffer;

(b) Answering a client's questions regarding an offer or counteroffer; and

(c) Assisting a client in preparing, communicating or negotiating an offer or counteroffer.

2. As used in NRS 645.320, the Commission will interpret the term "exclusive agency representation" to mean an agency relationship that consists of one broker and one client, including, but not limited to:

(a) An exclusive agency listing agreement;

(b) An exclusive buyer's brokerage agreement; or

(c) An exclusive right to sell or lease listing agreement.

3. The provisions of this section do not prohibit the creation of an agency relationship described in a form prepared pursuant to subsection 2 or 3 of NRS 645.193.

(Added to NAC by Real Estate Comm'n by R165-07, eff. 4-17-2008)

NAC 645.551 Exclusive buyer's brokerage agreements: Inclusion of certain provisions regarding compensation of broker. (NRS 645.050, 645.190) An exclusive buyer's brokerage agreement may authorize the broker specified in the agreement to receive compensation from the seller or lessor of the property or the broker of the seller or lessor and may provide that the purchaser or tenant is not required to compensate the broker if the property is purchased or leased solely through the efforts of the purchaser or tenant.

(Added to NAC by Real Estate Comm'n by R165-07, eff. 4-17-2008)

NAC 645.600 Responsibilities of broker regarding associated licensees, employees and operation of business; agreement to retain licensee as independent contractor. (NRS 645.050, 645.190)

1. Every real estate broker shall teach the licensees associated with him or her the fundamentals of real estate or time-share practice, or both, and the ethics of the profession. The broker shall supervise the activities of those licensees, the activities of his or her employees and the operation of his or her business.

2. The supervision described in subsection 1 includes, without limitation, the establishment of policies, rules, procedures and systems that allow the real estate broker to review, oversee and manage:

(a) The real estate transactions performed by a licensee who is associated with the real estate broker;

(b) Documents that may have a material effect upon the rights or obligations of a party to such a real estate transaction;

(c) The filing, storage and maintenance of such documents;

(d) The handling of money received on behalf of a real estate broker;

(e) The advertising of any service for which a real estate license is required; and

(f) The familiarization by the licensee of the requirements of federal and state law governing real estate transactions, including, without limitation, prohibitions against discrimination.

3. In establishing such policies, rules, procedures and systems, the real estate broker shall consider the number of licensees associated with the real estate broker, the number of employees employed by the real estate broker and the number and location of branch offices operated by the real estate broker.

4. A real estate broker shall establish a system for monitoring compliance with such policies, rules, procedures and systems. The real estate broker may use a real estate broker-salesperson to assist in administering the provisions of this section so long as the real estate broker does not relinquish overall responsibility for the supervision of the acts of the licensees associated with the real estate broker.

5. A real estate broker may enter into a written agreement with each licensee associated with the real estate broker to retain the licensee as an independent contractor. If such an agreement is entered into, it must:

gned and dated by the real estate broker and the licensee; and

de the material aspects of the relationship between the real estate broker and the licensee, including, without
.............., he supervision by the real estate broker of the activities of the licensee for which a real estate license is
required.

[Real Estate Adv. Comm'n, § VII subsec. 1, eff. 10-31-75] — (NAC A by Real Estate Comm'n, 4-27-84;
R111-01, 12-17-2001; R031-04, 11-30-2004)

NAC 645.605 Considerations in determining certain misconduct by licensee. (NRS 645.050, 645.190, 645.633)
In determining whether a licensee has been guilty of gross negligence or incompetence under paragraph (h) of subsection
1 of NRS 645.633 or conduct which constitutes deceitful, fraudulent or dishonest dealing under paragraph (i) of that
subsection, the Commission will consider, among other things, whether the licensee:

1. Has done his or her utmost to protect the public against fraud, misrepresentation or unethical practices related to
real estate or time shares.

2. Has ascertained all pertinent facts concerning any time share or property for which the licensee accepts an agency.

3. Has attempted to provide specialized professional services concerning a type of property or service that is outside
the licensee's field of experience or competence without the assistance of a qualified authority unless the facts of such
lack of experience or competence are fully disclosed to his or her client.

4. Has disclosed, in writing, his or her interest or contemplated interest in any property or time share with which the
licensee is dealing. The disclosure must include, but is not limited to, a statement of:

(a) Whether the licensee expects to receive any direct or indirect compensation, dividend or profit from any person or
company that will perform services related to the property and, if so, the identity of the person or company;

(b) The licensee's affiliation with or financial interest in any person or company that furnishes services related to the
property;

(c) If the licensee is managing the property, his or her interest in or financial arrangement with any person or company
that provides maintenance or other services to the property;

(d) If the licensee refers one of his or her clients or customers to another person or company, such as a contractor, title
company, attorney, engineer or mortgage banker, the licensee's expectation of a referral fee from that person or company;
and

(e) If the licensee receives compensation from more than one party in a real estate transaction, full disclosure to and
consent from each party to the real estate transaction. A licensee shall not accept compensation from more than one party
in a real estate transaction, even if otherwise permitted by law, without full disclosure to all parties.

5. Has kept informed of current statutes and regulations governing real estate, time shares and related fields in which
he or she attempts to provide guidance.

6. Has breached his or her obligation of absolute fidelity to his or her principal's interest or his or her obligation to
deal fairly with all parties to a real estate transaction.

7. Has ensured that each agreement for the sale, lease or management of property or time shares is contained in a
written agreement that has been signed by all parties and that his or her real estate broker and each party to the real estate
transaction has a copy of the written agreement.

8. Has obtained all changes of contractual terms in writing and whether such changes are signed or initialed by the
parties concerned.

9. Understands and properly applies federal and state statutes relating to the protection of consumers.

10. Has acquired knowledge of all material facts that are reasonably ascertainable and are of customary or express
concern and has conveyed that knowledge to the parties to the real estate transaction.

11. Has impeded or attempted to impede any investigation of the Division by:

(a) Failing to comply or delaying his or her compliance with a request by the Division to provide documents;

(b) Failing to supply a written response, including supporting documentation, if available;

(c) Supplying false information to an investigator, auditor or any other officer of the Division;

(d) Providing false, forged or altered documents; or

(e) Attempting to conceal any documents or facts relating to a real estate transaction.

(Added to NAC by Real Estate Comm'n, eff. 8-21-81; A 8-26-83; 4-27-84; 6-3-86; A by Real Estate Div., 3-
31-94; 3-1-96; A by Real Estate Comm'n by R111-01, 12-17-2001; R031-04, 11-30-2004)

NAC 645.610 Restrictions on advertising; use of name under which licensee is licensed. (NRS 645.050,

1. In addition to satisfying the requirements set forth in NRS 645.315:

(a) An advertisement of the services of a licensee for which a license is required under chapter 645 of NRS must not be false or misleading.

(b) Except as otherwise provided in this paragraph, a licensee shall not use his or her name or telephone number or the name or telephone number of another licensee of the brokerage firm with which the licensee is associated in any advertisement which contains the words "for sale by owner," "for lease by owner" or similar words. A licensee may use his or her name or telephone number in an advertisement for property if the licensee has an ownership interest in the advertised property and the advertisement contains:

(1) If the licensee is a real estate broker, the words "for sale by owner-broker," "for lease by owner-broker" or substantially similar words; or

(2) If the licensee is an agent, the words "for sale by owner-agent," "for lease by owner-agent" or substantially similar words.

(c) The name of a brokerage firm under which a real estate broker does business or with which a real estate broker-salesperson or salesperson is associated must be clearly identified with prominence in any advertisement. In determining whether the name of the brokerage firm is identified with prominence, the Division shall consider, without limitation, the style, size and color of the type or font used and the location of the name of the brokerage firm as it appears in the advertisement.

(d) A licensee shall not publish or cause to be published any advertisement or place any sign that makes any reference to the availability of a specific property which is exclusively listed for sale by another broker unless the licensee obtains the prior written consent of the broker with whom the property is listed. Such consent must not be given or withheld by the listing broker without the knowledge of the owner of the property.

(e) A licensee shall not advertise or otherwise conduct business under a name, including a nickname, other than the name under which he or she is licensed to engage in business.

2. If advertising under the name of a franchise, a broker shall incorporate in a conspicuous way in the advertisement the real, fictitious or corporate name under which the broker is licensed to engage in business and an acknowledgment that each office is independently owned and operated.

3. In addition to the provisions of paragraph (a) of subsection 1, a licensee who represents a seller or lessor under an exclusive agency listing agreement or an exclusive right to sell or lease listing agreement shall not advertise any property that is subject to the agreement as "for sale by owner" or otherwise mislead a person into believing that the licensee does not represent the seller or lessor.

4. As used in this section, "advertisement" includes, without limitation:

(a) Any unsolicited printed material and any broadcast made by radio, television or electronic means, including, without limitation, by unsolicited electronic mail and the Internet, billboards and signs; and

(b) Business cards, stationery, forms and other documents used in a real estate transaction.

[Real Estate Adv. Comm'n, § VII subsecs. 2 & 3, eff. 10-31-75] — (NAC A by Real Estate Comm'n, 8-21-81; 12-16-82; 4-27-84; 12-27-91; A by Real Estate Div., 3-1-96; A by Real Estate Comm'n by R186-99, 1-21-2000; R111-01, 12-17-2001; R031-04, 11-30-2004; R165-07, 4-17-2008)

NAC 645.611 Advertisement of services: Use of terms "team" and "group." (NRS 645.050, 645.190) A licensee may use the term "team" or "group" to advertise the services provided by the licensee if:

1. The use of the term does not constitute the unlawful use of a trade name and is not deceptively similar to a name under which any other person is lawfully doing business;

2. The team or group is composed of more than one licensee;

3. The members of the team or group are employed by the same broker;

4. The name of the team or group contains the last name of at least one of the members of the team or group; and

5. The advertising complies with all other applicable provisions of this chapter and chapter 645 of NRS.

(Added to NAC by Real Estate Comm'n by R031-04, eff. 11-30-2004)

NAC 645.613 Dissemination of certain unsolicited information through Internet or electronic mail. (NRS 645.050, 645.190) A licensee disseminating unsolicited information concerning real property or marketing real property through the Internet or electronic mail:

1. Shall be deemed to be engaged in advertising and shall comply with the applicable provisions of this chapter and chapter 645 of NRS relating to advertising.

2. Shall make all disclosures, obtain appropriate signatures and follow all requirements set forth in this chapter and chapter 645 of NRS before entering into a relationship as the agent of a client. The clicking of an acceptance box on the Internet or in an electronic mail is insufficient to create such a relationship between the licensee and the client. As used in this subsection, "appropriate signature" means the legal signature of the client.

(Added to NAC by Real Estate Comm'n by R031-04, eff. 11-30-2004)

NAC 645.615 Use of sign to identify business. (NRS 645.050, 645.190, 645.560)

1. The sign which NRS 645.560 requires each broker to erect and maintain in a conspicuous place upon the premises of the broker's place of business must be readable from the nearest public sidewalk, street or highway.

2. If the broker's place of business is located in an office building, hotel or apartment house, the broker's sign must be posted on the building directory or on the exterior of the entrance to the business.

3. Upon request by the Division, the broker shall furnish a photograph of his or her sign as proof of compliance with NRS 645.560 and this section.

[Real Estate Adv. Comm'n, § VI subsecs. 5-7, eff. 10-31-75] — (NAC A by Real Estate Comm'n, 8-21-81; 12-16-82; 4-27-84; A by Real Estate Div., 11-30-87; A by Real Estate Comm'n by R092-00, 8-29-2000)

NAC 645.620 Use of fictitious name. (NRS 645.050, 645.190)

1. A broker shall not operate under a fictitious name unless the broker complies with chapter 602 of NRS and files with the Division a certified copy of the certificate issued by the county clerk. The Division shall not issue more than one license nor register more than one owner-developer under the same name.

2. If a broker changes or assumes a fictitious name under which business is conducted, the broker shall file a certified copy of the certificate issued by the county clerk to the Division within 10 days after the certificate is issued.

3. A broker may not use more than one name for each license under which he or she operates.

[Real Estate Adv. Comm'n, § VI subsec. 3, eff. 10-31-75] — (NAC A by Real Estate Comm'n, 8-21-81; A by Real Estate Div., 3-1-96; A by Real Estate Comm'n by R186-99, 1-21-2000)

NAC 645.627 Location of office. (NRS 645.050, 645.190)

1. A broker shall establish an office in a location which is easily accessible to the public. If the broker chooses to establish an office in a private home or in conjunction with another business, he or she shall set aside a separate room or rooms for conducting his or her real estate business. The broker's office must comply with local zoning requirements.

2. A broker who is licensed in Nevada but who maintains an active license in another state shall maintain and operate a Nevada office.

(Added to NAC by Real Estate Comm'n, eff. 8-21-81)

NAC 645.630 Prompt tender of offers. (NRS 645.050, 645.190) A licensee shall promptly deliver:

1. To the seller, every bona fide offer, complete with all terms and conditions of purchase, which he or she obtains.

2. To the purchaser and seller, copies of each acceptance of an offer or counteroffer.

[Real Estate Adv. Comm'n, § VII, subsecs. 4 & 6, eff. 10-31-75]

→ Must Be Disclosed

NAC 645.632 Notification of rejection of offer or counteroffer. (NRS 645.050, 645.190)

1. If a licensee represents a seller in a transaction, and if the seller does not accept an offer within a reasonable time after an offer has been presented to the seller, the licensee shall provide to the buyer or the representative of the buyer written notice signed by the seller which informs the buyer that the offer has not been accepted by the seller.

2. If a licensee represents a buyer in a transaction, and if the buyer does not accept a counteroffer within a reasonable time after a counteroffer has been presented to the buyer, the licensee shall provide to the seller or the representative of the seller written notice signed by the buyer which informs the seller that the counteroffer has not been accepted by the buyer.

NAC 645.635 Disclosure of unmerchantable title. (NRS 645.050, 645.190, 645.252) A licensee may not attempt to sell, or offer to sell, any real property or any time share with knowledge that the title is unmerchantable unless the licensee notifies the prospective purchaser of that fact before the payment of any part of the purchase price.

NAC 645.637 Disclosure of relationship as agent or status as principal. (NRS 645.050, 645.190, 645.252) In each real estate transaction involving a licensee, as agent or principal, the licensee shall clearly disclose, in writing, to his or her client and to any party not represented by a licensee, the relationship of the licensee as the agent of his or her client or the status of the licensee as a principal. The disclosure must be made as soon as practicable, but not later than the date and time on which any written document is signed by the client or any party not represented by a licensee, or both. The prior disclosure must then be confirmed in a separate provision incorporated in or attached to that document and must be maintained by the real estate broker in his or her files relating to that transaction.

(Added to NAC by Real Estate Div., 11-8-88, eff. 7-1-89; A by Real Estate Comm'n, 12-27-89; R186-99, 1-21-2000; R111-01, 12-17-2001; R123-06, 6-1-2006)

NAC 645.640 Disclosure of interest of licensee in certain transactions. (NRS 645.050, 645.190, 645.252)

1. A licensee shall not acquire, lease or dispose of any time share, real property or interest in any time share or real property for himself or herself, any member of his or her immediate family, his or her firm, or any member thereof, or any entity in which the licensee has an interest as owner unless the licensee first discloses in writing that:

(a) He or she is acquiring, leasing or disposing of the time share or property for himself or herself or for a member, firm, or entity with which the licensee has such a relationship; and

(b) He or she is a licensed real estate broker, licensed real estate broker-salesperson or licensed real estate salesperson, whether his or her license is active or inactive. This disclosure may be accomplished with a reference to himself or herself as an agent, licensee, salesperson, broker or broker-salesperson, whichever is appropriate.

2. If a licensee advertises any time share or real property or his or her wish to enter into a transaction which is subject to the provisions of subsection 1, the licensee shall include in the advertisement the disclosure required by that subsection.

[Real Estate Adv. Comm'n, § VII subsec. 8, eff. 10-31-75] — (NAC A by Real Estate Comm'n, 12-16-82; 4-27-84; A by Real Estate Div., 11-30-87; A by Real Estate Comm'n by R186-99, 1-21-2000; R031-04, 11-30-2004)

NAC 645.645 Inspections and audits by Division: Cooperation by broker; form for permission. (NRS 645.190, 645.195, 645.310, 645.313) A broker shall, upon demand, provide the Division with the documents and the permission necessary for the Division to complete fully an inspection and audit, including an inspection and audit of any money accounts as provided in NRS 645.310 and 645.313. Permission may be given on a form provided by the Division. The form must provide a bank, depositor or other holder of information with release from liability which might result from disclosure of the information required by the Division.

[Real Estate Adv. Comm'n, § VII subsec. 15, eff. 10-31-75] — (NAC A by Real Estate Comm'n by R031-04, 11-30-2004)

NAC 645.650 Periods for maintenance of certain records by broker and for provision of certain paperwork to broker. (NRS 645.050, 645.190)

1. A broker shall keep complete real estate transaction and property management records for at least 5 years after the date of the closing or the last activity involving the property, including, without limitation, offers that were not accepted and transactions that were not completed, unless otherwise directed by the Division.

2. A salesperson or broker-salesperson must provide any paperwork to the broker with whom he or she is associated within 5 calendar days after that paperwork is executed by all the parties.

[Real Estate Adv. Comm'n, § VII subsecs. 7 & 10 par. c, eff. 10-31-75] — (NAC A by Real Estate Comm'n, 8-21-81; A by Real Estate Div., 3-1-96; A by Real Estate Comm'n by R186-99, 1-21-2000; R031-04, 11-30-2004)

NAC 645.655 Records of transactions; trust accounts. (NRS 645.050, 645.190, 645.195, 645.310, 645.633)

1. Each real estate transaction of a brokerage must be numbered consecutively or indexed to permit audit by a representative of the Division.

2. A complete record of each real estate transaction, together with records required to be maintained pursuant to NRS 645.310, must be:

(a) Kept in this State; and

(b) Open to inspection and audit by the Division upon its request during its usual business hours, as well as other hours during which the licensee regularly conducts his or her business.

3. If any records the Division requests to inspect or audit pursuant to subsection 2 are stored electronically, access to a computer or other equipment used to store the information must be made available to the Division for use in its inspection or audit.

4. The real estate broker shall give written notice to the Division of the exact location of the records of the real estate broker and shall not remove them until he or she has delivered a notice which informs the Division of the new location.

5. A licensee shall not maintain a custodial or trust account from which money may be withdrawn without the signature of a licensee. A signature applied by use of a rubber stamp does not constitute the signature of a licensee for the purposes of this subsection.

6. A real estate salesperson may not be the only required signatory on a custodial or trust fund account. A real estate salesperson may be a cosigner of an account with his or her real estate broker.

7. A real estate broker who files for relief under the bankruptcy laws of the United States shall immediately terminate each trust account established pursuant to NRS 645.310 and deposit all money from each trust account into escrow with executed instructions to the escrow agent or officer to disburse the money pursuant to the agreement under which it was originally deposited.

8. A real estate broker who is engaged in property management for one or more clients shall maintain two separate property management trust accounts distinct from any trust account that the real estate broker may have for other real estate transactions. One trust account must be used solely for activities relating to rental operations, and the other trust account must be used solely for security deposits. A real estate broker shall maintain a ledger account for each unit of property he or she manages regardless of whether the client owns more than one unit under the real estate broker's management. All rents and deposits for each unit must be deposited into and credited to each property's management trust account, and all authorized repairs and expenses must be paid out of the corresponding ledger account. For the purposes of this subsection, "unit" means one single-family dwelling unit.

9. Property management and real estate transaction trust accounts must be reconciled monthly by the real estate broker or the designee of the real estate broker within 30 days after receipt of the bank statement. A real estate broker who permits any trust account, including any ledger account, to fall into deficit and remain in deficit for more than 45 consecutive days in 1 year is subject to discipline pursuant to paragraph (h) of subsection 1 of NRS 645.633 or other applicable charges, or both.

[Real Estate Adv. Comm'n, § VII subsec. 10 pars. a, b, d & e, eff. 10-31-75] — (NAC A by Real Estate Comm'n, 6-3-86; A by Real Estate Div., 3-1-96; A by Real Estate Comm'n by R111-01, 12-17-2001; R031-04, 11-30-2004, eff. 7-1-2005)

NAC 645.657 Payment of deposits. (NRS 645.050, 645.190, 645.310) A licensee who receives a deposit on any transaction in which he or she is engaged on behalf of a broker or owner-developer shall pay over the deposit to that broker or owner-developer, or to the escrow business or company designated in the contract, within 1 business day after receiving a fully executed contract.

(Added to NAC by Real Estate Comm'n, eff. 8-21-81; A 12-16-82; R031-04, 11-30-2004; R123-06, 6-1-2006)

NAC 645.660 Disclosure of certain interests required before deposit of money. (NRS 645.050, 645.190) A licensee shall not deposit money received by the licensee in any escrow business or company in which the licensee or anyone associated with him or her in the real estate or time-share business has an interest without disclosing this association to all parties to the transaction.

NAC 645.665 Absence of broker from business for prolonged period. (NRS 645.050, 645.190) A broker shall not be absent from his or her business for 30 days or more if the broker is the only broker in his or her office unless the broker inactivates his or her license or otherwise notifies the Division in advance. Failure to observe this requirement is a ground for suspension. If a broker will be absent from his or her business for 30 days or more, the broker must designate an office manager in accordance with NAC 645.178 or make other arrangements approved by the Division in advance.

[Real Estate Adv. Comm'n, § VII subsec. 12, eff. 10-31-75] — (NAC A by Real Estate Comm'n, 4-27-84; R031-04, 11-30-2004)

NAC 645.670 Conduct of inspections by Division. (NRS 645.050, 645.190, 645.195, 645.310)

1. The Division may use a form of its design to conduct any inspection and require the broker or office manager in charge of the office being inspected to sign such a form.
2. Such an inspection must include, but need not be limited to:
(a) The address of the real estate office or time-share office.
(b) The sign identifying the office.
(c) The procedure used to deposit money.
(d) The trust records.
(e) The indexing or numbering system used in filing records.
(f) Advertising.
(g) The availability of current statutes and regulations at the place of business.
(h) Any affiliation with a developer as defined in chapter 119 or 119A of NRS.
(i) Any documentation required by chapter 119 or 119A of NRS or the federal Land Sales Act.

[Real Estate Adv. Comm'n, § VII subsec. 17, eff. 10-31-75] — (NAC A by Real Estate Comm'n, 8-21-81; 4-27-84)

NAC 645.675 Agreements for advance fees. (NRS 645.050, 645.190, 645.324)

1. Each agreement for an advance fee used in Nevada must:
(a) Be in writing;
(b) Contain a definite and complete description of the services to be rendered;
(c) Specify the total amount of the fee involved and clearly state when the fee is due;
(d) Not imply or purport to guarantee that the real property involved will be purchased, sold, rented, leased or exchanged as a result of the services rendered;
(e) Specify the date of full performance of the services contracted for;
(f) Not imply or purport to represent to purchasers and prospective purchasers of the advertising or promotional services offered that a buyer for the property is immediately or soon available; and
(g) Provide that a full refund will be made to the customer if the services for which the advance fee is being received are not substantially or materially provided to the customer.
2. Any oral representation or promise made to a purchaser or a prospective purchaser of the advertising and promotional services offered pursuant to an agreement for an advance fee to induce the purchaser or prospective purchaser of the services to sign the agreement is incorporated into the agreement. The agreement must not relieve or exempt the vendor of the services from any oral representation or promise incorporated into the agreement.

[Real Estate Adv. Comm'n, § IX subsecs. 1 & 2, eff. 10-31-75] — (NAC A by Real Estate Comm'n by R031-04, 11-30-2004)

NAC 645.678 Duties of broker operating agency which lists rentals for advance fee. (NRS 645.050, 645.190) A broker operating an agency which lists rentals for an advance fee shall:

1. Not publish, advertise or distribute information concerning a rental without first receiving approval from the owner of the rental.
2. Provide for full refunds to customers if the services for which payment was received was substantially or materially not received by the customer.
3. Inform each customer in writing of the term for which the rental service is to be provided.
4. Make no additional charge for services rendered during the period for which the services were initially purchased.

NAC 645.680 Form for complaints; investigations of licensees; action by Administrator on report of investigation. (NRS 645.050, 645.190)

1. The Division shall prepare and require a standard form or affidavit for use in making a citizen's complaint. This form may require any information the Division considers pertinent.

2. If a complaint is made or if the Division requests an investigation of a licensee, the Administrator shall appoint a member of the staff of the Division to investigate any action of a licensee which appears to violate a provision of chapter 113, 116, 119, 119A, 119B, 645, 645C or 645D of NRS or the regulations adopted pursuant thereto. An investigation that is initiated by a complaint need not be limited to the matter in the complaint.

3. A licensee shall disclose all facts and documents pertinent to an investigation to members of the Division's staff conducting the investigation.

4. A person appointed to investigate a matter pursuant to this section shall submit a written report to the Administrator which describes the results of the investigation.

5. The Administrator shall review a report submitted pursuant to subsection 4 and based upon the review shall:

(a) Dismiss the matter that is the subject of the investigation;

(b) Impose an administrative fine pursuant to NAC 645.695;

(c) Negotiate a resolution of the matter that is the subject of the investigation, which may include, without limitation, administrative sanctions pursuant to NAC 645.695;

(d) Create an advisory committee to review the matter that is the subject of the investigation pursuant to NAC 645.490, if the licensee who is the subject of the investigation agrees to participate in an informal conference with an advisory committee; or

(e) Schedule a hearing that must be conducted pursuant to NAC 645.810.

[Real Estate Adv. Comm'n, § VIII, eff. 10-31-75] — (NAC A by Real Estate Comm'n, 8-21-81; 4-27-84; R146-99, 1-21-2000; R031-04, 11-30-2004)

NAC 645.690 Correction of certain deficiencies upon notice and request by Division. (NRS 645.050, 645.190)

1. The Division may grant a licensee up to 10 days to correct any deficiency involving advertising, business location, office operation or a broker's sign. A notice of the deficiency and a request to correct the deficiency will be mailed to the licensee. Failure to comply with the request is a ground for the suspension or revocation of the license. The notice must state the deficiencies or violations, the recommended action, and the date by which the deficiencies must be corrected.

2. The Division may grant an extension for a definite time to correct the deficiency whenever the correction may, practicably, require additional time.

[Real Estate Adv. Comm'n, § VII subsec. 14, eff. 10-31-75] — (NAC A by Real Estate Comm'n, 8-21-81; R031-04, 11-30-2004)

NAC 645.695 Administrative fines and other sanctions. (NRS 645.050, 645.190, 645.575, 645.630, 645.633, 645.635, 645.660)

1. The Administrator may require a licensee to pay an administrative fine in the amount set forth in this subsection for each violation of the following provisions:

	For each Offense
NRS 645.252..	$500
Subsection 4, 5 or 6 of NRS 645.310...................	1,000
NRS 645.530..	100 per license
NRS 645.550..	500
NRS 645.560..	500
Subsection 1 of NRS 645.570............................	250
Subsection 2 of NRS 645.570............................	500
Subsection 1 of NRS 645.580............................	250
Paragraph (a), (b), (c), (e), (f), (i), (j), (k) or (l) of subsection 1 of NRS 645.630...........................	500
Paragraph (g) of subsection 1 of NRS 645.630.......	1,000
Paragraph (c), (e), (g), (h), (j), (k) or (l) of subsection 1 of NRS 645.633...........................	500
Paragraph (a) or (f) of subsection 1 of NRS 645.633....	250
Paragraph (i) of subsection 1 of NRS 645.633........	1,000
Subsection 1, 2, 3, 4, 5 or 6 of NRS 645.635.........	500

98

	For each Offense
Subsection 7 or 8 of NRS 645.635...................................	1,000
Subsection 3 of NRS 645.660.......................................	1,000
NAC 645.4442..	100
NAC 645.448..	100
NAC 645.610..	500
NAC 645.620..	500
NAC 645.627..	500
NAC 645.632..	500
NAC 645.637..	500
NAC 645.640..	500
NAC 645.645..	500
NAC 645.650..	1,000
NAC 645.655..	1,000
NAC 645.855..	2,000

2. In addition to or in lieu of imposing an administrative fine pursuant to subsection 1, the Administrator may:

(a) Recommend to the Commission that the license of the licensee and any permit of the licensee be suspended or revoked;

(b) Require a licensee to complete continuing education; or

(c) Take any combination of the actions set forth in paragraphs (a) and (b).

(Added to NAC by Real Estate Comm'n., eff. 5-14-96; A by R059-98, 7-1-98; R146-99 & R186-99, 1-21-2000; R092-00, 8-29-2000; R111-01, 12-17-2001; R031-04, 11-30-2004; R123-06, 6-1-2006; R093-10, 5-30-2012)

REVISER'S NOTE.

The regulation of the Real Estate Commission filed with the Secretary of State on May 30, 2012 (LCB File No. R093-10), which amended this section, contains the following provisions not included in NAC:

"1. The amendatory provisions of section 1 of this regulation [NAC 645.4442] apply only to first-time licensees whose licenses expire on or after July 1, 2012.

2. The amendatory provisions of section 3 of this regulation [NAC 645.448] apply only to licensees whose licenses expire on or after July 1, 2013.

3. The amendatory provisions of section 4 of this regulation [NAC 645.695] apply only to:

(a) A first-time licensee whose license expires on or after July 1, 2012.

(b) A licensee whose license expires on or after July 1, 2013."

REGULATION OF OWNER-DEVELOPERS

NAC 645.700 Registration required. (NRS 645.190) An owner-developer must obtain a registration for each recorded subdivision which he or she intends to sell.

[Real Estate Adv. Comm'n, § XVI subsec. 3 par. g, eff. 10-31-75]

NAC 645.710 Application for registration. (NRS 645.190, 645.285, 645.287)

1. An application for an original registration as an owner-developer must be completed by the owner-developer, unless the applicant is a partnership or corporation, and in that case the application must be completed by a partner or the principal officer. The application must be filed with an office of the Division and must be accompanied by fingerprint cards. The applicant's fingerprints must be taken by a regular law enforcement agency or other authorized entity acceptable to the Division. If a search of criminal records has been requested by the Division, an application for registration is not complete until the Division has received the appropriate information.

2. The applicant must provide in the application:

(a) A statement of the applicant's arrests and convictions, if any, and any proceedings against him or her brought by governmental agencies;

(b) A brief history of his or her business;

(c) The legal description of the property to be covered by the registration, as shown on a recorded map, which shows all the certificates of approval required by law;

(d) The location of each of his or her sales offices;

(e) A statement which shows his or her financial condition; and

(f) A history of his or her bankruptcies, if any.

3. The application must be accompanied by:

(a) The applicant's sworn verification of the truthfulness of the matters stated in the application and its attachments; and

(b) A statement that the applicant understands the responsibilities of an owner-developer pursuant to this chapter and chapter 645 of NRS and that he or she could be subject to disciplinary action pursuant to this chapter and chapter 645 of NRS.

4. The fee for the original registration must accompany the application and is not refundable after the owner-developer has been registered.

5. If the applicant is a partnership or corporation, it must file with the Division a certified or verified copy of the partnership agreement or articles of incorporation.

6. The application must be submitted with a copy of:

(a) The applicant's notice of exemption under subsection 5 of NRS 119.120;

(b) The applicant's business license, if one is required by the local government;

(c) If the applicant is a partnership or corporation, the provisions authorizing it to employ salespersons to sell the lots and residences; and

(d) The applicant's certificate of fictitious name, if such a certificate has been filed.

7. An application by a registered owner-developer to enlarge the geographical area covered by his or her registration must be made on a form prepared by the Division. The applicant must provide the Division with the same information as is required for an original application, and the application must be accompanied by the appropriate fee.

[Real Estate Adv. Comm'n, § XVI subsec. 1, eff. 10-31-75; A 2-20-76] — (NAC A by Real Estate Comm'n, 8-21-81; 12-16-82; 6-3-86; R031-04, 11-30-2004)

NAC 645.730 Status of registration; required notices. (NRS 645.190)

1. The Division's registration of a person as an owner-developer does not constitute a licensure. Such a registrant may not use the term "licensed" either in his or her advertising or oral presentations to prospective purchasers, but this section does not preclude him or her from using the term "licensed contractor."

2. An owner-developer shall keep at each of his or her sales offices a copy of the letter of registration sent to the owner-developer by the Division.

3. Every owner-developer shall within 10 days give written notice to the Division of any change of name, address, or status affecting the owner-developer, or any licensed real estate broker-salesperson or salesperson in his or her employ. The notice must be prepared on a form provided by the Division and be given within 10 days after the change occurs. The proper fee must accompany the notice. The owner-developer shall also notify the Division of the location of the sales office which is to be used by the owner-developer's licensed broker-salesperson or salesperson.

4. The registration of an owner-developer will be annulled at such time as the owner-developer fails to employ licensed real estate broker-salespersons or salespersons.

5. Inactive status is not available for owner-developers.

[Real Estate Adv. Comm'n, § XVI subsec. 3 pars. a-f, eff. 10-31-75] — (NAC A by Real Estate Comm'n, 8-21-81; 12-16-82)

NAC 645.740 Expiration of registration. (NRS 645.190)

1. A registration for an owner-developer is effective for 1 year after the date of issuance. An owner-developer may renew his or her registration by paying the required fee and submitting the appropriate form to the Division. There is no limit on the number of annual renewals.

2. If an owner-developer fails to renew his or her registration, the licenses of all salespersons in his or her employ who have renewed will immediately be placed on inactive status.

3. If the registration of an owner-developer is cancelled, suspended, or revoked, the owner-developer shall immediately terminate all activities pursuant to his or her registration and shall deliver to the Division all of the licenses of his or her employees.

[Real Estate Adv. Comm'n, § XVI subsec. 3 pars. j-1, eff. 10-31-75] — (NAC A by Real Estate Comm'n, 8-21-81)

NAC 645.750 Limitations on licensees. (NRS 645.050, 645.190, 645.330)

1. A licensee associated with an owner-developer may only sell, lease, rent, or offer and negotiate to sell, lease or rent the registered development for an owner-developer, and may not engage in any other activity listed in NRS 645.030.

2. A licensee employed by an owner-developer may not be associated with a real estate broker at the same time.

3. Real estate brokers working for owner-developers must change their status to real estate broker-salespersons.

4. An employee of an owner-developer is prohibited from erecting, displaying or maintaining any sign or billboard or advertising under his or her own name unless the advertisement is located at the office of his or her employer. The name of the employee may not dominate the owner-developer's sign in any way.

5. Except as otherwise provided in subsection 6, the time during which a licensee is employed by an owner-developer does not satisfy the requirement of prior experience set forth in subsection 4 of NRS 645.330.

6. The Commission may permit an applicant to satisfy the requirement of prior experience set forth in subsection 4 of NRS 645.330 if the applicant has been employed by an owner-developer. The Commission will consider the prior experience of an applicant with an owner-developer at its next regularly scheduled meeting if the applicant:

(a) Files a petition with the Commission; and

(b) At the meeting of the Commission, demonstrates that the quality, quantity and variety of experience that the applicant received during his or her employment with an owner-developer was substantially equivalent to the experience of a person who has been actively engaged as a full-time licensed real estate broker-salesperson or salesperson in private practice.

[Real Estate Adv. Comm'n, § XVI subsecs. h, i, m & t, eff. 10-31-75; § XVI subsec. t, eff. 12-20-75] — (NAC A by Real Estate Comm'n, 8-21-81; A by Real Estate Div., 11-30-87; 3-31-94; A by Real Estate Comm'n by R111-01, 12-17-2001)

NAC 645.760 Records of sales; limitation on sales. (NRS 645.190, 645.195)

1. All records pertaining to the sale of any single-family residence in the subdivision of a registered owner-developer must be maintained at his or her principal place of business and be available for inspection by the Division. Upon request, the owner-developer shall send copies of those records to the appropriate office of the Division.

2. The owner-developer may not sell any lot in his or her subdivision pursuant to this chapter unless:

(a) The lot contains a single-family residence not previously sold; or

(b) A single-family residence is to be constructed upon the lot, and the residence is purchased under the same agreement as the sale of the land.

[Real Estate Adv. Comm'n, § XVI subsecs. n, q & s, eff. 10-31-75; § XVI subsecs. r & s, eff. 12-20-75] — (NAC A by Real Estate Comm'n, 8-21-81; 12-16-82)

NAC 645.770 Disciplinary action; investigation of financial status. (NRS 645.190, 645.610, 645.630, 645.633)

1. The Commission may fine an owner-developer, revoke or suspend the registration of an owner-developer, or impose a fine and revoke or suspend the registration of an owner-developer for any violation of chapter 113, 116, 119, 119A, 645, 645C or 645D of NRS or the regulations adopted pursuant thereto.

2. If the Administrator has reason to believe that there has been a substantial change in the financial status of the owner-developer since his or her original application, the Administrator shall investigate the financial status of the owner-developer. If the Administrator determines that the owner-developer is financially incompetent to maintain his or her business, the Administrator shall bring a complaint for revocation of the registration of the owner-developer.

[Real Estate Adv. Comm'n, § XVI subsec. o, eff. 10-31-75] — (NAC A by Real Estate Comm'n, 8-21-81; 4-27-84; R031-04, 11-30-2004)

REGULATION OF PROPERTY MANAGERS

NAC 645.799 Applicability of certain provisions regarding management of common-interest communities. (NRS 645.050, 645.190) A person who holds a permit and engages in the management of a common-interest community is subject to the provisions of chapter 116 of NRS and chapters 116 and 116A of NAC relating to managers of common-interest communities.

(Added to NAC by Real Estate Comm'n by R136-99, eff. 4-3-2000)

NAC 645.800 Permit to engage in property management: General requirements; fees; effective date. (NRS 645.190, 645.6052)

1. A person who wishes to obtain a permit to engage in property management must submit to the Division:

(a) A completed application on a form prescribed by the Division;

(b) A fee of $40; and

(c) A certificate of completion, in a form that is satisfactory to the Division, that indicates the person's successful completion of the 24 classroom hours of instruction in property management required by paragraph (a) of subsection 2 of NRS 645.6052.

2. The 24 classroom hours of instruction in property management required pursuant to paragraph (a) of subsection 2 of NRS 645.6052 must include, without limitation:

(a) Four hours of instruction relating to:

(1) Contracts for management services;

(2) Leases of real property;

(3) Applications to rent real property;

(4) The Fair Credit Reporting Act, 15 U.S.C. §§ 1681 et seq.; and

(5) The Fair Debt Collection Practices Act, 15 U.S.C. §§ 1692 to 1692o, inclusive;

(b) Two hours of instruction relating to the maintenance of records of money deposited in trust accounts and the requirements for reporting to the Division set forth in chapter 645 of NRS;

(c) One hour of instruction relating to the use of a computerized system for bookkeeping;

(d) Two hours of instruction relating to the laws of this State governing property management;

(e) Two hours of instruction relating to the disclosure of required information in real estate transactions, including, without limitation:

(1) Disclosures required pursuant to NRS 645.252; and

(2) Disclosures related to environmental issues as governed by state and federal law;

(f) Five hours of instruction relating to:

(1) The Americans with Disabilities Act of 1990, 42 U.S.C. §§ 12101 et seq.;

(2) The Residential Landlord and Tenant Act as set forth in chapter 118A of NRS;

(3) The Nevada Fair Housing Law as set forth in chapter 118 of NRS; and

(4) State and federal law governing unlawful discrimination based on sex, including, without limitation, sexual harassment;

(g) Three hours of instruction relating to property management for a common-interest community as set forth in chapter 116 of NRS;

(h) One hour of instruction relating to the duties and responsibilities of a real estate broker, including the supervision of employees and real estate salespersons and real estate broker-salespersons associated with the real estate broker;

(i) Two hours of instruction relating to risk management, including, without limitation:

(1) The maintenance of real property;

(2) The health and safety of a tenant;

(3) Fire insurance;

(4) Rental insurance; and

(5) Disability insurance; and

(j) Two hours relating to the management of commercial property.

3. The Division may accept a course in property management from a nationally recognized or accredited organization to fulfill the requirements set forth in paragraphs (a), (b), (c), (h), (i) and (j) of subsection 2, if the successful completion of that course would qualify the applicant to engage in property management pursuant to the requirements of that organization.

4. The applicant must complete the hours of instruction set forth in paragraphs (d), (e), (f) and (g) of subsection 2 at an accredited educational institution in this State.

5. A permit to engage in property management initially issued by the Division is effective on the date the application for the permit is submitted to the Division or the date on which the fee for the permit is paid, whichever occurs later.

6. As used in this section and paragraph (a) of subsection 2 of NRS 645.6052, the Commission will interpret the term "successfully completed" or "successful completion" to include, without limitation, passing an examination which is prepared and administered by an organization designated by the Division, with a score of at least 75 percent that:

(a) Includes the subject matter presented in the hours of instruction required pursuant to subsection 2; and

(b) Consists of at least 50 multiple-choice questions.

The fee for the examination is $75.

NAC 645.8005 Permit to engage in property management: Additional requirements for person designated to apply on behalf of certain organizations. (NRS 645.190, 645.6052) In addition to the requirements set forth in NRS 645.6052 and the regulations adopted pursuant thereto, to obtain a permit pursuant to NRS 645.6052, a person who is designated to engage in property management on behalf of a partnership, corporation, limited-liability company or sole proprietor pursuant to NRS 645.6054 must be a broker or a broker-salesperson with 2 years of full-time active experience within the 4 years immediately preceding the date the person applies for a permit to engage in property management on behalf of a partnership, corporation, limited-liability company or sole proprietor pursuant to NRS 645.6054.

(Added to NAC by Real Estate Comm'n by R092-00, eff. 8-29-2000)

NAC 645.802 Permit to engage in property management: Requirements and fee for renewal; effective date of renewal; date of expiration. (NRS 645.190, 645.6052)

1. The Division may renew a permit to engage in property management if the holder of the permit submits to the Division:

(a) A request for the renewal of the permit with the holder's application to renew his or her license as a real estate broker, real estate broker-salesperson or real estate salesperson;

(b) A renewal fee of $40; and

(c) Documentation of his or her successful completion of the requirements for continuing education required by paragraph (a) of subsection 4 of NRS 645.6052.

2. The hours of continuing education used to fulfill the requirements set forth in paragraph (c) of subsection 1 must include:

(a) Instruction relating to any amendments to the laws of this State governing property management; and

(b) If the holder of the permit is a manager of a common-interest community pursuant to chapters 116 and 116A of NAC, 3 hours of instruction relating to the laws of this State that are applicable to the responsibilities and duties involved in the management of a common-interest community.

3. The renewal of a permit is effective on the date on which the application for renewal of a license is submitted to the Division or on the date on which the renewal fees for the license and the permit are paid, whichever occurs later.

4. A permit expires on the same date as the holder's license expires.

NAC 645.804 Approval of courses for educational requirements. (NRS 645.190, 645.6052)

1. For an applicant to receive credit for a course of instruction in property management that is designed to fulfill the educational requirements for the issuance of a permit which are described in paragraph (a) of subsection 2 of NRS 645.6052, the course must be approved by the Commission.

2. An educational institution that wishes to obtain approval to offer courses that meet the educational requirements for the issuance or renewal of a permit to engage in property management must apply to the Division pursuant to the applicable procedures set forth in NAC 645.400 to 645.467, inclusive.

(Added to NAC by Real Estate Comm'n by R059-98, eff. 7-1-98; A by R031-04, 11-30-2004)

NAC 645.805 Termination of association of person designated to apply on behalf of certain organizations. (NRS 645.050, 645.190, 645.6054)

1. Except as otherwise provided in subsection 4, if a person to whom a permit is issued pursuant to NRS 645.6054 ceases to be connected or associated with the partnership, corporation, limited-liability company or sole proprietor for whom the person is acting as a property manager, the partnership, corporation, limited-liability company or sole proprietor shall not engage in the business of property management unless, not later than 30 days after that person ceases to be connected or associated with the partnership, corporation, limited-liability company or sole proprietor, the partnership, corporation, limited-liability company or sole proprietor designates another person to hold the permit on behalf of the partnership, corporation, limited-liability company or sole proprietor pursuant to the requirements set forth in subsection 3 of NRS 645.6054.

2. The real estate broker of a partnership, corporation, limited-liability company or sole proprietorship who is required pursuant to NRS 645.310 to maintain a trust account for money received for property management shall:

(a) Request a statement from the bank in which the trust account is being held not later than 5 days after the date that the designated property manager ceases to be connected or associated with the partnership, corporation, limited-liability company or sole proprietor; and

(b) Submit to the Division, on a form provided by the Division, a reconciliation of the trust account for the 30 days immediately preceding the date that the designated property manager ceases to be connected or associated with the partnership, corporation, limited-liability company or sole proprietor.

3. A reconciliation required pursuant to paragraph (b) of subsection 2 must be submitted to the Division not later than 15 days after the designated property manager ceases to be connected or associated with the partnership, corporation, limited-liability company or sole proprietor or by the end of the month in which the designated property manager ceases to be connected or associated with the partnership, corporation, limited-liability company or sole proprietor, whichever occurs later.

4. A partnership, corporation, limited-liability company or sole proprietor may petition, in writing, the Administrator for an extension of time in which to designate another property manager after the designated property manager ceases to be connected or associated with the partnership, corporation, limited-liability company or sole proprietor. The Administrator may grant such an extension, in writing, if he or she finds the partnership, corporation, limited-liability company or sole proprietor has a severe hardship resulting from circumstances beyond the control of the partnership, corporation, limited-liability company or sole proprietor which has prevented the partnership, corporation, limited-liability company or sole proprietor from meeting the requirements of subsection 1.

(Added to NAC by Real Estate Comm'n by R059-98, eff. 7-1-98)

NAC 645.806 Trust accounts: Annual accounting required; maintenance of records. (NRS 645.050, 645.190, 645.310)

1. On or before the date of expiration of his or her license as a real estate broker, a broker who engages in property management or who associates with a property manager who engages in property management shall provide to the Division, on a form provided by the Division, an annual accounting as required by subsection 5 of NRS 645.310 which shows an annual reconciliation of each trust account related to property management that he or she maintains.

2. The reconciliation required pursuant to subsection 1 must include the 30 days immediately preceding the expiration date of his or her license as a real estate broker.

3. A broker who engages in property management or who associates with a property manager who engages in property management shall maintain complete accounting records of each trust account related to property management that he or she maintains for at least 5 years after the last activity by the broker which involved the trust account. If the records are maintained by computer, the broker shall maintain an additional copy of the records on computer disc for at least 5 years after the last activity by the broker which involved the trust account.

(Added to NAC by Real Estate Comm'n by R059-98, eff. 7-1-98; A by R092-00, 8-29-2000)

NAC 645.807 Trust accounts: Execution of checks by certain broker-salespersons. (NRS 645.050, 645.190) A real estate broker-salesperson who holds a permit to engage in property management may sign checks on a trust account without the signature of the real estate broker who employs him or her if the broker-salesperson has obtained the written permission of the broker authorizing him or her to do so. A signature applied by use of a rubber stamp does not constitute the signature of a real estate broker-salesperson for the purposes of this section.

(Added to NAC by Real Estate Comm'n by R059-98, eff. 7-1-98; A by R031-04, 11-30-2004)

PROCEEDINGS BEFORE COMMISSION

NAC 645.810 Procedure at hearing; receipt of evidence; date of decision. (NRS 645.190)

1. The presiding officer of a hearing shall:

(a) Ascertain whether all persons commanded to appear under subpoena are present and whether all documents, books, records and other evidence under subpoena are present in the hearing room.

(b) Administer the oath to the reporter as follows:

Do you solemnly swear or affirm that you will report this hearing to the best of your stenographic ability?

(c) Administer the oath to all persons whose testimony will be taken:

Do you and each of you solemnly swear or affirm to tell the truth and nothing but the truth in these proceedings?

(d) Ascertain whether either party wishes to have a witness excluded from the hearing except during the testimony of the witness. A witness may be excluded upon the motion of the Commission or upon the motion of either party. If a witness is excluded, the witness will be instructed not to discuss the case during the pendency of the proceeding. The respondent will be allowed to remain present at the hearing. The Division may designate a person who is a member of the staff of the Division and who may also be a witness to act as its representative. Such a representative will be allowed to remain present at the hearing.

(e) Ascertain whether a copy of the complaint or decision to deny has been filed and whether an answer has been filed as part of the record in the proceedings.

(f) Hear any preliminary motions, stipulations or orders upon which the parties agree and address any administrative details.

(g) Have the discretion to limit the opening and closing statements of the parties.

(h) Request the Division to proceed with the presentation of its case.

2. The Division may not submit any evidence to the Commission before the hearing except for the complaint and answer.

3. The respondent may cross-examine witnesses in the order that the Division presents them.

4. Witnesses or counsel may be questioned by the members of the Commission at any time during the proceeding.

5. Evidence which is to be introduced:

(a) Must first be marked for identification; and

(b) May be received by the Commission at any point during the proceeding.

6. When the Division has completed its presentation, the presiding officer shall request the respondent to proceed with the introduction of evidence and calling of witnesses on his or her behalf.

7. The Division may cross-examine witnesses in the order that the respondent presents them.

8. When the respondent has completed his or her presentation, the Division may call any rebuttal witnesses.

9. When all testimony for the Division and respondent has been given and all evidence submitted, the presiding officer may request the Division and the respondent to summarize their presentations.

10. The Commission may waive any provision of this section if necessary to expedite or ensure the fairness of the hearing.

11. The date of decision for the purpose of subsection 2 of NRS 645.760 is the date the written decision is signed by a Commissioner or filed with the Commission, whichever occurs later.

12. In the absence of the President of the Commission, any matter which must be acted upon may be submitted to the Vice President or to the Secretary.

13. Upon the presentation of evidence that the respondent received notice of the hearing and has not filed an answer within the time prescribed pursuant to NRS 645.685, the respondent's default may be entered and a decision may be issued based upon the allegations of the complaint.

[Real Estate Adv. Comm'n, § XVII subsecs. 1 & 2 pars. b-q, eff. 10-31-75] — (NAC A by Real Estate Comm'n, 8-21-81; 4-27-84; 6-3-86; A by Real Estate Div., 11-30-87; A by Real Estate Comm'n by R111-01, 12-17-2001; R031-04, 11-30-2004; R123-06, 6-1-2006)

NAC 645.820 Procedures for rehearing. (NRS 645.190) The following procedures are used for a rehearing in a case where a ruling or decision of the Commission is against the licensee:

1. The licensee may within 10 days after his or her receipt of the decision petition the Commission for a rehearing.

2. The petition does not stay any decision of the Commission unless the Commission so orders.

3. The petition must state with particularity the point of law or fact which in the opinion of the licensee the Commission has overlooked or misconstrued and must contain every argument in support of the application that the licensee desires to present.

4. Oral argument in support of the petition is not permitted.

5. The Division may file and serve an answer to a petition for a rehearing within 10 days after it has received service of the petition.

6. If a petition for rehearing is filed and the Commission is not scheduled to meet before the effective date of the penalty, the Division may stay enforcement of the decision appealed from. When determining whether a stay is to be granted, the Division shall determine whether the petition was timely filed and whether it alleges a cause or ground which may entitle the licensee to a rehearing.

7. A rehearing may be granted by the Commission for any of the following causes or grounds:

(a) Irregularity in the proceedings in the original hearing;

(b) Accident or surprise which ordinary prudence could not have guarded against;

(c) Newly discovered evidence of a material nature which the applicant could not with reasonable diligence have discovered and produced at the original hearing; or

(d) Error in law occurring at the hearing and objected to by the applicant during the earlier hearing.

8. A petition for a rehearing may not exceed 10 pages of standard printing.

9. The filing of a petition for rehearing, or the decision therefrom, does not stop the running of the 30-day period of appeal to the district court from the date of the decision of the Commission for the purpose of subsection 2 of NRS 645.760.

[Real Estate Adv. Comm'n, § XVII subsec. 3, eff. 10-31-75] — (NAC A by Real Estate Comm'n, 8-21-81; 4-27-84)

NAC 645.830 Procedures for obtaining and granting continuances. (NRS 645.190) The procedures for obtaining and granting continuances of Commission hearings are as follows:

1. The time of the hearing may be continued by the Commission upon the written petition of the licensee or upon the written petition of the Division for good cause shown, or by stipulation of the parties to the hearing.

2. A continuance will not be granted unless it is made in good faith and not merely for delay.

3. A request for a continuance made before the hearing must be served upon the Commission as set forth in subsection 4 of NRS 645.050. If the Secretary of the Commission is not available to review and rule upon the continuance before the hearing, the continuance must be reviewed and ruled upon by the:

(a) President of the Commission; or

(b) If the President is unavailable, the Vice President of the Commission.

[Real Estate Adv. Comm'n, § XVII subsec. 4, eff. 10-31-75] — (NAC A by Real Estate Comm'n, 4-27-84; R111-01, 12-17-2001; R123-06, 6-1-2006)

NAC 645.835 Amendment or withdrawal of complaint. (NRS 645.190)

1. A complaint may be amended at any time.

2. The Commission will grant a continuance if the amendment materially alters the complaint or a respondent demonstrates an inability to prepare for the case in a timely manner.

3. A complaint may be withdrawn at any time before the hearing begins.

(Added to NAC by Real Estate Comm'n by R031-04, eff. 11-30-2004)

NAC 645.840 Motions. (NRS 645.190)

1. All motions, unless made during a hearing, must be in writing.

2. A written motion must be served on the opposing party and the Commission at least 10 working days before the time set for the hearing on the motion.

3. An opposing party may file a written response to a motion within 7 working days after the receipt of the motion by serving the written response on all parties and the Commission, except that a written response may be filed less than 3 working days before the time set for the hearing on the motion only with the permission of the Commission upon good cause shown.

4. The Commission may require oral argument or the submission of additional information or evidence to decide the motion.

(Added to NAC by Real Estate Comm'n by R031-04, eff. 11-30-2004)

NAC 645.845 Rules of evidence; informality of proceedings. (NRS 645.190)

1. In conducting any investigation, inquiry or hearing, the Commission, its officers and the employees of the Division are not bound by the technical rules of evidence, and any informality in a proceeding or in the manner of taking testimony does not invalidate any order, decision, rule or regulation made, approved or confirmed by the Commission. The rules of evidence of courts of this State will be followed generally but may be relaxed at the discretion of the Commission if deviation from the technical rules of evidence will aid in determining the facts.

2. Any evidence offered at a hearing must be material and relevant to the issues of the hearing.

3. The Commission may exclude inadmissible, incompetent, repetitious or irrelevant evidence or order that presentation of that evidence be discontinued.

4. A party who objects to the introduction of evidence shall briefly state the grounds of the objection at the time the evidence is offered. The party who offers the evidence may present a rebuttal argument to the objection.

5. If an objection is made to the admissibility of evidence, the Commission may:

(a) Note the objection and admit the evidence;

(b) Sustain the objection and refuse to admit the evidence; or

(c) Receive the evidence subject to a subsequent ruling by the Commission.

NAC 645.850 Submission or exclusion of documentary evidence of respondent. (NRS 645.190)

1. Not less than 5 working days before a hearing before the Commission, the respondent must provide to the Division a copy of all documents that are reasonably available to the respondent which the respondent reasonably anticipates will be used in support of his or her position. The respondent shall promptly supplement and update any such documents.

2. The respondent shall provide, at the time of the hearing, 10 copies of each document he or she wishes to have admitted into evidence at the hearing.

3. If the respondent fails to provide any document required to be provided by the provisions of this section, the Commission may exclude the document.

(Added to NAC by Real Estate Comm'n by R031-04, eff. 11-30-2004)

NAC 645.855 Attendance of certain brokers required at disciplinary hearing. (NRS 645.190) If a person licensed as a real estate salesperson or real estate broker-salesperson is accused of violating any provision of this chapter or chapter 645 of NRS, the broker of record with whom the person licensed as a real estate salesperson or real estate broker-salesperson was associated at the time of the alleged violation and the broker with whom the person licensed as a real estate salesperson or real estate broker-salesperson is currently associated shall attend any disciplinary hearing before the Commission concerning that licensee.

(Added to NAC by Real Estate Comm'n by R031-04, eff. 11-30-2004; A by R123-06, 6-1-2006)

NAC 645.860 Failure of party to appear at hearing. (NRS 645.190) If a party fails to appear at a hearing scheduled by the Commission and a continuance has not been requested or granted, upon an offer of proof by the Division that the absent party was given proper notice and upon a determination by the Commission that proper notice was given, the Commission may proceed to consider the case without the participation of the absent party and may dispose of the matter on the basis of the evidence before it. If the respondent fails to appear at the hearing or fails to reply to the notice, the charges specified in the complaint may be considered as true.

(Added to NAC by Real Estate Comm'n by R031-04, eff. 11-30-2004)

NAC 645.865 Voluntary surrender of license, permit, registration or certificate. (NRS 645.190) The Commission may accept the voluntary surrender of a license, permit, registration or certificate in lieu of imposing any other disciplinary action set forth in chapter 645 of NRS.

(Added to NAC by Real Estate Comm'n by R031-04, eff. 11-30-2004)

NAC 645.870 Reporting of disciplinary action or denial of application. (NRS 645.190) The Commission may report any disciplinary action it takes against a licensee or any denial of an application for a license to:

1. Any national repository which records disciplinary actions taken against licensees;

2. Any agency of another state which regulates the practice of real estate; and

3. Any other agency or board of the State of Nevada.

(Added to NAC by Real Estate Comm'n by R031-04, eff. 11-30-2004)

NAC 645.875 Petitions for regulations. (NRS 645.190)

1. Any person may by petition, request the Commission to adopt, file, amend, or repeal any regulation. The petition must clearly identify in writing the change requested of the regulation and must contain all relevant data, views and arguments regarding the change.

2. The Commission will consider the petition at the next regularly scheduled meeting which occurs more than 10 working days after the submission of the petition.

[Real Estate Adv. Comm'n, § II subsec. 3, eff. 12-30-76] — (NAC A by Real Estate Comm'n, 8-21-81) — (Substituted in revision for NAC 645.090)

PERMIT TO ENGAGE IN BUSINESS AS BUSINESS BROKER

NAC 645.901 Definitions. (NRS 645.190, 645.863) As used in NAC 645.901 to 645.919, inclusive, unless the context otherwise requires, the words and terms defined in NAC 645.903 to 645.909, inclusive, have the meanings ascribed to them in those sections.

(Added to NAC by Real Estate Comm'n by R123-06, eff. 6-1-2006)

NAC 645.903 "Applicant" defined. (NRS 645.190, 645.863)   "Applicant" means a licensee who is applying for a permit.
(Added to NAC by Real Estate Comm'n by R123-06, eff. 6-1-2006)

NAC 645.905 "Business broker" defined. (NRS 645.190, 645.863)   "Business broker" has the meaning ascribed to it in NRS 645.0075.
(Added to NAC by Real Estate Comm'n by R123-06, eff. 6-1-2006)

NAC 645.907 "License" defined. (NRS 645.190, 645.863)   "License" means a license as a real estate broker, real estate broker-salesperson or real estate salesperson.
(Added to NAC by Real Estate Comm'n by R123-06, eff. 6-1-2006)

NAC 645.909 "Permit" defined. (NRS 645.190, 645.863)   "Permit" means a permit to engage in business as a business broker.
(Added to NAC by Real Estate Comm'n by R123-06, eff. 6-1-2006)

NAC 645.911 "Engage in business as a business broker" interpreted. (NRS 645.050, 645.190, 645.863)   As used in chapter 645 of NRS, the Commission will interpret the term "engage in business as a business broker":
   1. Except as otherwise provided in subsection 2, to include engaging in the business of:
   (a) Selling, exchanging, optioning or purchasing;
   (b) Negotiating or offering, attempting or agreeing to negotiate the sale, exchange, option or purchase of; or
   (c) Listing or soliciting prospective purchasers of,
☐ any business, the individual assets of any business or any ownership interest in any business, including, without limitation, any stock, partnership interest or membership interest in a limited-liability company, for which income and expenses have been reported to the Internal Revenue Service in the previous calendar or fiscal year on Form 1040, Form 1065, Form 1120 or Form 1120S, or any combination thereof, unless 50 percent or more of the gross reported income, excluding net capital gain, was earned by the rental of real estate reported on Form 8825.
   2. Not to include engaging in the business of:
   (a) Selling, exchanging, optioning or purchasing;
   (b) Negotiating or offering, attempting or agreeing to negotiate the sale, exchange, option or purchase of; or
   (c) Listing or soliciting prospective purchasers of,
☐ real property and a related business, if more than 50 percent of the gross income from the related business is directly derived from the use of the real property, including, without limitation, income derived from the transfer of tenant leases or management agreements and income derived from storage facilities, hotels, motels, ranches or any other business that would have no value but for the concurrent transfer of the real property.
(Added to NAC by Real Estate Comm'n by R123-06, eff. 6-1-2006; A by R077-07, 1-30-2008)

NAC 645.913 General requirements; fees; background investigation. (NRS 645.190, 645.863)
   1. A licensee who wishes to obtain a permit must:
   (a) Submit to the Division:
      (1) A completed application on a form prescribed by the Division;
      (2) A fee of $40;
      (3) A fee of $75 for the examination required by paragraph (b); and
      (4) A certificate of completion, in a form satisfactory to the Division, indicating that the applicant has successfully completed the 24 hours of classroom instruction relating to business brokerage required by paragraph (a) of subsection 2 of NRS 645.863; and
   (b) Pass an examination which is prepared and administered by an organization designated by the Division, with a score of at least 75 percent. The examination must:
      (1) Include the subject matter presented in the hours of classroom instruction required pursuant to subsection 2; and
      (2) Consist of at least 50 multiple-choice questions.
   2. The 24 hours of classroom instruction relating to business brokerage required by paragraph (a) of subsection 2 of NRS 645.863 must include, without limitation:

(a) Eight hours of instruction relating to financial statements, including, without limitation:
    (1) Income statements, balance sheets and cash flow statements;
    (2) Reformatting and recasting income statements and balance sheets; and
    (3) Terms and concepts used in financial statements;
(b) Six hours of instruction relating to the valuation of a business, including, without limitation:
    (1) Business value and alternative purchase offers;
    (2) Cash equivalent value;
    (3) Business purchase price and seller carry-back notes;
    (4) Investment value and fair market value;
    (5) Determining the value of goodwill;
    (6) The significance of a business's assets in creating market value;
    (7) The market value of a franchised business; and
    (8) The rules of thumb of business valuation;
(c) Six hours of instruction relating to purchase offer and sale considerations, including, without limitation:
    (1) Structuring the transaction;
    (2) Describing the business;
    (3) Asset sales and stock sales;
    (4) Describing the tangible assets being acquired;
    (5) Describing the goodwill being acquired;
    (6) Including real property in the transaction;
    (7) Describing the assets included in the purchase;
    (8) Describing the assets excluded from the purchase;
    (9) Cash on hand;
    (10) Method and terms of payment;
    (11) Assumption by the buyer of liabilities of the seller;
    (12) Notification of creditors of the seller;
    (13) Method for the calculation of the purchase price of a business when the buyer of the business assumes the liabilities of the seller;
    (14) Adjustments at the close of escrow to the liabilities of the seller assumed by the buyer; and
    (15) Summarizing the structure of the transaction; and
(d) Four hours of instruction relating to business brokerage and professional practices, including, without limitation:
    (1) Business opportunity contracts, agreements and disclosure forms;
    (2) Marketing, preparing a business for sale and advertising a business for sale;
    (3) Understanding the significance of the "potential" of a business;
    (4) Offering prospectus and confidentiality agreement;
    (5) Issues of business brokerage compensation;
    (6) Purchase offer and acceptance forms used for business opportunities; and
    (7) Business broker and business appraiser associations.
  3. The Division may accept a course in business brokerage from a nationally recognized or accredited organization to fulfill the educational requirements set forth in subsection 2 if the successful completion of that course would qualify the applicant to engage in business as a business broker pursuant to the requirements of that organization.
  4. Each applicant must pay a fee determined by the Division for the costs of an investigation of the applicant's background.
  5. Each applicant must, as part of his or her application and at the applicant's own expense:
(a) Arrange to have a complete set of his or her fingerprints taken by a law enforcement agency or other authorized entity acceptable to the Division; and
(b) Submit to the Division:
    (1) A completed fingerprint card and written permission authorizing the Division to submit the applicant's fingerprints to the Central Repository for Nevada Records of Criminal History for submission to the Federal Bureau of Investigation for a report on the applicant's background and to such other law enforcement agencies as the Division deems necessary; or
    (2) Written verification, on a form prescribed by the Division, stating that the fingerprints of the applicant were taken and directly forwarded electronically or by other means to the Central Repository and that the applicant has given written permission to the law enforcement agency or other authorized entity taking the fingerprints to submit the

fingerprints to the Central Repository for submission to the Federal Bureau of Investigation for a report on the applicant's background and to such other law enforcement agencies as the Division deems necessary.

6. The Division may:

(a) Unless the applicant's fingerprints are directly forwarded pursuant to subparagraph (2) of paragraph (b) of subsection 5, submit those fingerprints to the Central Repository for Nevada Records of Criminal History for submission to the Federal Bureau of Investigation and to such other law enforcement agencies as the Division deems necessary; and

(b) Request from each such agency any information regarding the applicant's background as the Division deems necessary.

NAC 645.915   Expiration date; requirements and fee for renewal. (NRS 645.190, 645.863)

1. A permit expires on the same date as the license of the holder of the permit expires.

2. The Division may renew a permit if the holder of the permit submits to the Division:

(a) A request for the renewal of the permit with the application to renew his or her license;

(b) A renewal fee of $40; and

(c) Documentation indicating that the holder of the permit has successfully completed the continuing education required by paragraph (a) of subsection 4 of NRS 645.863.

(Added to NAC by Real Estate Comm'n by R123-06, eff. 6-1-2006)

NAC 645.917   Effective date of renewal. (NRS 645.190, 645.863)   The renewal of a permit is effective on the date on which the applicant submits to the Division an application to renew his or her license or the applicant pays the renewal fees for the license and the permit, whichever occurs later.

(Added to NAC by Real Estate Comm'n by R123-06, eff. 6-1-2006)

NAC 645.919   Approval of courses for educational requirements. (NRS 645.190, 645.863)

1. For an applicant to receive credit for a course of instruction in business brokerage that is designed to fulfill the educational requirements for the issuance or renewal of a permit, the Commission must approve the course.

2. An educational institution that wishes to obtain the approval of the Commission to offer courses that meet the educational requirements for the issuance or renewal of a permit must apply to the Division pursuant to the procedures set forth in NAC 645.400 to 645.467, inclusive.

(Added to NAC by Real Estate Comm'n by R123-06, eff. 6-1-2006)

STATE LAW
Practice Test 1

1. A Seller's Real Property Disclosure document is required for all of the following properties, EXCEPT a(n):

   A. For Sale by Owner
   B. New Home
   C. Resale
   D. Home that has been inspected by a certified home inspector.

2. A Nevada licensee must give the Duties Owed by a Nevada Licensee form to prospective purchasers/tenants:

   A. before they are shown any properties.
   B. at an open house.
   C. at the close of escrow
   D. no later than the time of entering an agreement to purchase or lease.

3. The licensing law of Nevada requires that the:

   A. broker keep all information confidential that the seller has provided about the property.
   B. broker disclose everything that the sellers tells him or her.
   C. broker disclose information that materially affects the property even when the buyer does not ask for it.
   D. seller disclose all facts that might affect the sale.

4. If a Nevada licensee tells the lender that the sales price on a property is something other than its actual sale price, the:

   A. licensee has done nothing wrong as long as the appraisal substantiates the price.
   B. buyer is likely to receive an interest rate discount.
   C. licensee can have his/her license suspended or revoked.
   D. buyer can receive a lower mortgage amount.

5. Under the terms of the contract, a seller is required to provide a termite certification. The seller requests his listing agent to order one. The agent does so, knowing he will receive a referral fee from the pest control company. Is this a violation of the Nevada license law?

   A. No, if the referral fee is less than $25.
   B. No, because undisclosed referral fees are not a violation of the Nevada license law.
   C. Yes, because a salesperson may not receive compensation from anyone other than his employing broker.
   D. Yes, because only the seller may compensate a salesperson.

6. All of the following are grounds for disciplinary action EXCEPT a licensee:

   A. trying to negotiate a sale of property directly with an owner while that owner is currently exclusively listed with another broker.
   B. giving information on a rental to a tenant without the landlord's permission.
   C. refusing to write a low offer that the licensee knows will not be accepted.
   D. refusing to show property to a prospective purchaser due to poor credit.

7. What are the three types of agency recognized in Nevada?

   A. Single Agency, Dual Agency, and Assigned Agency
   B. Seller Agency, Buyer Agency, Assigned Dual Agency
   C. Subagency, Dual Agency, Seller Agency
   D. Fiduciary Agency, Universal Agency, Multiple Agency

8. A broker may collect a commission from both the seller and the buyer if:

   A. the broker holds a state license.
   B. the buyer and the seller are at non-arm's length.
   C. both parties give their informed, written consent.
   D. both parties have legal representation.

9. A Nevada real estate salesperson, associated with Hammond Realty, who wishes to place her house on the market for sale and a sign on the property must:

   A. identify the broker on the sign and may identify the salesperson.
   B. identify both her name and the brokerage name.
   C. identify her name and contact information.
   D. indicate her status as a REALTOR.

10. All funds received by the broker on behalf of the principal must be deposited in the trust account or escrow opened:

    A. within three days of receiving the offer.
    B. within 10 business days of execution of the contract.
    C. within five calendar days of receiving the offer.
    D. within one banking day of acceptance of the offer.

11. Broker-Salesperson Harrigan accepts an earnest money deposit from his buyer, payable to his brokerage, when writing the offer. Under Nevada law, Harrigan must:

    A. deposit the money in his trust account immediately.
    B. hold the check in a secure location until acceptance of the offer then open escrow.
    C. deposit the funds in a separate trust account solely for that transaction.
    D. turn the funds over to his broker promptly.

12. Salesperson Harriet engages in blockbusting and discriminatory activities and also deposited an earnest money check in her personal checking to purchase a new car. Harriet's broker, John, was completely unaware of these activities. What is the impact of Harriet's behavior on John when the violations are brought before the Commission?

    A. John may be disciplined for failure to supervise.
    B. John is liable for Harriet's actions, but not Harriet as she is only a salesperson.
    C. John will be disciplined only for violations of the Fair Housing Act.
    D. John must surrender his license.

13. Several weeks after the close of escrow, a broker-salesperson received a nice thank you note with a bonus check from the seller. The broker-salesperson cashed the check and kept the funds for her own use. Which of the following is TRUE?

    A. This is a violation of Nevada regulations and the broker-salesperson may be disciplined.
    B. This is perfectly legitimate only if the check was payable to the broker-salesperson.
    C. This is acceptable provided the broker is aware.
    D. This is legal as long as the bonus check is not in excess of $500.

14. Every Nevada real estate office is required to keep transaction records for:

    A. three years from last activity.
    B. five years from last activity.
    C. seven years from last activity.
    D. None of the Above

15. Regarding time share promotional meetings,:

    A. division employees may attend.
    B. recording devises are not allowed.
    C. verbal statements may enhance written advertising.
    D. shills are permitted.

16. Who is responsible for investigating transaction files and trust records of brokers and owner-developers?

    A. the Nevada Real Estate Commission
    B. the Attorney General
    C. the Division interloper.
    D. The Administrator and the Division.

17. Three weeks before Nick begins his real estate pre-licensing course, he offers to help his neighbor sell her house. The neighbor agrees to pay Nick a 5% commission. An offer is accepted while Nick is still taking the course and closes the day after he passes the PSI exam. The neighbor then refuses to pay Nick the commission. Can Nick sue to recover payment?

    A. No. Only the broker can sue for commissions.
    B. No. State law prohibits the suit since Nick was unlicensed at the time of listing.
    C. Yes. Nick performed under the listing agreement.
    D. Both A&B

18. Which of the following are CIC liens that are NOT the basis of foreclosure?

    A. Unpaid monthly dues
    B. Unpaid special assessments
    C. Fines for health or safety hazards
    D. Fines for other violations of the CC&Rs

19. An owner-developer may employ all of the following EXCEPT:

    A. a licensed salesperson.
    B. a licensed broker-salesperson.
    C. a licensed broker.
    D. an unlicensed hostess.

20. Which of the following could result in the suspension, revocation, or fine in an exclusive right to sell listing agreement?

    A. a specified commission rate
    B. no broker protection clause
    C. no specific termination date
    D. no automatic renewal clause

21. The Farmers listed their house for sale with Broker Simmons on February 1st. The listing was to last 6 months. In April, the Farmers decided they no longer wanted to sell the property. Which of the following statements is TRUE?

    A.   The sellers have ended the listing agreement and there are no penalties.
    B.   The sellers have in effect withdrawn the broker's right to sell and may be liable to the broker.
    C.   The Farmers are required to leave the house on the market until July 31st.
    D.   None of the Above

22. A buyer has just entered into a contract to buy a condominium unit from a person who originally purchased the unit from the developer and the buyer has lived there for the last 10 years. The buyer has a right to cancel the contract within:

    A. 3 business days
    B. 5 days of the contract date.
    C. 10 days of receipt of the certificate of resale.
    D. There is no right of cancellation

23. All of the following contracts must be in writing EXCEPT:

    A. exclusive agency listing
    B. open listing
    C. exclusive right to sell listing
    D. real estate sales contract

24. A California broker wants to broker lots in Nevada to California investors. The California broker may do this if he:

    A. relocates to Nevada.
    B. obtains a cooperative certificate
    C. pays a Nevada broker a referral fee.
    D. This cannot be done.

25. All of the following are requirements of a property manager permit holder EXCEPT:

    A. 24 hours of pre-permit education.
    B. 3 hours of continuing education in property management.
    C. a real estate license.
    D. a broker's license.

26. Who MUST have a real estate license?

    A. The owner of the property being sold or leased
    B. An executor of an estate
    C. A bankruptcy trustee
    D. A property manager

27. A Nevada licensee had her Arizona license suspended for failure to account and commingling. She:

    A. may have her Nevada license suspended because of the Arizona suspension.
    B. will NOT be disciplined in Nevada for the Arizona offense.
    C. will automatically have her Nevada license suspended.
    D. does not have to disclose the Arizona incident to the Real Estate Division of Nevada.

28. Which of the following MAY have an active Nevada real estate license?

   A. depository financial institution
   B. Division employee
   C. suspended licensee
   D. Nonresident of Nevada

29. In Nevada, a partnership, association, or corporation will be granted a Nevada real estate licenses only if:

   A. there is a member who meets the qualifications of a broker.
   B. every member actively participating in the brokerage business has a broker's license.
   C. all papers are filed with the Secretary of State
   D. All of the Above

30. In Nevada, an unlicensed assistant may perform all of the following activities EXCEPT:

   A. compute commission checks,
   B. assemble disclosure documents required for a closing.
   C. explain simple contract documents to prospective purchasers.
   D. prepare mailings and promotional materials.

31. Brown, a nonresident of Nevada, applies for a Nevada broker-salesperson's license. She must file with the Division a:

   A. Certificate of Habitability.
   B. Consent to Service of Process.
   C. Certificate of Resale.
   D. Corpus Delicti.

32. A Nevada broker may have his license suspended or revoked for all of the following EXCEPT:

   A. failing to keep adequate records.
   B. depositing earnest money directly into the firm's trust account.
   C. helping a student cheat on the licensing exam.
   D. displaying a for sale sign on a property without the authorization of the owner.

33. In Nevada, real estate commissions are:

   A. limited by the real estate Division.
   B. determined by a group of prominent brokers.
   C. set by what is customary and has always been the norm.
   D. negotiable between the client and the broker.

34. A net listing in Nevada is:

    A. illegal.
    B. advisable.
    C. permissible with approval of the Division.
    D. permissible if the seller understands and agrees.

35. How are members of the Commission selected to serve?

    A. Chosen by the Council on Housing Matters (CHM)
    B. Appointed by the Nevada Governor
    C. Elected through public elections
    D. Hand-picked by HUD

36. The Nevada Real Estate Commission consists of :

    A. four active real estate brokers or broker-salespersons and one public member.
    B. a combination of licensees and members of the public.
    C. five actively licensed brokers or broker-salespersons.
    D. five actively licensed brokers or salespersons.

37. Who may receive compensation from ERRF?

    A. A broker whose commission was refuted by his client
    B. A seller who pays a commission to a broker under false pretenses
    C. A buyer who paid a brokerage fee under a brokerage agreement
    D. A cooperating agency which did not receive their share of the commission from the listing firm

38. What is the maximum fine for a violation of NRS 645.630, NRS 645.633, or NRS 645.635 (the major violations)?

    A. $500 per offense
    B. $5,000 per offense
    C. $10,000 per offense
    D. $20,000 per offense

39. Salesman Clem tells his clients not to worry about the air conditioning unit in the house they are buying. "This entire house was checked out from head to toe two weeks ago by a licensed inspector." Although Clem was told this by the Seller, and Clem was just repeating what the seller told Clem, Clem is presumed guilty of:

    A. misrepresentation.
    B. fraud.
    C. twisting.
    D. All of the Above

40. Agent Denise accepts an earnest money check from her purchasers, the Smithers, in the amount of $2,000 to accompany an offer the Smithers wish her to present to the bank. Denise, in some financial trouble, deposits the money in her own checking account to pay some bills knowing she will be able to replace the funds after her next closing due to close the following week.

A. Denise may do so legally provided she replaces the funds immediately after her next closing.
B. Denise must hold up on presenting the offer to the bank as there is no earnest money to accompany the offer.
C. Denise, but not her broker, can be disciplined as this is conversion.
D. None of the Above

STATE LAW
Practice Test 2

1. A seller is required to provide the buyer a Seller's Real Property Disclosure document in all of the following transactions, EXCEPT:

   A. a private sale with no broker.
   B. a commercial transaction
   C. a home that was professionally inspected within the last 30 days
   D. a three unit residential building

2. A real estate broker representing a seller knows the house has a cracked foundation and that the husband committed suicide in the house. The broker must disclose:

   A. neither fact.
   B. both facts.
   C. the suicide but not the foundation.
   D. the foundation but not the suicide.

3. The licensing law of Nevada requires that the:

   A. broker keep all information confidential that the seller has provided about the property.
   B. broker disclose everything that the sellers tells him or her.
   C. broker disclose information that materially affects the property even when the buyer does not ask for it.
   D. seller disclose all facts that might affect the sale.

4. The listing salesperson is showing his listing to very interested buyers. The asking price is $249,000. The salesperson suggests to the buyers that hey make an offer of $230,000 because the salesperson believes that might be accepted by his sellers. Has the salesperson violated the licensing law?

   A. No, because he is representing the buyers whenever he writes an offer on their behalf.
   B. No, because the salesperson is attempting to generate some sort of purchasing activity on the property.
   C. Yes, because he offered the property at a price not authorized by the sellers and is breaching his fiduciary duty.
   D. Yes, because the offer is not a bona fide offer.

5. Broker Mark procures a ready, willing, and able buyer for his seller. The seller accepts the offer in writing and then experiences a change of heart 3 days later by withdrawing his acceptance. In this situation, Mark:

   A. cannot collect a commission as the transaction will not close.
   B. may sue the buyer.
   C. may well be entitled to collect a commission.
   D. may retain the deposit in lieu of a commission.

6. A seller's listing agreement has expired and the seller lists with a different brokerage. Jim, the original listing agent, now has a buyer interested in the seller's property. Jim:

   A. must be an assigned agent.
   B. cannot disclose to the buyer information about the physical condition of the property.
   C. cannot represent the buyer due to his prior relationship with the seller.
   D. cannot disclose to the buyer offers received on the seller's property or an acceptable selling price to the seller.

7. What are the three types of agency recognized in Nevada?

   A. Single Agency, Dual Agency, and Assigned Agency
   B. Seller Agency, Buyer Agency, Assigned Dual Agency
   C. Subagency, Dual Agency, Seller Agency
   D. Fiduciary Agency, Universal Agency, Multiple Agency

8. Salesperson Judy has been working with buyers to find their dream home. After locating a property, the buyers ask Judy if she can recommend a home warranty program. Judy knows of a company who will pay a referral fee for referring them. Can Judy make this recommendation?

   A. No. This is illegal per Nevada licensing law.
   B. No, if Judy's broker has an alliance with a home warranty company.
   C. Yes, if Judy discloses the referral fee and it is paid through her broker.
   D. Yes, if the home warranty company is the cheapest.

9. A buyer sees a property listed with Value Realty but does NOT wish to enter into a buyer brokerage agreement. A salesperson, other than the listing agent, from Value Realty can sell the buyer the listing if:

   A. the salesperson discloses she is a buyer's broker.
   B. the salesperson acts as a dual agent.
   C. she represents the seller only.
   D. she indicates her status as a REALTOR.

10. Paul, an associate with Hummingbird Realty, lists a property with sellers, Fitzsimmons. After discussing it with his wife, Paul decide he and his wife would like to purchase the property themselves from the Fitzsimmons. As a Nevada licensee, Paul:

    A. must be a dual agent.
    B. cannot purchase his own listing as it is a conflict of interest.
    C. must maintain his duties as the sellers' agent.
    D. must be a buyer's agent only and have his broker re-assign the listing and arrange for seller representation.

11. Broker A enters into a listing with the seller. Salesperson B learns of the listing through the MLS and finds a buyer ready, willing, and able to purchase. Typically in Nevada, Salesperson B:

    A. is a sub-agent to Broker A.
    B. is an agent of the buyer only with an executed buyer brokerage agreement.
    C. must represent bother the seller and the buyer.
    D. has a fiduciary to the buyer.

12. What is the purpose for the Consent to Act form?

    A. the parties to the transaction acknowledge and agree to a dual agency transaction.
    B. to spell out the actions the agent will provide to the client and the client's consent to the same.
    C. the fiduciary's consent for the broker to act on the client's behalf.
    D. All of the Above

13. Salesperson Jeanette paid the local newspaper company to run an ad in the real estate section. Jeanette's ad promotes "Jeanette sells Vegas" including her accomplishments, production awards, market share, and contact information. Jeanette must also include in the ad:

    A. the registered name of her brokerage firm.
    B. her real estate license number.
    C. the wording, "This ad approved by the Nevada Real Estate Division".
    D. All of the Above

14. Every Nevada real estate office is required to keep transaction records for:

    A. three years from last activity.
    B. five years from last activity.
    C. seven years from last activity.
    D. None of the Above

15. Broker-salesperson Adam hires a marketing firm to design a web site to promote Adam's real estate career. Which of the following omissions from the web site could result in a fine from the Nevada Real Estate Division?

    A. the brokerage name.
    B. Adam's cell phone number.
    C. pictures of the properties Adam wishes to advertise.
    D. None of the Above.

16. What is the most standard real estate brokerage commission in Las Vegas?

    A. 3%
    B. 4%
    C. 6%
    D. None of the Above

17. Which of the following statements is TRUE regarding an earnest money deposit?

    A. Cash is not permitted.
    B. A promissory note is illegal in Nevada.
    C. An earnest money deposit of some sort is legally required with an offer.
    D. It can be anything of value that is acceptable to the offeree.

18. In Nevada, must a Broker maintain a trust account?

    A. Yes.
    B. Yes and the account information must be on file with the Commission.
    C. No, only if the Division has exempted the Broker from maintaining one.
    D. No.

19. An owner-developer may employ all of the following EXCEPT:

    A. a licensed salesperson.
    B. a licensed broker-salesperson.
    C. a licensed broker.
    D. an unlicensed hostess.

20. Which of the following could result in the suspension, revocation, or fine in an exclusive right to sell listing agreement?

    A. a specified commission rate
    B. no broker protection clause
    C. no specific termination date
    D. no automatic renewal clause

21. In Nevada, a real estate salesperson may lawfully collect a commission from:

   A.   either the buyer or the seller as long as the correct agency disclosure is made.
   B.   the salesperson's broker.
   C.   a licensed title or escrow firm registered in Nevada.
   D.   All of of the Above

22. Broker Johnson is in the process of opening a branch office in Sparks, Nevada. Johnson
    applies for a branch office license and clearly identifies the relationship with his main office.
    The broker appoints salesperson Kelly as the branch office manager. Which of the following is
    TRUE?

   A. Kelly must be a resident of Sparks.
   B. Johnson will be granted a branch office license as he has named a branch office manager.
   C. Johnson cannot promote his Las Vegas listings in Sparks.
   D. Johnson's application will be denied.

23. All of the following contracts must be in writing EXCEPT:

   A. exclusive agency listing
   B. open listing
   C. exclusive right to sell listing
   D. real estate sales contract

24. In Nevada, in order for a listing broker to sue for a commission, all of the following are
    necessary for her to show entitlement for that commission EXCEPT:

   A. there was a brokerage agreement.
   B. the property successfully closed escrow.
   C. the broker produced a ready, willing, and able purchaser who met price and terms
      acceptable to the seller.
   D. The broker was properly licensed at the time of procurement.

25. How is a broker's commission determined in a real estate transaction?

   A. it is determined by what is customary in the marketplace.
   B. the commission percentage rate is set by local real estate brokers in the community.
   C. it is determined by the seller.
   D. it is negotiated between seller and broker and confirmed in the listing agreement.

26. Regarding signage for a Nevada real estate brokerage firm, the broker must have a sign:

    A. unless the brokerage activities will be conducted in her home.
    B. at the main office with identical signs at any branch offices.
    C. with letters of at least 5 inches in height.
    D. visible from the nearest public sidewalk, street, or highway, on the building directory, or at the entry of the business.

27. James Wickitt has offices in nine western states including Nevada. He is the broker to over 7,600 licensed associates. If any one associate in any one location makes a misrepresentation to a client, Wickett:

    A. may be disciplined for failure to supervise.
    B. should have offered better training and management.
    C. cannot be disciplined because he would have no way to know of the misrepresentation..
    D. will have his license suspended until a monetary fine is paid.

28. A broker must disclose all of the following to the Nevada Real Estate Division within 10 days of their occurrence EXCEPT:

    A. a change of address for the brokerage.
    B. the termination of a licensee.
    C. a name change of the brokerage such as the addition of a franchise name.
    D. completion of mandatory continuing education courses.

29. Which of the following continuing education courses is NOT required for a broker-salesperson to renew his license:

    A. property management
    B. broker management
    C. agency relationships
    D. law and ethics

30. In Nevada, an unlicensed assistant may perform all of the following activities EXCEPT:

    A. typing and filing.
    B. assemble documents and organize files.
    C. tell prospective clients the prices and details of homes advertised for sale.
    D. order termite, roof, and general property inspections.

31. Common Interest Community documents are:

    A. only required on new construction.
    B. required to be provided by the association which may charge a reasonable fee.
    C. due by the close of escrow.
    D. always paid for by the seller.

32. A qualified intermediary handles:

    A. homeowners association disputes.
    B. delayed 1031 tax deferred exchanges.
    C. income tax audits.
    D. disputes between the broker and an associated licensee.

33. Hustlin' Harry is desperately looking for listings in his farm area. In an attempt to get a quick listing, he door knocks and tells the homeowners that a particular ethnic group is buying all the homes in the neighborhood.

    A. Harry is creating "panic selling".
    B. Harry is "blockbusting".
    C. Harry may be fined and have his license suspended or revoked.
    D. All of the Above

34. A net listing in Nevada is:

    A. illegal.
    B. advisable.
    C. permissible with approval of the Division.
    D. permissible if the seller understands and agrees.

35. In Nevada, the age of legality is:

    A. 17
    B. 18
    C. 21
    D. None of the Above

36. The Nevada Real Estate Commission consists of :

    A. four active real estate brokers or broker-salespersons and one public member.
    B. a combination of licensees and members of the public.
    C. five actively licensed brokers or broker-salespersons.
    D. five actively licensed brokers or salespersons.

37. Waiver of pre-licensing educational requirements for brokers and broker-salespersons is made for active, full-time experience if the applicant can show:

    A. 15 credits for every two years.
    B. 16 credits for every two years.
    C. 8 credits for every one year.
    D. There is no waiver for experience.

38. What is the maximum fine for a violation of NRS 645.630, NRS 645.633, or NRS 645.635 (the major violations)?

    A. $500 per offense
    B. $5,000 per offense
    C. $10,000 per offense
    D. $20,000 per offense

39. A broker candidate applying for a license as a broker, must do all of the following EXCEPT:

    A. provide a three year work history.
    B. supply his previous real estate experience
    C. disclose any past felony convictions
    D. disclose any past licensing penalties

40. Homeowner Smithers refuses to show his house for rent to any members of African descent. Upon being refused an opportunity to preview the house because of their ethnicity, the Thompsons file a complaint with the Nevada Real Estate Division. Upon confirmation of the discrimination, the Division will:

    A. start a formal investigation to affirm or deny the allegations.
    B. issue an injunction against Smithers
    C. assist the Thompsons with a legal suit against Smithers
    D. do nothing, as the Division has no jurisdiction over an unlicensed person.

State Law Practice Test – 1 KEY

1. B
2. D
3. C
4. C
5. C
6. D
7. A
8. C
9. A
10. D
11. D
12. A
13. A
14. B
15. A
16. D
17. D
18. D
19. C
20. C
21. B
22. D
23. B
24. B
25. D
26. D
27. A
28. D
29. A
30. C
31. B
32. B
33. D
34. D
35. B
36. C
37. B
38. C
39. A
40. D

State Law Practice Test – 2 KEY

1. B
2. D
3. C
4. C
5. C
6. D
7. A
8. C
9. A
10. D
11. D
12. A
13. A
14. B
15. A
16. D
17. D
18. D
19. C
20. C
21. B
22. D
23. B
24. B
25. D
26. D
27. A
28. D
29. A
30. C
31. B
32. B
33. D
34. D
35. B
36. C
37. B
38. C
39. A
40. D

DUTIES OWED BY A NEVADA REAL ESTATE LICENSEE

does not constitute a contract for services nor an agreement to pay compensation.

licensee is required to provide a form setting forth the duties owed by the licensee to:
whom the licensee is acting as an agent in the real estate transaction, and
nted party to the real estate transaction, if any.

see in the real estate transaction is _____

whose license number is _____. The licensee is acting for [client's name(s)] _____

_____ who is/are the ☐ Seller/Landlord; ☐ Buyer/Tenant.

Broker: The broker is *Zabdie LLC* _____, whose company is _____.

Are there additional licensees involved in this transaction? ☐ Yes ☐ No **If yes, Supplemental form 525A is required.**

Licensee's Duties Owed to All Parties:
A Nevada real estate licensee shall:
1. Not deal with any party to a real estate transaction in a manner which is deceitful, fraudulent or dishonest.
2. Exercise reasonable skill and care with respect to all parties to the real estate transaction.
3. Disclose to each party to the real estate transaction as soon as practicable:
   a. Any material and relevant facts, data or information which licensee knows, or with reasonable care and diligence the licensee should know, about the property.
   b. Each source from which licensee will receive compensation.
4. Abide by all other duties, responsibilities and obligations required of the licensee in law or regulations.

Licensee's Duties Owed to the Client:
A Nevada real estate licensee shall:
1. Exercise reasonable skill and care to carry out the terms of the brokerage agreement and the licensee's duties in the brokerage agreement;
2. Not disclose, except to the licensee's broker, confidential information relating to a client for 1 year after the revocation or termination of the brokerage agreement, unless licensee is required to do so by court order or the client gives written permission;
3. Seek a sale, purchase, option, rental or lease of real property at the price and terms stated in the brokerage agreement or at a price acceptable to the client;
4. Present all offers made to, or by the client as soon as practicable, unless the client chooses to waive the duty of the licensee to present all offers and signs a waiver of the duty on a form prescribed by the Division;
5. Disclose to the client material facts of which the licensee has knowledge concerning the real estate transaction;
6. Advise the client to obtain advice from an expert relating to matters which are beyond the expertise of the licensee; and
7. Account to the client for all money and property the licensee receives in which the client may have an interest.

Duties Owed By a broker who assigns different licensees affiliated with the brokerage to separate parties.
Each licensee shall not disclose, except to the real estate broker, confidential information relating to client.

Licensee Acting for Both Parties:
The Licensee

MAY [_____/_____] **OR** **MAY NOT [_____/_____]**

in the future act for two or more parties who have interests adverse to each other. In acting for these parties, the licensee has a conflict of interest. Before a licensee may act for two or more parties, the licensee must give you a "Consent to Act" form to sign.

I/We acknowledge receipt of a copy of this list of licensee duties, and have read and understand this disclosure.

Seller/Landlord: _____ *Date:* _____ *Time:* _____

Seller/Landlord: _____ *Date:* _____ *Time:* _____
OR
Buyer/Tenant: _____ *Date:* _____ *Time:* _____

Buyer/Tenant: _____ *Date:* _____ *Time:* _____

CONSENT TO ACT

This form does not constitute a contract for services nor an agreement to pay compens

DESCRIPTION OF TRANSACTION: The real estate transaction is the ☐ sale and purchase; c

Property Address: _____

_____.

In Nevada, a real estate licensee may act for more than one party in a real estate transaction however, before the licensee does so, he or she must obtain the written consent of each party. This form is that consent. Before you consent to having a licensee represent both yourself and the other party, you should read this form and understand it.

Licensee: The licensee in this real estate transaction is _____ ("Licensee") whose

license number is _____ and who is affiliated with _____ ("Brokerage").

Seller/Landlord _____

          Print Name

Buyer/Tenant _____

         Print Name

CONFLICT OF INTEREST: A licensee in a real estate transaction may legally act for two or more parties who have interests adverse to each other. In acting for these parties, the licensee has a conflict of interest.

DISCLOSURE OF CONFIDENTIAL INFORMATION: Licensee will not disclose any confidential information for 1 year after the revocation or termination of any brokerage agreement entered into with a party to this transaction, unless Licensee is required to do so by a court of competent jurisdiction or is given written permission to do so by that party. Confidential information includes, but is not limited to, the client's motivation to purchase, trade or sell, which if disclosed, could harm one party's bargaining position or benefit the other.

DUTIES OF LICENSEE: Licensee shall provide you with a "Duties Owed by a Nevada Real Estate Licensee" disclosure form which lists the duties a licensee owes to all parties of a real estate transaction, and those owed to the licensee's client. When representing both parties, the licensee owes the same duties to both seller and buyer. Licensee shall disclose to both Seller and Buyer all known defects in the property, any matter that must be disclosed by law, and any information the licensee believes may be material or might affect Seller's/Landlord's or Buyer's/Tenant's decisions with respect to this transaction.

NO REQUIREMENT TO CONSENT: You are not required to consent to this licensee acting on your behalf. You may
- Reject this consent and obtain your own agent,
- Represent yourself,
- Request that the licensee's broker assign you your own licensee.

CONFIRMATION OF DISCLOSURE AND INFORMATION CONSENT

BY MY SIGNATURE BELOW, I UNDERSTAND AND CONSENT: I am giving my consent to have the above identified licensee act for both the other party and me. By signing below, I acknowledge that I understand the ramifications of this consent, and that I acknowledge that I am giving this consent without coercion.

I/We acknowledge receipt of a copy of this list of licensee duties, and have read and understand this disclosure.					
Seller/Landlord	*Date*	*Time*	*Buyer/Tenant*	*Date*	*Time*
Seller/Landlord	*Date*	*Time*	*Buyer/Tenant*	*Date*	*Time*

Approved Nevada Real Estate Division
Replaces all previous editions

Page 1 of 1

524
Revised 05/01/05

131

CONFIRMATION REGARDING REAL ESTATE AGENT RELATIONSHIP
This form does not constitute a contract for services

Property Address

In the event any party to the real estate transaction is also represented by another licensee who is affiliated with the same Company, the Broker may assign a licensee to act for each party, respectively. As set forth within the *Duties Owed* form, no confidential information will be disclosed. **This is ☐ is not ☐ such a transaction.**

I/We confirm the duties of a real estate licensee of which has been presented and explained to me/us. My/Our representative's relationship is:

_____ is the AGENT of | _____ is the AGENT of

☐ Seller/Landlord Exclusively ② ☐ Buyer/Tenant Exclusively ③ | ☐ Buyer/Tenant Exclusively ③ ☐ Seller/Landlord Exclusively ②

☐ Both Buyer/Tenant & Seller/Landlord ① | ☐ Both Buyer/Tenant & Seller/Landlord ①

① IF LICENSEE IS ACTING FOR MORE THAN ONE PARTY IN THIS TRANSACTION, you will be provided a **Consent to Act form for your review, consideration and approval or rejection. A licensee can legally represent both the Seller/Landlord and Buyer/Tenant in a transaction, but ONLY with the knowledge and written consent of BOTH the Seller/Landlord and Buyer/Tenant.**

② A licensee who is acting for the Seller/Landlord exclusively, is not representing the Buyer/Tenant and has no duty to advocate or negotiate for the Buyer/Tenant.

③ A licensee who is acting for the Buyer/Tenant exclusively, is not representing the Seller/Landlord and has no duty to advocate or negotiate for the Seller/Landlord.

by _____ | by _____
Seller's/Landlord's Company | *Buyer's/Tenant's Company*
_____ | _____
Licensed Real Estate Agent | *Licensed Real Estate Agent*

_____ | _____
Date   *Time* | *Date*   *Time*

_____ | _____
Seller/Landlord   Date   Time | Buyer/Tenant   Date   Time

_____ | _____
Seller/Landlord   Date   Time | Buyer/Tenant   Date   Time

Approved Nevada Real Estate Division
Replaces all previous editions

560
Revised 4/1/99

D UTIES OWED BY A
NEVADA LICENSEE

I MPACT FEES

S OIL REPORT

C OMMON-INTEREST
COMMUNITIES

L IEN FOR DEFERRED
TAXES

O PEN RANGE

S ELLER'S REAL PROPERTY
DISCLOSURE

U SED MOBILE HOMES

R ESIDENTIAL POOL SAFETY
AND DROWNING PREVENTION

E NVIRONMENTAL HAZARDS

S EWER AND WATER
RATES

Nevada Real Estate Division

RESIDENTIAL DISCLOSURE GUIDE

A few things you need to know before buying or selling a home in Nevada.

Revised October 2015

State of Nevada
Department of Business & Industry
Real Estate Division

Table of Contents

Important

BEFORE YOU PURCHASE PROPERTY IN COMMON-INTEREST COMMUNITY

DID YOU KNOW . . .

1. YOU GENERALLY HAVE 5 DAYS TO CANCEL THE PURCHASE AGREEMENT?

When you enter into a purchase agreement to buy a home or unit in a common-interest community, in most cases you should receive either a public offering statement, if you are the original purchaser of the home or unit, or a resale package, if you are not the original purchaser. The law generally provides for a 5-day period in which you have the right to cancel the purchase agreement. The 5-day period begins on different starting dates, depending on whether you receive a public offering statement or a resale package. Upon receiving a public offering statement or a resale package, you should make sure you are informed of the deadline for exercising your right to cancel. In order to exercise your right to cancel, the law generally requires that you hand deliver the notice of cancellation to the seller within the 5-day period, or mail the notice of cancellation to the seller by prepaid United States mail within the 5-day period. For more information regarding your right to cancel, see Nevada Revised Statutes 116.4108, if you received a public offering statement, or Nevada Revised Statutes 116.4109, if you received a resale package.

2. YOU ARE AGREEING TO RESTRICTIONS ON HOW YOU CAN USE YOUR PROPERTY?

These restrictions are contained in a document known as the Declaration of Covenants, Conditions and Restrictions. The CC&Rs become a part of the title to your property. They bind you and every future owner of the property whether or not you have read them or had them explained to you. The CC&Rs, together with other "governing documents" (such as association bylaws and rules and regulations), are intended to preserve the character and value of properties in the community, but may also restrict what you can do to improve or change your property and limit how you use and enjoy your property. By purchasing a property encumbered by CC&Rs, you are agreeing to limitations that could affect your lifestyle and freedom of choice. You should review the CC&Rs, and other governing documents before purchasing to make sure that these limitations and controls are acceptable to you. Certain provisions in the CC&Rs and other governing documents may be superseded by contrary provisions of chapter 116 of the Nevada Revised Statutes. The Nevada Revised Statutes are available at the Internet address http://www.leg.state.nv.us/nrs/.

Approved Nevada Real Estate Division
Replaces all previous versions
Page 1 of 4
584
Revised 10/1/09

135

OU WILL HAVE TO PAY OWNERS' ASSESSMENTS FOR AS LONG AS OU OWN YOUR PROPERTY?

As an owner in a common-interest community, you are responsible for paying your share of expenses relating to the common elements, such as landscaping, shared amenities and the operation of any homeowners' association. The obligation to pay these assessments binds you and every future owner of the property. Owners' fees are usually assessed by the homeowners' association and due monthly. You have to pay dues whether or not you agree with the way the association is managing the property or spending the assessments. The executive board of the association may have the power to change and increase the amount of the assessment and to levy special assessments against your property to meet extraordinary expenses. In some communities, major components of the common elements of the community such as roofs and private roads must be maintained and replaced by the association. If the association is not well managed or fails to provide adequate funding for reserves to repair, replace and restore common elements, you may be required to pay large, special assessments to accomplish these tasks.

4. IF YOU FAIL TO PAY OWNERS' ASSESSMENTS, YOU COULD LOSE YOUR HOME?

If you do not pay these assessments when due, the association usually has the power to collect them by selling your property in a nonjudicial foreclosure sale. If fees become delinquent, you may also be required to pay penalties and the association's costs and attorney's fees to become current. If you dispute the obligation or its amount, your only remedy to avoid the loss of your home may be to file a lawsuit and ask a court to intervene in the dispute.

5. YOU MAY BECOME A MEMBER OF A HOMEOWNERS' ASSOCIATION THAT HAS THE POWER TO AFFECT HOW YOU USE AND ENJOY YOUR PROPERTY?

Many common-interest communities have a homeowners' association. In a new development, the association will usually be controlled by the developer until a certain number of units have been sold. After the period of developer control, the association may be controlled by property owners like yourself who are elected by homeowners to sit on an executive board and other boards and committees formed by the association. The association, and its executive board, are responsible for assessing homeowners for the cost of operating the association and the common or shared elements of the community and for the day to day operation and management of the community. Because homeowners sitting on the executive board and other boards and committees of the association may not have the experience or professional background required to understand and carry out the responsibilities of the association properly, the association may hire professional community managers to carry out these responsibilities. Homeowners' associations operate on democratic principles. Some decisions require all homeowners to vote,

Approved Nevada Real Estate Division
Replaces all previous versions

Page 2 of 4

584
Revised 10/1/09

136

some decisions are made by the executive board or other boards or committees established by the association or governing documents. Although the actions of the association and its executive board are governed by state laws, the CC&Rs and other documents that govern the common-interest community, decisions made by these persons will affect your use and enjoyment of your property, your lifestyle and freedom of choice, and your cost of living in the community. You may not agree with decisions made by the association or its governing bodies even though the decisions are ones which the association is authorized to make. Decisions may be made by a few persons on the executive board or governing bodies that do not necessarily reflect the view of the majority of homeowners in the community. If you do not agree with decisions made by the association, its executive board or other governing bodies, your remedy is typically to attempt to use the democratic processes of the association to seek the election of members of the executive board or other governing bodies that are more responsive to your needs. If you have a dispute with the association, its executive board or other governing bodies, you may be able to resolve the dispute through the complaint, investigation and intervention process administered by the Office of the Ombudsman for Owners in Common-Interest Communities, the Nevada Real Estate Division and the Commission for Common Interest Communities. However, to resolve some disputes, you may have to mediate or arbitrate the dispute and, if mediation or arbitration is unsuccessful, you may have to file a lawsuit and ask a court to resolve the dispute. In addition to your personal cost in mediation or arbitration, or to prosecute a lawsuit, you may be responsible for paying your share of the association's cost in defending against your claim.

6. YOU ARE REQUIRED TO PROVIDE PROSPECTIVE PURCHASERS OF YOUR PROPERTY WITH INFORMATION ABOUT LIVING IN YOUR COMMON-INTEREST COMMUNITY?

The law requires you to provide a prospective purchaser of your property with a copy of the community's governing documents, including the CC&Rs, association bylaws, and rules and regulations, as well as a copy of this document. You are also required to provide a copy of the association's current year-to-date financial statement, including, without limitation, the most recent audited or reviewed financial statement, a copy of the association's operating budget and information regarding the amount of the monthly assessment for common expenses, including the amount set aside as reserves for the repair, replacement and restoration of common elements. You are also required to inform prospective purchasers of any outstanding judgments or lawsuits pending against the association of which you are aware. For more information regarding these requirements, see Nevada Revised Statutes 116.4109.

Approved Nevada Real Estate Division
Replaces all previous versions

Page 3 of 4

584
Revised 10/1/09

137

7. YOU HAVE CERTAIN RIGHTS REGARDING OWNERSHIP IN A COMMON-INTEREST COMMUNITY THAT ARE GUARANTEED YOU BY THE STATE?

Pursuant to provisions of chapter 116 of Nevada Revised Statutes, you have the right:

(a)   To be notified of all meetings of the association and its executive board, except in cases of emergency.

(b)   To attend and speak at all meetings of the association and its executive board, except in some cases where the executive board is authorized to meet in closed, executive session.

(c)   To request a special meeting of the association upon petition of at least 10 percent of the homeowners.

(d)   To inspect, examine, photocopy and audit financial and other records of the association.

(e)   To be notified of all changes in the community's rules and regulations and other actions by the association or board that affect you.

8. QUESTIONS?

Although they may be voluminous, you should take the time to read and understand the documents that will control your ownership of a property in a common-interest community. You may wish to ask your real estate professional, lawyer or other person with experience to explain anything you do not understand. You may also request assistance from the Office of the Ombudsman for Owners in Common-Interest Communities, Nevada Real Estate Division, at:

OR

2501 E. Sahara Ave, Suite 202
Las Vegas, NV 89104-4137
Voice: (702) 486-4480
or toll free at (877) 829-9907
Fax: (702) 486-4520

788 Fairview Dr, Ste 200
Carson City, NV 89701
Voice: (775) 687-4280

I/We acknowledge that I/we have received the above-information.		
_____ *Purchaser*	_____ *Date*	_____ *Time*
_____ *Purchaser*	_____ *Date*	_____ *Time*

Test Question

Disclosure of Information on Lead-Based Paint and/or Lead-Based Paint H

Lead Warning Statement

Every purchaser or any interest in residential real property on which a residential dwelling was built prior to (1978) is notified that such property may present exposure to lead from lead-based paint that may place young children at risk of developing lead poisoning. Lead poisoning in young children may produce permanent neurological damage, including learning disabilities, reduced intelligence quotient, behavioral problems, and impaired memory. Lead poisoning also poses a particular risk to pregnant women. The seller of any interest in residential real property is required to provide the buyer with any information on lead-based paint hazards from risk assessments or inspections in the seller's possession and notify the buyer of any known lead-based paint hazards. A risk assessment or inspection for possible lead-based paint hazards is recommended prior to purchase.

Seller's Disclosure

(a) Presence of lead-based paint and/or lead-based paint hazards (check (i) or (ii) below):

    (i) _____ Known lead-based paint and/or lead-based paint hazards are present in the housing (explain).

_____

    (ii) _____ Seller has no knowledge of lead-based paint and/or lead-based paint hazards in the housing.

(b) Records and reports available to the seller (check (i) or (ii) below):

    (i) _____ Seller has provided the purchaser with all available records and reports pertaining to lead-based paint and/or lead-based paint hazards in the housing (list documents below).

_____

    (ii) _____ Seller has no reports or records pertaining to lead-based paint and/or lead-based paint hazards in the housing.

Purchaser's Acknowledgment (initial)

(c) _____ Purchaser has received copies of all information listed above.

(d) _____ Purchaser has received the pamphlet *Protect Your Family from Lead in Your Home*.

(e) Purchaser has (check (i) or (ii) below):

    (i) _____ received a 10 day opportunity (or mutually agreed upon period) to conduct a risk assessment or inspection for the presence of lead-based paint and/or lead-based paint hazards.

    (ii) _____ waived the opportunity to conduct a risk assessment or inspection for the presence of lead-based paint and/or lead-based paint hazards.

Agent's Acknowledgment (initial)

(f) _____ Agent has informed the seller of the seller's obligations under 42 U.S.C. 4852d and is aware of his/her responsibility to ensure compliance.

Certification of Accuracy

The following parties have reviewed the information above and certify, to the best of their knowledge, that the information they have provided is true and accurate.

_____   _____   _____   _____
Seller   Date   Seller   Date

_____   _____   _____   _____
Purchaser   Date   Purchaser   Date

_____   _____   _____   _____
Agent   Date   Agent   Date

Seller will sign and send back to the buyer.

SELLER'S REAL PROPERTY DISCLOSURE FORM

.n accordance with Nevada Law, a seller of residential real property in Nevada must disclose any and all known conditions and aspects of the property which materially affect the value or use of residential property in an adverse manner *(see NRS 113.130 and 113.140).*

Date _____

Property address _____

Do you currently occupy or have you ever occupied this property? YES ☐ NO ☐

Effective October 1, 2011: A purchaser may not waive the requirement to provide this form and a seller may not require a purchaser to waive this form. *(NRS 113.130(3))*

Type of Seller: ☐ Bank (financial institution); ☐ Asset Management Company; ☐ Owner-occupier; ☐ Other: _____

Purpose of Statement: (1) This statement is a disclosure of the condition of the property in compliance with the Seller Real Property Disclosure Act, effective January 1, 1996. (2) This statement is a disclosure of the condition and information concerning the property known by the Seller which materially affects the value of the property. Unless otherwise advised, the Seller does not possess any expertise in construction, architecture, engineering or any other specific area related to the construction or condition of the improvements on the property or the land. Also, unless otherwise advised, the Seller has not conducted any inspection of generally inaccessible areas such as the foundation or roof. This statement is not a warranty of any kind by the Seller or by any Agent representing the Seller in this transaction and is not a substitute for any inspections or warranties the Buyer may wish to obtain. Systems and appliances addressed on this form by the seller are not part of the contractual agreement as to the inclusion of any system or appliance as part of the binding agreement.

Instructions to the Seller: (1) ANSWER ALL QUESTIONS. (2) REPORT KNOWN CONDITIONS AFFECTING THE PROPERTY. (3) ATTACH ADDITIONAL PAGES WITH YOUR SIGNATURE IF ADDITIONAL SPACE IS REQUIRED. (4) COMPLETE THIS FORM YOURSELF. (5) IF SOME ITEMS DO NOT APPLY TO YOUR PROPERTY, CHECK N/A (NOT APPLICABLE). EFFECTIVE JANUARY 1, 1996, FAILURE TO PROVIDE A PURCHASER WITH A SIGNED DISCLOSURE STATEMENT WILL ENABLE THE PURCHASER TO TERMINATE AN OTHERWISE BINDING PURCHASE AGREEMENT AND SEEK OTHER REMEDIES AS PROVIDED BY THE LAW *(see NRS 113.150).*

Systems / Appliances: Are you aware of any problems and/or defects with any of the following:

Must advise to Get One

	YES	NO	N/A		YES	NO	N/A
Electrical System	☐	☐	☐	Shower(s)	☐	☐	☐
Plumbing	☐	☐	☐	Sink(s)	☐	☐	☐
Sewer System & line	☐	☐	☐	Sauna / hot tub(s)	☐	☐	☐
Septic tank & leach field	☐	☐	☐	Built-in microwave	☐	☐	☐
Well & pump	☐	☐	☐	Range / oven / hood-fan	☐	☐	☐
Yard sprinkler system(s)	☐	☐	☐	Dishwasher	☐	☐	☐
Fountain(s)	☐	☐	☐	Garbage disposal	☐	☐	☐
Heating system	☐	☐	☐	Trash compactor	☐	☐	☐
Cooling system	☐	☐	☐	Central vacuum	☐	☐	☐
Solar heating system	☐	☐	☐	Alarm system	☐	☐	☐
Fireplace & chimney	☐	☐	☐	owned.. ☐ leased.. ☐			
Wood burning system	☐	☐	☐	Smoke detector	☐	☐	☐
Garage door opener	☐	☐	☐	Intercom	☐	☐	☐
Water treatment system(s)	☐	☐	☐	Data Communication line(s)	☐	☐	☐
owned.. ☐ leased.. ☐				Satellite dish(es)	☐	☐	☐
Water heater	☐	☐	☐	owned.. ☐ leased.. ☐			
Toilet(s)	☐	☐	☐	Other_____	☐	☐	☐
Bathtub(s)	☐	☐	☐				

EXPLANATIONS: Any "Yes" must be fully explained. Attach explanations to form.

_____ _____
Seller(s) Initials

_____ _____
Buyer(s) Initials

Nevada Real Estate Division
Replaces all previous versions

Page 1 of 4

140

Seller Real Property Disclosure Form 547
Revised 04/29/16

Property conditions, improvements and additional information: .... <u>YES</u>   <u>NO</u>   <u>N/A</u>

Are you **aware** of any of the following?:

1. Structure:

   (a) Previous or current moisture conditions and/or water damage? .... ☐ ☐

   (b) Any structural defect? .... ☐ ☐

   (c) Any construction, modification, alterations, or repairs made without

   required state, city or county building permits? .... ☐ ☐

   (d) Whether the property is or has been the subject of a claim governed by

   NRS 40.600 to 40.695 (construction defect claims)? .... ☐ ☐

   (If seller answers yes, FURTHER DISCLOSURE IS REQUIRED)

2. Land / Foundation:

   (a) Any of the improvements being located on unstable or expansive soil? .... ☐ ☐

   (b) Any foundation sliding, settling, movement, upheaval, or earth stability problems

   that have occurred on the property? .... ☐ ☐

   (c) Any drainage, flooding, water seepage, or high water table? .... ☐ ☐

   (d) The property being located in a designated flood plain? .... ☐ ☐

   (e) Whether the property is located next to or near any known future development? .... ☐ ☐

   (f) Any encroachments, easements, zoning violations or nonconforming uses? .... ☐ ☐

   (g) Is the property adjacent to "open range" land? .... ☐ ☐

       (If seller answers yes, FURTHER DISCLOSURE IS REQUIRED under NRS 113.065)

3. Roof: Any problems with the roof? .... ☐ ☐

4. Pool/spa: Any problems with structure, wall, liner, or equipment................................. ☐ ☐ ☐

5. Infestation: Any history of infestation (termites, carpenter ants, etc.)? .... ☐ ☐

6. Environmental:

   (a) Any substances, materials, or products which may be an environmental hazard such as

   but not limited to, asbestos, radon gas, urea formaldehyde, fuel or chemical storage tanks,

   contaminated water or soil on the property? .... ☐ ☐

   (b) Has property been the site of a crime involving the previous manufacture of Methamphetamine

   where the substances have not been removed from or remediated on the Property by a certified

   entity or has not been deemed safe for habitation by the Board of Heath? .... ☐ ☐

7. Fungi / Mold: Any previous or current fungus or mold? .... ☐ ☐

8. Any features of the property shared in common with adjoining landowners such as walls, fences,

road, driveways or other features whose use or responsibility for maintenance may have an effect

on the property? .... ☐ ☐

9. Common Interest Communities: Any "common areas" (facilities like pools, tennis courts, walkways or

other areas co-owned with others) or a homeowner association which has any

authority over the property? .... ☐ ☐

   (a) Common Interest Community Declaration and Bylaws available? .... ☐ ☐

   (b) Any periodic or recurring association fees? .... ☐ ☐

   (c) Any unpaid assessments, fines or liens, and any warnings or notices that may give rise to an

   assessment, fine or lien? .... ☐ ☐

   (d) Any litigation, arbitration, or mediation related to property or common area? .... ☐ ☐

   (e) Any assessments associated with the property (excluding property taxes)? .... ☐ ☐

   (f) Any construction, modification, alterations, or repairs made without

   required approval from the appropriate Common Interest Community board or committee? .... ☐ ☐

10. Any problems with water quality or water supply? .... ☐ ☐

11. <u>Any other conditions</u> or aspects of the property which materially affect its value or use in an

adverse manner? .... ☐ ☐

12. Lead-Based Paint: Was the property constructed on or before 12/31/77? .... ☐ ☐

   (If yes, additional Federal EPA notification and disclosure documents are required)

13. Water source: Municipal ☐ Community Well ☐ Domestic Well ☐ Other ☐

   If Community Well: State Engineer Well Permit # _____ Revocable ☐ Permanent ☐ Cancelled ☐

   Use of community and domestic wells may be subject to change. Contact the Nevada Division of Water Resources

   for more information regarding the future use of this well.

14. Wastewater disposal: Municipal Sewer ☐ Septic System ☐ Other ☐

15. This property is subject to a Private Transfer Fee Obligation? .... ☐ ☐

   EXPLANATIONS: Any "Yes" must be fully explained. Attach explanations to form.

```



```

   _____ _____   _____ _____

     Seller(s) Initials   *Buyer(s) Initials*

Nevada Real Estate Division   Page 2 of 4   **Seller Real Property Disclosure Form 547**
Replaces all previous versions   **Revised 04/29/16**

141

Buyers and sellers of residential property are advised to seek the advice of an attorney concerning their rights and obligations as set forth in Chapter 113 of the Nevada Revised Statutes regarding the seller's obligation to execute the Nevada Real Estate Division's approved "Seller's Real Property Disclosure Form". For your convenience, Chapter 113 of the Nevada Revised Statutes provides as follows:

CONDITION OF RESIDENTIAL PROPERTY OFFERED FOR SALE

NRS 113.100 Definitions. As used in NRS 113.100 to 113.150, inclusive, unless the context otherwise requires:

1. "Defect" means a condition that materially affects the value or use of residential property in an adverse manner.

2. "Disclosure form" means a form that complies with the regulations adopted pursuant to NRS 113.120.

3. "Dwelling unit" means any building, structure or portion thereof which is occupied as, or designed or intended for occupancy as, a residence by one person who maintains a household or by two or more persons who maintain a common household.

4. "Residential property" means any land in this state to which is affixed not less than one nor more than four dwelling units.

5. "Seller" means a person who sells or intends to sell any residential property.

(Added to NRS by 1995, 842; A 1999, 1446)

NRS 113.110 Conditions required for "conveyance of property" and to complete service of document. For the purposes of NRS 113.100 to 113.150, inclusive:

1. A "conveyance of property" occurs:

(a) Upon the closure of any escrow opened for the conveyance; or

(b) If an escrow has not been opened for the conveyance, when the purchaser of the property receives the deed of conveyance.

2. Service of a document is complete:

(a) Upon personal delivery of the document to the person being served; or

(b) Three days after the document is mailed, postage prepaid, to the person being served at his last known address.

(Added to NRS by 1995, 844)

NRS 113.120 Regulations prescribing format and contents of form for disclosing condition of property. The Real Estate Division of the Department of Business and Industry shall adopt regulations prescribing the format and contents of a form for disclosing the condition of residential property offered for sale. The regulations must ensure that the form:

1. Provides for an evaluation of the condition of any electrical, heating, cooling, plumbing and sewer systems on the property, and of the condition of any other aspects of the property which affect its use or value, and allows the seller of the property to indicate whether or not each of those systems and other aspects of the property has a defect of which the seller is aware.

2. Provides notice:

(a) Of the provisions of NRS 113.140 and subsection 5 of NRS 113.150.

(b) That the disclosures set forth in the form are made by the seller and not by his agent.

(c) That the seller's agent, and the agent of the purchaser or potential purchaser of the residential property, may reveal the completed form and its contents to any purchaser or potential purchaser of the residential property.

(Added to NRS by 1995, 842)

NRS 113.130 Completion and service of disclosure form before conveyance of property; discovery or worsening of defect after service of form; exceptions; waiver.

1. Except as otherwise provided in subsection 2:

(a) At least 10 days before residential property is conveyed to a purchaser:

(1) The seller shall complete a disclosure form regarding the residential property; and

(2) The seller or the seller's agent shall serve the purchaser or the purchaser's agent with the completed disclosure form.

(b) If, after service of the completed disclosure form but before conveyance of the property to the purchaser, a seller or the seller's agent discovers a new defect in the residential property that was not identified on the completed disclosure form or discovers that a defect identified on the completed disclosure form has become worse than was indicated on the form, the seller or the seller's agent shall inform the purchaser or the purchaser's agent of that fact, in writing, as soon as practicable after the discovery of that fact but in no event later than the conveyance of the property to the purchaser. If the seller does not agree to repair or replace the defect, the purchaser may:

(1) Rescind the agreement to purchase the property; or

(2) Close escrow and accept the property with the defect as revealed by the seller or the seller's agent without further recourse.

2. Subsection 1 does not apply to a sale or intended sale of residential property:

(a) By foreclosure pursuant to chapter 107 of NRS.

(b) Between any co-owners of the property, spouses or persons related within the third degree of consanguinity.

(c) Which is the first sale of a residence that was constructed by a licensed contractor.

(d) By a person who takes temporary possession or control of or title to the property solely to facilitate the sale of the property on behalf of a person who relocates to another county, state or country before title to the property is transferred to a purchaser.

3. A purchaser of residential property may not waive any of the requirements of subsection 1. A seller of residential property may not require a purchaser to waive any of the requirements of subsection 1 as a condition of sale or for any other purpose.

4. If a sale or intended sale of residential property is exempted from the requirements of subsection 1 pursuant to paragraph (a) of subsection 2, the trustee and the beneficiary of the deed of trust shall, not later than at the time of the conveyance of the property to the purchaser of the residential property, or upon the request of the purchaser of the residential property, provide:

(a) Written notice to the purchaser of any defects in the property of which the trustee or beneficiary, respectively, is aware; and

(b) If any defects are repaired or replaced or attempted to be repaired or replaced, the contact information of any asset management company who provided asset management services for the property. The asset management company shall provide a service report to the purchaser upon request.

5. As used in this section:

(a) "Seller" includes, without limitation, a client as defined in NRS 645H.060.

(b) "Service report" has the meaning ascribed to it in NRS 645H.150.

(Added to NRS by 1995, 842; A 1997, 349; 2003, 1339; 2005, 598; 2011, 2832)

_____   _____   _____   _____
Seller(s) Initials   *Buyer(s) Initials*

Nevada Real Estate Division   Page 3 of 4   **Seller Real Property Disclosure Form 547**
Replaces all previous versions   **Revised 04/29/16**

142

NRS 113.135 Certain sellers to provide copies of certain provisions of NRS and give notice of certain soil reports; initial purchaser entitled to rescind sales agreement in certain circumstances; waiver of right to rescind.

1. Upon signing a sales agreement with the initial purchaser of residential property that was not occupied by the purchaser for more than 120 days after substantial completion of the construction of the residential property, the seller shall:

(a) Provide to the initial purchaser a copy of NRS 11.202 to 11.206, inclusive, and 40.600 to 40.695, inclusive;

(b) Notify the initial purchaser of any soil report prepared for the residential property or for the subdivision in which the residential property is located; and

(c) If requested in writing by the initial purchaser not later than 5 days after signing the sales agreement, provide to the purchaser without cost each report described in paragraph (b) not later than 5 days after the seller receives the written request.

2. Not later than 20 days after receipt of all reports pursuant to paragraph (c) of subsection 1, the initial purchaser may rescind the sales agreement.

3. The initial purchaser may waive his right to rescind the sales agreement pursuant to subsection 2. Such a waiver is effective only if it is made in a written document that is signed by the purchaser.

(Added to NRS by 1999, 1446)

NRS 113.140 Disclosure of unknown defect not required; form does not constitute warranty; duty of buyer and prospective buyer to exercise reasonable care.

1. NRS 113.130 does not require a seller to disclose a defect in residential property of which he is not aware.

2. A completed disclosure form does not constitute an express or implied warranty regarding any condition of residential property.

3. Neither this chapter nor chapter 645 of NRS relieves a buyer or prospective buyer of the duty to exercise reasonable care to protect himself.

(Added to NRS by 1995, 843; A 2001, 2896)

NRS 113.150 Remedies for seller's delayed disclosure or nondisclosure of defects in property; waiver.

1. If a seller or the seller's agent fails to serve a completed disclosure form in accordance with the requirements of NRS 113.130, the purchaser may, at any time before the conveyance of the property to the purchaser, rescind the agreement to purchase the property without any penalties.

2. If, before the conveyance of the property to the purchaser, a seller or the seller's agent informs the purchaser or the purchaser's agent, through the disclosure form or another written notice, of a defect in the property of which the cost of repair or replacement was not limited by provisions in the agreement to purchase the property, the purchaser may:

(a) Rescind the agreement to purchase the property at any time before the conveyance of the property to the purchaser; or

(b) Close escrow and accept the property with the defect as revealed by the seller or the seller's agent without further recourse.

3. Rescission of an agreement pursuant to subsection 2 is effective only if made in writing, notarized and served not later than 4 working days after the date on which the purchaser is informed of the defect:

(a) On the holder of any escrow opened for the conveyance; or

(b) If an escrow has not been opened for the conveyance, on the seller or the seller's agent.

4. Except as otherwise provided in subsection 5, if a seller conveys residential property to a purchaser without complying with the requirements of NRS 113.130 or otherwise providing the purchaser or the purchaser's agent with written notice of all defects in the property of which the seller is aware, and there is a defect in the property of which the seller was aware before the property was conveyed to the purchaser and of which the cost of repair or replacement was not limited by provisions in the agreement to purchase the property, the purchaser is entitled to recover from the seller treble the amount necessary to repair or replace the defective part of the property, together with court costs and reasonable attorney's fees. An action to enforce the provisions of this subsection must be commenced not later than 1 year after the purchaser discovers or reasonably should have discovered the defect or 2 years after the conveyance of the property to the purchaser, whichever occurs later.

5. A purchaser may not recover damages from a seller pursuant to subsection 4 on the basis of an error or omission in the disclosure form that was caused by the seller's reliance upon information provided to the seller by:

(a) An officer or employee of this State or any political subdivision of this State in the ordinary course of his or her duties; or

(b) A contractor, engineer, land surveyor, certified inspector as defined in NRS 645D.040 or pesticide applicator, who was authorized to practice that profession in this State at the time the information was provided.

6. A purchaser of residential property may waive any of his or her rights under this section. Any such waiver is effective only if it is made in a written document that is signed by the purchaser and notarized.

(Added to NRS by 1995, 843; A 1997, 350, 1797)

The above information provided on pages one (1) and two (2) of this disclosure form is true and correct to the best of seller's knowledge as of the date set forth on page one (1). **SELLER HAS DUTY TO DISCLOSE TO BUYER AS NEW DEFECTS ARE DISCOVERED AND/OR KNOWN DEFECTS BECOME WORSE** *(See NRS 113.130(1)(b)).*

Seller(s): _____ Date: _____

Seller(s): _____ Date: _____

BUYER MAY WISH TO OBTAIN PROFESSIONAL ADVICE AND INSPECTIONS OF THE PROPERTY TO MORE FULLY DETERMINE THE CONDITION OF THE PROPERTY AND ITS ENVIRONMENTAL STATUS. Buyer(s) has/have read and acknowledge(s) receipt of a copy of this Seller's Real Property Disclosure Form and copy of NRS Chapter 113.100-150, inclusive, attached hereto as pages three (3) and four (4).

Buyer(s): _____ Date: _____

Buyer(s): _____ Date: _____

Nevada Real Estate Division
Replaces all previous versions

Page 4 of 4

Seller Real Property Disclosure Form 547
Revised 04/29/16

143

Nevada Real Estate Division

The Nevada Law and Reference Guide

A legal resource guide for Nevada real estate licensees.

FOURTH EDITION, 2014

FUNDED BY THE REAL ESTATE EDUCATION & RESEARCH FUND
AUTHORIZED BY THE NEVADA REAL ESTATE COMMISSION

NEVADA REAL ESTATE DIVISION, DEPT. OF BUSINESS & INDUSTRY

Nevada Real Estate Division

The Nevada Law and Reference Guide

A legal resource guide for Nevada real estate licensees.

ACKNOWLEDGEMENTS

Funding for this project was provided by the Nevada Real Estate Division, Department of Business & Industry, State of Nevada, through the Nevada Education Research and Recovery Fund.

The Guide was conceived and given its nativity under the auspices of Gail J. Anderson, Real Estate Division Administrator (2002-2007), and the 2005-2006 Nevada Real Estate Commissioners: Benjamin Green, Washoe County; Lee Gurr, Elko County; Curry Jameson, Washoe County; Charlie Mack, Clark County; and Beth Rossum, Clark County. The format, chapter topic suggestions and problem areas were identified with a series of round table discussion groups composed of real estate industry practitioners. Their insight and comments when the project was just beginning were invaluable.

Debra March, Executive Director of The Lied Institute of Real Estate Studies, College of Business of the University of Nevada, Las Vegas, served as administrative project manager. Her extensive background in real estate education and administration/management kept the project moving forward.

Melody L. Luetkehans, JD, researched and wrote the Guide under contract with the Lied Institute. Previously, she was General Counsel for the Nevada Association of Realtors® and manned their Legal Hotline for years. She continues to teach real estate law and is currently with the National Judicial College on the University of Nevada, Reno campus.

Sarah Zita, of Zita Group, Inc., Las Vegas, Nevada, designed and provided the wonderful graphics, photographs, layout, formatting, technical and editorial corrections, and the artwork. The beauty and functionality of the Guide is all her.

Nothing of this scope is possible without extensive review. The written material was reviewed by the late Gail Brown Fox, long-time corporate broker in Clark County; Matt D'Orio, formerly Education/Information Officer with the Real Estate Division; Lee Gurr, previous NV Real Estate Commissioner and broker/owner; Deanna Rymarowicz, Esq., legal counsel for the Greater Las Vegas Association of Realtors®; Ben Scheible, Esq., author and real estate educator; and Robert Aalberts, JD. professor of law at UNLV, who was also a member of the review committee. Current RED Administrator Ann M. McDermott, along with Safia Anwari, Education & Information Officer of the Real Estate Division, reviewed and edited the text to ensure its timeliness. The Real Estate Division would like to acknowledge the contribution of Bruce Alitt, Chief Investigator, in reviewing and suggesting edits

Finally, much thanks goes to the current Commissioners and Real Estate Division Administrator for seeing this project through to its finalization: RED Administrator Ann M. McDermott; Beth Rossum, Commission President, from Clark County; Janice Copple, vice-president, Washoe County; Bert Gurr, secretary, Elko County; Marc Sykes, Washoe County; and Soozi Jones Walker, Clark County.

TABLE OF CONTENTS

I. NEVADA LAW ON REAL ESTATE AGENCY

TABLE OF CONTENTS

1. 2A Corpus Juris Secundum, Agency §4 (c), (1972).

2. NRS 111.450.

3. Seigworth v. State , 91 Nev. 536, 538 (1975).

4. NRS 645.0045.

5. NRS 645.005.

6. NRS 645.0045(2).

"The Real Estate Division specifically rejects the use of the term "dual agency". The position statement may be found at http://www.red.state. nv.us/publications/ PositionStatements/ MULTI%20REP%20 FINAL%20SEP%2007.pdf

Here we examine the nature of real estate agency as identified in Nevada statute, regulation, and as amplified by case law. We review Nevada's laws on real estate licensee agency and its parameters - what it is and isn't, its raison d'être. We look at how real estate agency is created, the legally recognized types of agency in Nevada, the legal sources of the licensee's agency duties, the minimum legal parameters of agency, what activities aren't included in real estate agency and what terminates an agency relationship.

A. REPRESENTING THE CLIENT

1. GENERAL AGENCY LAW

Under general agency law, agency occurs when one person (the agent), with the consent of another person (the principal), undertakes to represent and act on the principal's account with third-persons and usually in business matters. It is voluntary, consensual and as a rule - when dealing with real property - is founded upon an express or implied contract.[1]

Nevada recognizes two types of agency concerning real property: first, there is general agency in which the agent is authorized under a general power-of-attorney to perform all duties for the principal that the principal could perform to convey real property (general agency requires a written power-of-attorney with its special recording requirements);[2] second, there is special agency in which the agent is given limited authority to act for the client within certain restrictions and for specific transactions.[3] Real estate brokerage agreements create a special agency wherein the broker's authority is limited to facilitating a real estate transaction for his or her principal. Unless otherwise noted, all agency referred to in

The Nevada Law and Reference Guide, is concerned with real estate agency in which the broker is the agent of the client.

Nevada's real estate brokerage statutes (NRS 645) define "agency" as the relationship between a principal (client) and an agent (broker) arising out of a brokerage agreement in which the agent agrees to do certain acts on behalf of the principal in dealings with a third party.[4] Real estate related acts are identified in the definition of "brokerage agreement" and include the broker assisting, soliciting or negotiating the sale, purchase option, rental or lease of real property, or the sale, exchange, option or purchase of a business.[5] However, by statute, an agency relationship cannot be established solely from a licensee's negotiations or communications with a client of another broker if the licensee has received written permission from that party's broker.[6]

A brokerage agreement is an employment contract wherein the broker agrees to provide real estate related services for valuable consideration or compensation. It may be either oral or written. The client does not need to be the one paying the

I - 3

broker's compensation. The compensation may be paid to the broker by either the client or another person.[7] Though the brokerage agreement is an employment contract, without some type of alternative agreement, a real estate broker is an independent contractor and not the employee of the client.

Real estate related services include, but are not limited to, any of the following acts: the negotiation of, or the sale, exchange, option, purchase, rent or lease, of any interest in real estate (improved or unimproved); any modular, used manufactured or mobile home (when conveyed with any interest in the underlying real estate); public lands; or in a business. It also covers the listing or soliciting of prospective purchasers, lessees or renters, or the taking of an advance fee.[8]

Once agency is established, all the duties and responsibilities of representation attach to the broker (and through the broker, to the broker-salesperson or salesperson). Those duties are found in statute (NRS), administrative regulation (NAC), and as expanded upon in case law (Nevada Reports).

Nevada does not recognize "transactional" agency, or limited agency representation. Transactional agency is where the broker agrees that he or she is not representing either party but only is hired to facilitate the transaction. Limited agency is a truncated form of agency wherein the broker contractually limits his duties and liabilities with the client by agreeing to perform only certain acts of representation. In Nevada, with one exception, no duty of a licensee as found in NRS 645.252 or NRS 645.254, may be waived.[9] This is true even if a client and broker agree by contract to limit the broker's duties; legally, the broker is always vested with the full duties, responsibilities and liabilities of representation identified in law.
To ensure a client understands the

licensee's basic duties, the licensee is required to provide the client and each unrepresented party with a state mandated form called the "Duties Owed by a Nevada Real Estate Licensee".[10]

a. Single or sole agency – Single agency is the most common form of agency and the one least likely to create liability for a broker. Single agency is where the broker represents only one party in a given transaction. The broker's duty, loyalty and responsibilities are focused on promoting the interests of that client.

b. "Acting for More Than One Party to the Transaction" – Nevada law provides that a broker may represent more than one party in a real estate transaction. "The same person or entity may act as the agent for two parties interested in the same transaction when their interests do not conflict and where loyalty to one does not necessarily constitute breach of duty to the other."[11] When representing more than one party in a transaction, the broker must disclose this representation and obtain the written consent of each party before proceeding.[12]

7. NRS 645.005.

8. NRS 645.030.

9. NRS 645.255. The exception is when a client authorizes in writing the broker to waive the duty to present all offers (NRS 645.254(4).

10. NRS 645.252(3).

11. Young v. Nevada Title Co., 103 Nev. 436, 439 (1987).

12. NRS 645.252(1)(d).

"Transactional agency" – where the broker agrees he or she is not representing either party and is only hired to facilitate the transaction.

13. Keystone Realty v. Glenn Osterhus, 107 Nev. 173, 177 (1991).

14. NRS 645.253.

15. NRS 645.252(1)(e).

There are several types of possible multiple representations. The most typical is where a broker seeks to represent both the buyer and seller. Not as prevalent but more common in sellers markets (where there are more buyers than properties), is when the broker represents two or more buyers in competition with each other for a single property. Theoretically, a broker could also simultaneously represent a seller and multiple competing buyers. Under existing law, regardless of which parties are being represented, seller and buyer or another mixture, each party must be given a Consent to Act form and the opportunity to reject this type of agency relationship.

Even though a licensee acting for more than one party to the transaction is permitted by law, the law does not provide for any modification of a broker's duties when representing multiple clients with adverse interests. The broker (and each licensee under him or her) owes to each client all of the duties provided for in law. The law does acknowledge such representation creates a conflict of interest in the licensee as the clients have interests opposed to one another.

The state mandated disclosure form, called "Consent to Act", outlines for the client the consequences of the licensee's multiple representation and requires the client's written authorization before the licensee may proceed with such representation. The Consent to Act form is designed with the seller/landlord and buyer/tenant relationship in mind but may be reasonably altered to reflect various combinations of conflicts of interests, i.e., buyer versus buyer.

Every licensee must be aware of the appearance of such undisclosed representation. For example, undisclosed representation may inadvertently occur when a licensee representing a seller provides the buyer with client services such that the buyer is under the reasonable expectation that the licensee is working for him.[13] Another scenario is when a seller's agent seeks to concurrently represent a buyer in the sale of the buyer's other properties without disclosing that relationship to the seller. Unless the licensee makes each party fully aware of the licensee's lines of representation, the licensee may be participating in an undisclosed multiple representation.

c. Assigned Agency – To lessen the conflict of interest impact created when a broker represents more than one party in a transaction, the law provides an "Ethical Wall" wherein the broker is allowed to assign a separate agent to each client. Upon this assignment the broker does not need to use the "Consent to Act" disclosure form nor receive the approval of the clients.

Black's Law Dictionary defines an "Ethical Wall" as a legal construct designed to shield (in our case) a broker from the liability of multiple party representation. It prohibits the respective assigned agents from exchanging the confidences of the clients and restricts the transfer and distribution of the clients' personal information and documents. The statute reiterates the licensee's duty of confidentiality to his or her assigned client.[14] To ensure a client's confidences are not inadvertently disclosed, the broker should assure that assigned client's files are kept apart and secured.

d. Change in Licensee's Relationship – A licensee must disclose to each party in a real estate transaction when the licensee's relationship with any party changes.[15] The disclosure must be made as soon as practicable and must be in writing. A new Duties Owed form should be provided to each client. If a client's consent is required (as in when acting for two or more parties to the transaction) consent must be obtained – disclosure alone is insufficient to ensure consent.

I- 5

2. AGENCY DISCLOSURE FORMS

When an agency relationship is established the broker is required to provide the client with a state mandated disclosure form called the "Duties Owed by a Nevada Real Estate Licensee".[16] Should the broker at any point in a transaction be deemed to represent more than one party, the broker must also provide the parties with a "Consent to Act" form and receive their permission before proceeding with the representation. The appropriate agency disclosure form (Duties Owed or Consent to Act if applicable) must be used in all real estate agency relationships regardless of the type of representation, i.e., single, more than one party, and assigned; or the type of real estate transaction, e.g., purchase, property management. The Duties Owed form must also be given when a licensee is a principal in a transaction.[17]

The forms are prepared and distributed by the Real Estate Division and reflect not only the requirements of statute (NRS 645.252(1)) but also of the real estate administrative code (NAC 645.637).[18] Each form must be fully filled-in, signed and kept in the broker's transaction file for five years.[19]

It is important to note that an agency relationship is not created because a party signs either a Duties Owed or Consent to Act form. These forms are strictly disclosure documents. Each form specifically states that it does not constitute a contract for services nor an agreement to pay compensation.[20] Accordingly, it is irrelevant whether a brokerage agreement is oral or written, or whether a licensee is acting on his or her own behalf, a Duties Owed form or Consent to Act form, must be given to and signed by the licensee's client. Additionally, if a party is unrepresented the broker must keep that party's signed form with their client's transaction file.[21]

A licensee who refers a potential client to another licensee does not need to provide the Duties Owed disclosure form if the referring licensee's only activity is the referral.[22] For example, a seller contacts a broker about representing him in the sale of his Fallon ranch. The broker does not regularly deal with ranch or rural properties therefore, he refers the client to a broker who regularly works with this type of property. The first broker is not required to provide the rancher with a Duties Owed form.

a. Duties Owed By A Nevada Real Estate Licensee form – The Duties Owed By A Nevada Real Estate Licensee form (Duties Owed) is divided into three main sections and several subsections. The first section is a box for the identification of the licensee, his or her license number, the client's name, the broker's and brokerage's names, and finally, the name of client who the licensee is representing, e.g., seller, buyer, landlord, or tenant.[23]

The second section is a paraphrase of the statutes outlining the licensee's duties to all parties in the transaction and those duties specific to the licensee's representation of the client. There is a single sentence reference to a licensee's duty of confidentiality under assigned agency and a notice of the activities which require the licensee to provide the client with the Consent to Act form.

The third section is where the client signs acknowledging receipt of a copy of the form. The client, in signing the acknowledgement, also attests that he or she has read and understands the disclosure.

16. NRS 645.252(3).

17. NAC 645.637.

18. NRS 645.193.

19. NAC 645.650.

20. See Real Estate Division forms "Duties Owed by a Nevada Real Estate Licensee" and "Consent to Act".

21. NRS 645.252(3).

22. Real Estate Division Position Statement, Joan Buchanan, Administrator, March 10, 1999.

23. The Duties Owed form may be found at: http://www.red.state.nv.us/Forms/525.pdf

DUTIES OWED BY A NEVADA REAL ESTATE LICENSEE
This form does not constitute a contract for services nor an agreement to pay compensation.

In Nevada, a real estate licensee is required to provide a form setting forth the duties owed by the licensee to:
   a) **Each party for whom the licensee is acting as an agent in the real estate transaction, and**
   b) **Each unrepresented party to the real estate transaction, if any.**

Licensee: The licensee in the real estate transaction is _____

whose license number is _____. The licensee is acting for [client's name(s)] _____

_____ who is/are the ☐Seller/Landlord; ☐Buyer/Tenant.

Broker: The broker is _____, whose

company is _____.

Licensee's Duties Owed to All Parties:
A Nevada real estate licensee shall:
1. Not deal with any party to a real estate transaction in a manner which is deceitful, fraudulent or dishonest.
2. Exercise reasonable skill and care with respect to all parties to the real estate transaction.
3. Disclose to each party to the real estate transaction as soon as practicable:
   a. Any material and relevant facts, data or information which licensee knows, or with reasonable care and diligence the licensee should know, about the property.
   b. Each source from which licensee will receive compensation.
4. Abide by all other duties, responsibilities and obligations required of the licensee in law or regulations.

Licensee's Duties Owed to the Client:
A Nevada real estate licensee shall:
1. Exercise reasonable skill and care to carry out the terms of the brokerage agreement and the licensee's duties in the brokerage agreement;
2. Not disclose, except to the licensee's broker, confidential information relating to a client for 1 year after the revocation or termination of the brokerage agreement, unless licensee is required to do so by court order or the client gives written permission;
3. Seek a sale, purchase, option, rental or lease of real property at the price and terms stated in the brokerage agreement or at a price acceptable to the client;
4. Present all offers made to, or by the client as soon as practicable, unless the client chooses to waive the duty of the licensee to present all offers and signs a waiver of the duty on a form prescribed by the Division;
5. Disclose to the client material facts of which the licensee has knowledge concerning the real estate transaction;
6. Advise the client to obtain advice from an expert relating to matters which are beyond the expertise of the licensee; and
7. Account to the client for all money and property the licensee receives in which the client may have an interest.

Duties Owed By a broker who assigns different licensees affiliated with the brokerage to separate parties.
Each licensee shall not disclose, except to the real estate broker, confidential information relating to client.

Licensee Acting for Both Parties: You understand that the licensee _____ **may or** _____ may not, in the future act
                                                                         (Client Init)   (Client Init)
for two or more parties who have interests adverse to each other. In acting for these parties, the licensee has a conflict of interest. Before a licensee may act for two or more parties, the licensee must give you a "Consent to Act" form to sign.

I/We acknowledge receipt of a copy of this list of licensee duties, and have read and understand this disclosure.					
Seller/Landlord	*Date*	*Time*	*Buyer/Tenant*	*Date*	*Time*
Seller/Landlord	*Date*	*Time*	*Buyer/Tenant*	*Date*	*Time*

b. The Consent to Act form – The Consent to Act form[24] is used when a broker (broker-salesperson or salesperson), is acting for two or more parties to a transaction. The form is divided into approximately seven parts. Parts one and three are informational giving the property address, licensee's name and license number, brokerage, seller's and buyer's names. Part two recites the legal authorization that allows a broker to act for more than one party in a real estate transaction and states the requirement for written client authorization. Part four identifies the licensee's conflict of interest, the duty of confidentiality, and the requirement for each client to have also received a Duties Owed form. Part five lets the client know he or she is not required to consent to this type of representation. Part six is the client's acknowledgment of receipt of the form and a statement that consent is being granted without coercion. Part seven is the client's signatures box.[25]

A substantial number of division disciplinary hearing cases concern agency disclosure form violations. These violations include forms not given to clients, forms not completed correctly, and those lacking required signatures or missing necessary information.[26] The Real Estate Commission, the body charged with hearing the Division's disciplinary cases, has found the incorrect execution of these forms amounts to gross negligence by the licensee, therefore, it is incumbent upon each broker to ensure the Duties Owed and Consent to Act forms are properly completed and signed. Anytime there is a change in the identity of the parties or licensees, a new form must be completed and signed.[27]

3. CREATION OF AGENCY

Historically, an agency relationship could have been created in several ways: by expressed statement, wherein both the client and the broker agreed to the

agency; or by unintentional or implied agency. Unintentional agency is where the licensee did not intend to create or continue with the representation of the client, however; the client reasonably assumed the licensee was representing him or her. Implied agency is where the licensee acts as the agent of the client with the intention of representation and the client tacitly accepts those services even though there is no expressed (oral or written) brokerage agreement.[28]

In 2007, the Nevada legislature defined "agency" for real estate licensees as the relationship between a principal and an agent arising out of a brokerage agreement in which the agent is engaged to do certain acts on behalf of the principal in dealings with a third party.[29] Therefore, to create an agency relationship, there must first be a brokerage agreement.

A brokerage agreement is defined as an oral or written contract between a client and a broker in which the broker agrees to provide real estate related services in exchange for valuable consideration.[30]

This definition of agency seems to preclude the trap of unintentional agency, however; as brokerage agreements may be oral, there is the possibility that a licensee's conduct may lead a party to the reasonable expectation that an oral brokerage agreement exists and therefore, the licensee is that party's agent.

The Nevada Supreme Court found agency when a licensee's representation and advice were sufficient to support a client's conclusion that the licensee impliedly agreed to the agency. In Keystone Realty v. Glenn Osterhuse (1985), the Osterhuses contacted Keystone Realty, who represented a builder/developer, about purchasing a new home lot in the Northwood Estates subdivision. The real estate agent went to the buyers' home, explained certain terms of the purchase

24. Consent to Act form

25. NRS 645.252(1)(d).

26. Real Estate Commission Disciplinary Fine Report 1-95 through 9-30-04.

27. NRS 645.252(1)(e).

28. Keystone Realty v. Glenn Osterhus, 107 Nev. 173, 177 (1991).

29. NRS 645.0045.

30. NRS 645.005.

31. Real Estate Division Position Statement, Joan Buchanan, Administrator, March 10, 1999.

32. NRS 645.635 (2). This statute also seeks to prevent the possible tort "intentional reference with a contractual relationship."

33. NRS 645.0045 (2)

34. See RED form "Authorization to Negotiate Directly with Seller."

agreement and answered the couple's questions. The agent also told them he would ensure that the developer delivered their deed to them as payment was being held outside of escrow on the advice of the agent. Additionally, the purchase agreement was contingent on the sale of the couple's current residence which the agent agreed to sell for them. At no time did the agent inform the Osterhuses he only represented the developer. When the Osterhuses did not receive their deed after they moved into their new home, they made inquiries and discovered title to their home was still in the developer's name and that the developer had declared bankruptcy. The couple filed a law suit against the developer and brokerage for breach of agency and negligence.

The broker argued there was no agency relationship with the Osterhuses as the broker only represented the developer. Without agency, there was no duty to the Osterhuses to ensure they received their title. The court rejected this argument and said,

> "[A]fter reviewing the record, we conclude that the interrelated transactions of the parties, along with the representations and advice given by [the agent], constituted substantial evidence to support the conclusion that the [brokerage] impliedly agreed to act as the [couple's] agent in their purchase of the Northwood Estates lot and home."

Furthermore, the court held the agent negligent in that representation when he failed to ensure proper title was given. The Osterhuses were awarded approximately $58,000.

The assumption of the existence of agency rests with the client's reasonable expectations. To determine whether the client's expectations are reasonable, the court will look at the licensee's statements, representations and actions.

Referral – A licensee who refers a client to another licensee does not create an agency relationship with the person being referred if the licensee's only activity was the referral. However, a referring licensee must still be careful not to create in the clients' minds the perception that the licensee continues to represent them.[31]

Authorization to Negotiate - To forestall implied agency, a licensee is prohibited from negotiating a sale, exchange or lease of real estate with another broker's client unless that licensee has received written authorization from the other broker for such direct communication. [32] By law, such direct communication does not create an agency relationship between the authorized broker and the other broker's client. [33]

To this end, the Real Estate Division has created a form authorizing a buyer's broker to negotiate directly with a seller.[34] The type of communication authorized by the RED form is limited to the delivery, communication, or facilitation of an offer, counteroffer, or proposal; discussion and review of the terms of an offer, counteroffer, or proposal; and the preparation of any responses as directed.

Even with a signed "Authorization" form, if the buyer's broker starts performing agency duties for the seller outside those authorized by statute, the broker may be held liable for creating an "implied agency". When the "Authorization" form is used, the buyer's broker still retains all the agency duties and responsibilities to his or her client, the buyer. This authorization is not a "Consent to Act" form substitute.

I - 9

CONSENT TO ACT
This form does not constitute a contract for services nor an agreement to pay compensation.

DESCRIPTION OF TRANSACTION: The real estate transaction is the ☐ sale and purchase *or* ☐ lease of

Property Address: _____

_____

In Nevada, a real estate licensee may act for more than one party in a real estate transaction; however, before the licensee does so, he or she must obtain the written consent of each party. This form is that consent. Before you consent to having a licensee represent both yourself and the other party, you should read this form and understand it.

Licensee: The licensee in this real estate transaction is _____ ("Licensee") whose

license number is _____ and who is affiliated with _____ ("Brokerage").

Seller/Landlord _____
Print Name

Buyer/Tenant _____
Print Name

CONFLICT OF INTEREST: A licensee in a real estate transaction may legally act for two or more parties who have interests adverse to each other. In acting for these parties, the licensee has a conflict of interest.

DISCLOSURE OF CONFIDENTIAL INFORMATION: Licensee will not disclose any confidential information for one year after the revocation or termination of any brokerage agreement entered into with a party to this transaction, unless Licensee is required to do so by a court of competent jurisdiction or is given written permission to do so by that party. Confidential information includes, but is not limited to, the client's motivation to purchase, trade or sell, which if disclosed, could harm one party's bargaining position or benefit the other.

DUTIES OF LICENSEE: Licensee shall provide you with a "Duties Owed by a Nevada Real Estate Licensee" disclosure form which lists the duties a licensee owes to all parties of a real estate transaction, and those owed to the licensee's client. When representing both parties, the licensee owes the same duties to both seller and buyer. Licensee shall disclose to both Seller and Buyer all known defects in the property, any matter that must be disclosed by law, and any information the licensee believes may be material or might affect Seller's/Landlord's or Buyer's/Tenant's decisions with respect to this transaction.

NO REQUIREMENT TO CONSENT: You are not required to consent to this licensee acting on your behalf. You may
- Reject this consent and obtain your own agent,
- Represent yourself,
- Request that the licensee's broker assign you your own licensee.

CONFIRMATION OF DISCLOSURE AND INFORMATION CONSENT

BY MY SIGNATURE BELOW, I UNDERSTAND AND CONSENT: I am giving my consent to have the above identified licensee act for both the other party and me. By signing below, I acknowledge that I understand the ramifications of this consent, and that I acknowledge that I am giving this consent without coercion.

I/We acknowledge receipt of a copy of this list of licensee duties, and have read and understand this disclosure.					
Seller/Landlord	*Date*	*Time*	*Buyer/Tenant*	*Date*	*Time*
Seller/Landlord	*Date*	*Time*	*Buyer/Tenant*	*Date*	*Time*

Approved Nevada Real Estate Division
Replaces all previous editions

Page 1 of 1

524
Revised 05/01/05

NEVADA LAW ON REAL ESTATE AGENCY I - 10

158

STATE OF NEVADA
DEPARTMENT OF BUSINESS AND INDUSTRY
REAL ESTATE DIVISION
788 Fairview Drive, Suite 200 * **Carson City**, NV 89701-5453 * (775) 687-4280
2501 East Sahara Avenue, Suite 102 * **Las Vegas**, NV 89104-4137 * (702) 486-4033
Email: realest@red.state.nv.us   http://www.red.state.nv.us

AUTHORIZATION TO NEGOTIATE DIRECTLY WITH SELLER

Nevada law permits a real estate licensee to negotiate a sale or lease directly with the seller or lessor with written permission from the listing broker. This form grants that permission with respect to the below-named Seller(s) and the listed property.

- Seller agrees, and the Seller's broker authorizes, that a Buyer's agent or broker may present offers (including subsequent counteroffers) and negotiate directly with the Seller.

- "Negotiate" means (a) delivering or communicating an offer, counteroffer, or proposal; (b) discussing or reviewing the terms of any offer, counteroffer, or proposal; and/or (c) facilitating communication regarding an offer, counteroffer, or proposal and preparing any response as directed.

- Seller understands and agrees that, after accepting an offer, additional contact from the Buyer's agent may be required to obtain disclosures and other documents related to the transaction.

- Seller acknowledges and agrees that Buyer's agent does not represent the Seller, and negotiations pursuant to this authorization do not create or imply an agency relationship between the Buyer's agent and the Seller. Seller understands that he/she should seek advice from Seller's broker and/or financial advisers or legal counsel.

- Seller acknowledges that Seller's broker will provide a copy of this authorization to the Buyer's agent or broker upon request, prior to presenting an offer.

Seller's Name(s): _____

Seller's Signature(s): _____ _____ / ____ ____
                                                                                              Date   Time

Property Address: _____ -

City: _____ Zip: _____ Contract Listing Date: _____

Company Name: _____

Seller's Agent Name: _____ Signature: _____
                                                                                       ____ / ____ ____
                                                                                       Date   Time

Seller's Broker Name: _____ Signature: _____
                                                                                        ____ / ____ ____
                                                                                        Date   Time

06/26/2007   637

I-11

B. DUTIES — SOURCES

A real estate licensee when performing real estate related activities is subject to certain duties and legal responsibilities to the client, broker, peers, the public, and the Real Estate Division. These duties are found in statute, regulation, and expounded upon in case law.

The main sources of a licensee's duties are found in both Nevada and federal law, i.e., the Nevada Revised Statutes (NRS) and the United States Code (U.S.C.).[35] Duties may also be found in state or federal administrative regulation - Nevada Administrative Code (NAC) and the Code of Federal Regulations (C.F.R.). Nevada regulations (NAC) have the force and effect of law.[36]

Traditionally, real estate agency law originated with the common law. The common law is that body of law derived from judicial decisions rather than from statutes or constitutions.[37] Most duties emanated from the common law and though, by statute, the common law is abrogated where a duty is statutorily defined the common law may still be used today to illuminate how the statutes should be interpreted and what behavior to avoid.

The replacement of common law duties by statute is limited to those duties identified in NRS 645.252 to 645.254.[38] However, the statutes alone may not give a licensee specific direction as to what behavior a duty requires or what behavior must be avoided. For this the licensee must look to case law. For example, NRS 645.252(1)

(a) requires the licensee to disclose any material fact relating to the property which he knows, or which by the exercise of reasonable care and diligence, should have known. The question remains what constitutes a material fact. We find in case law that "A fact is material… if it is one which the agent should realize would be likely to affect the judgment of the principal in giving his consent to the agent to enter into the particular transaction on the specified terms."[39]

A broker may also have duties to the client which were agreed to by contract. Some contracts extend the authority of the licensee to act for the client beyond the traditional limits of special agency. For example, a property manager is given a greater range of authority to act for the landlord than the usual authority afforded to a listing broker.[40] This extension of authority for a property manager is found in contract as authorized by statute. A breach of a contractual duty can create liability and either party (broker or client) may file a civil law suit to obtain a remedy.

A licensee's duties are divided into two types; affirmative prescriptions - "you shall", and prohibitions - "you shall not". An example of an affirmative duty would be NAC 645.605(6) that states a licensee has an "obligation to deal fairly with all parties to a real estate transaction", while a prohibition would be NRS 645.3205, "[a] licensee shall not deal with any party to a real estate transaction in a manner which is deceitful, fraudulent or dishonest."

35. For example, the federal law of RESPA, the Real Estate Settlement Procedures Act, 12 U.S.C. 2601. "U.S.C." stands for the United States Code.

36. NRS 233B.040(1).

37. Black's Law Dictionary, 7th ed. (1999).

38. NRS 645.251.

39. Holland Rlty. v. Nev. Real Est. Comm'n, 84 Nev. 91, 98 (1968), quoting the Restatement of Agency § 390.

40. NRS 645.6056.

41. Fleshman v.
Hendricks,
93 Nev. 103 (1977).

Breach of NRS 645.3205 creates liability, while NAC 645.605(6) is used by the Commission to determine if a licensee is guilty of a breach.

The law recognizes three types of behavior that can create liability - not doing what one is required to do, doing what one is not supposed to do, and doing something one is supposed to do but doing it in a wrong (negligent) way. The legal terms are nonfeasance, malfeasance, and misfeasance.

Nonfeasance occurs when a licensee is supposed to act and does not. For example, NRS 645.252(1)(e) requires a licensee to disclose to each party to the real estate transaction when there is any change in his relationship to a party in that transaction. If a licensee is removed from the transaction by the broker, the parties are required to be informed that the licensee is no longer representing the client. A broker would be guilty of nonfeasance if he or she failed to inform the parties.

Malfeasance is a wrongful or unlawful act. For example, NRS 645.254(4) requires a licensee to present all offers to the client as soon as practicable. If a licensee intentionally withholds from the client another broker's offer, that is malfeasance.

Obviously, it is not malfeasance if a client has signed an appropriate waiver under NRS 645.254(4).

Misfeasance is where a licensee performs a lawful act but in an unlawful or negligent manner. In Fleshman v. M. Hendricks (1977) broker Hendricks took a listing from Fleshman.[41] The listing stated the property was subject to a non-transferable lease. The broker obtained a buyer who was ready and willing to purchase the property but who would not take it with the lease. When the transaction failed because the seller refused to break the lease (he would have been sued by the tenant), and the buyer refused to purchase with the lease in place, the broker sued the seller for his commission. The court found that in order for the broker to collect his commission he would have had to produce a ready, willing and able buyer. This buyer would not purchase because of the lease. The court stated it was the broker's misfeasance in not ensuring the buyer would purchase with the lease in place that caused the transaction to fall apart therefore, the broker should not "be permitted to recover by virtue of his own misfeasance."

I - 13

42. NRS 645.259(1).

43. Prigge v. South Seventh Realty, 97 Nev. 640 (1981). The treatise was 2 Restatement (Second), Agency §348, Comment b, at 113 (1958).

Just as there are affirmative duties and prohibitions, the law specifically restricts a licensee's liability in certain areas.

C. THINGS FOR WHICH A LICENSEE IS NOT LIABLE

1. CLIENT'S MISSTATEMENT

A licensee may not be held liable for the misrepresentations made by his client unless the licensee knew of the misrepresentation and failed to inform the person to whom the misrepresentation was made.[42] In Prigge v. South Seventh Realty (1981), a purchaser sued both the seller and the listing broker for misrepresentation as to how the property was constructed. The purchaser declared that both the seller and the broker misrepresented the property as being a frame and stucco house when in fact it was not. The broker argued that he had taken the word of the seller and should not be held liable for the seller's misrepresentations. The court relying on established agency principles found for the broker and refused to find him liable. The court quoted a learned treatise in finding

> [A]n agent who makes untrue statements based upon the information given to him by the principal is not liable because of the fact that the principal knew the information to be untrue. An agent can properly rely upon statements of the principal to the same extent as upon statements from any other reputable source.[43]

This protection has its limitations. The court in the same case said it was making its findings on the limited arguments presented in the appeal. It went on to state that the buyer failed to argue that the broker "knew or should have known the true facts through the exercise of reasonable care". If the buyer had argued this level of diligence, the outcome of the case could have been different.

The "knew or should have known" criteria is found as an affirmative prescription in NRS 645.252(1) which states a licensee shall disclose any material and relevant facts, data or

44. See SB 319, Nevada's 73rd Legislative Session (2005).

45. NRS 645.259(2).

46. NRS 113.130 and NRS 113.135.

47. NRS 645.257(3).

48. Prigge v. South Seventh Realty, 97 Nev. 640, 641 (1981).

49. NRS 645.252(4)(a).

50. NRS 645D.060.

information which he knows, or which by the exercise of reasonable care and diligence he should have known, relating to the property. In Prigge the question could have been whether the broker "should have known" the house was not a frame and stucco building. This level of diligence – should have known - is so well established in law that it has withstood legislative attempts to remove it.[44]

2. ITEMS OF PUBLIC RECORD

A licensee cannot be held liable for a seller's failure to disclose information that is of public record and which is readily available to the client.[45] Under current Nevada law, a seller of a residential property is required to complete a state mandated form called the Seller's Real Property Disclosure.[46] Answers to many of the questions asked on the form would only be known by the seller who must disclose what he or she knows. Some of those items may be of public record thereby, theoretically, available to anyone. Should the seller not disclose a material fact that is of public record, this statute provides that the licensee cannot be charged with non-disclosure if the licensee reasonably had no knowledge of the item and the public record was readily available to the client. The licensee is not required to search the public records to ensure the seller told the truth.

The caveat is that the licensee must reasonably not know of the client's misstatement or concealed fact. If a material fact, data or information concerning the property is readily discernable to the licensee or, it is a fact, data or information that a reasonably prudent licensee would have knowledge of, the licensee will be held liable for the non-disclosure even if that item is of public record.[47] The Nevada Supreme Court in Prigge found that parallel courts in other jurisdictions, "have refused, in similar circumstances, to hold an agent for a disclosed seller responsible for an independent search for concealed facts, in the absence of any information which would

have put the agent on notice". (emphasis added)[48]

3. PROPERTY INSPECTIONS

Unless otherwise agreed to in writing, a licensee owes no duty to any party to the real estate transaction to independently verify the accuracy of a statement made by an inspector certified under NRS 645D, or by any other appropriate licensed or certified expert.[49]

NRS 645D is the set of statutes that require the certification of inspectors generally known as "home inspectors", who perform the physical examination of the mechanical, electrical or plumbing systems of a structure.[50] Other experts may include, but are not limited to, licensed contractors, pest inspectors, roofers, electricians, plumbers, appraisers, and any of the other licensed or certified building-trade professionals.

There is a caveat to this release from liability; it is that the professional is certified or licensed. A real estate licensee will not be released from liability if the "professional" upon whose word or inspection report the licensee is relying, is unlicensed or uncertified. For example, a licensee cannot escape liability by relying on the proclamation of a local handyman that the house's wiring is in good order. It is also incumbent upon the licensee, if the licensee has a reasonable doubt as to the

I - 15

accuracy of a material fact or an inspection report, to tell the client of that doubt and urge the client to verify the inspection. In Ewing v. Bissell (1989), Jaeger, a real estate licensee acting as a dual agent, sold the Ewing's a parcel of land in Las Vegas which reportedly contained 1.34 acres.[51] The plat map identified the parcel as having 1.34 acres and the purchase agreement stated there were approximately 1.34 acres. Jaeger testified he "inspected the property and thought there might be a question as to the total acreage of the lot; however, he could not determine the actual size of the lot by viewing it." Also, he "knew that a better legal description of the property was needed." Jaeger told the sellers, but not the buyers, they could get a survey of the property. Additionally, the buyer had informed Jaeger acreage was important to him as he wanted to place two homes on the property and the zoning law required .50 acres per home. Acreage was therefore a material fact for the buyers.

After the close of escrow, the Clark County Assessor informed the buyers they had received only .83 acres. The buyers sued the sellers, brokerage and agent for the difference between what they received and what they thought they were purchasing. The court found for the buyers allowing them an abatement of the purchase price by reducing the price by the percentage of acreage the buyers did not receive. The court reviewed Jaeger's testimony as to his concern about the size of the lot and held him liable. It said Jaeger was the individual in the best position to ensure the size of the lot was ascertained before escrow closed and Jaeger was under the duty to disclose material facts that may affect the buyer's decision to purchase.

At the same time, a licensee is not required to re-inspect or personally verify the accuracy of a valid inspection. In the Ewing case above, if a survey had been done, Jaeger would not have had to verify the accuracy of the surveyor's work.[52]

Additionally, the licensee is not required to become a property inspector by conducting the investigation of the condition of the property which is the subject of the real estate transaction.[53] However, this clause should not be used by the licensee in an attempt to remove from the licensee his or her responsibility to disclose "material and relevant facts, data or information which the licensee knows, or by the exercise of reasonable care and diligence… should have known relating to the property." (emphasis added).[54] The licensee is always charged with reasonable care and diligence. It is not reasonable that a licensee ignore patent or observable problems or questions about the property's condition because he or she "owes no duty to investigate." The level of investigation stated here is the level expected of a professional in a particular field such as a licensed property inspector. The licensee owes no duty to reach that level of investigation.

51. Ewing v. Bissell, 105 Nev. 488 (1989).

52. NRS 645.252(4).

53. NRS 645.252(4)(c).

54. NRS 645.252(1).

55. NRS 645.252(4)(b).

56. NRS 645.254(3)(c).

57. Charles v. Lemons & Assoc. et al., 104 Nev. 388 (1988).

4. FINANCIAL AUDIT OF A PARTY

A licensee owes no duty to conduct an independent investigation of the financial condition of a party to the real estate transaction.[55] Nevertheless, a licensee is still responsible for disclosing to his or her client all material facts of which the licensee has knowledge concerning the transaction.[56] For example, if a licensee representing a buyer has knowledge of the seller being in bankruptcy, it is incumbent upon the licensee to disclose that information to the client. However, the licensee has no duty to personally examine the financial condition of a party.

Nor does the licensee have a duty to review a principal's credit history. This may specifically come into play if the client participates in alternative forms of financing such as the seller carrying back some of the purchase price. A seller "carries back" when he or she acts as a lender to the purchaser by "carrying" some of the purchase price in the form of a promissory note which is usually secured by a deed of trust on the property.

The caveat on this limitation of liability is that the licensee can waive this protection by his or her statements or actions. If a licensee presumes to investigate a principal's financial condition, gives specific credit or financial advice or guidance, reviews a party's credit report, or designs an alternative financing plan for the parties, the licensee may have waived any protection this statute could provide.

In Charles v. Lemons & Associates, (1988) the sellers, Mr. & Mrs. Charles, sued their brokerage and agent, Century Realty and Larry Geisendorf, for misrepresentation and failure to disclose material information.[57] Geisendorf negotiated the sale of the Charles' home with some buyers wherein the buyers would assume the existing first mortgage, obtain a second in the buyers' names, and have the sellers carry back a third deed of trust. The Charles claimed Geisendorf told them the buyers were financially capable of purchasing the property and that they were qualified to make payments on the loans. What Geisendorf failed to tell his clients was that the buyers had a combined income of only $2,400 per month, that they expected to use the income from a speculative gold investment to meet their financial obligations, and that the buyer's second mortgage had an APR of 30.85%.

When the buyers did not make any payments, the Charles' sued their agent and brokerage. They stated they would not have made the deal with the buyers if it hadn't been for the statements by Geisendorf concerning the buyers' financial soundness. That, coupled with their agent's failure to disclose material facts about the transaction, i.e., the buyers' tenuous loan arrangements, breached the agent's fiduciary duty to the sellers and caused the sellers loss.

I - 17

5. PROVIDING OTHER "PROFESSIONAL" SERVICES

A licensee is not required to perform services or give advice if the service or advice requires expertise outside the realm of real estate related services or for which a separate certification or license is required.[58] Again, this protection may be waived should the licensee undertake to provide such services or advice.

A licensee who performs unauthorized services may be held liable not only to the client, but to the various licensing entities and to any third-party who acts on the licensee's representations and is damaged. In Epperson v. Roloff. Epperson, a buyer, sued the Roloffs who were the sellers, and Alexander, the sellers' agent, for fraud and breach of contract. The sellers told their agent the property had "a solar storage area for auxiliary heating". Alexander, without ensuring a solar heating system existed, told the buyers and their agent that "solar really saves on your gas bill" and proceeded to make other statements of fact about the system. Needless to say, there was no solar heating system. When the buyers sued, the court stated the agent could be held liable to the third-party buyers if they justifiably relied on the agent's statements or advice.[59]

Giving legal advice or determining the market value of a property are services a licensee is most commonly asked to provide.[60] Because these activities are so intricately woven into the fabric of a real estate transaction the licensee can easily slip into giving answers and thus providing unauthorized services. If a licensee does so, he or she not only violates NRS 645, but also the statutes regulating those professions.

Other services a licensee may be asked to provide include but are not limited to, home inspection,[61] tax and income advice (accountant),[62] and property management.[63] The fact that these activities, or some semblance of them, are performed daily by licensees does not in and of itself transform the activities from being unauthorized or illegal unless the licensee is duly certified or licensed in that profession. A licensee must be especially conscientious when asked to do any of the above activities and always refer the client to the appropriate professional.[64]

To that end, a licensee must be aware of the pitfall of relying on a client's request or permission to perform unauthorized activities. No client can authorize a licensee to perform services for which a certification or license is required and a licensee cannot escape liability just because the client requested such service or advice. The Nevada Supreme Court has stated "that one may not legitimize his otherwise unlawful practice of the law by contractually obligating himself to achieve legal effectiveness."[65] Thus, as with many areas of real estate agency law, a client's instruction does not make an illegal act legal or place it within the scope of the licensee's authority. Should a licensee be requested to perform services beyond the licensee's expertise or authorization, the licensee has an affirmative duty to advise the client the matter is beyond his or her expertise and suggest the advice or service be obtained from an appropriate certified or licensed professional. Otherwise, a licensee will be subject to Commission discipline if found guilty of attempting to provide specialized professional services or advice that are outside the licensee's licensed authority.[66]

58. NRS 645.254(3)(d).

59. Epperson v. Roloff, 102 Nev. 206 (1986).

60. NRS 7.285 (1) prohibits the unauthorized practice of law and NRS 645C.260 requires the licensure of anyone doing appraisals.

61. NRS 645D.900.

62. NRS 628.540.

63. NRS 645.6054.

64. NRS 645.254 (3)(d).

65. Pioneer Title Insurance & Trust Co., v. State Bar of Nevada, 74 Nev. 186, 192 (1958).

66. NRS 645.254 (3)(d) and see NAC 645.605 (3).

67. NRS 645.254(2).

68. NRS 645.320(2).

D. TERMINATION OF AGENCY

Nevada has no specific statute that provides which event or action terminates agency. Agency can end in various ways, such as:

- when the object of the agency is fulfilled, or

- the agency agreement terminates by contract date, or

- the broker and client mutually agree to terminate the agency, or

- the agency is abandoned, or

- the agency is terminated due to a party's breach, or

- it ends because of the death of either the broker or the client.

Here we must draw a distinction between the end of the agency and the termination of a party's rights under the brokerage agreement. An agency relationship may end but each party may continue to have certain rights stemming from that relationship. Some of those rights, such as the licensee's duty of confidentiality, are statutorily identified as extending past the revocation or termination of the brokerage agreement - in the case of confidentiality it is one year.[67] Other rights include the broker's right to compensation. The broker may have a right to collect compensation even if the agency has ended and the broker is no longer providing real estate related services to the client.

1. END OF TRANSACTION OR CONTRACT DATE

Most special agency relationships, such as real estate agency, terminate when the object of the agency ends. In real estate, this is usually when there has been a successful transaction and the object for which the agency was created, the sale or lease of real property, has been fulfilled.

Agency may also end when the brokerage agreement has an end or termination date and that date comes and goes without the broker's efforts procuring a successful transaction. Each exclusive representation brokerage agreement is required to have in writing a specified and complete termination date.[68] That date is generally read as ending the agency. A licensee should be aware that the licensee's statements or actions may extend the agency past the termination date and create an unintentional agency.

2. MUTUAL AGREEMENT

Unless there is an agreement to the contrary, a brokerage agreement may be terminated by either party.[69] Depending on the circumstances, this end of agency may be conditional or unconditional. An unconditional release is when both the broker and the client mutually agree to end the agency. At this point the broker and client walk away from their agency relationship without any obligation to the other. A conditional release is when the broker agrees to stop representing the client but holds the client to the client's obligations, such as the payment of compensation.

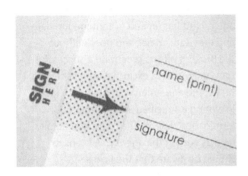

3. ABANDONMENT OR INVOLUNTARY TERMINATION – CLIENT OR BROKER

Another, more difficult type of termination is when the agency is abandoned or involuntarily terminated (being fired) by either the client or the broker.

Abandonment occurs when one party ceases to continue with the relationship. It may happen suddenly or through lack of contact over a period of time. There is no set time frame in which lack of communication between the broker and client creates abandonment. The courts look at whether a reasonable period of time has elapsed. What makes a "reasonable" period of time is fact specific. In one case, Reese v. Utter (1976), the broker, Utter, had an exclusive listing with Reese. During the listing period Utter submitted an offer which Reese rejected. After the rejection Utter abandoned all efforts at negotiating the sale of the property. A year after the listing expired, Reese sold the property to the original offeror on substantially different terms and without the assistance or participation of Utter. Utter then sued Reese for his commission. The court found Utter was not entitled to a commission as he had abandoned his efforts to sell the property and there was no hint of fraud or bad faith on the part of the seller.[70]

A client may abandon a broker. In Bartsas Realty v. Leverton (1966), Mary Bartsas, a broker, responded to an open listing agreement from an institutional seller, First National Bank of Nevada, to find a buyer for an estate of which First National was the executor. Mrs. Bartsas submitted an offer from Davidson, president of a construction company. Without communicating with Bartsas, Davidson then contacted broker Leverton and resubmitted a similar offer through him. When First National told Leverton of the first offer (which had not yet been

69. Kaldi v. Farmers Ins. Exch., 117 Nev. 273, 279 (2001).

70. Reese v. Utter, 92 Nev. 377, 380 (1976).

71. Bartsas Realty v. Leverton, 82 Nev. 6, 7 (1966).

72. Kaldi v. Farmers Ins. Exch., 117 Nev. 273, 279 (2001).

73. NRS 645.252(1)(e).

74. NRS 645.633(1)(b), and NAC 645.605(6).

75. Wayman v. Torreyson, 4 Nev. 124, 135 (1868).

76. NRS 148.420 and NRS 148.330.

77. NAC 645.350(2).

accepted or rejected), Leverton replied "Well, he (Davidson) has changed brokers and he has come to me now." (Italics added.)[71] Mrs. Bartsas was then told by First National of the second offer. She attempted to speak with Davidson who never again communicated with her. She attempted to communicate with Leverton without satisfaction. Leverton continued the negotiations with First National and eventually the sale was consummated. Bartsas sued Leverton and First National. The court held for Bartsas finding that a client cannot in bad faith ignore or abandon the broker or otherwise intervene so as to deprive a broker of his or her commission. The broker must be given an opportunity to consummate the sale if the broker has not abandoned the negotiations.

A client or broker can "fire" the other at any time. The Nevada Supreme Court stated "[a]bsent a contractual provision to the contrary, an independent contractor/principal agency relationship is terminable at any time at the will of the principal or the agent." [72]

Once fired, a broker is required to stop representing the client and inform the other parties in the transaction of the change in his or her agency status.[73] A client can refuse to be represented by, or work with, a broker-salesman or salesman; however, the brokerage agreement continues in force as the agency is with the broker not the salesperson. At this juncture, the broker may release the client (conditionally or unconditionally), or the parties may agree to have another licensee under the broker continue with the representation. The fact that a client does not want to continue being represented by a certain licensee does not automatically release the client from an obligation to pay compensation under the brokerage agreement.

It is important to remember that certain duties of the licensee to the client remain in full force and effect even if active agency has ended. For example, the licensee may not divulge the client's confidences for one year, nor may the licensee take any action in violation of the provisions of NRS 645 which may harm the ex-client.[74]

4. DEATH – CLIENT OR BROKER

It is old law in Nevada that a client's death terminates the agency.[75] Nevertheless, the broker may still have rights under the original brokerage agreement for the collection of compensation.[76]

Upon the death of a licensee (broker, broker-salesperson, or salesperson) his or her real estate license automatically expires.[77] Without a valid real estate license, there can be no legal representation. Since the brokerage agreement is with the broker, if a broker-salesperson or salesperson dies, the brokerage agreement continues in place. It is then between the broker and client to determine if the brokerage agreement should continue with the services of a different broker-salesperson or salesperson or whether the brokerage agreement will be canceled. If the broker dies, the broker's agency representation as evidenced by the brokerage agreement ends. In either case, whether the death is of the broker or his or her broker-salesman or salesman, the client continues to be responsible for paying any compensation earned by the broker before the licensee's death.

I - 21

E. REVIEW

The basis of all real estate brokerage representation is founded upon agency law. This law encompasses the duties and responsibilities of the broker (and by extension all licensees under him or her). In Nevada, the broker's duties and responsibilities are codified – turned into statute and made a part of the NRS or NAC. Case law explains by example how those statutory duties (and their common law antecedents) are applied by the courts. Most agency occurs with the representation by a broker of one party to a real estate transaction. Nevertheless, Nevada law allows the broker to represent multiple parties with conflicting interests when such representation is disclosed to, and approved of, by the parties. To that end, Nevada requires each licensee to provide a written agency disclosure form called the Duties Owed by a Nevada Real Estate Licensee, and if there is multiple representation, the licensee is required to have the clients complete the Consent to Act form. The law limits the licensee's liability in certain situations with caveats and exceptions to such liability waiver. Finally, the broker's agency relationship may be terminated in various ways from fulfilling the terms of the brokerage contract to the death of the client or broker.

II. NEVADA LAW ON FIDUCIARY DUTIES

TABLE OF CONTENTS

1. NRS 1.030.

2. NRS 645.251.

Federal statutes are found in the United States Code (U.S.C.). Federal regulations are in the Code of Federal Regulations (C.F.R.).

Common, or case law, is law identified through judicial decisions in lawsuit cases.

The laws and regulations that govern the licensee and the real estate transaction come from various sources. The main three sources are statute, regulation, and common law. Besides state law, the licensee is governed by applicable federal statutes and regulations. The focus here is on state law and regulation as they are modified by applicable case law.

A. EVOLUTION OF THE COMMON LAW TO STATUTORY DUTIES

The common law has its origins in previous judicial decisions. The United States derives its common law from England. When deciding a case, a judge looks at how similar cases were previously decided. This helps the judge and the legal system to maintain consistency.

Over the years a body of law was compiled from these cases addressing common topics such as contracts, agency, and real property. Nevada has adopted this English common law. [1] It covers any legal issue not addressed by statute or regulation. Statutes or regulations control unless otherwise stated. In 1995, many of the licensee's common law duties were put into statute and for

these duties (NRS 645.252, 645.253, and NRS 645.254) the common law was expressly rejected. [2] Even so, judicial decisions and traditional common law terms direct how statutes or regulations are interpreted.

Common Law Terms: The rules of agency evolved from the common law. Agency law defines the duties and responsibilities a real estate licensee has to the client. However, the legislators, when writing the statutes, often used traditional common law terms but did not define them. Without an understanding of what those common law terms mean, the licensee will not know what must be done or avoided. For example, a licensee must have absolute fidelity to the client's interest. (NAC 645.605(6)) What is

II - 3

absolute fidelity? The licensee must look at case law to understand the parameters of absolute fidelity.

Common Law Agency: Under common law, a broker's main duty is to ensure the client's business and interests are carried out to the client's best advantage.[3] This is the broker's fiduciary duty. It includes:

1. Absolute fidelity to the client's interests;

2. Honesty;

3. The broker's use of reasonable skill and care in all aspects of the transaction, and

4. Full disclosure of all issues and facts concerning the property or the transaction.[4]

3. Lemon v. Landers, 81 Nev. 329, 332 , 462 P.2d 648 (1965).

4. Lowe v. State Dep't of Commerce, 89 Nev. 488, 494, 515 P. 2d 388 (1973), see also Jory v. Bennight, 91 Nev. 763, 542 P.2d 1400, 1404, (1975).

NEVADA LAW ON FIDUCIARY DUTIES TO THE CLIENT II - 4

5. NAC 645.605 (6).

6. Lemon v. Landers, 81 Nev. 329, 332, 462 P.2d 648 (1965).

7 & 8. Holland Realty v. NV Real Estate Comm., 84 Nev. 91, 98, 436 P.2d 422 (1968).

9. NRS 645.252 (1)(b) & (c); NRS 645.633 (1) (g); NAC 645.605 (4); NAC 645.610 (1)(b)(1-2); NAC 645.637 and NAC 645.640.

10. NRS 645.280.

B. CLIENT BEFORE SELF– ABSOLUTE FIDELITY

A licensee has the duty of absolute fidelity to the client's interests.[5] Absolute fidelity means a licensee must put the client's interests ahead of the licensee's interest. A licensee "will not be permitted to pervert his authority to his own personal gain in severe hostility to the interest of his principal."[6]

For example, absolute fidelity is breached when a licensee withholds an offer from the client in order to purchase the property himself. In Holland Realty v. Nevada Real Estate Commission (1968)[7] Grant Holland, a Las Vegas broker, sued the Real Estate Division when it revoked his license. The Real Estate Commission had found him guilty of violating NRS 645 for misrepresentation, making false promises to induce performance, and receiving a secret and undisclosed profit.

Holland had double escrowed a property without disclosure to either party and kept the profit. In that transaction, he misrepresented who was taking title, his agency status, and who were the real parties. He then sold the property a third time as an undisclosed buyer's agent while acting as the seller's agent under a net listing agreement. He did not disclose to the seller the property's true sale price. Again, he kept the difference.

After the Commission revoked his license, Holland sued the Division. The court upheld the Division's discipline and found Holland's behavior breached his basic fiduciary duty of absolute fidelity to his clients. The court stated:

[a] broker when pursuing his own interest cannot ignore those of his principal and will not be permitted to enjoy the fruits of an advantage taken of a fiduciary relationship, whose dominant characteristic is the confidence reposed by one in another.'[8]

There are two prongs to the duty of absolute fidelity. First, the duty to disclose the licensee's interest and, secondly, the prohibition against taking advantage of any situation, even if disclosed, that would harm the client's interests.

1. DISCLOSURE OF LICENSEE'S INTEREST

A licensee must disclose in writing to the parties whenever the licensee has a personal interest in either the transaction or the property. Such disclosure ensures everyone is aware of the licensee's potential conflicting loyalties.[9]

The licensee should be aware that some laws prohibit certain acts even if the licensee's interest is disclosed. As an example, a salesperson may not receive compensation from anyone other than his or her broker: taking such payment is illegal whether or not it is disclosed.[10]

a. Interest in the Transaction – Any time the licensee has an interest in the transaction, that interest must be disclosed in writing. An "interest in the transaction" occurs when:

II - 5

1. The licensee receives, or expects to receive, compensation from more than one party;[11]

2. Is a party in the transaction, or

3. Has a personal relationship with one of the principals.

Compensation: The licensee is under an affirmative duty to disclose to each party to the real estate transaction each "source" from which the licensee will receive compensation.[12] The statute does not require the licensee to disclose the amount of the compensation, only its source - the identity of the person or company giving the compensation.[13]

Compensation includes referral fees and other payment such as fees received from vendors to be on a broker's list of service providers. Even though the broker may give a service provider list to a client without charge, the broker must disclose if a vendor paid to be on that list.[14]

Compensation includes money the broker may accept, give or charge as a rebate or direct profit on expenditures made for the client.[15] For example, a buyer asked the broker to have a new air conditioning unit installed. The buyer paid for the unit in escrow. The air conditioning manufacturer offered a $200 rebate. The broker, when he purchased the unit, applied for and kept the rebate without disclosing it to his buyer. This is a violation of the broker's absolute fidelity to the client.

Party to the Transaction: When a licensee is acting as a principal, it is a material fact and must be disclosed.[16] This ensures all parties to the transaction are fully aware of where the licensee's loyalties may lie. Moreover, the licensee may not acquire (purchase), lease or dispose of (sell), any time-share or real property without revealing the licensee's licensed status.[17]

Relationship with a Principal: The licensee must disclose whenever he or she has a personal relationship with a principal to the transaction.[18] A licensee (including permitted property managers) must disclose the licensee's affiliation with, or financial interest in, any person or entity that furnishes maintenance or other services related to the property.[19]

RESPA: RESPA (Real Estate Settlement Procedures Act) prohibits referrals from one business to another business when owned by the same company unless there is full disclosure. These are affiliated business arrangements.[20] If a licensee has an ownership interest in a business and refers clients to that business, the licensee must disclose that ownership interest.

b. Interest in the Property – A licensee, whether acting as an agent or a principal, has an "interest in the property" whenever the licensee has, or anticipates, an ownership interest.[21] Failure to disclose the licensee's interest is an element in the Real Estate Commission's determination of whether the licensee was deceitful or dishonest.[22]

Any anticipated interest must be disclosed even if it is only a pass-through interest. For example, a licensee must disclose when the licensee takes title, however briefly, during a "double escrow."[23] Engaging in an undisclosed double escrow transaction is a breach of the licensee's absolute fidelity to the client. The Nevada Supreme Court has found it illegal when,

> [t]he broker or salesman purchases a principal's property in the first escrow, and sells it to a third party at a profit in a second escrow without a full disclosure to both the principal and the third party. The broker or salesman receives a commission on the sale in the first escrow and a secret profit on the closing in the second escrow. [24]

11. NAC 645.605 (4)(e).

12. NRS 645.252 (1)(b).

13. NAC 645.605 (4).

14. Judy Bendure, "Preferred Vendor Lists," Real Estate Division Open House, vol. 25, issue 1, Winter 2000, at p. 4. The Open House is the Real Estate Division's information bulletin.

15. NRS 645.633 (1)(g).

16. NRS 645.252 (1)(c); NAC 645.637.

17 & 18. NAC 645.640 (1).

19. NAC 645.605 (4)(b).

20. 12 U.S.C. § 2607.

21. NRS 645.252 (1)(c) and NAC 645.640.

22. NAC 645.605 (4).

23. Alley v. NV Real Estate Div., 94 Nev. 123, 125, 575 P.2d 1334 (1978).

24. Tahoe Village Realty v. DeSmit, 95 Nev. 131, 134, 590 P.2d 1158 (1979).

The Real Estate Settlement Procedures Act (RESPA), federal law, prohibits a licensee from receiving or giving kickbacks and unearned fees even if such kickbacks or fees are disclosed. (RESPA, 12 U.S.C. § 2607).

The relationships that must be disclosed are when a principal is a member of the licensee's immediate family, or a member of the licensee's firm, or an entity (such as a corporation) in which the licensee has an ownership interest.

25. Lemon v. Landers, 81 Nev. 329, 332, 462 P.2d 648 (1965).

26. NAC 645.637.

27. NAC 645.640 (1).

28. American Fidelity Fire Ins. v. Adams, 97 Nev. 106, 108, 635 P.2d 88 (1981).

29. NAC 645.640 (2).

30. NAC 645.610 (1)(b) (1-2).

31. Real Estate Division form, Consent to Act, 05/01/05..

32. NRS 645.254 (2).

33. NRS 645.252 (1)(a).

34. Holland Realty v. NV Real Estate Comm., 84 Nev. 91, 98, 436 P.2d 422 (1968).

35. NRS 40.770.

A defect is "a condition that materially affects the value or use of property in an adverse manner." NRS 113.100(1).

A licensee may not take an undisclosed profit at the expense of another party, nor may the licensee purchase or sell the property of a client through the use of a third person without full disclosure and the client's consent.[25]

2. DISCLOSURE IN WRITING

Whether the licensee's interest is in the transaction or in the property, the disclosure must be in writing - an oral disclosure does not satisfy the regulations.[26] When disclosing the licensee's interest in the property, the disclosure must state the licensee is acquiring or selling the property for him or herself and that the licensee is a broker, broker-salesperson, or salesperson. The Real Estate Division will recognize the disclosure if the licensee includes the term "agent," "licensee," or "broker, broker-salesperson, salesperson," whichever designation is appropriate.[27]

Timing: The disclosure must be made "as soon as practicable," but not later than the date and time on which any written document is signed by the parties. The Nevada Supreme Court has defined "as soon as practicable" to mean "promptly" or "within a reasonable length of time" considering the facts and circumstances of each particular case.[28]

Advertising: If the licensee advertises a property, the advertisement must identify the licensee's licensed status. This disclosure must be made whether the licensee is acting as an agent or as a principal.[29] Accordingly, the licensee must state "for sale by owner-broker" (agent, salesperson, etc.)[30] or substantially similar words in any advertisement for the property in which the licensee is a principal.

3. CONFIDENTIALITY

A licensee may obtain confidential information during the course of the brokerage relationship when the licensee is told, or inadvertently discovers, information harmful to the client's interests.

What constitutes a client's confidential information varies from transaction to transaction and from client to client. The Real Estate Division has previously identified confidential information as "the client's motivation to purchase, trade or sell, which if disclosed, could harm one party's bargaining position or benefit the other."[31] It includes any information that a reasonable person would expect, or request, to be kept confidential. The licensee should consider confidential any information that, if disclosed to the other party, would harm the client's position. A licensee is under the duty not to disclose the client's confidential information for one year after the revocation or termination of the brokerage agreement.[32]

Disclosure Duty: At no time does a client's request for confidentiality control the licensee's disclosure duty. A licensee must disclose to all parties any material and relevant facts relating to the property.[33] This affirmative duty overrides a client's request that the licensee not disclose relevant property facts such as defects. What facts are material and relevant? Any fact about the property that is likely to influence a principal about the property's desirability.[34]

Confidential Material Facts: By law, certain facts that a party may consider material, are deemed not material. Since the law says those facts are not material, the seller and licensee may consider them confidential. The licensee is not liable for their non-disclosure.[35]

II - 7

In Nevada, it is not material if the property was the site of a homicide, suicide or death. The exception is if the property caused the death, for example, someone was electrocuted by the home's bad wiring.

It is not material if the property was occupied by a person with AIDS or any other disease not transmitted through occupancy of the property.

With one exception, it is not material if the property was the site of a felony. The exception is if the property was used to manufacture methamphetamine and the property was not rehabilitated.

It is not material if the property is located near a licensed facility under NRS 449.0055, transitional living for released offenders. (This does not include a halfway house for recovering alcohol and drug abusers.)

Finally, by law it is not material if a sex offender lives, or is expected to live, in the community. This information does not need to be disclosed unless the broker and a buyer have agreed otherwise.

The licensee may not be held liable to the other party for non-disclosure of any of the above items. However, a buyer-client and licensee may agree the licensee will disclose the information if the licensee knows the answer. Any such agreement should be in writing and cleared with the broker.

No Misinformation: A licensee is not allowed to lie or give misinformation. If asked a direct question regarding a confidential matter, the licensee should state the information is confidential and refuse to answer. The client may authorize the licensee to direct the individual to a reliable source.

Required Disclosure: When may a licensee disclose confidential information? The law provides protection for disclosure of confidential information under any one of four circumstances: first, when a court of competent jurisdiction orders disclosure; second, when the client authorizes disclosure;[36] third, when the licensee discloses information to the broker;[37] and fourth, when the information is required to be disclosed by law. The courts will not allow the licensee to hide behind a client's instruction to keep information confidential that the licensee is obligated by law to disclose.

The right of confidentiality is held by the client, not the licensee. That means it is the client's decision on whether confidential information may be disclosed. If there is any question whether a fact or information is confidential, the licensee must clear it with the client before disclosure.

36. NRS 645.254 (2).

37. NRS 645.253.

AIDS stands for acquired immune deficiency syndrome, a deadly disease caused by infection and transmitted through blood or bodily secretions.

Methamphetamine (meth) is an illegal street drug. During the making of meth toxic fumes seep into the walls, floors, sinks and counters. General cleaning or painting does not remove the residue. The property must be "rehabilitated" (made habitable again). Only the government (for example, a health department) or a certified entity can legally rehabilitate a meth property NRS 40.770(6).

NRS 179D.400 defines a "Sex Offender" as a person who is: (a) Convicted of a sexual offense listed in NRS 179D.410; or (b) Found guilty by a court of a sexual offense, such as: (1) A sexually violent predator, or (2) A nonresident sex offender who is a student or worker within this state.

NRS 209.081 "Offender" means any person convicted of a crime under the laws of this state and sentenced to imprisonment in the state prison.

38. NRS 645.3205.

39. NRS 645.633 (1).

40. Holland Realty v. NV Real Estate Comm., 84 Nev. 91, 98, 436 P.2d 422 (1968).

41. NRS 645.630 (1)(a) & (b).

42. NRS 645.633 (1)(e).

43. NRS 645.635 (10).

44. NAC 645.525.

45. NRS 645.993.

46. NRS 645.645.

47. NAC 645.650.

48. Letter to Licensees, from Gail Anderson, Real Estate Division Administrator, "Disclosure of fees and what they are labeled". December, 2002, as a violation of NRS 645.3205.

49. NAC 645.605 (6).

"Moral turpitude" is conduct contrary to justice, honesty, or morality and includes offenses involving fraud, breach of trust, perjury and intentional dishonesty for personal gain. State Bar of Nevada v. Claiborne, 104 Nev. 115, 756 P.2d 464 (1988). See also RED Open House, Fall 2007, page 3.

C. DUTY OF HONESTY

1. NO DECEIT, FRAUD OR DISHONESTY

Whether acting as a principal or an agent, a licensee has a duty to all parties not to be deceitful, fraudulent or dishonest.[38] Deceit is the act of intentionally or recklessly giving a false impression or statement, so that another person will rely on it. It includes any conviction involving bad faith, dishonesty, a lack of integrity, or moral turpitude.[39] Dishonesty is the act of not telling the truth. In other words, the licensee must at all times be honest. Webster's defines honesty as "adherence to the facts."

Licensee's Personal Affairs: The duty of honesty extends past the licensee's business activities and into his or her personal affairs. Nevada's Supreme Court found,

> [t]here can be no justification of an interpretation of the licensing act which would allow a broker to be honest as a broker and dishonest as a property owner. A broker who is dishonest or incompetent in the real estate activities in which he is involved as owner, is not likely to be honest or competent in his activities which are purely brokerage in nature. The purpose of real estate licensure is to bar the dishonest or incompetent from entry into this occupation. 'We believe that a single standard of honesty and competency should guide a broker's real estate activities whether performing as broker or owner.'[40]

Dishonest Activities: Activities that constitute deceitful, fraudulent or dishonest behavior include, but are not limited to, any material misrepresentation or false promises of a character likely to influence, persuade or induce the listener's reliance on the misrepresentation;[41] guaranteeing future profits on the resale of property;[42] submitting any false or fraudulent appraisal to a financial institution or other interested person;[43] naming false consideration in a document;[44] filing with the Division any false documents with willful, material misstatements of fact,[45] and misrepresentation in the sale of home protection insurance.[46]

How certain brokerage fees are labeled may cause RED concern. Calling a charge a name that implies the fee is required by law when it is not, will subject the broker to RED discipline. For instance, regulations require a broker to maintain brokerage transaction files for five years.[47] Some brokers have charged their clients for this file storage by calling the charge, among other terms, a "regulatory compliance fee." The Division has stated this is misleading "conduct which constitutes deceitful, fraudulent or dishonest dealing... ."[48]

The licensee's duty of honesty includes the duty to deal fairly with all parties to a transaction, not just the client.[49]

II - 9

Discipline: The Real Estate Commission may discipline any licensee convicted of any crime involving fraud, deceit, misrepresentation or moral turpitude. It may discipline whether or not the licensee pled nolo contendere (no contest) or guilty. The Division may file criminal charges against any person, licensee or not, who sells real property by intentional misrepresentation, deceit or fraud.[50]

2. SILENCE AS DECEIT

A corollary to the duty to be honest is the duty to speak the whole truth and not be misleading by silence.[51] Generally, mere silence is not a misrepresentation unless there is a duty to speak. Licensees have such a duty. Nevada's agency laws impose upon the licensee the duty to disclose to each party all known material facts about the property.[52] Additionally, the licensee must disclose to the client all known facts about the transaction.[53]

Nevada's Supreme Court has said a licensee's willful silence in the face of a client's expressed misunderstanding is "more deceit than any other category that the court can find... ."[54] A party may have a mistaken belief about the property, elements of the transaction, or be ignorant of a material aspect or defect. If the licensee knows of the mistaken impression, the licensee has the duty to correct the misunderstanding. If the licensee remains silent, this is deceit as much as an affirmative lie.

If a fact is required to be disclosed by the licensee, no instruction from a client can absolve the licensee from liability for willfully withholding the information.

50. NRS 645.990 (1)(b).

51. Northern NV Mobile Home Brokers v. Penrod, 96 Nev. 394, 398, 610 Nev. 724 (1980).

52. NRS 645.252 (1).

53. NRS 645.254 (3)(c).

54. Holland Realty v. NV Real Estate Comm., 84 Nev. 91, 97, 436 P.2d 422 (1968).

55. NRS 645.254 (1).

56. NRS 645.257 (3).

57. NRS 645.633 (1)(h).

58 & 59. NRS 645.252 (2) and NAC 645.605 (5).

60. NAC 645.600 (3) & (4).

61. NRS 645.633 (1)(h) and NAC 645.605.

62. Doud v. Las Vegas Hilton Corp., 109 Nev. 1096, 1100, 864 P.2d 1272 (1993).

63. Turney v. Sullivan, 89 Nev. 554, 555, 516 P.2d 672 (1973).

64. Hammerstein v. Jean Dev. West, 111 Nev. 1471, 1476, 907 P.2d 975 (1995).

Black's Law Dictionary defines negligence as "culpable carelessness".

D. REASONABLE SKILL AND CARE: COMPETENCY

1. STANDARD OF CARE

In any transaction, the licensee is required to exercise reasonable skill and care.[55] What is "reasonable skill and care?" It is the degree of care that a reasonably prudent real estate licensee would exercise in similar circumstances.[56] In other words, the licensee must not act incompetently or with gross negligence.[57]

At a minimum, a licensee is expected to have the knowledge required to obtain a then current real estate license and to act on that knowledge.[58] The minimum is just that, a minimum. A licensee may be held to a higher level of competency and skill if a licensee has, or claims to have, greater knowledge, expertise, or a specialization.

The licensee must keep informed of the current laws and regulations that impact the licensee's real estate practice.[59] Brokers who have agents are required to familiarize their licensees with all relevant current federal and state laws. Additionally, the broker must ensure there is a system in place for monitoring the licensee's compliance with this regulation.[60]

2. NEGLIGENCE

The licensee will have liability if the licensee's gross negligence causes harm.[61] What is negligence? Negligence is a legal term used to identify unreasonable, but generally unintentional behavior that causes another damage or harm.

Elements of Negligence: Briefly, there are four elements to negligence. All four must exist before there is a legal cause of action. Those elements are duty, breach, cause and harm.[62]

To have liability there must first be a duty.[63] The licensee's duties are found in statute, regulation, common law, and contract. Those sources outline what must be done and avoided in the licensee's relationship with his or her client, other parties in the transaction, the public, the licensee's peers and broker, and the Real Estate Division.

The second element is a breach of that duty. A licensee may breach a duty by not doing something one is obligated to do ("nonfeasance"); by doing something one is not supposed to do ("malfeasance"); or by doing something in a careless or haphazard manner ("misfeasance"). For example, it is nonfeasance if the licensee does not provide a copy of the brokerage agreement to the client (NRS 645.300); malfeasance if the licensee discloses a client's confidences (NRS 645.254(2)); and misfeasance when a licensee overlooks some material term of the purchase agreement (NRS 645.254(4)).

The third element requires the breach of duty to have caused the harm.[64] For instance, a listing agent inadvertently tells the buyers that the sellers are divorcing and need to sell quickly. This is an unauthorized disclosure of a seller confidence. Several weeks later the buyers, unhappy with the property condition, terminate the escrow. The sellers have lost the sale. In this scenario the listing agent breached his duty to the sellers when he disclosed the sellers' confidential information; however, the sellers' loss was not a result of the agent's breach. There is no causal link between the licensee's breach and the sellers' harm. The agent's negligent act of disclosing the divorce was not the cause of the buyers rejecting the property.

Nevertheless, this does not mean the sellers are without recourse for the agent's breach. The sellers may file a complaint with the Division and the licensee may be subject to regulatory discipline.[65]

Finally, there must be damages or harm. Harm occurs when the licensee breaches a duty and that breach causes an injury, loss or detriment to the client. Often, a client's loss may be remedied by money (damages).[66] There are various legal restrictions on the amount and type of damages a person may claim under negligence. At no time should a licensee discuss negligence damages with a client.

Strict Liability: Under certain circumstances the law may impose liability strictly for violating a statute or regulation without anyone being harmed.[67] For example, failing to put a definite termination date on an exclusive brokerage agreement eliminates the broker's right to collect a commission regardless of whether the client was harmed.[68]

"Gross negligence" is negligent behavior with a reckless disregard for the consequences of one's actions. It requires the licensee to have understood and ignored the potential harm.[69] The statutes generally impose regulatory liability on the licensee for the licensee's gross negligence.

NAC 645.605 lists a series of actions that if not followed, the Commission may consider the lack of doing those things, gross negligence.

65. NRS 645.633 (1)(b).

66. Arnesano v. State, Dep't Trans., 113 Nev. 815, 821, 942 P.2d 139 (1997).

67. NRS 645.630, 645.633 and 645.635.

68. Bangle v. Holland Realty Inv. Co., 80 Nev. 331, 393 P.2d 138 (1964).

69. Hart v. Kline, 61 Nev. 96, 116 P.2d 672 (1941). See also NAC 645.605

70. NRS 645.252 (1)(a).

71. NRS 645.257 (3).

72. NRS 645.252.

73. Garff v. J.R. Bradley Co., 84 Nev. 79, 85, 436 P.2d 428 (1968).

74. Woods v. Label Investment Corp., 107 Nev. 419, 812 P.2d 1293 (1991) and Collins v. Burns, 103 Nev. 394, 741 P.2d 819 (1987).

75. NRS 645.252 (1)(a).

76. Lowe v. Real Estate Division, 89 Nev. 488, 490, 515 P.2d 388 (1973).

E. DISCLOSURE: "SHOULD HAVE KNOWN" – DUTY TO INVESTIGATE

1. SOURCE

The licensee has a duty to disclose to each party to the transaction any material and relevant facts, data, or information which he or she knows, or which, by the exercise of reasonable care and diligence, should have known, relating to the property.[70]

Standard of Care: The standard of care is the legal level against which a person's behavior is judged. It stems from the idea that a "reasonable person" will act in a certain way - usually with prudence, diligence, and care not to harm anyone or anything. This is the general standard of care.

A real estate licensee is assumed to have a superior knowledge of real estate transactions. With that superior knowledge there is a heightened standard of care. For a real estate licensee, the minimum standard of care is the knowledge to pass a then current real estate license exam.[71]

This heightened standard of care requires a licensee to know and follow all the duties imposed by law. Disclosure is a core duty. A licensee must disclose any material facts relating to the property of which the licensee has actual knowledge.[72]

Actual Knowledge: What is actual knowledge? The court has found,

> [a]ctual knowledge consists not only of what one certainly knows, but also consists in information which he might obtain by investigating facts which he does know and which impose upon him a duty to investigate.[73]

The law will not allow a licensee to ignore "danger signals" or "red lights,"[74] to gloss over conflicting information, or to act carelessly in obtaining material facts about the property under the excuse that the licensee did not "know for certain" relevant facts.

The question becomes what facts, data or information must the licensee investigate and how thoroughly? A licensee is required to investigate "any material and relevant facts, data or information relating to the property" using "reasonable care and diligence."[75]

2. RELATING TO THE PROPERTY

The duty to investigate covers those facts relating to the property. "Relating to the property" normally means items specific to the individual property, but may include the investigation of some information which may impact the property or its use such as a proposed highway, shopping center, or school.[76]

a. When Must A Licensee Investigate – Generally, a licensee is responsible for the reasonable investigation of information, data or facts if: 1) the information concerns an item that directly impacts the property; 2) the licensee has volunteered, or claims an expertise in, any relevant information; 3) the information is required to be disclosed by law; or 4) the broker has explicitly contracted with the client to be responsible for obtaining certain information.

Impacts the Property: The licensee must investigate any item directly related to, or that impacts, the physical condition of

II - 13

the property. For example, in Epperson v. Roloff, (1986),[77] the listing agent was told by the seller the home had a "solar implication." The agent did not ask the client to explain what a solar implication might be. Nevertheless, he told potential buyers the house had a solar feature which really saves on winter heating costs. The feature turned out to be a hole in the roof covered with corrugated sheet metal painted black. The buyers sued the broker and sellers for misrepresentation. The listing agent had a duty to the buyers to disclose all relevant facts about the property. He breached that duty by not investigating and disclosing what the "solar feature" really was.

The level of investigation imposed by the law does not require the licensee to become a "property inspector," NRS 645.252(4)(c) but it does require reasonable and common sense inquiry into the physical condition of the property.

Volunteered Information: When the licensee has volunteered specific information or claims an expertise in a certain topic, the licensee will be held responsible for its reasonable accuracy. This does not mean the licensee guarantees the information; however, the licensee must take reasonable steps to insure the information is up-to-date and sufficiently correct. For example, a property fronts an extensive tract of undeveloped land. If the licensee states the land is controlled by the Bureau of Land Management and won't be developed, that volunteered statement must be accurate and current. Before the licensee volunteers facts, he or she has a duty to investigate the truthfulness of any statement.

Disclosure Required by Law: A licensee has a duty to investigate property facts that may require certain disclosures obligatory by law. For example, Washoe County, Nevada, has a Solid-Fuel Burning Device (wood stove) regulation.[78]

The real estate licensee has a duty to investigate whether or not a unit has a fireplace or wood burning stove and then to provide the seller with the required disclosure form.[79] However, the licensee would not be required to determine if an existing wood stove was in compliance with Code. (That type of inspection requires a county certificate.)

Contracted Investigation: Finally, the broker may, by contract, assume a duty to investigate and disclose facts that are beyond those required by law. For example, the broker and client may agree that the broker will investigate whether the property can be zoned for a particular future use. At all times the broker must be careful not to provide services requiring a license, permit or certification which the broker does not have.

Remember, the purpose of the duty to investigate is to find and disclose material and relevant facts about the property so that a principal may make an informed decision.

b. What Must Be Investigated – When a fact relates to the property, the licensee is required to investigate if it is "material and relevant." The Nevada Supreme Court, quoting the Restatement of Agency §390, stated,

> A fact is material… if it is one which the agent should realize would be likely to affect the judgment of the principal …which he should realize [is] likely to have a bearing upon the desirability of the transaction…[80]

Anything impacting the physical condition of the property is material and relevant. Anything that affects the property's value or use is material and relevant.

77. Epperson v. Roloff, 102 Nev. 206, 719 P.2d 799 (1986).

78. Washoe County, District Board of Health Regulation Governing Air Quality Management, Section 040.051§A(2)(b).

79. NRS 645.252 (4)(b).

80. Holland Realty v. NV Real Estate Comm., 84 Nev. 91, 98, 436 P.2d 422 (1968).

Professional property inspectors are licensed by the state and regulated by the Real Estate Division under NRS 645D.

81. NRS 40.770.

82. NRS 40.770 (4).

83. NRS 645.252.

84. Prigge v. South Seventh Realty, 97 Nev. 640, 641, 637 P.2d 1222 (1981).

85. NRS 645.257 (2).

86. NRS 645.259 (2).

87. NRS 645.259 (1).

88. NRS 645.259 (2) referring to NRS 645.252.

89. Woods v. Label Investment Corp.107 Nev. 419, 426, 812 P.2d 1293 (1991).

90. NRS 645.254 (3)(c).

91. NRS 645.252 (4)(b).

A "material fact" is one that is significant or essential to the issue or matter at hand.

See "Confidential Material Facts" on page II - 7.

c. Exemptions – Certain material facts that may be relevant to the client are by law not considered material to the transaction. With certain restrictions, these facts are exempted from the licensee's duty of disclosure and investigation. Thus, the licensee does not have any liability if those facts are not disclosed.[81]

There are restrictions to each of these that the licensee must know. For example, a seller does not need to disclose if the property was a site of a felony. The restriction is if the property was the site of a meth lab and not "rehabilitated," then the seller, and licensee, must disclose. These exemptions may be waived if the broker has an agreement with the client to investigate or disclose any of the above.[82]

Statements by Experts: A licensee is not responsible for investigating or verifying any statements of, or work performed by, a licensed or certified professional, expert, or property inspector licensed under NRS 645D.[83] For example, if a licensed roofer has given the buyer a report that the roof is sufficient, the licensee is not responsible for climbing on the roof to verify the roofer's professional opinion.

d. Representations of the Client – The licensee has the right to rely on the client's representations about the property unless the licensee knows, or should know, the information is false. The Nevada Supreme Court has said it will not "hold an agent… responsible for an independent search for concealed facts, in the absence of any information which would have put the agent on notice."[84]

By law, it cannot be assumed that the licensee has the client's knowledge about the property.[85] Furthermore, a licensee cannot be held liable for the Seller's non-disclosure of information on the Seller's Real Property Disclosure Statement, if:

1. The licensee did not know of the non-disclosure, and

2. The information is of public record.[86]

The licensee will be held liable for non-disclosure if the licensee knows the client made a misrepresentation and did not tell the recipient that the statement was false.[87] As with absolute fidelity, the courts will not allow a licensee who knew better to hide behind a client's misrepresentation.[88] The bottom line? The licensee may rely on information provided by the client unless such reliance is unreasonable. If a licensee,

> has information which would serve as a "red light" to any normal person of her intelligence and experience [or]… is aware of facts from which a reasonable person would be alerted to make further inquiry, then he or she has a duty to investigate further and is not justified in relying on the seller's description of the property.[89]

3. CONCERNING THE TRANSACTION

Facts that concern the transaction must be disclosed to the licensee's client.[90] This disclosure may require the licensee to reasonably investigate certain aspects of the transaction. These may include, but are not limited to, facts about the escrow, relevant loan information, or the status of other transactions (for example, contingency sale property).

However, a licensee is not required and has no duty to conduct an independent inspection of the financial condition of a party to a real estate transaction. The licensee should not be acting as a loan officer, financial or tax consultant.[91] A licensee should not request, investigate, or review a party's credit report.

A licensee may reasonably rely on financial information provided by the client. In Collins v. Burns (1987),[92] Golanty was the listing agent of a small liquor store owned by Burns. He prepared a sales-and-expense fact sheet and a profit chart using financial figures provided by his client. Relying on the chart and the licensee's fact sheet, Collins purchased the store. She later defaulted on the note and Burns sued for the unpaid principal. Collins countersued and claimed she was defrauded as the information on the fact sheet and chart were grossly inaccurate. The court found for Collins. Although Golanty drafted the chart and fact sheet, he was not a party to the Supreme Court case. He had reasonably relied on the information provided by his client and there was nothing in that information that would have alerted Golanty to his client's misrepresentation.

4. LEVEL OF INVESTIGATION

A licensee is not required to conduct an investigation of the condition of the property which is the subject of the real estate transaction. (NRS 645.252(4)(c)) This statute relieves the licensee of the duty to act as a property inspector. Property inspectors are licensed individuals and are experts in their field. Under this statute, a licensee is not required to perform acts that should be done by licensed property inspectors. However, this does not relieve the licensee from his or her duty to exercise reasonable care and diligence. If a question arises as to the condition of the property, the licensee must address that issue by referring the client to a qualified expert. A licensee will not escape liability for not exercising reasonable care and diligence by using the argument that he or she has no duty to investigate.

Once a licensee is required to investigate, how detailed should that investigation be? The statute says the licensee must investigate using reasonable care and diligence.[93] Reasonable care is taking the time and effort necessary to gather the required paperwork and review it for "red lights". It means looking at the property and comparing it with the seller's statements to ensure the property is what is represented. During this review, the licensee is looking for something out of the ordinary that either contradicts what has been stated, differs from what the licensee knows, or is otherwise amiss.

This reasonable level of investigation does not mean a licensee should interpret documents, determine their legal consequences, or act as an appraiser, property inspector, loan officer, lawyer, or private investigator. As discussed elsewhere, the licensee should not attempt to perform any service not specific to the real estate transaction.

The duty to investigate does require the licensee to have sufficient knowledge to identify any warning signs and to point out these warning signs to the client. Once a concern is identified, the licensee should suggest the client obtain further professional services.

92. Collins v. Burns, 103 Nev. 394, 741 P.2d 819 (1987).

93. NRS 645.252 (1)(a).

"Statement" refers not just to what is said, but to all the various representations of the seller such as the multiple listing service property profile print-out, the Seller's Real Property Disclosure Form, and relevant advertising.

F. SUPPLEMENTARY SERVICES

1. BEYOND THE LICENSEE'S EXPERTISE

If a licensee is asked by a client to perform services outside the licensee's expertise, the client must be told the matter is beyond the licensee's current proficiency and advise the client to obtain guidance from an expert.[94]

This does not mean the licensee cannot expand into new areas. It does mean if the licensee is unfamiliar with a property type or service, the licensee is required to disclose that fact to the client and obtain the assistance of a qualified authority before proceeding.

2. BEYOND THE LICENSEE'S AUTHORITY

A licensee may be disciplined for providing specialized professional services outside the licensee's authority.[95] It does not matter if the advice is accurate or the service well done. Liability lies in doing the thing, not in its result. "Matters beyond the expertise of the licensee" include, but are not limited to, activities that requires a license, permit or professional certification. If the licensee does not have such a license, permit or certification, the activity is automatically beyond the licensee's authority.

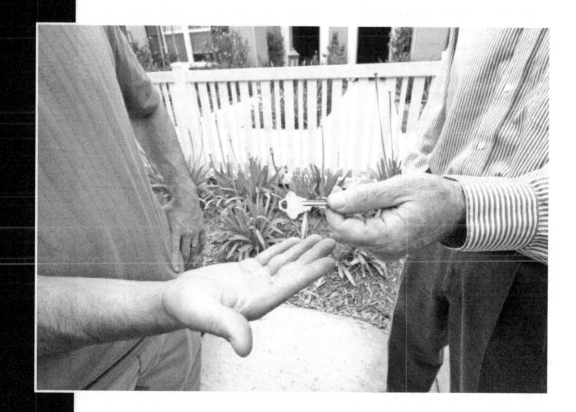

A licensee must be aware of the boundary between authorized real estate services and unauthorized services. Often a licensee is requested by a client to advise or act on a matter for which the licensee is not authorized. Sometimes however, the licensee, willingly and without instruction, crosses this boundary.

In Goldstein v. Hanna (1981),[96] Callahan was the listing agent for a condominium owned by Hanna. Goldstein and Hanna signed a lease with option to purchase to close by December 9, "unless exercised prior thereto." During the lease period, Goldstein exercised the option and signed a purchase agreement with another buyer using a double escrow. Both closing dates were set for August 29. Prior to the closing, the ultimate buyer backed out. Goldstein contacted Callahan who advised him the option was still good until December 9. This was both a misstatement of the law and beyond Callahan's authority. Goldstein, justifiably relying on Callahan's statement, did not close on August 29. The seller then cancelled the escrow and attempted to get the property back. Goldstein sued Hanna for specific performance citing his reliance on Callahan's statement. Though the court's decision was split, Hanna eventually lost the property.

The two areas in which a licensee is most likely to provide unauthorized services are with legal and appraisal activities.[97] Clients will ask a licensee to tell them their rights under a contract, or ask what their legal options are. Additionally, clients often ask the licensee what a property is worth or the value of a business. Because these activities are so intricately woven into the fabric of a real estate transaction, the licensee can easily slip into providing unauthorized answers and services. If he or she does so, it is a violation of not only NRS 645, but of the statutes regulating those professions.

Unauthorized Practice of Law: The unauthorized practice of law is strictly prohibited in Nevada.[98] It is monitored by the State Bar of Nevada under the control of the Nevada Supreme Court.[99] Unfortunately, there is no statute or regulation which defines what activities constitute the practice of law. Through case law, the courts have provided a list of some activities that are considered "practicing law." These include discussing with a client the legal effect of an act; interpreting legal provisions in a document; discussing the rights or responsibilities of the parties; selecting and providing pre-printed legal documents; or determining the legal sufficiency of any action or document.[100]

Many of the actions done daily by real estate licensees come close to those listed above. Some of these are found in the very definition of a real estate broker.[101] Some are required by the broker's statutory duties.[102] Other activities are inherent in the nature of the broker/client relationship.[103] Nevertheless, the unauthorized practice of law is a very fine line which the licensee must stringently guard against stepping over. As with any question of unauthorized professional counsel, the licensee should suggest the client obtain advice from an expert.[104]

Appraisal and the BPO: An "appraisal" is "an analysis, opinion or conclusion, written or oral, relating to the nature, quality, value… of, identified real estate for or with the expectation of receiving compensation." [105] In Nevada, only appraisers are authorized to prepare an appraisal. [106] Appraisers are licensed and regulated by the Real Estate Division. [107]

96. Goldstein v. Hanna, 97 Nev. 559, 635 P.2d 290 (1981), Justices Mowbray and Manoukian dissenting.

97. Real Estate Commission Disciplinary Fine Report, 1/95 through 9/30/04.

98. NRS 7.285 (1).

99. NRS 7.725.

100. Pioneer Title Insurance & Trust Co., v. State Bar of Nevada, 74 Nev. 186, 326 P.2d 408 (1958).

101. NRS 645.035.

102. NRS 645.252(3).

103. NRS 645.252(2).

104. NRS 645.254(3)(d).

105. NRS 645C.030.

106. NRS 645C.040.

107. NRS 645C.260.

An option once exercised, even if before the option's ultimate cut-off date, terminates the option and the contract becomes a bilateral purchase agreement. Once the option is exercised, if the sale isn't completed, the option cannot be resurrected.

Ubiquity does not remove illegality.

108. SB 184, sec 8

109. NRS 645C.150 (4).

110. SB 184, sec. 1,
NAC 645.05 (3)
and NRS 645C.260.

111. SB 184, sec. 1

112 NRS 645.254 (3)(d).

One common real estate activity is often confused with an appraisal. A broker's price opinion (BPO) is a compilation of recent sales of similar properties in the general location of the target property. Real estate agents may prepare a BPO for prospective clients to help establish an estimated sale price. [108] A real estate licensee is exempt from the appraisal statutes only when providing limited services within the scope of a real estate license. [109]

Often lenders and other interested entities will request a licensee to give them an estimate of value for a fee without intending to utilize the licensee's real estate services. A licensee providing this service would be in breach of appraisal and real estate brokerage laws, and subject to discipline from both the Real Estate Commission and the Appraisal Commission.[110]

To avoid crossing into appraisal services, the law (NRS 645) now defines the BPO, and sets forth the persons for whom and the purposes for which a BPO may be prepared for a fee by a real estate licensee whose "license is in good standing." It creates limitations on the uses to which opinions prepared for specified clients may be put and requires the inclusion of a disclaimer in all BPOs stating that it is "not an appraisal of the market value of the property" for which the "services of a licensed or certified appraiser must be obtained." [111]

Other Services: Even though client requests for legal and appraisal services are most common, those are not the only professional services a client may ask for – or an enthusiastic licensee may attempt to provide. Other services include, but are not limited to, home inspection, tax and income advice, and property management. When asked to do any unauthorized activity, the licensee must either have the appropriate license, permit or certification, or refer the client to the appropriate professional.[112]

The licensee must be aware of the pitfall of relying on a client's authorization to perform any unauthorized activity. As with many areas of real estate agency law, a client's instruction does not make an illegal act legal.

II - 19

G. REVIEW

The licensee's duties are found in statute, regulation, and in the common law. Most codified duties evolved from the common law using common law terms such as "fiduciary," "absolute fidelity," "negligence," and "should have known." Generally, these terms are not defined in statute or regulation.

Absolute fidelity means putting the client's interests before the licensee's interest. A licensee may have an interest in the property or in the transaction. This interest must be disclosed in writing. Sometimes, even if an interest is disclosed, a licensee may not act on that interest if it would harm the client.

A licensee must be honest and not act in a deceitful, fraudulent or dishonest manner in either the licensee's personal or professional Life. Silence, when there is a duty to speak, is deceit.

The licensee must exercise reasonable skill and care toward all parties in the transaction. This includes not acting in a negligent manner. Negligence is unreasonable, but generally unintentional, behavior that causes harm.

The term "should have known" creates the duty to investigate. The licensee must reasonably investigate material and relevant information relating to the property and the transaction. This duty has limitations and restrictions, but those restrictions do not allow the licensee to ignore obvious warning signs that something is amiss.

Lastly, the licensee should be cautious of activities outside the licensee's expertise or authority, especially legal or appraisal services.

III. NEVADA LAW ON BROKERAGE AGREEMENTS

TABLE OF CONTENTS

The brokerage agreement is one of the most important contracts with which a licensee must deal. It defines the relationship between the client and the broker. Discussed in this chapter are the legal parameters to the creation and termination of the brokerage agreement, the two types of representation found in Nevada (open or exclusive), legal aspects to compensation, and some characteristics of specialized brokerage agreements.

A. CREATION AND TERMINATION

1. EMPLOYMENT AGREEMENT

A broker's legal relationship with the client starts with an employment contract called a brokerage agreement. In the brokerage agreement, the broker promises to provide real estate related services for valuable consideration. Real estate related services include the broker assisting, soliciting, or negotiating on behalf of the client for the sale, purchase, option, rental or lease of real property. The consideration may be paid either by the client or another person.[1]

A listing contract is a seller's brokerage agreement; a buyer's brokerage agreement is with a buyer. Specialized brokerage agreements such as commercial, advance fee, manufactured home, and listing with option to purchase, as well as property management agreements, are discussed in their own sections.

2. BROKER REPRESENTS CLIENT

There are only two parties to a brokerage agreement, the client and the broker. Though a licensed broker-salesperson or salesperson may represent the brokerage,[2] the legal relationship is between the broker and the client regardless of whether or not the broker knows the individual client. The broker always retains overall responsibility for the brokerage relationship.[3]

Only a broker may collect compensation for real estate related services. No broker-salesperson or salesperson may accept compensation from, or pay compensation to, any person other than a broker (or owner-developer) with whom, at the time of the transaction, he or she is licensed.[4] If a non-broker licensee does accept or pay compensation to anyone other than the broker, that licensee is subject to a fine up to $10,000, and may have conditions placed on his or her license, such as suspension, revocation, or denied renewal.[5]

a. Independent Contractor – Most non-broker licensees (salesperson and broker-salesperson) are independent contractors; nevertheless, by law they cannot enter into their own brokerage agreements with clients. NRS 645 restricts a non-broker licensee from being hired independent of a broker. For example, broker-salespersons or salespersons:

1. May not perform real estate related services without being associated with a licensed broker;[6]

III - 3

2. May not accept compensation from anyone other than the broker;[7]

3. May not advertise without the broker's supervision;[8] and

4. May not hold a client's funds, but must "promptly" turn over any money to the broker.[9]

The broker is the entity that represents the client. This is true even if the person dealing with the client is a salesperson or broker-salesperson. The broker's salesperson actually represents the broker and all of the salesperson's activities are done through, and in the name of, the brokerage. Thus, in a technical sense, when a salesperson is referred to as the "client's agent" the wording is incorrect - it is the broker who is the client's agent.

b. Broker Liability – The broker gives the salesperson, or broker-salesperson, authority to act for the broker. For example, a broker may give an agent the authority to sign a brokerage contract, to negotiate compensation, and to set the level of services or representation.[10] However, at no time does this transfer of authority transfer the broker's liability. The broker must always supervise any agents and is ultimately responsible for the agents' actions.[11]

This does not remove the salesperson's individual responsibilities. Each broker-salesperson or salesperson has legal duties toward the client, the broker, professional peers, and the public, and may be held personally liable if those duties are breached.[12]

c. Who Pays – For a valid brokerage agreement, the client does not need to be the one who pays the broker. Legally binding agreements may occur regardless of whether the broker's compensation is paid by the client, the other party's broker, or some agreed upon third person.[13]

3. FORM OF BROKERAGE AGREEMENT

Brokerage Agreements are employment contracts and like other contracts, they have the same formation requirements. There must be a "meeting of the minds"; the contract must have definite terms as to: subject matter, parties, compensation (payment), and time of performance, and there must be consideration. At a minimum, there must be the mutual understanding that the broker will accept valuable consideration from the client or a third person for the performance of real estate related services.[14]

Brokerage agreements may be oral or written.[15] Nevada has no mandatory brokerage agreement form. Though there is no required form, Nevada's Attorney General has stated the Real Estate Division is within its authority to adopt regulations governing the content of brokerage agreements.[16] Since there is no mandatory form, with a few exceptions, all of the terms of the contract depend on the agreement of the parties.

Oral Contracts: Oral brokerage agreements are legal contracts in which a broker agrees to represent a client with the intention or expectation of compensation and there is no written contract. No oral brokerage agreement may be exclusive.[17]

With an oral listing contract, the seller is only obligated to compensate the broker if the broker's services were the procuring cause of a successful transaction.[18] Regardless of the amount of time, energy or money a listing broker expends representing a client, if the broker is not the procuring cause the client is not obligated to pay.[19]

7. NRS 645.280.

8. NRS 645.315 (2).

9. NRS 645.310 (2), NRS 645.630 (1)(i) & NAC 645.657.

10. NRS 645.300, recognizes a non-broker licensee may prepare a written brokerage agreement, and NRS 645.320 (4).

11. NAC 645.600 (1).

12. NAC 645.605 (6), NRS 645.252, 645.254, 645.630, 645.633, 645.635.

13, 14, 15. NRS 645.005.

16. AGO 97-28 (12-31-1997).

17. NRS 645.320.

18. Morrow v. Barger, 104 Nev. 247, 250, 737 P.2d 1153 (1987).

19. Sahara Realty Corp. v. Adelson, 89 Nev. 147, 508 P.2d 1210 (1973).

The term "independent contractor" as applied to real estate licensees is most often used as a federal tax income designation. 26 USC §3508, also see (AGO) 1956-160 (1956). But Nevada law provides for various other designations (See NRS 612.133 and NRS 616A.220).

20. NRS 645.320.

21. NRS 645.300.

22. NRS 645.633 (1)(f).

23. NAC 645.650.

"Valuable consideration" includes any type of compensation: the commission, finder's fee, referral fee, advanced fee, payment, or gift if given in exchange for services. It can be anything of value, not just money.

As with most oral agreements, should a dispute arise the broker would have to satisfactorily establish to the court the existence and terms of the contract. Additionally, in order to collect a commission, the broker will have to prove he or she was the procuring cause of the transaction.

Written Contracts: Though it is legal to have oral brokerage agreements, all exclusive agency brokerage agreements must be in writing. Under Nevada law, written brokerage contracts have certain statutory requirements regarding terms, form, and distribution.[20]

Client Must Receive a Copy: If the brokerage agreement is in writing, once it is signed by the broker and the client, the client must receive a copy.[21] The copy should be given to the client when it is signed or as soon thereafter as possible. To verify that the client received the copy, the broker may have a "receipt acknowledgment" incorporated into the form.

Should the broker fail to leave a copy of the agreement with the client, the broker is subject to a disciplinary fine of up to $10,000, and administrative action.[22] To verify compliance with these laws, the Real Estate Division requires each brokerage agreement be kept by the broker for five years from the date of closing or last activity on the transaction.[23]

III - 5

4. A WORD ABOUT ELECTRONIC BROKERAGE AGREEMENTS

Generally, Nevada law authorizes an electronic format for any transaction or contract in which the parties agree to conduct their business electronically.[24] By law, an electronic record satisfies any statute that requires the contract to be in writing. An electronic signature satisfies any statute requiring a signature.[25]

There is a difference between an electronic signature and a digital signature. An electronic signature is an electronic sound, symbol or process attached to, or logically associated with, an electronic record and executed or adopted by a person with the intent to sign the record.[26] No particular type of electronic signature is required. A digital signature is an electronic signature that uses an asymmetric cryptosystem to verify to the reader the identity of the signer.[27]

Some software packages, such as Microsoft Office, use certain technology to enable the writer to digitally sign a file by using a preset certificate. This internal certificate is a piece of technology that confirms the file or document originated from the signer and that it has not been altered by unauthorized third persons. The internal or self-signed certificates are considered unauthenticated when the document is sent to another computer unless the certificate was issued by a formal certification authority. A person must apply to a commercial certification authority to obtain an authenticated digital certificate. As with all modern technology, electronic formats are changing rapidly. What is cutting edge today will be passé tomorrow.

Intend to be Bound: Before entering into any electronically created brokerage agreement, the licensee should be aware of an issue concerning NRS 719, the statutes regulating electronic contracts, and NAC 645, the administrative code regulating real estate licensees. NRS 719 allows for the creation of a valid contract purely electronically. NAC 645.613 requires the licensee to "obtain appropriate signatures before entering into a relationship as the agent of a client." The regulation goes on to state that " 'appropriate signature' means the legal signature of the client." NRS 719 allows for a legal signature to be created electronically.

The intent of the Real Estate Commission in NAC 645.613 was to require proof a client agreed to sign the brokerage agreement. Specifically, the Commissioners did not want only "the clicking of an acceptance box,"[28] either on the internet or in an e-mail, to create a binding brokerage agreement. The prospective client must know he or she is signing a contract and must intend to be bound by it – regardless of whether the contract is created orally, in writing, or electronically.

5. TERMINATION

a. Events Causing Termination – As with all contracts, certain events will terminate the contract. Generally, and unless the contract provides otherwise, these events are:

- Completion of the contract's purpose;
- Termination by contract term;
- Mutual agreement;
- Impossibility of performance;
- Breach;
- Operation of law; or
- A party's death.

24. NRS 719.220 (2).

25. NRS 719.240.

26. NRS 719.100.

27. NRS 720.060.

28. NAC 645.613.

29. NRS 645.254 (2).

30. Humphrey v. Knobel, 78 Nev. 137, 147, 369 P.2d 872 (1962).

31. NRS 645.633 (1)(f).

32. NRS 645.320(2).

33. Kaldi v. Farmers Ins. Exch, 117 Nev. 273, 279, 21 P.3d 16 (2001).

Some professional associations, such as the National Association of Realtors®, have more stringent behavior guidelines. For example, NAR's Code of Ethics, Article 2, has no time limit on keeping the client's confidences.

A word about dates: when the contract calls for a date, each licensee should have access to a calendar that identifies nonjudicial days and holidays. Nonjudicial days are days when the courts are closed. Often these are the major national and state holidays. NRS 1.130

Completion of the contract's purpose: The purpose of any brokerage agreement is the employment of a broker by a client to perform real estate related services for compensation. Once the contract is fully performed, the purpose of the contract is ended and the contract terminates.

Though a brokerage agreement ends, each party may continue to have certain responsibilities stemming from the contract. Some of these, such as the licensee's duty of confidentiality, are statutorily identified as extending past the revocation or termination of the brokerage agreement - in the case of confidentiality, it is one year.[29]

Termination by contract term: The contract may state it will terminate upon a certain event. Usually, that event is a certain date, but it may be any agreed upon event. With an oral brokerage agreement, if the contract does not have a termination date it will remain effective for a "reasonable time."[30] How long is a reasonable time? It is subject to the court's determination and decided case by case.

All written brokerage agreements must have a set termination date.[31] Each exclusive representation brokerage agreement is required to be in writing and have a definite, specified and complete termination date.[32] That date legally ends the representation, but not necessarily the right to compensation or other statutory obligations.

A brokerage agreement may end upon the occurrence of a specific event. For example, a seller may be attempting to sell a home due to a job transfer. The listing contract has both a specific termination date and alternatively, a clause that provides the brokerage agreement will terminate 24 hours after the seller gives the broker proof of her transfer date. The idea being if the home is not sold by either the contract's termination date or the transfer date, then, the client's employer's relocation company will acquire the home.

Termination by mutual agreement: A brokerage agreement may be terminated by either party.[33] Depending on the circumstances, the termination may be conditional or unconditional.

An unconditional release is when both the broker and the client mutually agree to terminate the brokerage agreement and end the relationship. At this point the broker and client part without any further

III - 7

contractual obligation to the other. The termination of the brokerage agreement does not release the broker from certain statutory duties such as confidentiality.

A <u>conditional release</u> is when the broker stops representing the client but holds the client to the payment of compensation. This type of termination usually occurs when the client or broker "fires" the other.

The Nevada Supreme Court stated "[a]bsent a contractual provision to the contrary, an independent contractor/principal agency relationship is terminable at any time at the will of the principal or the agent."[34]

A client has the right to refuse to work with any specific broker-salesman or salesman; however, as the brokerage agreement is with the broker, the brokerage agreement continues in force. When this happens, the broker may transfer the client to another agent or release the client from the brokerage agreement. The broker has no right to force a client to work with a particular agent. However, if the client refuses to work with the brokerage without cause, the client has breached the employment agreement.

Impossibility of performance: A contract will terminate if, through no fault of either party, the contract becomes impossible to perform. For example, the seller's property burns down - now there is nothing to sell. The seller could terminate the brokerage agreement based on the impossibility of performance. The performance need not be totally impossible, only highly impractical. The act creating the impossibility must have been reasonably unforeseeable.[35]

Breach: The brokerage agreement may be terminated when either party breaches it. A breach occurs when the client or the broker does not perform obligations under the contract.

If the client is claiming the broker breached the contract, the broker may not be entitled to any compensation. The client may sue for any actual damages the client suffered due to the broker's breach.[36]

If the broker believes the client has breached the contract, the broker is entitled to any compensation originally agreed to and earned before the breach, or may sue for any alternative remedies provided in the contract.

Recording a Lis Pendens: The brokerage agreement is a contract for services. The only way to enforce its terms is either through ADR or court action. Unfortunately, some licensees believe they can record a lis pendens to stop the ex-client's escrow when there is a dispute about compensation or the brokerage agreement.

A lis pendens is a notice recorded in the county Recorder's Office that lets the world know there is litigation pending about the title to, or possession of, real property. It may only be recorded after a legal complaint is filed with the court (NRS 14.010).

As an employment contract, the brokerage agreement is not a claim for title to, or possession of, real property. Therefore, no authorization or right is given to the broker to record a lis pendens against a seller's property. Should a broker inappropriately record a lis pendens, the broker is subject to a counter-suit for slander of title.

"Operation of Law": Most contracts will terminate when the parties cannot perform their obligations under the contract because of a legal change in the status of a party. Usually, the parties do not intend for the law to change their rights or liabilities, but it happens anyway. For example, by "operation of law" a duly executed brokerage agreement may be avoided by a client who is a minor.

34. Kaldi v. Farmers Ins. Exch, 117 Nev. 273, 279, 21 P.3d 16 (2001).

35. Nebaco, Inc. v. Riverview Realty Co, Inc., 87 Nev. 55, 482 P.2d 305 (1971).

36. NRS 645.257 (1).

"ADR" stands for "alternative dispute resolution" and includes mediation, arbitration, or conciliation.

A broker, broker-salesman, or salesman may be a corporation. The corporate legal entity may be dissolved, but unless legally dissolved, the corporation does not die.

37. NRS 62A.030 (1)(a) & NRS 129.010.

38. Wayman v. Torreyson, 4 Nev. 124, 135 (1868).

39. NRS 148.420 & NRS 148.330.

40. NAC 645.350 (2).

41. NAC 645.350 (3).

42. NRS 645.350 (2)(a).

43. NRS 78.060 (1)(d).

44. NRS 645.370.

45. NRS 645.252 (1)(e), NRS 645.310 (1), NRS 645.254 (2).

46. Nollner v. Thomas, 91 Nev. 203, 533 P.2d 478 (1975).

The Broker Protection Period is also known as a "grace period."

In Nevada, anyone under eighteen years old is a child and cannot legally enter into a contract.[37] Therefore, any contract signed by the minor is not enforced by the other party. The contract is voidable by the minor by "operation of law".

A Party's Death: It is old law in Nevada that a client's death terminates the agency.[38] Nevertheless, the broker may still have rights under the original brokerage agreement for the collection of compensation.[39] For example, a broker has a listing contract with a client. The broker finds a buyer for the client's property and the parties sign a purchase agreement. Toward the end of the escrow the seller dies; however, the client's estate chooses to proceed with the escrow. The broker does not automatically represent the estate since her client, the seller, has died. Nevertheless, the broker has fulfilled her contractual obligations by procuring a ready, willing and able buyer, and is entitled to the agreed upon compensation. The broker has rights under the original brokerage agreement and could sue the estate should it not pay her.

A Licensee's Death: Upon the death of a licensee, his or her real estate license automatically expires.[40] Without a valid real estate license, there can be no legal representation. If the broker-salesperson or salesperson dies, the brokerage agreement continues in place because the brokerage agreement is with the broker. If the broker dies, historically, the brokerage agreement automatically ends; however, by regulation, another licensed broker may act in the deceased's broker's place for up to sixty (60) days after the original broker's death. The new broker must submit an affidavit to the Division within 7 business days from the date of death.[41] In either case, the client or the client's estate is responsible for paying any compensation earned by the broker before death.

When the Broker is a Corporation: A broker may be a corporation.[42] Corporations have perpetual existence.[43] Every corporation that files for a broker's license must designate one of its officers its corporate broker. That officer must have a broker's license.[44] If the designated corporate broker dies, the broker corporation still exists, but its officers must immediately designate another corporate officer, who is licensed as a broker, as the corporation's broker.

b. After Termination - When the brokerage agreement terminates, the broker must stop representing the client, remove any personal property from the seller's property (such as signs), account to the client for all funds, keep the client's confidences, and do nothing to harm the ex-client or interfere with the transaction even if the broker believes he or she is still owed a commission.[45]

Broker Protection Period: Most exclusive representation agreements have a "broker protection period." This is a contract clause that gives the broker the right to collect a commission for a set time after the brokerage agreement ends. To collect a commission, the broker must have introduced the property or buyer to the client during the brokerage agreement period. Unless the brokerage agreement allows for the broker to collect if the broker is the procuring cause, upon the end of the broker protection period, the seller may sell the property to a buyer procured by the broker and not owe the broker a commission.[46]

The broker protection period does not allow the broker to continue marketing the property, nor is the broker entitled to a commission if he or she negotiates with a new buyer.

III - 9

Not all brokerage agreements are created equal. There are two types of representation recognized in Nevada — open or exclusive. Open contracts allow the client to hire several brokers. Exclusive contracts require the seller to work with just one broker. Other forms of brokerage agreements focus not on the type of representation but on how the broker is to be paid, such as in net listings or option listings.

47. Humphrey v. Knobel, 78 Nev. 137, 144, 369 P.2d 872 (1962).

48. Morrow v. Barger, 103 Nev. 247, 252, 737 P.2d 1153 (1987).

B. TYPES OF REPRESENTATION

1. "OPEN" BROKERAGE AGREEMENT

An open brokerage agreement is where the broker has no exclusive representation of the client – the client may hire any number of other brokers. An open brokerage agreement allows the seller to sell the property without owing a commission. The courts favor the client in determining the level of representation. The more "open" the contract, the better for the client.

Open brokerage agreements may be oral or written. All oral brokerage contracts are considered "open." All written brokerage agreements are also presumed to be open unless the contract's terms or title state it is exclusive.

Unless otherwise specified in contract, a broker earns a commission with an open agreement only if the broker is the "procuring cause" of the transaction - that is, the broker finds a buyer ready, willing and able to purchase on the seller's precise terms. "Precise terms" does not mean the property must be sold at list price: it may be sold at any price the seller agrees to accept.[47]

The court will usually find the other brokers' open agreements terminated as soon as the client accepts one broker's offer. This is the case even if another broker subsequently produces a ready, willing and able prospective buyer. If the other agreements did not automatically terminate, the client could be liable for several commissions.

Implied Brokerage Agreements: Though not favored by the courts, under some circumstances, a court will find a broker is owed compensation under an implied brokerage agreement.

In Morrow v. Barger, (1987),[48] the court found an implied brokerage agreement after the written listing ended. Claire Morrow was a broker who had a written open listing with the Bargers to sell their ranch. During the listing period, Morrow showed the property to three potential buyers. When the written brokerage agreement ended, the sellers instructed Morrow to continue marketing the property – which she did. After a while, the sellers stopped communicating with Morrow. Eventually, Morrow learned that the Bargers personally sold the property to all three buyers in a complicated escrow. Morrow sued for her commission and won. The court said Morrow had an implied open listing; therefore, she was entitled to a commission.

49. Morrow v. Barger, 103 Nev. 247, 250, 737 P.2d 1153 (1987). See footnote 2 of the case. See also R165-07, sections 2 and 4 for definitions of exclusive agency and exclusive right to sell or lease listing agreements.

50. NRS 645.635 (2) & NAC 645.535(3).

51. NRS 645.635 (2), NAC 645.535(3) & NRS 645.0045 (2).

52. NAC 645.535 (4).

53. NRS 645.320.

54. R-165-07, section 3.

54a. Joan Buchanan, "Duties Owed Mandates 'Reasonable Skill and Care' ", Real Estate Division Open House, vol. 22, issue 1, Winter 1997, at p. 9.

If a seller is aware of the broker's continuing efforts to secure a buyer and the seller does not affirmatively stop the broker, the seller cannot deprive the broker of a commission by ignoring (or firing) the broker and conducting the final negotiations.

2. "EXCLUSIVE" REPRESENTATION AGREEMENTS

a. General – Exclusive agency representation occurs when the broker is the client's sole real estate agent. Generally, there are two types of exclusive agreements; those in which the broker will get paid regardless of who is the procuring cause (with listings, commonly known as an Exclusive Right To Sell), and those in which the client hires the broker as an exclusive agent, but retains the right to sell or find a property without paying a commission (commonly known as an Exclusive Agency).[49]

Exclusive representation protects the broker from interference by other licensees with the client-broker relationship. A licensee, property manager or owner-developer may not negotiate the sale, exchange or lease of real estate with a principal if the client has an exclusive agency agreement in force with another broker.[50] (An exception is made if the broker has given written permission to a requesting licensee to negotiate directly with the client. Nevada has a state mandated authorization form.)[51] A broker who holds an exclusive agency agreement must cooperate with other brokers whenever it is in the client's best interest.[52]

b. Specific Terms - The law identifies only four provisions that must be included in an enforceable exclusive brokerage agreement. These are:

1. The agreement must be in writing;

2. It must be signed by both the broker and the client or their authorized representatives;

3. The contract must have a definite termination date; and

4. The agreement may not require the client to notify the broker of the client's intention to cancel the exclusive features of the brokerage agreement once the agreement is terminated.[53]

By and large, other than certain requirements for specialized brokerage agreements, all other contract terms are negotiable.

c. Buyer's Brokerage Agreements – In a written buyer's brokerage agreement, all the required terms of the exclusive listing agreement apply. [54] Additionally, though not law, the Real Estate Division has identified various elements that, at a minimum, should be in a buyer's brokerage agreement. These include:

"specified terms, duration, compensation, services agreed upon, and the ability of a client to cancel for non-performance. ... Any special services, circumstances and/ or conditions should be spelled out in the agreement."[54a]

d. Missing Elements = No Compensation – If an exclusive brokerage agreement is not in writing or if it is missing a necessary legal provision, the broker will be unable to collect a commission.[55] A faulty exclusive brokerage agreement cannot become an open brokerage agreement. Failure to include a fixed termination date makes the agreement voidable by the client and removes the broker's ability to claim payment under alternative legal theories of compensation.[56]

In Bangle v. Holland Realty Inv., Co., (1964),[57] Nevada's Supreme Court found that Holland, a licensed real estate broker, could not collect $38,800 for commissions earned from selling Bangle's houses. Holland had not followed the statute requiring a definite termination date in the exclusive agency brokerage agreement. The court found NRS 645.320 had specific statutory elements for a valid exclusive contract. If those elements were missing, the contract failed and could not be converted to an open contract. Therefore, Holland's listing contract, by not having a definite termination date as required by statute, was unenforceable. The court held "the purpose of NRS 645.320 is best served by denying any relief to a broker or salesman, who claims an exclusive agency to sell, unless the requirements of the statute are complied with."

3. LIMITED SERVICE CONTRACTS AND LIABILITY

a. No Transactional Agency – Nevada does not recognize "transactional" agency. Transactional agency is a limited form of agency in which the broker does not represent either party but is hired to facilitate the transaction. A transactional "agent" is more similar to an escrow officer than to a traditional real estate agent. At this time, with the exception of one duty, a broker may not limit the broker's liability to, or representation of, a client. If a broker provides any real estate related services

to anyone for any compensation, the broker takes on all legal duties and their related liability.[58]

b. Limited Service Contracts – There is a difference between the right of the parties to contract for certain services and the broker's level of legal liability. Some services are dictated by statutory duties whether or not stated in the contract.

By law, a licensee cannot "contract away" or a client "waive" the statutory duties of NRS 645.252 or NRS 645.254. The public has the right to expect the licensee will adhere to the law and abide by all of the licensee's legal duties. A broker can be held responsible for not performing all of the stated duties whether or not the client and broker have agreed otherwise.

The sole exception concerns NRS 645.254 (4), which states a licensee has the duty to present all offers made to or by the client as soon as practicable unless the client signs a written waiver. The waiver must be on a state mandated form (Waiver Form) and signed by both the client and the broker.

A licensee and client cannot agree by contract to do an illegal thing – such a contract is automatically void. For example, the broker cannot agree with the client to discriminate against a protected class.[59] The RED may bring a complaint against a licensee who breaks the law regardless of the terms of any brokerage agreement.

Non-statutory services may be contractually limited. For example, the broker and client may agree that the broker does not have to hold an open house or personally show the property. The broker may have a menu of discretionary services and charge the client piece-meal for those services.

55. Bangle v. Holland Realty Inv. Co, 80 Nev. 331, 393 P.2d 138 (1964).

56. Morrow v. Barger, 103 Nev. 247, 252, 737 P.2d 1153 (1987).

57. Bangle v. Holland Realty Inv. Co, 80 Nev. 331, 393 P.2d 138 (1964).

58. NRS 645.030 & NRS 645.260. See also NRS 645.255, no duty in NRS 645.252 or NRS 645.254 may be waived.

59. NRS 645.321.

A "void" contract never had legal sufficiency or effect – it is as if the contract never existed.

STATE OF NEVADA
DEPARTMENT OF BUSINESS AND INDUSTRY
REAL ESTATE DIVISION
788 Fairview Drive, Suite 200 * **Carson City**, NV 89701-5453 * (775) 687-4280
2501 East Sahara Avenue, Suite 102 * **Las Vegas**, NV 89104-4137 * (702) 486-4033
Email: realest@red.state.nv.us   http://www.red.state.nv.us

WAIVER FORM

In representing any client in an agency relationship, a real estate licensee has specific statutory duties to that client. Under Nevada law only one of these duties can be waived. NRS 645.254 requires a licensee to "present all offers made to or by the client as soon as practicable." This duty may be waived by the client.

"Presenting all offers" includes without limitation: accepting delivery of and conveying offers and counteroffers; answering a client's questions regarding offers and counteroffers; and assisting a client in preparing, communicating and negotiating offers and counteroffers.

In order to waive the duty, the client must enter into a written agreement waiving the licensee's obligation to perform the duty to present all offers. **By signing below you are agreeing that the licensee who is representing you will <u>not</u> perform the duty of presenting all offers made to or by you with regard to the property located at:**

_____.
Property Address   City

AGREEMENT TO WAIVER

By signing below I agree that the licensee who represents me shall not present any offers made to or by me, as defined above. I understand that a real estate transaction has significant legal and financial consequences. I further understand that in any proposed transaction, the other licensee(s) involved represents the interests of the other party, does not represent me and cannot perform the waived duty on my behalf. I further understand that I should seek the assistance of other professionals such as an attorney. I further understand that it is my responsibility to inform myself of the steps necessary to fulfill the terms of any purchase agreement that I may execute. I further understand that this waiver may be revoked in writing by mutual agreement between client and broker.

WAIVER NOT VALID UNTIL SIGNED BY BROKER.

_____   _____   _____   _____
Client   Date   Licensee   Date

_____   _____   _____   _____
Client   Date   Broker   Date

06/26/2007   636

III - 13

4. INTERFERENCE WITH BROKERAGE AGREEMENT

a. By Other Brokers – Once a valid exclusive brokerage agreement is in place, a licensee may not, for personal gain, induce any party to break that contract in order to substitute a new agreement. A licensee who violates this statute may be subject not only to civil action from the harmed broker, but the Real Estate Commission may impose a $10,000 fine and other administrative sanctions.[60]

b. By the Client – A client cannot in bad faith ignore the broker or intervene in the transaction so as to deprive a broker of earned compensation. Nevada's Supreme Court determined that a seller must give the broker an opportunity to finish the transaction with the ultimate buyer if the broker initially produced the buyer and has not abandoned negotiations. The seller, in order not to be liable for a commission, must notify the procuring broker of any subsequent offers by such buyers and give the broker a reasonable time to protect the broker's commission – or the seller must decline the sale.[61]

The brokerage agreement is an employment contract between the client and the broker. A seller and buyer cannot, in their purchase agreement or through escrow instructions, attempt to modify the terms of the brokerage agreement without the consent of the broker.

60. NRS 645.630 (1)(l).

61. Bartsas Realty, Inc. v. Leverton, 82 Nev. 6, 9, 409 P.2d 627 (1966).

62. NRS 645.280 (2).

63. Ramezzano v. Avansino, 44 Nev. 72, 81, 189 Pac. 681 (1920).

64. Close v. Redelius, 67 Nev. 158, 166, 215 P.2d 659 (1950).

NRS 645 covers those real estate related services that are provided by a broker with the intention or expectation of receiving compensation. "Compensation" is anything of value. It may be cash, property (real or personal), a promise to pay (promissory note), or the exchange of services with a cash value. For example, a broker who helps a carpenter sell his house in exchange for the carpenter converting the broker's garage, is receiving compensation. Compensation includes any commission, finder's fee, referral fee, advanced fee, payment, thing of value, or gift if given in exchange for services.

C. COMPENSATION

1. ONLY THE BROKER IS PAID

Under Nevada law, only a broker is authorized to collect compensation for real estate related services, whether preformed by the broker or by the broker's agent.[62] A broker-salesperson or salesperson cannot accept compensation from any person other than the broker (or owner-developer) with whom he or she is licensed at the time of the transaction. Therefore, only a broker may be employed by a client.

2. RIGHT TO COMPENSATION

In purchase transactions, the listing broker earns compensation by securing a buyer within the time specified in the contract. The buyer must be ready, willing, and able to purchase at the price designated by the seller.[63] "Able" means financially able. The money does not have to be immediately available as long as funds are available to close the deal within the time required.[64] The "price designated by the principal," includes any sale price to which the seller agrees regardless of the initial list price.

III - 15

A subsequent default by buyer will not limit the broker's right to commission. Some purchase agreements require the parties to have an on-going relationship; for example, a Lease with Option to Purchase or where the seller is carrying a portion of the purchase price. Should the buyer default, unless otherwise agreed between the broker and seller, the seller cannot refuse to pay, nor require the broker to refund, the broker's earned commission. If a buyer defaults after closing a transaction, it is the buyer who is liable to the seller for all of the damages caused by the default including any broker's commission already paid. The seller's remedy is against the buyer.

In Chicago Title v. Schwartz, (1993),[65] Schwartz sold a property to the Wrights. Chicago Title was the escrow holder. Chenin was the seller's listing agent. Originally, the transaction was a straight purchase and Chenin's commission was to be paid at the close of escrow. Because the Wrights had financial difficulties, Schwartz agreed to an installment contract and unilaterally instructed Chicago Title to alter the commission order to pay Chenin at the end of the installment period. However, Chicago Title paid the commission at the close of escrow.

When the Wrights defaulted on the installment contract, Schwartz sued Chicago Title for the early release of the commission. The court held that regardless of the buyers' later default, Chenin was owed her compensation when she earned her commission per the listing contract. Therefore, even if Chicago Title had mistakenly released the commission, Schwartz was not harmed because Schwartz already owed the money to Chenin. If Schwartz was harmed, he had to look to the defaulting buyer for reimbursement.

a. When Earned and When Due – In a purchase transaction, unless the broker and client contract otherwise, the broker's commission is earned when the broker fulfills the terms of the brokerage agreement. In an open listing, the broker earns the commission when he or she finds a buyer ready, willing and able to purchase on the agreed terms. For purchase transactions, payment is typically due upon close of escrow. The Nevada Supreme Court has stated, "[t]he law supports the theory that the broker's commission was owed at the close of escrow… ."[66] For non-purchase transactions, payment is due after the services are tendered. Nevertheless, the parties may agree to defer the payment until a specific time or event.

In exclusive agency agreements, compensation is generally owed when the broker fulfills the terms of the agreement. The payment terms must be clear and unambiguous.[67] In an exclusive agency agreement, the broker's commission is not dependent upon the broker being the "procuring cause" of the buyer. Alternatively, the seller and broker may agree the property must sell only at a certain price or under specific conditions before the broker gets paid.

Advanced fee: An advance fee is compensation collected by a broker from a client before services are rendered.[68] It may be collected in advance for listing or advertising a property or a business for sale or lease.[69] Most advanced fees are for the sale of prospecting lists. Any broker who charges an advance fee must give the client an accounting of that fee within three months after collecting it, whether or not the property was actually sold or leased.[70]

b. Procuring Cause – When there is an open listing, in order to be entitled to a real estate commission, a broker must show an employment contract existed and that the broker was the procuring cause of the sale. If a real estate broker has been the "procuring" or "inducing" cause of a sale, he or she is entitled to the agreed commission regardless of who eventually closes the transaction.

65, 66. Chicago Title Agency v. Schwartz, 109 Nev. 415, 418, 419, 851 P.2d 419 (1993).

67. Nollner v. Thomas, 91 Nev. 203, 533 P.2d 478 (1975).

68. NRS 645.323.

69. NRS 645.002.

70. NRS 645.322.

"Procuring cause" is also known as the "inducing cause," "efficient cause," or "proximate cause."

71, 72, 73. Bartsas Realty, Inc. v. Leverton, 82 Nev. 6, 9 - 10, 409 P.2d 627 (1966).

74. Humphrey v. Knobel, 78 Nev. 137, 369 P.2d 872 (1962).

What actions must a broker take to show he or she was the procuring cause? The court has said it is impossible to specify which acts must be present to show "procuring cause," but those acts require the broker to demonstrate "conduct that is more than merely trifling."[71] To be the procuring cause of the sale, the broker must do more than contribute indirectly or incidentally to the sale. Merely introducing the buyer to the seller is not enough. Just imparting information about the property is insufficient. The broker must set in motion a chain of events which, without break in their continuity, cause the buyer and seller to come to terms.

If a broker is the procuring cause of the sale, the broker has a "vested" right to the commission.[72] The right continues even if a seller includes a compensation clause in the purchase agreement that provides the commission will go to another broker. Such a clause is only the client's personal promise to pay a commission to another broker. It does not affect the procuring broker's right to payment.

If a broker is the procuring cause of a sale, it does not matter whom the clients choose to be their final agent. In Bartsas Realty v. Leverton, (1966),[73] Mary Bartsas, a broker, had an open listing agreement with First National Bank of Nevada. She submitted an offer from Davidson to First National. Without communicating with Bartsas, Davidson hired Leverton as his broker who resubmitted a similar offer to First National. When First National told Leverton of the Bartsas's previous offer, Leverton replied, "Well, he (Davidson) has changed brokers and he has come to me now." Eventually, Davidson purchased the property. Bartsas sued Leverton and First National under a claim of procuring cause. The court ruled in favor of Bartsas.

Whether a broker's efforts constitute the procuring cause of a sale is a complicated question based on the particular facts of the matter. Davidson had the right to be represented by any broker of his choice. He was not required to hire Bartsas as his exclusive agent; however, that did not eliminate Bartsas's right to a commission as the procuring cause of the transaction. In this case, both Bartsas and Leverton may have earned a commission - Bartsas as the procuring cause and Leverton as Davidson's agent.

Unless specifically agreed to in the brokerage agreement, a seller cannot refuse to pay a broker because the property was listed at one price but the seller accepted a lower price. A seller may not refuse an offer from a buyer, wait until the brokerage agreement has expired, and then sell the property to that buyer in order to not pay the broker's commission. [74]

III - 17

3. SOURCE AND AMOUNT

Since compensation may only be paid to a broker, only the broker has the right to determine who to accept compensation from and the value of services. This right is modified by legal restrictions and regulations concerning a broker's compensation. Most of these deal with the amount of the compensation and disclosure.

Generally, the source and amount of compensation is determined by agreement between the broker and the client. They should agree on the source of compensation up-front. For example, they should agree on whether the client will pay the broker, or whether the broker will seek his or her compensation from a third party (such as a seller). A broker may rebate the client of a particular transaction a portion of the broker's commission on that transaction without violating the statute (AGO 97-28, 1997).

The amount of compensation is negotiable between the broker and the client. It may be determined as a percentage of the value of the property's sale price, a flat fee (allocated in various ways), or by law. For example, in a probate where the broker is selling a deceased's unimproved real property, Nevada law provides the maximum commission is 10% of the property's sale price.[75]

It is unlawful for any licensee to offer, promise, allow, give or pay, directly or indirectly, any part or share of his or her commission, compensation or finder's fee to any person who is not a real estate licensee, in consideration for services.[76] No broker-salesperson or salesperson may accept compensation from, or pay compensation to, any person other than a broker (or owner-developer) with whom he or she is licensed at the time of the transaction.[77]

a. Source and MLS – There are only two sources of compensation, from the client or from a third party. Most listing agreements have the compensation paid directly by the client. Most buyer brokerage agreements are oral and have the compensation paid by a third party, usually the listing broker. Other third party compensation sources include referral fees from other brokers or compensation paid by relocation companies.

Multiple Listing Service: A multiple listing service is a member-only information dissemination service and a forum for the unilateral offer of compensation. Member brokers place descriptions of listed properties with the MLS so that other members may see what is available for sale. Along with the property description there is a unilateral offer for compensation from the listing broker to any cooperating broker. To earn the stated compensation, the cooperating broker must be the procuring cause of the buyer in a successful transaction. In this instance, the source of the buyer's broker's commission is the listing broker, not the seller.

b. Determining Amount – The most common way of determining a broker's commission is as a percentage of the property's sale price. Nevertheless, there are other ways of calculating the broker's compensation. These include flat fee arrangements, net listings, and a "fee for services" arrangement where the client selects from a menu of services and selectively pays for each service chosen. Each broker and client may mix and match how the broker's compensation will be calculated.

Flat Fee: The broker may charge a client a set or flat fee regardless of the value of the property or the type of service rendered.

75. NRS 148.110.

76. NRS 645.280 (1).

77. NRS 645.280.

Many written buyer brokerage agreements require payment from the buyer-client, with the broker crediting the buyer for any amounts the broker receives from other sources (such as the seller or listing broker).

The cooperating broker is the other party's broker. The term usually refers to the buyer's broker. The buyer's broker may also be known as the "selling" broker.

78. Flamingo Realty, Inc. v. Midwest Development, 110 Nev. 984, 994, 879 P. 2d 69 (1994), Justice J. Young in his dissent sites "net listing" formulas for alternative compensation themes. See also, Shell Oil Co. v. Ed Hoppe Realty Inc., 91 Nev. 576, 581, 540 P.2d 107 (1975).

79. Humphrey v. Knobel, 78 Nev. 137, 369 P.2d 872 (1962).

80. Close v. Redelius, 67 Nev. 158, 167, 215 P.2d 659 (1950).

The net listing brokerage agreement is also known as a "special contract."

The brokerage agreement will not be considered a net listing if the broker's compensation is stated as a percentage of the sales price.

Some brokers charge a flat fee to the client for their portion of the commission with the client agreeing to pay a percentage of the sale price to any cooperating broker. Most advance fee arrangements are flat fees.

Menu (unbundled services): Recently, the idea of menu services has become popular. Menu services are distinct services, each offered for a fee. The client chooses from the menu what services the broker will provide and the broker's compensation is based on the set value of those services. Regardless of the services chosen, the broker cannot refuse to perform a statutory duty because the client did not pay for it.

Net Listings: In a broker's net listing contract, a fixed or net amount must be paid to the seller and the broker's compensation is limited to the excess

of the sale price over the net amount specified. Some states prohibit net listings; however, in Nevada they have been allowed by the courts.[78]

Normally, whoever drafts or provides a contract is held responsible for any deficiencies of that contract. With most brokerage agreements, the broker provides the written agreement and often any dispute over contract terms is decided in the client's favor. However, with a net listing, the courts may construe the construction of the contract against the seller since it is the seller who usually dictates the terms of the net listing.[79]

With a net listing, the client must give the broker a fair chance to earn a commission. The client cannot refuse to accept offers above the net price waiting for the brokerage agreement to terminate and then accept a lower offer. In Close v. Redelius, (1950),[80] Hazel Close hired Redelius, a broker, under an open oral net listing to sell her Reno beauty salon. Redelius, introduced and worked with Wygant to purchase the salon for $1,200 over the net list price. The $1,200 would have been Redelius' commission. Close then told Redelius she decided not to sell at that time. Eventually, Wygant and Close, without including Redelius, agreed to purchase the property at the net amount, thereby cutting Redelius from the deal. The court found for Redelius and stated that a seller with a net listing cannot interfere with the transaction until the broker has had a reasonable opportunity to sell the property at a profit.

III - 19

On the other side, net listings are considered by prominent real estate professional organizations to be ripe for potential unethical conduct by the broker. The concern is that with a net listing, the broker becomes a speculator in the client's property.[81] Additionally, many multiple listing services refuse to take net listings as the co-operating broker's commission, if any, cannot be reasonably determined.

Net listings are still used with hard to sell properties, such as rural land and environmentally damaged property. They are more popular when there is a buyer's market.

c. Quantum Meruit – Quantum meruit is a legal theory used to establish the compensation rate when there is no express agreement or when the agreement fails but the court finds it would be inequitable not to give the broker a commission. Quantum meruit allows the broker to be paid the reasonable value of his or her services.[82] The court will look at "established customs" when determining the worth of the broker's services. [83]

Quantum meruit cannot be used to collect compensation when there is a faulty exclusive brokerage agreement.

4. RESPA AND ANTI-TRUST

Two important sets of laws impact a broker's compensation: RESPA and the anti-trust laws.

a. RESPA – RESPA stands for the Real Estate Settlement Procedures Act.[84] RESPA is federal law passed in 1974 and it is periodically amended. It regulates the behavior of settlement service providers who deal with federally related loans in residential real estate transactions. Real estate licensees are specifically identified as being settlement service providers.[85] A "settlement service provider" is anyone who provides services in connection with a real estate transaction.

Among other items, RESPA regulates who can give and receive compensation for settlement services. No person may give or accept any fee, kickback, or thing of value strictly for a referral to a settlement service provider.[86] RESPA does not review whether the commission is reasonable, nor does it cover broker-to-broker referral fees.

b. Anti-trust - There are two sources for anti-trust laws for Nevada brokers – state law (NRS 598A) and federal law (Sherman Act[87] and the Clayton Act[88]). The object of these laws is to regulate trade to ensure a competitive market for the protection of the consumer. The United States Supreme Court, when defining "trade", said the term included all occupations in which men are engaged for a livelihood.[89] That includes real estate licensees. There are certain jurisdictional issues in applying the federal anti-trust laws to local (Nevada) brokerage services. Nevertheless, some activities dealing with the broker's commission may still fall under the law's shadow.

The main area of regulation concerning a broker's compensation is price fixing. This is where a group of brokers determine a fixed rate of compensation, thereby eliminating competition. Also, it applies to any activity that would tend to establish a uniform practice, for example, setting the length of listing periods.

A broker may set the commission rate in his or her brokerage without being in violation of price fixing. The problem arises when two or more brokers from various firms act in concert to establish industry wide fixed commissions. To avoid even the appearance of price fixing, brokers should have written policies stating their commission rates and establishing their independent business justification for those rates.

81. National Association of Realtors®, Code of Ethics and Arbitration Manual, 2006, case interpretation #1-3.

82. Morrow v. Barger, 103 Nev. 247, 252, 737 P.2d 1153 (1987).

83. Flamingo Realty v. Midwest Devel., 110 Nev. 984, 988, 879 P.2d 69 (1994).

84. 12 U.S.C. § 2600 et seq.

85. 12 U.S.C. § 2602 (3), and Reg. X § 3500.2(b).

86. 12 U.S.C. § 2606, RESPA § 8 (a), and Reg. X § 3500.14.

87. 15 U.S.C. § 1 (1973).

88. 15 U.S.C. § 17 (1973).

89. United States v. National Association of Real Estate Boards, 339 U.S. 485 (1950). NAREB was the precursor to NAR.

A "buyer's market" is when there are more properties on the market than there are buyers. Therefore, the seller has a harder time selling the property and the buyer can get a better deal.

"Quantum Meruit" is Latin. Literally it means "as much as he deserves." It refers to the reasonable value of a person's services.

90. NRS 598A.060.

91. AGO 97-28
(12-31-1997).

A federally related loan is any loan that is either insured by, or subject to, federal regulation or made for the purchase of a residence. It includes conventional as well as FHA or VA loans.

"Commodity" is defined as any tangible property including real property. "Service" is any activity performed for economic gain. (NRS 598A.020

General price uniformity within a profession for a specific locale is not, in and of itself, illegal. However, if it can be shown the players acted in unison to establish a fixed commission, the possibility of an anti-trust violation increases dramatically.

Additionally, brokers should not have set listing periods. It may be problematic if two or more independent brokers require the same, set listing time frames (ex: all listings are 6 months). Listing periods or broker protection periods should be individually set between a broker and the client.

Nevada's anti-trust law: Nevada has its own anti-trust law that covers the sale of any commodity or the performance of any service. Nevada's law makes it an unlawful restraint of trade to price fix. Additionally, agreements between competitors to divide territories, allocate customers, or monopolize an area, are illegal.[90]

c. Rebates to Clients – Both Nevada law and federal law (RESPA) allow a broker to rebate or refund part of the commission to the client.[91] There is a caveat to this type of refund. The broker must acknowledge receipt of the full amount of the commission before refunding a portion back to the client. This is to ensure complete and accurate income accounting. For example, a buyer's broker promises to rebate $1,000 of his commission to the client on the close of escrow. The commission is $5,000. The broker should, even if only on paper, receive the $5,000, and then pay the rebate; otherwise, it may appear the broker is receiving only $4,000, which would be an inaccurate and potentially illegal accounting of the broker's income.

III - 21

5. DISCLOSURE

A licensee must disclose to each party to a transaction (client or not), each source from which he or she will receive compensation.[92] The Real Estate Commission can discipline any licensee found guilty of accepting, giving, or charging, any undisclosed commission by a fine of up to $10,000 per charge, and they may suspend or revoke the licensee's license.[93]

A licensee may also be charged with deceitful, fraudulent or dishonest dealing.[94] The Commission may discipline a licensee if it finds the licensee has not disclosed, in writing, that the licensee:

• expects to receive any direct or indirect compensation from any person who will perform services related to the property,[95]

or

• received compensation from more than one party.

If a broker anticipates receiving compensation from more than one party, the broker must obtain each party's consent.[96] The amount of the compensation does not need to be disclosed, only its source.

The licensee should note that disclosure alone does not make the receipt of certain compensation legal. For example, a salesperson or broker-salesperson may not accept compensation directly from a client under NRS 645.280, even if that compensation is fully disclosed to all parties.

92. NRS 645.252 (1)(b).

93. NRS 645.633 (1)(g).

94. NRS 645.3205.

95. NAC 645.605 (4)(a).

96. NRS 645.252 (1)(b) & NAC 645.605 (4)(e).

97. NRS 645.8711.

98. NRS 645.8705.

99, 100. NRS 645.8761.

101. NRS 645.002 & NRS 645.004.

102. NRS 645.323.

Some brokerage agreements concern specialized property or services and are subject to specific laws.

D. SPECIALIZED BROKERAGE AGREEMENTS

1. COMMERCIAL BROKERAGE AGREEMENTS

Nevada law allows a broker to collect the broker's commission from a commercial real estate transaction by recording a special type of claim called the Broker's Commercial Claim. This claim is not a lien on real property.

Commercial real estate is any real estate in Nevada except:

1. Improved property with four or less residential units (condominiums, houses, townhouses);

2. Improved property with more than four residential units, but where each unit is sold individually (such as condominiums); and

3. Unimproved property upon which no more than four residential units may be developed or zoned.[97]

To be protected by the commercial claim law, the brokerage agreement must be in writing and state what services the broker will provide and what disposition the client desires: for example, sale, purchase, exchange or lease of the commercial real estate.[98] By definition the "owner" has an existing interest in the property, therefore the client will be either the seller or the landlord. The broker representing a buyer or tenant is not afforded claim rights under this section of the law.

Since a brokerage agreement is an employment agreement, it is a contract for services and not a claim on the real property. If the owner breaches the brokerage agreement, the broker's remedy is a claim upon the owner's net proceeds - in other words, a claim over the owner's personal property. The claim is not a claim or lien upon the seller's real estate and does not attach to the real property.[99]

The right to enforce a claim under this section belongs only to the broker. As such, the broker may waive the claim right. An agent for the broker may not waive the broker's claim right even if that agent is otherwise authorized to bind the broker to the brokerage agreement.[100] Any waiver of the broker's right must be done by the broker on or before the date the brokerage agreement is signed.

2. ADVANCE FEE AGREEMENTS

Another specialized brokerage agreement is the advance fee agreement. Any brokerage agreement that requires a client to provide money up-front for brokerage services qualifies as an advance fee agreement.[101] Any person requiring money up-front for real estate related services must have a real estate license.[102] An advance fee is a fee asked for, or given to, a broker for listing or advertising properties, lists of real estate service providers, or for the referral of potential

"Disposition" is the voluntary conveyance of any interest an owner has in the property. An "owner" is any person who holds any existing legal interest in the property and includes an assignee-in-interest. "Owner" does not include a mortgagee, trustee under a deed of trust, or an owner of a claim against the property. NRS 645.872-.8735.

"Net proceeds" are the owner's gross receipts from the disposition of the property minus existing encumbrances, claims or liens and escrow costs. NRS 645.8741.

III - 23

customers (buyers, sellers, landlords, tenants, etc.). Often it involves providing lists of rentals.

Though no specific forms are currently required, the Real Estate Commission is authorized to establish forms for advance fee brokerage agreements. It may also require reports and forms for the review and audit of advance fee agreements.[103]

An advance fee brokerage agreement must be in writing with a detailed description of the broker's services and a date of performance. The broker must identify the total amount of the advance fee and when payment is due.[104]

Full Refund: A special provision includes a statement that the broker will provide a full refund if the services are not substantially or materially provided.[105] For example, if a broker collects advertising costs in advance from a client and the broker does not provide the advertising as stated, the client is entitled to a refund. This provision does not require the property to have been actually sold or leased.

No Guarantee: Additionally, the brokerage agreement cannot imply or guarantee there are tenants or buyers immediately or soon to be available, nor that the property will be purchased, sold, exchanged or leased due to the broker's services.[106]

Oral Promises: Any oral representations or promises made by the broker to induce potential clients into paying an advance fee are by law incorporated into the agreement. Unlike many contracts, there can be no provision in the brokerage agreement that relieves or exempts the broker from those oral representations or promises.[107]

3. BROKERAGE AGREEMENTS IN PROBATE AND GUARDIANSHIP

If a person dies with or without a will and owns real estate in Nevada, the personal representative (court approved/appointed executor or administrator) of the estate may enter into a listing agreement with one or more brokers. The brokerage agreement may be an Exclusive Right to Sell and provide for the payment of compensation to the broker out of the proceeds of the property's sale.

The maximum broker's compensation is set by Nevada law: 10% for the sale of unimproved real property and 7% for improved real property.[108] The payment of any commission must be confirmed by the court contingent upon the sale of the property through the broker's efforts. Even with a brokerage agreement, the court may determine which broker is the procuring cause of the sale and award that broker the commission.[109] The listing broker's commission must be divided between the listing broker and any cooperating broker.[110]

When an estate's personal representative signs the brokerage agreement, the representative has no personal liability to the broker and the estate itself is not liable to the broker unless a sale is made and confirmed by the court.

Similarly, a court-appointed guardian may enter into a brokerage agreement to sell a ward's real property. The requirements and commission restrictions are the same as for those properties being sold from probate. [111]

103. NRS 645.324.

104, 105, 106, 107. NAC 645.675.

108. NRS 148.110.

109. Bartsas Realty, Inc. v. Leverton, 82 Nev. 6, 409 P.2d 627 (1966).

110. NRS 148.120.

111. NRS 159.1385.

112. 11 U.S.C. § 327.

4. BANKRUPTCY

Bankruptcy is federal law that can have a profound effect on the sale of real property and any brokerage agreement.[112] There are various bankruptcy chapters a person may file under. Depending on the chapter, each debtor, and any contractor with that debtor, has certain rights and responsibilities. Considered here are general rules regarding the brokerage agreement when a party files for bankruptcy under Chapter 7 - liquidation or "straight" bankruptcy. Property management agreements and leases have other requirements not discussed here.

There are three major instances in which a broker may be confronted with a brokerage agreement subject to the bankruptcy law:

1. When the broker has an existing, valid listing agreement and the seller files for bankruptcy;

2. When the broker's buyer-client files for bankruptcy; and

3. When the broker is hired by the bankruptcy trustee to sell the bankrupt estate's real property.

Existing Listing Agreement: Usually, an existing listing agreement becomes an "executory contract" once the seller files for bankruptcy. As such, the bankruptcy trustee or the court (they are not the same) can either accept or reject the brokerage agreement. Even if the trustee accepts the contract, the court may reject it. If the trustee and court accept the existing brokerage agreement, the court may modify the compensation. If the contract is rejected, there is little recourse against the court or the trustee.

Buyer Files for Bankruptcy: As soon as the buyer files for bankruptcy, all of the buyer's assets (with certain exclusions) are subject to the control of the bankruptcy trustee. If the buyer has not executed a purchase agreement, any brokerage agreement the buyer has may be terminated since the debtor no longer has control over the assets necessary to purchase any property. If there is an executed purchase agreement, the court may set aside the purchase agreement. At this point the seller, or the buyer's broker, would have to file a Proof of Claim against the buyer's bankruptcy estate for any loss they suffer.

CAUTION! Bankruptcy law is highly technical and no broker should attempt to make a determination on the status of the brokerage agreement without consulting a bankruptcy attorney.

III - 25

Trustee Hires Broker: Many times the bankruptcy court or trustee will sell the debtor's real property assets. The trustee is authorized to hire professionals to help settle or distribute the bankruptcy estate. Under the Bankruptcy Code, a broker is considered a "professional" and therefore, compensation under the brokerage agreement must be approved by the bankruptcy court. The trustee may hire several brokers under an open listing agreement.

The broker may file a motion with the court to have the court appoint the broker and establish the commission. Once the court approves the broker, the commission becomes an administrative expense and is paid out of the assets of the estate before it is distributed to the debtor's creditors.

5. PROPERTY MANAGEMENT AGREEMENTS

Before a broker can engage in property management, the broker must obtain a permit or hire a designated property manager.[113] Every property manager must have a written property management agreement with each client.[114] By definition, a property manager's employment agreement is not a brokerage agreement;[115] it is a written employment contract between a client and broker in which the broker accepts compensation to manage the client's property.[116]

A property management agreement must be in writing - no oral agreements are enforceable. It must include the term of the employment; however, unlike general brokerage agreements that require a specific termination date, a property management agreement may contain an automatic renewal (roll-over) provision. If it does have a roll-over provision, the circumstances on how the agreement will be renewed must be clearly laid out as well as the term for each renewal.[117]

A property management agreement must state the broker's fee or compensation and whether it is calculated as a percentage of the rent, a flat fee, or by some other formula. There must be a provision on how the broker is to handle the retention and disposition of tenant rents and deposits during each term of the agreement. The agreement must outline the broker's authority to act as agent for the client, for example, whether or not the property manager may initiate eviction proceedings. Finally, it must state what conditions must occur if the agreement is cancelled during its term. The statute provides that a property management agreement may have a no-cause cancellation clause.[118]

6. MANUFACTURED HOUSING

A manufactured home, also known as a mobile home, is a residential structure which is built on a permanent chassis and designed to be transportable.[119] Manufactured homes are considered personal property unless legally converted to real property.[120] The laws dealing with their sale are administered by the Manufactured Housing Division of the Department of Business and Industry for the State of Nevada.[121] Manufactured housing may be located either in a mobile home park in which the home sits on rented space, or on a lot privately owned or rented.

113. NRS 645.230 (1)(b) & (c); NRS 645.013 & NRS 645.0195.

114. NRS 645.6056 (1).

115. NRS 645.005.

116. NRS 645.0192.

117, 118. NRS 645.6056.

119. NRS 489.113 & NRS 489.120.

120. NRS 361.244

121. NRS 489.091 & NRS 489.201.

122. NRS 645.042

123. NRS 645.258

124. Per Joan Hutchings, Licensing Officer, Manufactured Housing Division, Business and Industry Department, State of Nevada, Dec. 26, 2007.

A "slow market" occurs when there are more properties for sale than there are buyers, therefore listed homes stay on the market longer.

Real estate brokers, unless they have a dealer's permit, are only authorized to sell manufactured homes when:

1. The manufactured house is used and sits on private property (not in a mobile home park or rented space. NRS 645.030 (1)(a)) and

2. Both the real property and the home are being sold.

Manufactured Housing – A "used" manufactured or mobile home is one which has been sold, rented or leased and occupied before or after the sale or rental or its title of ownership has been previously registered with a state government entity. [122]

If the manufactured home has been converted to real property, any legal brokerage agreement may be used. If the manufactured home has not been converted, the broker must make certain disclosures; [123] however, as long as the broker is also selling the underlying real property, any legal brokerage agreement may be used. [124]

7. LISTING WITH OPTION TO PURCHASE AGREEMENT

More popular in slow real estate markets is the Listing with Option to Purchase Agreement. This option agreement provides that the broker will use his or her best efforts to sell the property, but should he or she be unable to do so, the broker will purchase the property from the client.

Obviously, this type of agreement is fraught with potential claims of broker abuse and conflict of interest. The concern is that with a Listing with Option to Purchase, the broker becomes a speculator in the client's property. Thus, for potential personal profit, the broker may not exercise his or her best efforts in selling the property. Nevada has no specific law restricting or prohibiting option contracts, but extensive disclosure is necessary.

III - 27

E. REVIEW

A broker's employment contract with a client is called a brokerage agreement. All brokerage agreements, being contracts, must have the general contract elements. Other than Nevada laws, certain laws, such as the federal Real Estate Settlement Procedures Act and anti-trust laws, affect what the licensee must do or disclose in a real estate transaction.

Special types of brokerage agreements require specific clauses or wording. Commercial brokerage, advanced fee, probate and guardianship, manufactured housing, and listing with option agreements are all specialized brokerage agreements. Property management agreements, though not technically brokerage agreements, are also specialized employment agreements between a client and a broker.

Brokerage agreements may be oral or written. Certain types of brokerage agreements must be in writing. For example, any brokerage agreement that authorized the broker to be the client's sole broker, called an exclusive agreement, must be in writing. Written contracts may be created with pen and paper, or electronically.

Exclusive brokerage agreements have several requirements. The agreement must contain a definite termination date; be signed by the broker and client or their authorized representatives; and must not require the client to notify the broker of the termination of the exclusive contract feature.

In the brokerage agreement, the broker may limit his or her services; however, at no time may the broker limit the liability for statutorily required duties or services.

Under Nevada law, only a broker is allowed to collect compensation. The salesperson or broker-salesperson may not receive or give compensation from or to, any person for real estate services other than the broker with whom he or she is licensed at the time of the transaction. The receipt of all compensation must be disclosed to the parties in the transaction.

IV. NEVADA LAW
ON OFFERS AND PURCHASE AGREEMENTS

TABLE OF CONTENTS

1. Frantz v. Johnson, 116 Nev. 455, 465, n.4. (2000).

2. McCall v. Carlson, 63 Nev. 390, 419, 172 P.2d 171 (1946).

3. NAC 645.630.

4. NAC 645.632.

GOOD FAITH
is a state of mind encompassing honesty; faithfulness to one's duty or obligation; the desire to observe the reasonable commercial standards of fair dealing; and made without the intent to defraud or to seek an unconscionable advantage.

An offer is the first step toward a legally binding purchase contract. Its terms will create the initial rights and responsibilities of the parties. Since the licensee will often help draft or review an offer, understanding its legal parameters is crucial.

A. OFFERS AND COUNTEROFFERS – GENERAL LAW

In typical real estate transactions, the buyer presents the offer to the seller who either accepts, modifies, or rejects it. The person who gives the offer is the offeror; the person receiving the offer is the offeree. Unless there are unusual circumstances, the brokers or principals' agents are not a party to the offer or purchase agreement. A counteroffer occurs when the offeree rejects the offer and proposes new, or modified, terms.

Intent: Under general contract law, the offer must express the parties' present intent to contract. Even if performance takes place in the future, at the time of contracting the parties must intend to be bound by their words or acts. In Nevada, all contracts are assumed to have an implied covenant of good faith.[1] However, good faith does not mean the parties have equal or balanced responsibilities, obligations, rights or benefits.

Clear Terms: When the client uses a broker, the broker is responsible for ensuring the offer is complete with clear and definite terms. Ambiguous words or contradicting terms can make the offer unenforceable or void. There must be no built-in vagueness. An example of an offer with vague or uncertain terms would be "close of escrow to be at the end of the month", or "seller accepts but retains the right to increase the purchase price." In those clauses, the close of escrow date is uncertain; the purchase price can be changed at the whim of seller - both conditions defeat the requirement for clear and definite terms.

Agreement: Both parties must agree to all the terms of the offer – there must be a "meeting of the minds".[2] A qualified or conditional acceptance turns the offer into a counteroffer which must, in turn, be accepted. Thus, a counteroffer is a modified rejection of the original offer and creates a new offer which must be accepted by both parties. The new offer will include those unchanged terms in the original offer if the old offer is incorporated by reference into the new one. If there are subsequent counteroffers, each must reference the previous offer/counteroffer. This ensures that those terms not in dispute are part of the final document.

Delivery: The offer or counteroffer, must be promptly delivered to the offeree (seller or buyer) who will then accept, counter, or reject it.[3] If it is rejected, the licensee is responsible for obtaining a written notice of the rejection from the client and providing that notice to the offeror within a reasonable time.[4] Once an offer (or counteroffer) is accepted and that acceptance it delivered to the offeror, the parties have a legal contract.

IV - 3

1. CREATING THE OFFER

An offer need not be in writing. Though verbal offers are legal, a verbal acceptance by the seller cannot create a legally binding contract for the sale of real property. Nevada's statute of frauds requires all purchase contracts for real property to be in writing. Therefore, to turn a verbal offer into an enforceable purchase agreement the contract must be in writing, state the consideration and be signed by the seller.[5]

In Nevada, most residential purchase offers are prepared using preprinted forms. There is no state mandated purchase form for real property.

Drafting an Offer for the Non-client: A listing broker is to promote the sale or lease of the seller's/landlord's property and one way of doing this is by putting all bona fide offers in writing and presenting them. The licensee has a duty, when requested, to reduce to writing a bona fide offer made in good faith.[6] Consequently, if a listing broker is requested by a non-represented party to write an bona fide offer, he or she must do so; however, drafting an offer does not automatically make the listing broker the buyer's agent, nor does it create multiple representation necessitating the use of a Consent to Act form.

If an unrepresented buyer requests a non-listing broker to draft an offer, the broker may require the buyer to enter into a brokerage agreement. No broker is required to work for free.

The licensee should be careful about unilaterally deciding an offer is not bona fide and refusing to present it. The licensee must present all offers to the client and let the client decide which offers are bona fide.[7] Obviously, this is not applicable if the licensee has a waiver from the client of the duty to present all offers.

2. WITHDRAWAL OF AN OFFER

Most written offers contain an expiration date and time. However, setting an expiration time does not require the offeror to hold the offer open until that time ends. In contract law, any offer, whether oral or written, may be withdrawn (revoked) by the offeror any time before it is accepted. A seller cannot demand the offeror keep the offer open until it expires.

After the expiration date the offer is no longer viable. Thus, an offer cannot be accepted by the offeree after the expiration date without the offeror agreeing to accept it. The parties may mutually agree to extend the expiration date. A licensee should verify any extension is in writing and signed by both parties. If no expiration time is stated in an offer, a court will impose a "reasonable" time for acceptance based on the facts of each case.

5. NRS 111.210.

6. NRS 645.635(7).

7. NRS 645.254 (4).

BONA FIDE
means an offer made in good faith, without fraud or deceit, where the offeror is sincere and genuine.

8. NRS 645.254 (4).

9. NRS 645.635 (8).

10. & 14. RED Informational Bulletin #001, Multiple Offers Guidelines of Licensees", revised 3/24/04.

11. NRS 645.254 (4).

12. NAC 645.630.

13. NRS 645.635 (8).

14. See sidenote #10.

15. See your local Realtor® Association.

16. Fannie Mae, Multiple Offers Notification form.

17. For example, ZipForm™, by RE FormsNet, LLC, Michigan.

3. PRESENTING THE OFFER

a. Time in Submitting Offer – Unless a client has signed a waiver, the licensee must present all offers made to or by the client as soon as practicable.[8] The listing broker is further required to present all written bona fide offers to the seller.[9] The issues of when, how and by whom offers are presented are determined by the client, not the licensee. There is no law or regulation stating how an offer is to be presented – whether the seller sees the offers in their submission order, all at once, the highest price first, or so forth. There is no law or regulation requiring the seller to reject one offer before seeing the next one. Clients have various desires on how they want to review any offers. A licensee must honor within the limits of the law, those desires.

Though not required by law, the Real Estate Division has stated in its Multiple Offers Guidelines for Licensees that a

> "representative of the cooperating broker has the right to be present when the offer is presented unless the seller gives written instruction to the contrary."[10]

If a seller does restrict the presentation of offers, the listing broker should get the instruction in writing, signed and dated by the seller. Regardless of whether the seller allows a buyer's agent to personally present his or her client's offer, the listing agent must still present all offers.

All offers must be submitted to the client as soon as practicable.[11] There is no statute defining "as soon as practicable". The Administrative Code requires a licensee to deliver all offers "promptly."[12] The Real Estate Commission may take action against any licensee who is found guilty of failing to submit all offers to a seller when the offers are "received".[13] Once the seller has accepted an offer in writing, the licensee may have some

leeway in presenting subsequent offers; however, all offers must still be presented.

Obviously, these laws are violated if a licensee "pockets" an offer. Pocketing an offer is when a licensee intentionally withholds presenting an offer. This is usually done when the licensee is waiting for another, preferred offer.

b. Multiple Offers - The Real Estate Division has issued guidelines for licensees should they receive multiple offers.[14] The guidelines list several alternatives for dealing with multiple offers, from the simple - "accept one offer in writing, and reject all other offers in writing", to the legally complex and technically hazardous – "counter all offers in writing." Individual brokerages, professional associations,[15] government sponsored entities[16] and stationery/ forms publishers[17] have designed various multiple offer forms. Regardless of the form used, the licensee should discuss with the seller how multiple offers will be handled. In a multiple offer situation, a client may mistakenly accept or become liable for two contracts on the sale of a single property. If there is ever a concern, the licensee should refer the client to appropriate legal counsel.

CAUTION!
When a seller issues multiple counteroffers, unless those counteroffers are carefully drafted, the seller may become obligated to more than one buyer.

IV - 5

REAL ESTATE DIVISION

realest@red.state.nv.us   www.red.state.nv.us

INFORMATIONAL BULLETIN #001

MULTIPLE OFFERS GUIDELINES FOR LICENSEES

When Taking the Listing

- ❖ Explain to the client that competing offers may be received.
- ❖ Discuss with the client options for handling multiple offers.
- ❖ The client decides how they want to handle multiple offers.
- ❖ Advise the client that they may wish to seek legal counsel if they do receive multiple offers.

Sellers Make the Decisions – Examples of Options

- ❖ Accept one offer in writing, and reject all other offers in writing.
- ❖ Reject all offers in writing and encourage higher offers.
- ❖ Counter one offer, reject other offers in writing.
- ❖ Delay the decision waiting for another offer informing all parties. Educate the seller that with this option the buyers may withdraw their offer.
- ❖ Alert one or more buyers that they are in a competing offer situation and need to submit their best offer. Reject other offers.
- ❖ Alert all buyers that they are in a competing offer situation.
- ❖ Counter all offers in writing.

Agent Communication

- ❖ Agents should make reasonable efforts to keep cooperating licensees informed of the decision of the client's instructions.

Presenting Offers

- ❖ The representative of the cooperating broker has the right to be present when the offer is presented unless the seller gives written instruction to the contrary.

Confidentiality

- ❖ The cooperating licensee does not have the right to be present at any subsequent discussion or evaluation of the offer by the seller and the listing broker.

NRS 645.253: Each licensee shall not disclose, except to the real estate broker, confidential information relating to a client in violation of NRS 645.254.

NRS 645.254, paragraph 2: A licensee who has entered into a brokerage agreement to represent a client in a real estate transaction … Shall not disclose confidential information relating to a client for 1 year after the revocation or termination of the brokerage agreement, unless he is required to do so pursuant to an order of a court of competent jurisdiction or he is

SOURCE: REAL ESTATE DIVISION.

18. NRS 645.254 (4). See RED: Waiver Form 636 and Authorization to negotiate Directly with Seller Form 637.

18a. NAC 645.254 as amended by R165-07, sec. 5

19. RED "Open House", Multiple Offers, p. 1, Vol. 26, Issue 1, Summer, 2004.

20. An "acceleration clause" in general contract or financing terms allows a lender to "accelerate" the terms of the loan should a borrower default, thereby making the loan immediately due and payable.

21. See #19 above.

c. Delivery - "Delivery" is the act of presenting to the other party the offeree's acceptance, rejection, or counteroffer. Delivery is important because it gives notice. The offeror cannot be bound by a contract until the accepted contract has been delivered to him or her.

Delivery to the other party's agent is considered delivery to the principal. Unless the offer specifically states a limited delivery method (for example, only by hand), delivery is accomplished when the signed offer is presented to the offeror's broker's office in any reasonable manner. This includes personal delivery (face-to-face), mail, facsimile, or e-mail (if an electronic format was previously agreed to). Once a signed offer is delivered, there is a binding purchase agreement.

4. EXCEPTIONS AND RESTRICTIONS

a. Waiver – A client may elect to waive the broker's duty to present all offers by signing a Waiver Form authorized by statute and created by the Real Estate Division.[18] The form restates the regulatory (NAC 645) definition of what "presenting all offers" encompasses to reflect the licensee's activities which often accompany the presentation of offers to the client.[18a] It provides that the broker is not obligated to accept delivery of or convey offers or counteroffers to the client; the broker is not required to answer the client's questions regarding the offers or counteroffers; and the broker is not require to assist the client in preparing, communicating or negotiating offers or counteroffers.

The waiver form must be signed by the client and the broker as the brokerage relationship is between the client and the broker, not the representing salesperson or broker-salesperson.
b. Disclosure of Offer Terms - Since a broker is hired to facilitate the sale or lease of the client's property, common thought is the broker should be able to

maximize his or her client's profit by having offerors bid against each other. To have an effective bidding process, the various offerors would need to know the terms of the competing offers. This would require the listing broker to disclose the terms and price of all other offers. The Real Estate Commission has identified this type of disclosure as a potential violation of NAC 645.605(6) - dealing fairly with all parties to a transaction.[19]

c. "Acceleration" Clauses (not what you think!) – The Division has stated it is a violation of fair dealing to insert what it identifies as an "acceleration" clause. This is not the "acceleration clause" found in general contract or financing law.[20] According to the Division, an acceleration clause is a clause in which the offeror promises to pay a certain set amount above the highest offered sale price and usually provides for a maximum or cap amount. The Division's example is, "I will pay $2,000 over the highest offer up to $300,000."[21] This type of clause automatically gives one offeror a stated advantage over other offerors and may not allow fair dealing for the other offerors.

IV - 7

Though the previous two activities (disclosing offer terms and inserting an acceleration clause) are not a direct violation of any law or regulation, and there is some controversy regarding this, nevertheless, the Real Estate Commission has found these practices to be highly suspect.

d. Discrimination – Regardless of any instruction or preference of the licensee's client, a licensee may never reject or modify an offer because the offeror is a member of a protected class. It is illegal to discriminate by denying a person an opportunity to engage in a real estate transaction because of that person's race, religious creed, color, national origin, disability, ancestry, familial status or sex (gender). A licensee cannot modify the terms and conditions of an offer to discriminate against, or provide a preference for, a person based on his or her protected class status.[22]

The licensee must be aware that a client seeking a preference for a person based on their protected class is also a violation of the law. For example, a licensee cannot follow a client's instruction to accept only offers from persons of a certain religious or racial background.

Nevada's protected classes are race, religious creed, color, national origin, disability, ancestry, familial status and sex.[23] Sexual orientation is not a protected class for housing in either Nevada or federal law.

5. REJECTION OF OFFER

Once an offer has been reviewed by the offeree, if it is rejected, the licensee must obtain a written notice signed by the offeree informing the offeror of the rejection.[24] There is no requirement that the notice explain why the offer is being rejected. The purpose of this regulation is to satisfy the offeror that his or her offer was actually presented, reviewed and rejected by the other party. Most Nevada preprinted purchase agreement forms contain a rejection clause with a place for the rejecting party to sign.
The rejection notice should be given to the offeror within a "reasonable" time. When there is no time frame specified, the courts will determine a "reasonable" time from the facts of each case. Once the rejection has been delivered, the offer is dead.

The Administrative Code requirement that the licensee have the offeree sign a rejection notice is only binding on the licensee, not on the client. There are times when a client, having rejected an offer, may refuse to sign a rejection notice. In these cases, the licensee is still charged with providing the offeror with a written rejection notice that states the client refused to sign the rejection.

22. NRS 645.321 (1)b).

23. The 1968 Fair Housing Act, as amended 1988, 42 U.S.C. § 3601 et seq. and NRS 118.

24. NAC 645.632.

25. Morrison v. Rayen Investments, Inc., 97 Nev. 58, 624 P.2d 11 (1981).

26. E. Allan Fransworth, Contracts, (3rd ed.) §§ 3.11, 3.18, Aspen Publishers, NY, 1999.

6. TERMINATION – LAPSE BY TIME

Most written offers contain an expiration clause which identifies a date and time after which the offer is invalid. This time frame is for the benefit of the offeror to allow him or her to move on to other transactions after a stated time and not be hampered by an outstanding, but unanswered, offer. The offer automatically lapses after the expiration time frame unless the date is extended by both parties. A late or defective acceptance becomes a counteroffer which must in turn be accepted by the original offeror.

In Morrison v. Rayen Investments, Inc. (1981),[25] Morrison, the buyer, offered to purchase Rayen Investments, Inc.'s property. The offer had a 15-day expiration period.

On the 16th day Rayen's president telegraphed the corporation's acceptance and instructed its agent to open escrow. The court found that since the telegraphed acceptance was outside the offer's required 15-day acceptance period, the offer had lapsed. Any attempt by the offeree to revive the offer became a counteroffer and Morrison, the original offeror, was required to accept that counteroffer before there was a binding contract. The court found that Morrison never accepted the counteroffer, therefore, there was never a legal purchase contract.

7. TERMINATION BY DEATH

There is no specific Nevada law saying what happens to an outstanding offer when either the seller or buyer dies. However, general contract law provides that if an offeree dies before accepting an offer, the offer immediately terminates.[26] If there is more than one offeree, the surviving offeree may accept the offer. If an offeror dies before the offer is accepted, the offer immediately terminates regardless of whether or not the offeree has notice of the offeror's death. If there is more than one offeror, the surviving offeror may reinstate the offer, but is not legally obligated to do so.

IV - 9

B. PURCHASE AGREEMENTS

27. NRS 129.010.

28. NRS 129.080.

29. 1916.

30. Seeley v. Goodwin, 39 Nev. 315, 156 P. 934 (1916).

See page IV-25 regarding the legal difference between a "contract of sale" and a "contract for sale".

Once an offer is accepted and delivered, it becomes a binding purchase agreement. A purchase agreement is a contract between a buyer and seller for the sale of real property. A purchase agreement contract may also be known as an O & A (offer and acceptance), contract of sale, or simply a sales contract. An installment contract (also known as a contract for sale) and an option contract are discussed separately.

At a minimum, general contract law requires what is called the four "P's" – parties, property, price and proof. The contract must identify the parties (the buyer and seller); what property is being sold; the price being paid; and proof the parties intend to be bound, i.e., consideration.

The majority of the conditions or terms found in real property purchase agreements are covered by general contract law. Reviewed here are only the legal requirements in Nevada statute and case law. These laws include public policy considerations and prohibited terms for purchase agreements; the licensee's duties when dealing with purchase agreements; and, a review of the legal requirements for specialized purchase agreements such as those for unimproved property and homes in common-interest communities.

1. GENERAL LEGAL REQUIREMENTS

To have an enforceable contract, each party signing the contract must be over the age of majority and legally competent.

In Nevada, the age of majority is 18 years old.[27] Contracts with minors are enforceable or voidable by the minor, but not enforceable by the other party if the minor chooses to rescind or disaffirm the contract. A minor may have legal emancipation giving him or her full majority rights.[28] Marriage alone does not give a minor legal emancipation.

A person must be legally competent to contract. A party's insanity, intoxication or lack of authority can make the contract void. It is old law in Nevada[29] that an intoxicated party (drugs or alcohol) cannot rescind or avoid a signed contract, unless the party was so inebriated as to be devoid of all reason and understanding. If the contract was notarized, that is prima facie evidence of legally sufficient signing, regardless of the signer's intoxication.[30] However, most purchase agreements are not notarized. If a licensee has any concern as to the signer's capacity, it is best to wait and have the contract signed at a different time.

A void contract was never legal, whereas a voidable contract, though legal on its face, is 'avoidable' by a party.

PRIMA FACIE
"Prima facie" evidence means evidence presumed by the court to be legally sufficient unless otherwise disproved or rebutted.

31. NRS 111.210.

32. NRS 111.450.

33. Zhang v. Dist. Court, 120 Nev. Adv. Op. 104 (2004).

34. Tomiyasu v. Golden, 81 Nev. 140, 141, 400 P.2d 415 (1965).

Statute of Frauds: Every purchase contract in Nevada must comply with the statute of frauds. It: 1) Must be in writing, 2) State the consideration given by the parties for the contract, and 3) Be signed by the owner (seller) or his or her lawfully authorized agent.[31] Unless the licensee has a separate, notarized and recorded, power-of-attorney from the client,[32] a client is not bound when a licensee signs the purchase agreement.

a. "Writing" Required – The "writing" clause required by Nevada's statute of frauds is intended to prove a contract exists; thereby preventing fraud and perjury. The writing may consist of a standard contract form, letter, or other written document and may consist of one or several related instruments that when read together, contain the legal requirements for a purchase contract. Emails may be sufficient to create a legal purchase agreement.

b. Consideration – All contracts require consideration. Consideration may be either the mutuality of obligation, or the receipt of a thing of value exchanged between the parties - from money to love and affection. If each party has some right (benefit) and responsibility (burden) there is mutuality of obligation and this is sufficient consideration, as is a promise given for a promise received.

Earnest money is not consideration - it is an inducement to negotiate. Earnest money is presented with an offer to indicate the genuineness of the offer. If the offer is accepted, the earnest money is usually incorporated into the purchase agreement as part of the buyer's down payment. If the offer is rejected, the earnest money is returned to the offeror.

Since each contract requires consideration, a contract without consideration is void. In Zhang v. Dist. Court (2004),[33] the seller defaulted on an existing purchase agreement. He then stated he would sell the property to the same buyer but at a higher price. To proceed with the transaction, the buyer agreed and signed the new purchase agreement. The buyer then sued to enforce the original contract. The court found for the buyer stating the seller was already obligated to sell to the buyer under the first contract when he required the buyer to sign the new contract. It found there was no consideration for the second contract. Without consideration, the second contract failed. Therefore, the buyer could enforce the first purchase agreement.

Inadequate consideration will not undo a contract. The Nevada Supreme Court has stated,

"mere inadequacy of price without proof of some element of fraud, unfairness, or oppression that could account for and bring about the inadequacy of price was not sufficient to warrant the setting aside of the [contract]."[34]

It is not up to the licensee to determine if the consideration is sufficient – that is the client's decision.

IV - 11

c. Who Signs and Various Entities –
Legally, only the seller or the seller's
lawfully authorized agent is required
to sign the purchase agreement.[35]
However, since most modern purchase
agreements require obligations from both
parties, seller and buyer, each must accept
those terms. That acceptance is proved
by the parties' signatures on the purchase
agreement.

A licensee must be aware of who has
the signing authority for a given entity.
When there is a question regarding a
party's authority to sign, the licensee
should request proof or verification at the
onset of the transaction. If there is any
question, the broker should require the
party's legal counsel to provide written
verification of authority. If the closing
is through an escrow company or title
insurance is being purchased, then the
escrow or title officer will determine who
is the appropriate legal entity. However,
that may not occur until well into the
transaction. If the licensee has been
dealing with an unauthorized principal,
the whole transaction may unravel at the
end. It is better to ensure upfront, who-is-
who and who has signing capacity.

Married Parties: Since Nevada is a
community property state, if a buyer
is married both spouses must sign the
purchase contract.[36] If a seller is selling
community property, the spouse does
not have to sign the purchase agreement
but will be required to execute the deed
transferring title.[37] Should the non-
signing spouse choose not to sign the
deed, the buyer may only sue the signing
spouse for breach of contract and could
bring an action against the broker for
negligence. A licensee should obtain
both spouses' signatures on any purchase
agreement, whether buyer or seller.

Co-ownership: If there are multiple
owners, each person on title will have
to sign the deed if the entire property is
being sold. If all owners do not sign the

purchase agreement, and the contract is
breached, the buyer will have recourse
only against the owners who signed.
Again, the licensee should be aware of a
possible negligence lawsuit against the
broker if the licensee fails to obtain all
necessary signatures.

Trusts and Guardianships: A trust is
created by an individual, called the
settlor, who allows the legal title to
specific property to be held in the name
of the trust for the benefit of others or
the settlor. A trust is controlled by one
or more trustees. Individuals named to
benefit by the trust's property are the
beneficiaries. Commonly, the trustee
has the authority, as granted by the
trust document, to sell or purchase
real property in the trust's name.[38] The
beneficiaries of the trust do not have the
authority to sell trust property. A trustee's
rights are outlined in law; however, trust
documents may modify the trustee's
responsibilities. A licensee should have
some written verification that the trustee
is solely authorized to sign the purchase
agreement.

The licensee should be aware that a
trustee who is not the settlor, usually
needs the approval of a court if the trustee
is personally purchasing property from,
or selling property to, the trust estate.[39]

A legally appointed guardian of an
incompetent ward may sign a brokerage
agreement to sell or to purchase real
property from the ward's estate.[40]
However, this authority also requires
court approval.[41]

Corporations: In Nevada, the statutes
Controlling most corporations are found
in NRS 78. Briefly, a corporation is owned
by the stockholders but managed by a
board of directors,[42] which has control
over the affairs of the corporation.[43]
Each corporation must have a president,
secretary and treasurer who are
accountable to the board of directors.[44]

35. NRS 111.210.

36. NRS 123.230 (4).

37. NRS 123.220 (3).

38. NRS 163.023.

39. NRS 163.050.

40. NRS 159.1385.

41. NRS 159.134.

42. NRS 78.115.

43. NRS 78.120.

44. NRS 78.130.

Title does not show all
ownership interests in a
property. A married man
may hold title as "sole and
separate" but his wife may
still have a community
property interest.

45. General partnerships NRS 87, limited partnerships NRS 88.

46. NRS 87.120.

47. NRS 87.090.

48. NRS 88.455.

49. NRS 86.301.

50. NRS 148.110.

51. NRS 148.060.

52. NRS 244.282 & NRS 244A.619.

53. NRS 266.267.

54. NRS 279.470.

55. NRS 361.595.

56. NRS 393.245 & University System NRS 396.430.

57. NRS 547.090.

58. NRS 111.160.

DEVISEE
A devisee is the person who gets property, usually real property, under a will.

All three positions may be held by the same person. The corporation's articles of incorporation, bylaws, or both, usually state the directors' and officers' authority to purchase or sell real property in the corporation's name. Therefore, each corporation may have different rules as to who is authorized to sign a purchase agreement. Often, but not always, the president of the corporation is authorized to sign. Nevertheless, when the corporation is selling its real property, the president may need a statement of ratification by the board of directors to strip the corporation of its assets.

Partnerships: Like other legal entities, partnerships are governed by Nevada law.[45] A general partnership may be composed of several individuals, each sharing the benefits and liabilities of the partnership. Unless otherwise provided in the partnership agreement, any partner in a duly formed general partnership may execute a purchase agreement in the partnership's name[46] and the partnership will be bound by the acts of that partner.[47]

Limited partnerships have both general and limited partners. The limited partners are liable only up to the amount they have invested in the partnership. The general partners share full liability. In limited partnerships, usually only a general partner has the right to execute a purchase agreement.

Limited Liability Company: A limited liability company is organized under NRS 86. It may acquire, own, and dispose of real property in its own name. Often, it is composed of a manager, or managers, charged with overseeing the company's affairs. It has members (similar to stockholders) and it may have agents, officers, or employees. Generally, the manager has the legal authority to execute documents for the acquisition or disposition of the company's property. A member may have the authority if the company is managed by its members, or

the company's articles of organization or operating agreement may provide that an agent, officer or employee can sign.[49]

Probate Executors or Administrators: Nevada law provides specific procedures on the sale of real property in probate. During probate, the court will grant authority over the deceased's estate to either an executor or court appointed administrator. The executor or administrator may sign brokerage agreements[50] and sell or purchase real property with court approval.[51] A devisee under a will, or an heir to an estate, does not have the right to sell real property still in the deceased's name.

Governments: Almost every government entity (e.g., state, county,[52] or city[53]) or quasi-government entity (e.g., Redevelopment agency,[54] abatement of pests' district,[55] school district,[56] or agricultural associations[57]) is given the statutory authority to purchase or sell real property. Each of these entities will have allocated a specific position that is authorized to execute purchase agreements and deeds for that entity. This position is not always the director, administrator, or chairman of the board or commission.

d. After-Acquired Title – A licensee should be aware that some sellers may attempt to sell property that they do not yet legally own. The majority of the time, the seller has a future interest in the property. For example, a devisee may attempt to sell his or her interest in a property that is still in the deceased's name. Or, a person may attempt to sell property he or she does not have title to but is in contract to purchase. These actions are not always illegal under Nevada's After-Acquired Title statute;[58] however, it is very unwise to participate in this type of transaction unless an attorney representing the proposed seller is willing to take responsibility for any liability the licensee and broker may incur.

IV - 13

Nevada's After-Acquired Title statute provides that if a person sells the fee simple absolute title to a property, which title is not yet in the seller's name, and afterwards acquires title to the property, the title immediately passes to the buyer. This is applicable only in very narrow, specific situations. It cannot be used to avoid transfer taxes – generally, the transfer tax can be assessed on each transaction. No broker should ever rely on this statute when taking a listing or when representing a buyer. If there is a question on ownership or title, the broker should consult with an attorney to establish the validity of the seller's authority.

e. "Signing" by Electronic Signature - Nevada law authorizes an electronic format for any transaction or contract in which the parties agree to conduct their business electronically.[59] An electronic record satisfies any statute that requires a writing and an electronic signature satisfies any statute requiring a sigNature.[60] If the signature must be notarized, it may be electronically notarized by the electronic signature of a notary together with all the information required to be included under other applicable law. That information must be attached to, or associated with, the electronic signature or record.[61]

f. Broker's Rights Under the Purchase Agreement – The parties to a purchase agreement are the buyer and seller – the parties' brokers are agents of the principals and not a party to the sale of the real property. The brokers' authority and contractual rights are found in the brokerage agreements, not the purchase agreement.[62] Since the brokers (or other licensees) are not a party to the contract, they lack standing (legal status) to sue on a breach of the purchase contract's terms. When a purchase agreement includes terms which indemnify the brokers, waive or disclaim their liability, state their compensation, or disclose their agency relationship, the licensee must understand those clauses may not be recognized as enforceable in a court of law.

59. NRS 719.220(2).

60. NRS 719.240.

61. NRS 719.280.

62. Seigworth v. State, 91 Nev. 536, 539, 539 P.2d 464 (1975).

63. J.A. Jones Constr. v. Lehrer McGovern Bovis, 120 Nev. Ad. Op. 32, p. 7 (2000).

64. J.A. Jones, Constr. at p. 8, citing Hilton Hotels v. Butch Lewis Productions, 107 Nev. 226, 232, 808 P.2d 919, 922-23 (1991).

65. NRS 40.453.

66. NRS 107.080-.100.

67. NRS 118.020.

68. NRS 645.321 (1).

69. NRS 111.237.

70. NRS 118.100.

71. NRS 207.300.

72. NRS 645.635 (9).

73. 42 U.S.C. §§ 3601 et seq.

74. NRS 113.040.

2. SPECIAL CLAUSES AND PROHIBITIONS

Along with the statutes outlining the minimum legal requirements for a purchase agreement, the law also provides for clauses or contract terms which affect the parties' various responsibilities or rights. These include public policy provisions which are automatically read into each contract, to prohibitions against certain restrictions or covenants.

a. Public Policy Provisions - All contracts contain some public policy clauses that are automatically considered part of the contract. For example, all contracts are presumed to have a clause requiring the parties to act in good faith. The Nevada Supreme Court has held that the

> "implied covenant of good faith and fair dealing exists in every Nevada contract ... [it] essentially forbids arbitrary, unfair acts by one party that disadvantage the other."[63]

No term in the contract can abrogate that implied covenant. The court stated,

> "We have held that when 'the terms of a contract are literally complied with but one party to the contract deliberately countervenes the intention and spirit . . ., that party can incur liability for breach of the implied covenant of good faith and fair dealing.'"[64]

Other public policy provisions include a prohibition against any clause which eliminates the statutory rights of a borrower (mortgagor or deed of trust grantor).[65] A borrower's rights include the right to receive default notices and the right to rely upon the statutory time-frames before foreclosure commences.[66]

Discrimination: It is against public policy for any seller or licensee to discriminate against any person because of that person's race, religious creed, color, national origin, disability, ancestry, familial status or sex (gender), by denying that person access to any opportunity to engage in a residential real estate transaction.[67] The prohibition includes any discriminatory wording or intent in the terms or conditions of a real estate transaction,[68] the addition of racial covenants or restrictions in a deed,[69] and the refusal to sell or make a residential property available to any person based on that person's status as a member of a protected class.[70] Such discriminatory behavior is not only a crime,[71] but will subject the licensee to discipline by the Real Estate Commission.[72] Nevada's protected classes echo the federal classes[73] and a licensee is subject to both laws.

b. If the Property is Destroyed – By statute, if the property is destroyed or taken by eminent domain while in escrow, the rights of the principals are predetermined unless the parties have contracted differently.[74]

When a property is substantially destroyed, if the buyer has not taken legal title or possession of the property and the buyer is not at fault in the property's destruction, then the seller cannot enforce the contract. The buyer may recover any portion of the price already paid. If the buyer has taken possession or legal title, and the seller is not at fault in the property's destruction, the seller may enforce the terms of the contract.

Likewise, while the property is in escrow, if it is taken by a government under eminent domain and the buyer has not taken possession or legal title, the seller is entitled to receive the value of the property from the taking entity, but he or she must refund any money the seller received from the buyer. If the buyer has taken possession or legal title, he or she

IV - 15

may receive the value of the property from the taking entity, but must pay to the seller the contract price.

c. If A Principal Dies – Should a principal die while in contract, his or her interest in the purchase agreement is determined by statute. Should the buyer die, the court appointed personal representative of the deceased (the executor or administrator) has several options. He or she may terminate the contract, continue with the purchase, or sell the deceased's rights under the contract.[75] The right to continue with the sale belongs to the buyer's estate, a seller cannot enforce the contract. If the seller dies while in contract, the buyers can require, with court approval, the seller's estate to continue with the sale.[76]

d. Solar Energy and the Flag – No purchase contract may have any clause restricting the buyer's right to obtain solar energy.[77] No contract may have any clause restricting the display of the American flag.[78] This includes restrictions in common-interest communities and CC & Rs (covenants, conditions and restrictions). There are some limitations on how the flag may be displayed.

e. Property Title & RESPA – Title is the legal evidence of ownership of a property. One of the basic assumptions when buying a property is that the buyer will receive clear title. When a property is subject to a financial obligation or use constraint, the title is encumbered. No property is completely free and clear of all title restrictions. All property may be subject to public restrictions (e.g., taxes, zoning) or private restrictions (e.g., C C & Rs, easements, financing obligations). Many purchase agreements have clauses disclosing these to the buyer. Often these clauses state the buyer will take title to the property in spite of the restriction if the restriction is common and reasonable, for example, property taxes.

The contract may or may not contain a time-frame which allows the seller to clear title defects or encumbrances. The right to extend the contract's time frame for the seller to clear title is not automatic and will only be granted if provided for in the contract or by agreement.[79]

Unmerchantable Title: An encumbrance, lien, restriction or claim can make the title unmarketable (e.g., unmerchantable). A real estate licensee may not offer or attempt to sell any property with an unmerchantable title unless the licensee notifies the prospective buyer of the title impairment before the buyer pays any part of the purchase price.[80]

Federal law (Real Estate Settlement Procedures Act – RESPA)[81] prohibits a seller from requiring a buyer to obtain title insurance from a specific title company. However, a seller may mandate a specific escrow company or lender.

This separation between escrow and title often confuses the new licensee. In the western United States, most title insurance companies are intimately associated with escrow companies where the purchase of title insurance and the purchase of escrow services seem seamless - both services and product coming as a package. In reality, title and escrow are separate and distinct services and entities. There are independent escrow companies that are not associated with a title insurance company and title insurance companies from which a buyer may purchase title insurance without using any escrow service.

75. NRS 148.330.

76. NRS 148.420.

77. NRS 111.239 and NRS 278.0208.

78. NRS 111.238.

79. Denison v. Ladd, 54 Nev. 186, 187-88, 10 P.2d 637 (1932).

80. NAC 645.635.

81. 12 U.S.C. § 2608.

An unmerchantable title is title that a reasonable buyer would refuse to accept because of use constraints, conflicting interests, or the possibility of litigation.

82. Epperson v. Roloff,
103 Nev. 206, 719 P.2d
799 (1986).

83. NRS 113.100-.150.

84. Mackintosh v. Jack
Matthews., 109 Nev.
628, 855 P.l2d 549 (1993)
(Justices Springer and
Young, dissenting).

f. The Integration Clause – An integration clause provides that the written contract represents the parties' complete and final agreement – that no verbal claims made by any party prior to the signing of the contract can be relied on or are a part of the contract. However, relying on the contract's integration clause will not shield a seller or licensee from their misrepresentations.

In one case, Epperson v. Roloff (1986),[82] the sellers attempted to claim that the contract's integration clause stopped the buyer from bringing a misrepresentation claim. In this case, the sellers and their agent, while showing the potential buyers the sellers' home, made reference to and gestured toward a "solar feature" in the house. After the buyers moved in, they discovered that the solar feature was a hole in the roof covered with corrugated metal painted black. When the buyers sued for misrepresentation, the sellers claimed they had made no affirmative statements about there being a solar panel. They then argued that the contract's integration clause prevented the buyers from relying on anything they had said unless it was in writing or in the contract. The court found that an integration clause does not bar a claim of misrepresentation when there is a duty to speak.

g. "As Is" Clause – Some laws concerning real property purchase contracts are found in statute, others are found in case law. The law concerning the "as is" clause is a common law creation. An "as is" clause requires the buyer to take the property with no warranties of fitness or condition and with all existing defects. Generally, if the property has a defect that is patent (exposed, accessible) the seller does not need to point out the defect unless there is a "special relationship" between the seller and buyer. If there is a special relationship, the seller is obligated to identify even patent defects.

The "as is" clause has its limitations. It cannot be used to force a buyer to purchase a property with a defect hidden by the seller. If the defect is latent (not readily discernable, hidden) and the seller knows of the defect, the seller must disclose it to the buyer regardless of any "as is" clause. The court found the seller has an affirmative duty to disclose to a potential buyer those adverse facts known only to the seller and which could not be reasonably discovered by the buyer. Since 1995 in Nevada, a residential property seller is required to complete the mandated Sellers Real Property Disclosure form identifying all property defects of which the seller is aware.[83]

Additionally, if a seller (or the agent) has fraudulently and affirmatively misrepresented the condition of the property (false representation) or has intentionally concealed known defects, the "as is" clause will not shield the seller from liability.

The most important Nevada case dealing with the "as is" clause is Mackintosh v. Jack Matthews and Company (1993).[84] Jack Matthews's brokerage was hired by California Federal Savings and Loan (Cal Fed) to sell a Carson City foreclosed property. Clark, an employee of Cal Fed, hired a local contractor to clean and paint the home. The contractor pointed out to Clark basement water leakage and other construction defects (cracked beam, broken water pipe, etc.). Clark told the contractor not to mention the water problem to anyone. Cal Fed then listed the property "as is."

The Mackintoshes were interested in purchasing the property. When they looked at it, the electricity was turned off and they had to use a flashlight while inspecting the basement. They noticed water in the basement but thought it was due to a recent repair of faulty plumbing. In the pest inspection report, the inspector noted "interior walls in

IV - 17

basement area are damaged and sheet rock is moldy from excessive moisture". The Mackintoshes reviewed and signed this report. They obtained their home loan from Cal Fed and closed escrow soon thereafter. After the close of escrow, the Mackintoshes became aware of the extensive water seepage problem and the other major construction defects.

The Mackintoshes sued Cal Fed, the brokerage and others for failure to disclose and for breach of fiduciary duty. Cal Fed argued the Mackintoshes were aware of a water problem but accepted the property, with this visible defect, "as is." It argued that as the seller, under general contract law, it owed no special duty to the buyers to disclose patent defects. The lower court granted summary judgment for Cal Fed and the other defendants. The Mackintoshes appealed.

The Nevada Supreme Court extensively reviewed the history of the "as is" clause from cases across the nation. It found generally, that when a property was sold "as is," the seller's nondisclosure of adverse information (e.g., defects) will not allow the buyer to rescind the contract or sue for damages. When a defect is patent, the buyer will only be able to rescind or get damages if the seller made actual false statements, not just remained silent.

Moreover, since the buyer was put on notice of a possible defect, the buyer had an affirmative duty to reasonably inquire as to the nature of the problem or defect— the traditional "should have known" rule. This principle provides that if a buyer knew, or should have known using reasonable diligence, of a defect, yet accepted the property anyway, the buyer waives any right to seek damages for that defect.[85] The court found that since the Mackintoshes were aware of some water damage, they were required to investigate further the potential water problem. Since they did not do this, under traditional

legal rules, they would lose their lawsuit. However, the court said in this case there was a "special relationship" between the parties thereby making the seller obligated to disclose even patent defects.

A special relationship occurs when one party confides in and relies on, the other party because of the nature of their relationship. In Mackintosh, the court found that Cal Fed was not only the seller but the lender as well. As their lender, the Mackintoshes confided personal and confidential information to Cal Fed - information a buyer would not normally share with a seller, and Cal Fed took the property as security for their loan - thereby reasonably leading the Mackintoshes to believe that there was a "special relationship" between themselves and Cal Fed. This special relationship invested Cal Fed with the requirement of full disclosure which nullified the onerous effects of the "as is" clause. Based on its finding of a special relationship, the court reversed the lower court's ruling and found for the Mackintoshes.

A licensee should never rely on an "as is" clause to shield him or her from non-disclosure liability. A licensee must always disclose, as soon as practicable and to each party to the transaction, all material and relevant facts, data or information relating to the property. This disclosure is required whether the licensee had actual knowledge of the information, or "should have known" of it using reasonable diligence.[86]

h. Unconscionability – No purchase agreement may have unconscionable clauses. The Nevada Supreme Court stated

> "[a] contract is unconscionable only when the clauses of that contract and the circumstances existing at the time of the execution of the contract are so one-sided as to oppress or unfairly surprise an innocent party."[87]

85. Thornton v. Agassiz, 106 Nev. 676, 799 P.2d 1106 (1990).

86. NRS 645.252 (1)(a).

87. Bill Stremmel Motors v. IDS Leasing Corp., 89 Nev. 414, 418, 514 P.2d 654 (1973).

An unconscionable clause is one that requires a party to do an act which affronts the sense of justice, decency, or reasonableness, or which requires a party to give-up a vested right.

88. NRS 645.633 (1)(h).

89. NRS 645.635 (3).

90. NRS 645.252 (2).

91. NRS 645.257 (3).

92. NAC 645.605 (5).

93. NAC 645.605 (9).

94. NAC 645.605 (2) and (10).

95. NRS 645.635 (1)(h).

96. Real Estate Division v. Soeller, 98 Nev. 579, 656 P.2d 224 (1982).

For example, a contract provision that provides for only one principal to pay the other principal's attorney fees regardless who is at fault, is unconscionable. As is a clause that allows one party to unilaterally alter the terms of the contract while still holding the other party accountable. For instance, an unconscionable seller's clause would be

> "seller reserves the right to increase the sale price or cancel this contract without penalty. Should seller exercise this right, buyer agrees to give up his right to mediate, arbitrate or seek damages or specific performance against seller."

The courts reserve to themselves the right to determine if various clauses are unconscionable. If they find a clause unconscionable, it may be stricken from the contract or the whole contract may be unenforceable.

3. LICENSEE DUTIES

A licensee has specific statutory duties to the client and other principals when handling a purchase agreement. These include general duties such as the requirement not to be negligent,[88] to specific duties such as ensuring a copy of the contract has been given to the client.[89]

a. Reasonable Skill and Care – A licensee has the duty to use reasonable skill and care with respect to all parties to the real estate transaction.[90] What is reasonable skill and care? It is the skill and care that a reasonably prudent licensee brings to any transaction by applying the licensee's knowledge of the law, the profession, and the property. The licensee, at a minimum, must have the degree of knowledge required to obtain a then current real estate license.[91] This requires the licensee to keep current with all real estate related laws[92] and to understand and properly adhere to those laws.[93] Additionally, reasonable skill and care includes the licensee reasonably obtaining knowledge of the material and pertinent facts about the property and the transaction.[94]

Reasonable care requires the licensee not to act in an irresponsible, careless or negligent manner.[95] Not being negligent entails understanding all the terms of the purchase agreement and completing the contract to ensure each term is lawful and represents the client's wishes. In Real Estate Division v. Soeller (1982),[96] Soeller was the listing broker for the Bennetts who were selling their Lake Tahoe property. Lund, a licensee with another brokerage, made a personal offer on the property. Soeller never reviewed Lund's offer before presenting it to his clients. He missed that Lund had not included a close of escrow date.

After the contract was signed, he did not verify if Lund had deposited the earnest money when she opened escrow. When a question arose, he instructed Lund

IV - 19

to negotiate directly with the Bennetts because he was going on vacation.

Eventually, Lund was unable to perform on the contract and verbally agreed with the Bennetts to cancel escrow. Nevertheless, she did not cancel the escrow nor did Soeller, the Bennett's broker, ever verify escrow was cancelled. Lund later found a buyer for the property (Howarth) and agreed to sell the Bennetts' property to Howarth in a double escrow for several thousands of dollars over the Bennetts' asking price. Because there was no close of escrow date on the purchase agreement and the escrow had not been cancelled, Lund proceeded to force the Bennetts to sell the property to her which she, in turn, immediately sold to Howarth. The profit was identified as "commission" to Lund's brokerage. Soeller received his full commission. When Soeller was sued, he claimed both the Bennetts and Howarth had full disclosure of the transaction as it was laid out in the escrow instructions. However, the court found there were at least three different sets of escrow instructions and there may have been more.

The Real Estate Commissioners found Lund, his brokers, and Soeller, in violation of NRS 645 for misconduct, negligence, lack of supervision, lack of honest dealing, and failure to protect the interests of their clients. Lund's license was revoked, Soeller's and the brokers' licenses were suspended. None of the licensees had used the reasonable skill or care necessary to protect the interests of their clients.

b. Writing Reviewed - A licensee must ensure all the terms and conditions of the purchase agreement are in writing and that it is properly signed by all parties.[97] The licensee must make certain each change or modification of the agreement is incorporated into the contract and signed or initialed by the appropriate parties.[98]

c. Authentic Terms - The purchase agreement must accurately reflect the authentic terms of the parties' agreement. For example, a licensee may not represent (either verbally or in writing) to any lender or other interested party, an amount in excess of the actual sale price, terms differing from those actually agreed upon,[99] or name any false consideration.[100] Any misstatement or concealment of a material fact to a lender is fraud and will subject that person to criminal and civil lawsuits as well as regulatory discipline.[101] A licensee who supplies false terms is in breach of NRS 645.3205[102] which states:

> "A licensee shall not deal with any party to a real estate transaction in a manner which is deceitful, fraudulent or dishonest."

Including a false term or fact or excluding any material term or fact from the purchase agreement in order to deceive anyone is fraud and such behavior is illegal. Anyone attempting to obtain anything of value using false pretense with the intent to deceive may be found guilty of a category B felony.[103] This prohibition includes submitting a false or fraudulent appraisal to any financial institution or other interested party.[104]

d. No Inducement to Breach - A licensee should not for personal gain, induce any party to the purchase agreement to breach it in order to substitute a new agreement.[105] The question becomes, what is the liability if the licensee presents an offer and the client breaks an existing contract in order to accept the new offer? The answer is, the licensee should not be liable as long as the licensee did not actively persuade the client to break the current contract.

Whenever a contract is breached, there is the potential for damage claims or a specific performance lawsuit from the non-breaching party. A licensee who encourages the breach of a contract may

97. NAC 645.605 (7).

98. NAC 645.605 (8).

99. NRS 645.635 (5).

100. NAC 645.525.

101. NRS 40.750 (2).

102. See also, NRS 645.633(1)(i).

103. NRS 205.380.

104. NRS 645.635 (10).

105. NRS 645.630 (1)(l).

A category B felony is one to six years in prison and/or a fine of $10,000 per charge.

In a specific performance lawsuit, the non-breaching party asks the court to enforce the terms of the contract – in other words to force the seller to sell the property.

106. Nolan v. State Dep't of Commerce-Real Estate Division, 85 Nev. 611, 460 P.2d 153 (1969) stricken as decisive of an incorrect issue, 86 Nev. 428, 470 P.2d 124 (1970).

107. NRS 645.254 (3)(b).

108. NAC 645.600 (2)(a).

109. NRS 645.635 (3).

110. NAC 645.605 (7).

111. NAC 645.650 (2).

112. NAC 645.650.

113. NRS 645.635 (4).

A tort is a civil wrong for which a remedy is available - usually it is money.

be liable in tort to both the seller and buyer and face disciplinary charges from the Real Estate Division.

In Nolan v. Real Estate Division (1969),[106] Joe Nolan, a broker, took a listing from the Wests. After his exclusive listing expired, the Wests gave him and another licensee, Stevens, open listings. Stevens eventually presented an offer to the Wests, which they accepted. Later that evening, Nolan presented another offer and he urged the Wests to disregard the Stevens' offer, stating that, in his opinion, the Wests would net a larger amount with his offer. When Mr. West expressed his concern about being sued, Nolan said he would pay the costs of any lawsuit and personally purchase the property if it didn't sell. The Wests then breached their contract with Stevens' client. Eventually, Stevens' client sued the Wests in district court for specific performance. They also filed a complaint with the Division. The Real Estate Commission held a hearing in which they found Nolan violated various provisions of the NRS and ordered his license suspended for three months. After several appeals, the case was sent back to the Commissioners to determine if Nolan's actions were motivated by the opportunity for his personal gain.

A licensee must be careful not to encourage a client to breach a contract otherwise the licensee, and his or her broker, may be liable under NRS 645, and in tort to the non-breaching party. In any situation in which the client is tempted to breach an existing contract, the licensee must advise the client to seek legal counsel before acting.[107] Brokers should always keep in mind they are ultimately responsible for their licensees' actions, including the drafting and handling of offers and the client's purchase agreement.[108]

e. Copies – Once an offer has been accepted and there is a completed and signed purchase agreement, the licensee must deliver a copy to the principals within a reasonable time.[109] The licensee also is required to provide the broker with a copy of the agreement[110] within five days after the paperwork is signed.[111] The broker must keep a copy of the purchase agreement (and all related records whether or not the transaction ever closed) for five years.[112]

f. Closing Documents – In Nevada, the majority of licensees and clients use escrow companies to coordinate and close the transaction. Other states and regions have different practices. In the Eastern half of the United States, most real estate transactions are settled in attorneys' offices. In other regions, closings may occur in a broker's office. However, even in Nevada, not all real estate transactions involve escrow companies. Because a closing may not occur in an escrow office, the licensee has a duty to ensure that within 10 business days after the transaction has closed, a complete, detailed closing statement is delivered to the principals. The seller's closing statement must show all the receipts and disbursements made by the broker for the seller. The buyer's closing statement must show all money received in the transaction, how and for what it was disbursed. A true copy of the closing statements must be kept in the broker's file.[113] The licensee is relieved of this duty if an escrow holder furnishes those statements.

4. REQUIREMENTS FOR SPECIALIZED PURCHASE AGREEMENTS

Not all real estate purchase agreements are created equal. Depending on the type of real estate being sold, there are specific clauses or provisions that must be incorporated into the purchase agreement before it is enforceable.

a. Common-Interest-Community Contracts – A residential common-interest-community property (CIC – also known as a homeowners' association) is "real estate with respect to which a person, by virtue of his ownership of a unit, is obligated to pay for real estate other than that unit."[114] In a CIC, a unit's owner must pay for the upkeep of common property, usually through a monthly assessment, fee or dues. The law governing CICs is found in NRS 116, which is administered by the Real Estate Division.[115] By statute, the common law supplements the CIC statutes.[116] However, no agreement or contract may modify or waive any homeowners' rights granted by statute.[117]

As with all contracts, no clause in the CIC purchase agreement may be unconscionable.[118] Additionally, each CIC purchase contract imposes the duty of good faith performance on each party.[119]

Sales of homes with a CIC are divided into the unit's first sale (where the seller is the "declarant") and resales. In a first sale, the declarant is required to provide the buyer with a copy of the Public Offering Statement.[120] This extensive disclosure document outlines the buyer's rights, including the right to cancel the purchase contract within five days after signing the contract. To exercise this right, the buyer (or his or her agent), must not have personally inspected the unit.[121] If they have inspected it, there is no right of cancellation. This right must also be stated in the purchase agreement.[122]

On resales, a buyer must be given a resale disclosure package at the unit owner's expense.[122a] The buyer may cancel the contract without penalty five days after he or she receives the package whether or not the unit was inspected.[123] The cancellation provision must also be in the purchase agreement.

In either cancellation case – new or resale - all payments made by the buyer before cancellation must be promptly refunded.

b. Unimproved Lots and Subdivisions – Both federal law and the NRS regulate the sale of unimproved and subdivided property.[124] The federal law is the Interstate Land Sales Full Disclosure Act[125] (ILSFDA), which regulates unimproved subdivided lots. Nevada's subdivided land law is found in NRS 119. Regardless of which law is used, the developer must provide the Nevada Real Estate Division with extensive information on the subdivision.[126] The information required includes a copy of the purchase agreement form the developer will be using.[127]

The developer/owner is ultimately responsible for the business acts of the brokers, salespeople, or representatives he or she has employed.[128] However, the broker of record, or the authorized salesperson, is required to sign the purchase contract. Therefore, the broker should be satisfied that the contract meets the minimum legal requirements.[129] The broker or salesman must understand the terms of the contract as he or she is required to review each document and disclosure with the prospective buyer.[130] If a question arises as to the meaning of a clause, the licensee should refer the buyers to their lawyer before getting into too much detail.

The broker must obtain a signed receipt from the buyer stating the buyer received the required documents. This receipt and a copy of the contract must be kept by the

114. NRS 116.021.

115. NRS 116.615.

116. NRS 116.1108.

117. NRS 116.1104.

118. NRS 116.1112.

119. NRS 116.1113.

120. NRS 116.4102.

121. NRS 116.4103 (1)(i).

122. NRS 116.4108.

122a. NRS 116.4109 as amended by SB 253.

123. NRS 116.4109 (2).

124. See also NRS 599A, Trade Regulations and Practices, Solicitation to Purchase Land, for further restrictions on sales practices.

125. 15 U.S.C. §§ 1701 to 1720.

126. NRS 119.119.

127. NRS 119.180 (1)(d) and NAC 119.150(9), NAC 119.220(5).

128. NRS 119.175.

129. NAC 119.330.

130. NRS 119.182 (1) and NAC 119.160(1).

In transactions governed by the ILSFDA, each purchase agreement has specific wording, disclosure, and revocation requirements.

131. NRS 119.182.

132. NAC 119.530, see also NAC 119.160.

133. NAC 119.530 (2).

134. NRS 119.182.

135. NAC 119.530(4).

136. NAC 119.530 (7).

137. NAC 119.530 (8).

138. NAC 119.530 (3).

139. NAC 119.530 (6).

140. NRS 119.170.

broker for three years or until one year after the final payment on a contract of sale, which ever is longer.[131]

Nevada requires specific wording and clauses in all subdivision purchase contracts. The regulations identify not only the wording but the format and size of print type that must be used.[132] Timing is important. Many of the required subdivision disclosures must be given to prospective buyers <u>before</u> the buyer signs any contract.

Each contract must contain the following statement in 12-point boldface type at the top of the contract:[133]

> This is a binding contract by which you agree to purchase an interest in real property. You should examine your rights of revocation contained elsewhere in this contract.

Also, the following wording must be clearly and conspicuously placed just above the buyer's signatures:

> The purchaser of any subdivision or any lot, parcel, unit or interest in any subdivision not exempted pursuant to the provisions of NRS 119.120 or 119.122 may cancel the contract of sale, by written notice, until midnight of the fifth calendar day following the date of execution of the contract, unless the contract prescribes a longer period for cancellation. The right of cancellation may not be waived. Any attempt by the developer to obtain such a waiver results in a contract which is voidable by the purchaser.

The notice of cancellation must be delivered personally to the developer or sent by certified mail or telegraph to the business address of the developer.

The developer shall, within 15 days after receipt of the notice of cancellation, return all payments made by the purchaser.[134] Whether the property being sold is located in Nevada or elsewhere, if the buyer is procured in Nevada, the contract must also contain the following statement:

> This contract is to be construed according to the laws of the State of Nevada and specifically chapter 119 of NRS, or

> This contract is to be construed according to the laws of _____. Any purchaser solicited in the State of Nevada retains those rights granted him under chapter 119 of NRS.[135]

The contract must list all major improvements in the subdivision. If a separate document contains the description of the major improvements, that document must be incorporated into the purchase agreement by reference. The Division will decide which improvements are considered major.[136]

If the deed won't be delivered to the buyer until 180 days after the close of escrow, the contract must say so. The buyer must be advised at signing that the contract should be recorded in the county where the property is located to give public notice of the buyer's interest in that property.[137]

The purchase contract <u>may not</u> contain any wording similar to: "[P]urchaser agrees that no representations, oral or implied, have been made to purchaser other than what is contained in this contract."[138]

Neither the developer, broker nor salesperson may make any written or oral statements, which change the true nature or legal significance of any document approved by the RED,[139] nor can they state that the subdivision was approved by the RED.[140]

The broker, salesperson, or developer may be sued by the buyer for any violation of NRS or NAC 119. The Division

IV - 23

may press criminal charges, as well as hold administrative hearings, against violators.[141]

c. Purchase Contracts Requiring Court Approval – Certain purchase agreements require court approval or confirmation. These may include contracts executed by an executor or administrator for a decease's estate; those where the owner is legally incompetent and under a guardianship; certain trust purchase agreements; or those contracts where the seller has filed for bankruptcy.

Trusts: A trustee is a fiduciary to the trust and, by extension, to the beneficiaries. The trustee cannot take personal advantage of his or her position. Therefore, a trustee must have the approval of a court when the trustee is personally purchasing property from, or selling property to, the trust estate.[142]

Probate: In a probate situation where an executor or administrator is selling the deceased's real property, public notice must be given, there must be a court hearing, and the court must review the purchase contract prior to confirming the sale. When an offer has been presented to the court for confirmation at a hearing, any would-be buyer may bid on it. If the second bid is within certain statutory guidelines, the court may accept that offer, order a new sale, or conduct a public auction in open court.[143] The licensee must be aware that no purchase contract for the sale of real property in probate is binding on the deceased's estate until confirmed by the court. [143]

Guardianship: In a guardianship, there is a court appointed guardian who administers the estate of the ward. A ward is a legally declared incompetent who is, by reason of mental or other incapacity, unable to properly manage and care for his or her property. A guardian may also be appointed for a minor. There are various types of guardians, e.g., guardian of the estate, guardian of the person, special guardian, and guardian ad litem, each with their own restrictions and authority.

Once a guardian is court appointed, all of the ward's property is put into a trust held for the ward's benefit. Generally, the guardian is given the authority to purchase or sell real property for the ward's estate. Each contract must be confirmed by the court before title passes. Much like probate, the sale of a ward's real property requires public notice, a court hearing, and confirmation. At the public hearing, other persons may bid against an existing purchase agreement.   The court may confirm a higher bid, thereby setting aside the original purchase contract. [144]

Bankruptcy: When a person files for bankruptcy[145] all of the property which the debtor owns, and the debtor's interests in other property, becomes part of the bankruptcy estate.[146] Depending on the bankruptcy chapter, the estate is under the control of a bankruptcy trustee[147] who may sell the estate's real property with court approval.[148]

If the debtor is in contract to purchase or sell real property prior to filing bankruptcy, the trustee has the authority to set aside that contract and cancel the transaction.[149] Also, under certain conditions, the trustee may undo a closed transaction if it was done within the recent past and was consummated to defraud creditors or strip the estate of value before the debtor filed bankruptcy.[150]

All purchase contracts accepted by the bankruptcy trustee must be approved at a court hearing.[151] Once approved, the property can be sold and the proceeds distributed to the debtor's creditors.

141. NRS 119.330.

142. NRS 163.050.

143. NRS 148.080 and NRS 148.220-270.

144. NRS 159.134-1415.

145. 11 U.S.C. §§ 101 et seq.

146. 11 U.S.C. § 541.

147. 11 U.S.C. § 704.

148. 11 U.S.C. §§ 327, 704.

149. 11 U.S.C. § 544.

150. 11 U.S.C. § 547.

151. 11 U.S.C. § 363.

152. In Title Insurance and Trust Co. v. Chicago Title Insurance Co., 97 Nev. 523, 634 P.2d 1216 (1981) the court used both "contract for sale" and "contract of sale" for the same document – an installment contract, while in Mackintosh v. Jack Matthews, 109 Nev. 628, 855 P.2d 549 (1993), the court used "contract for sale" for a traditional purchase agreement, compare with Goldston v. AMI Investments, Inc., 98 Nev. 567, 655 P.2d 521, where the court used "contract of sale" for a traditional purchase agreement.

Don't confuse "land contract" or "land sale contract" with a purchase agreement for unimproved or "raw" land.

CAUTION!
Drafting an installment contract is practicing law!

C. ALTERNATIVE CONTRACTS

There are other types of purchase contracts with which the licensee should be familiar—the installment contract and the option contract. Ordinary real property purchase contracts do not anticipate a long-term relationship between the buyer and the seller. However, the drafter of an installment contract needs to anticipate just such a relationship. These contracts act as financing instruments as well as purchase contracts.

The option contract does not in and of itself provide for the purchase of real estate. It is a distinct, separate agreement in which the seller agrees to hold available for a buyer the option to purchase the property at a certain price on some future date. Some option agreements are mated with lease agreements creating the hybrid "lease with option to purchase." That contract, depending on its wording, may have all the characteristics of a potential purchase agreement, a lease, an option and a mortgage.

1. INSTALLMENT CONTRACT

An installment contract may be called a land sale contract, land contract, contract for deed, bond for title, or articles of agreement for warranty deed. There is some confusion when referring to an installment contract as a "contract of sale" or a "contract for sale;" the Nevada courts have used both terms when referring to installment contracts and ordinary purchase agreements.[152]

In an installment contract, the buyer makes periodic payments to the seller, in return the buyer receives equitable title and often takes immediate possession of the property. Legal title is retained by the seller. Upon the successful conclusion of all the buyer's payments, the seller is obligated to transfer legal title to the buyer.

The licensee should not confuse an installment contract in which the seller retains legal title, with a contract in which the buyer gets legal title but pays the seller the purchase price in installments. The latter arrangement is a traditional mortgage, the buyer is the mortgagor and the seller is the mortgagee.

Some installment contracts "wrap" an existing loan into the buyer's installment payments. An example of a wrap situation is where the amount of the seller's existing mortgage payment is wrapped (included) in the buyer's payment to the seller.

A carefully drafted installment contract must ensure each party's rights. It should, at a minimum, address the party's obligations; assignment rights; payment of existing loans or liens; creation and payment of future loans or liens; identify tax obligations and deductions; allocate maintenance; address insurance rights and responsibilities; state default conditions and remedies; and establish final title transfer requirements and procedures. An installment contract is a legally complex document and should only be drafted by a licensed attorney.

IV - 25

Liability: Both buyer and seller need to be made aware of the potential liability inherent in an installment contract. For example, a seller may have a buyer that does not meet all the obligations under the installment contract, damages the property, or encumbers it with liens. Depending on the contract's wording, the seller may have to file for a judicial foreclosure to evict the buyer and then sue for damages.

On the other hand, keeping legal title in the seller's name can be a problem for the buyer. The seller may default on an existing loan; sell the property; further encumber it; or have a judgment or lien attach to the property; each of which could effect or terminate any rights of the buyer. The buyer could sue the seller for breach of contract, but may still lose the property.

One way to protect the buyer's rights is to record the installment contract. In Title Ins. and Trust Co. v. Chicago Title Ins. Co. (1981),[153] Moser lent Fullmer money secured by a deed of trust on Fullmer's property. Title Insurance Co. was the trustee. Fullmer then sold the property to Suleman under an installment contract, which was recorded. Suleman took possession and immediately constructed the Peter Pan Motel. Suleman later assigned his interest under the installment contract to Nazarali. Fullmer eventually defaulted on the note to Moser, who foreclosed under the deed of trust.

153. Title Insurance and Trust Co. v. Chicago Title Insurance Co., 97 Nev. 523, 634 P.2d 1216 (1981).

154: NRS 40.430.

155: NRS.40.050.

156: NRS 40.250 et seq.

At the trustee's foreclosure sale the property was sold to a third-party. Soon thereafter, the trustee, Title Insurance Co., discovered it had missed the recorded installment contract. The law requires a trustee to give notice of the trustee's sale to anyone who has an interest in the property. Under the installment contract Suleman, and through him Nazarali, his assignee, had an equitable title interest in the property. Therefore, Suleman was entitled to receive the foreclosure notice.

Neither Suleman nor Nazarali ever received a Notice of Default or a Notice of Trustee's Sale. In response to the lawsuit, the court voided the trustee's sale and Nazarali was given the opportunity to cure the default with Moser. "But for" the recorded installment contract, Suleman and Nazarali would have lost the property and their investments.

As a Financing Instrument: Depending on the contract's wording, the contract may be considered an executory contract for money owed, or a mortgage. This is significant. If the contract is breached, the remedies are different depending on how the installment contract is classified.

The law requires a mortgagee to foreclose before he or she can sue for damages under a breach of contract.[154] Thus, if the installment contract is classified as a mortgage, the seller will have to go through a judicial foreclosure before he or she can regain possession of the property.[155] One reason many sellers opt for an installment contract is to avoid this very situation.

If the installment contract is a contract for money owed, then the seller can use the unlawful detainer and eviction rules to remove the buyer, and immediately sue for damages.[156]

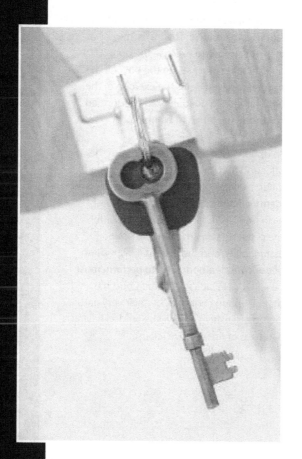

Historically, an installment contract would only be considered a mortgage if a deed was executed by the seller to the buyer and the seller reserved to him or herself a security interest.[157] However, depending on the contract's wording, today's courts may find an installment contract is a mortgage without the reservation right or a signed deed. It is more likely to be considered a mortgage if the contract contains onerous terms of forfeiture, or when the buyer has paid a considerable portion of the purchase price, or where the buyer has substantially improved the property, or when it would be inequitable not to allow the buyer more time to cure his or her default. The Court has said:

> [e]quity will relieve from forfeiture for default in payment of money under contract for sale of land if caused by accident, fraud, surprise, mistake, inadvertence, ignorance, or if default is unintentional and due to neglect which is not willful.[158]

It should be evident that installment contracts should not be drafted by real estate licensees nor should the licensee advise his or her client on offering or accepting an installment contract without also advising the client to seek legal advice.

2. OPTION TO PURCHASE AND LEASE WITH OPTION

An option contract is a separate, independent contract even though it may contain the necessary terms of the purchase agreement. An option requires the seller to hold open to the buyer, for a set time and with set terms, the right to purchase the property. Depending on its wording, the option's consideration may be independent of the purchase agreement and non-refundable, or it may be incorporated into the property's purchase price once the option is exercised. The seller is the optionor, the buyer is the optionee.

Unlike a purchase agreement, an option confers no interest in the property; it is merely a contractual right to acquire the property in the future. An option is a unilateral contract that becomes a bilateral contract once the option is exercised. It is unilateral in that only one party is required to perform. The buyer may or may not choose to exercise the option, but the seller must sell to the buyer if the buyer does exercise it. The exercise of the option must be unequivocally performed on its original terms to be binding.

As option contracts are distinct from the offer and purchase agreement, they need different types of terms. The parties should identify in the option contract what rights each one has regarding a party's death, the property's destruction, the option's assignability, and the eventual disposition of the consideration. Time to perform must be stated. Nevada's Supreme Court has said that all option contracts, by their very nature, are time sensitive and will be read as having a "time is of the essence" clause.[159]

157. Southern Pacific Co. v. Miller, 39 Nev. 169, 176, 154 P. 929 (1916).

158. Mosso v. Lee, 53 Nev. 176, 178, 295 P. 776 (1931).

159. McCall v. Carlson, 63 Nev. 390, 420, 172 P.2d 171 (1946).

A time is of the essence clause requires the parties to perform certain acts within the time frames set in the contract. Failure to perform by the stated time is a breach of the contract.

Unlike purchase contracts or offers, the death of a party does not terminate the option contract; however, rejection of the option does. The buyer's rejection of the option before the option's end-date ends the option and the seller is free to sell to another party.

Lease with Option to Purchase - Because the option is a separate, distinct contract, there is some confusion as to the nature of the hybrid "Lease with Option to Purchase." This document claims to be a rental agreement, thereby establishing a landlord and tenant relationship; an option contract, giving the tenant an option to purchase on set terms and conditions; and, depending on the contract's wording, an installment contract if a portion of the rent is used to build-up the tenant's equity.

A tenant may build equity depending on how the option's consideration or the rental security is applied and how the rental payments are apportioned. The buyer's payment may be solely rent or some of it may be applied to the down payment. Each choice has consequences as to how the contract will be interpreted by a court. Again, depending on the lease's wording, a breach of the lease terms will not always terminate the option. If the lease with option contract is not carefully drafted, the court may find the tenant has an equitable interest in the property. Once an equitable interest is established, eviction of a defaulting tenant/buyer requires a judicial foreclosure and the landlord/seller may have to refund money to the tenant/buyer.

D. REVIEW

An offer is only the first step toward a legally binding purchase contract. In Nevada, most residential purchase offers are prepared using preprinted forms even though there is no state mandated purchase form. When a broker is used, the licensee is responsible for ensuring the form is complete with clear and definite terms. The licensee has a duty, when requested, to put into writing all bona fide offers made in good faith. The licensee must always present all offers made to, or by, the client as soon as practicable. Regardless of any instruction or preference of the licensee's client, at no time may a broker reject or modify an offer because the offeror is of a protected class. Once an offer has been reviewed by the offeree, if it is rejected, the licensee is charged with obtaining a written notice, signed by the offeree, informing the offeror of the rejection.

Once an offer has been accepted, it turns into a purchase agreement. Every purchase agreement must comply with the statute of frauds. It 1) must be in writing, 2) state the consideration given by the parties for the contract, and 3) be signed by the owner (seller), or his or her lawfully authorized agent. Unless the licensee has a separate notarized and recorded power-of-attorney, the licensee is not authorized to sign the purchase agreement for the client. Nevada law authorizes an electronic format for any transaction or contract in which the parties agree to conduct their business electronically.

The law requires specific contract clauses which affect the parties' various responsibilities or rights. These include public policy provisions which are automatically read into each contract and prohibitions against certain restrictions or covenants. Additionally, the purchase agreement must accurately reflect the authentic terms of the parties' agreement. It cannot contain any discriminatory language indicating a preference for, or a bias against, anyone of a protected class.

Some purchase agreements must have certain clauses or provisions before they are enforceable. Others require court approval such as probate, guardianship, or bankruptcy contracts. Finally, the licensee should be aware of installment contracts and option contracts (including the lease with option to purchase).

A licensee has statutory duties when dealing with purchase agreements. These include general duties - not being negligent, and specific duties - ensuring a copy of the contract was given to the client. First among these is the duty to use reasonable skill and care with respect to all parties to the real estate transaction. A licensee may not induce any party to the purchase agreement to breach that agreement in order to substitute a new one if the licensee will secure personal gain from the breach.

Purchase contracts should not be drafted by real estate licensees nor should the licensee advise his or her client to accept an unknown or complicated contract type without also advising the client to seek legal advice.

V. NEVADA LAW ON DISCLOSURES

TABLE OF CONTENTS

1. Holland Realty v. NV Real Estate Comm., 84 Nev. 91, 98, 436 P.2d 422 (1968).

2. NRS 645.252 (1).

3. 42 USC §4852d (a)(4). The disclosure requirement is made applicable to licensees by statute.

4. NRS 645.252.

5. NRS 645.252, NRS 645.254. For a fuller discussion, see II. Nevada Law on Fiduciary Duties.

6. For example, NRS 119.182 deals with subdivisions and requires the licensee to disclose certain facts about the subdivision.

7. For example, NAC 119A.285 requires a licensee selling a time share to disclose if the licensee has an interest in the unit.

8. Federal Interstate Land Sales Full Disclosure Act (15 USC § 1701) and Nevada's Sale of Subdivided Land (NRS 119.119).

9. The federal department of Housing and Urban Development (HUD) requires the disclosure of the opportunity for a home inspection. (For Your Protection, Get a Home Inspection, form) HUD mortgage letter 99-18.

This chapter identifies the why, when, who, how and what of disclosure for the licensee. Discussed are generalized disclosure information and specific disclosure requirements broken down into the topics of agency, transaction, and property disclosures. Mandatory disclosure forms and summary disclosure tables are found in the Appendices.

A. GENERAL DISCLOSURE INFORMATION

There is an old saying in real estate that when in doubt – disclose, disclose, disclose. Because the licensee helps to facilitate most real estate transactions, the burden of disclosure falls heaviest on the agent. Over the years, extensive law and regulation has evolved requiring a host of disclosures by the licensee. Many disclosures concern the property, but the licensee must also disclose certain specifics about the licensee's agency and the transaction.

1. WHY DISCLOSE?

The purpose for full and honest disclosure is to ensure all parties to the transaction have sufficient information on key issues to make informed decisions.[1] These disclosures may be as broad as demanding the licensee disclose "any material and relevant facts, data or information ... relating to the property,"[2] to as narrow as requiring the licensee to disclose the possibility of lead-based paint on the property. [3]

The duty of disclosure varies with the licensee's relationship to a party. For example, the licensee owes to all parties the obligation of disclosing all material facts concerning the property as well as certain facts regarding the licensee's status and source of compensation.[4] In addition, the licensee owes to the client not only the above, but full and honest disclosure of all material facts concerning the transaction.[5]

2. SOURCES OF DISCLOSURE LAW

The laws requiring disclosure have a variety of sources – statute, regulation, common law, and contract. Statutes and regulations are found in federal, state and local laws, codes and ordinances. By contract, the licensee and client may agree to have the licensee make disclosures he or she would otherwise not be required by law to make.

Nevada statutes and regulations: Nevada's laws are codified in the Nevada Revised Statutes (NRS). Most real estate licensees are familiar with NRS Chapter 645, the laws governing real estate licensees; however, disclosure requirements are found throughout the NRS.[6]

NAC stands for the Nevada Administrative Code. Each state agency that licenses a profession has a set of regulations which govern that profession. These regulations are found in the NAC. Like the NRS, other sections of the NAC have disclosure requirements that are applicable to the real estate licensee, property or transaction.[7]

Federal laws and regulations: The federal government has applicable real estate disclosure laws. Some of these disclosures deal with the same topics as state law,[8] while others are specific to federal law.[9]

V - 3

Like Nevada, federal law has its statutes known as the United States Code (USC). These are the laws passed by Congress. Corresponding federal regulations are found in the Code of Federal Regulation (CFR). Additionally, various federal agencies, such as HUD, have their own statements of policy that are applicable to the real estate transaction.

Local laws: Some disclosures are required by local government entities such as counties and cities. These may be found in the respective government codes or ordinances.[10] Moreover, there are "hybrid" governing entities that take their authority from various federal and state laws. For example, the Tahoe Regional Planning Authority (TRPA) that controls and monitors development and land use practices in the Lake Tahoe basin, is a federally related agency with interstate jurisdiction.[11] The TRPA has its own Code of Ordinances that regulate land use. Any licensee dealing with Lake Tahoe properties must be aware of restrictions imposed by the TRPA and disclose relevant TRPA issues.

Common law: Historically, case law provided that a licensee was responsible for disclosing the condition of the property,[12] the condition of the neighborhood,[13] and conditions of the transaction that affected the client.[14]

Today, most common law disclosures have been codified into statute. However, sometimes the statute is not specific as to how or when a disclosure is to be made. At those times, a review of the original case law may bring into focus the edges of the disclosure's boundaries.

Contract: By contract, the broker may agree to disclose to the client items which the broker is otherwise exempt from disclosing. For example, a buyer's agent is not required by law to disclose if the property was the site of a death; however, the buyer and licensee may agree that the

agent will disclose if the licensee is aware of someone dying on the property.[15]

The licensee and client may not contract to do an illegal thing. For example, no agreement between a seller and the listing agent will relieve the licensee of liability for the nondisclosure of a material defect of the property.

3. DUTY OF INQUIRY AND "SHOULD HAVE KNOWN"

Disclosure is a core duty to agency. The licensee has a duty to disclose to each party to the transaction any material and relevant facts, data, or information which he or she knows, or which, by the exercise of reasonable care and diligence, should have known, relating to the property.[16] This includes information of which the licensee has actual knowledge as well as facts about which licensee must inquire.

The licensee should note that material "facts", not just problems or defects, must be disclosed. A "material fact" is any fact that is likely to influence a principal about the desirability of the property or the transaction.[17] Such facts include the licensee's agency status and loyalty, facts about the real estate transaction, certain facts about the property.

A licensee must disclose facts of which the licensee has actual knowledge.[18] What is actual knowledge? The Nevada Supreme Court has found,

> [a]ctual knowledge consists not only of what one certainly knows, but also consists in information which he might obtain by investigating facts which he does know and which impose upon him a duty to investigate.[19]

The law requires the licensee to inquire about facts or situations that would cause a reasonable person to question an item. A licensee will not be allowed to ignore

10. For example, the presence and compliance certification of a wood burning stove. Washoe County Health Department Regulation 040.051§§ A & D.

11. Federal Public Law 96-551 (12-19-80) [94 Stat. 3234], wherein the U.S. Congress established the Tahoe Regional Planning Agency (TRPA), administered in cooperation between the states of California and Nevada (see NRS 321.595 et seq., NRS 268.098).

12. Mackintosh v. Jack Matthews & Co, 109 Nev. 628, 855 P.2d 549 (1993).

13. Lowe v. Real Estate Division, 89 Nev. 488, 490, 515 P.2d 388 (1973).

14. Charles v. Lemons & Assoc., 104 Nev. 388, 760 P.2d 118 (1988).

15. NRS 40.770 (5).

16. NRS 645.252 (1)(a).

17. Holland Realty v. NV Real Estate Comm., 84 Nev. 91, 98, 436 P.2d 422 (1968).

18. NRS 645.252.

19. Garff v. J.R. Bradley Co., 84 Nev. 79, 85, 436 P.2d 428 (1968).

20. Woods v. Label Investment Corp., 107 Nev. 419, 812 P.2d 1293 (1991) and Collins v. Burns, 103 Nev. 394, 741 P.2d 819 (1987).

21. NRS 645.252 (1)(a).

22. NRS 40.770.

23. There remains an issue within HUD (US Dept. of Housing and Urban Development) whether, even if allowed by law, a licensee can disclose this under Fair Housing laws.

A "stigmatized" property is a property considered "damaged" because of an event that occurred there; for example, a murder. Generally, it does not refer to actual physical damage or a property defect.

NRS 179D.400 defines a "Sex Offender" as a person who is: (a) Convicted of a sexual offense listed in NRS 179D.410; or (b) Found guilty by a court of a sexual offense, such as: (1) A sexually violent predator, or (2) A nonresident sex offender who is a student or worker within this state.

"RELEASED OFFENDERS" are persons who have been released from prison and who require assistance with reintegration into the community. NRS 449.0055

"danger signals" or "red lights";[20] to gloss over conflicting information; or to act carelessly in obtaining material facts about the property, under the excuse that the licensee did not "know for certain" or did not have "actual knowledge" of relevant facts.

This does not mean the licensee must become a property inspector, private eye or lawyer. It does mean the licensee is required to use "reasonable care and diligence" to investigate "any material and relevant facts, data or information relating to the property."[21]

4. EXEMPTIONS AND EXCEPTIONS

When reviewing any disclosure law, the licensee should identify the statute's exemptions or exceptions to ensure the law is properly followed.

a. Stigmatized property - Nevada's stigmatized property law contains a list of certain facts that a licensee does not need to disclose.[22]

These exempted facts include:
1. Whether the property was the site of a homicide, suicide or a death by any other means, except deaths caused by a condition of the property (for example, faulty wiring);

2. Whether the property was occupied by a person with human immunodeficiency virus or HIV, or any other disease that is not known to be transmitted by living in the property;

3. Whether the property was the site of a felony or any other crime, except if the crime was the manufacture of methamphetamine and the property has not been rehabilitated;

4. Whether a sex offender resides or is expected to reside in the community; and

5. Whether the property is located near a licensed facility for transitional living for released offenders.

Waiver Can Create Broker Liability: If the licensee is exempt from disclosing certain facts, the broker may waive the exemption by contract. NRS 40.770 (5) provides that a buyer's broker can agree to be liable to the buyer for not disclosing the property was the site:

1. Of a homicide, suicide or death;

2. Of a crime punishable as a felony; or

3. Occupied by a person with AIDS.[23]

Additionally, the broker and buyer may agree to have the broker disclose:

4. The fact that a sex offender resides in the community; or

5. That the property is located near a facility for transitional living for released offenders.

The statute only states a buyer's broker may agree to make these disclosures; however, there is no statute stopping a seller and listing broker from agreeing to disclose to a buyer information the broker is not otherwise required to disclose. For example, the seller may allow the listing broker to disclose that the seller has received a notice from the local law enforcement agency that a sex offender is living in the neighborhood.

Should a broker consent to take on such liability to make those disclosures, the parties' contract controls the how, when and to whom the disclosure will be made.

V - 5

b. Client Misrepresentations - By law, it cannot be assumed that the licensee has the client's knowledge about the property.[24] In Prigge v. South Seventh Realty, (1981)[25] Prigge purchased a property and then sued South Seventh Realty for falsely representing in the listing that the home was frame and stucco, which it was not. Prigge argued that the brokerage should be liable for all facts, false or not, contained in a listing. South Seventh Realty argued it had simply relied upon the statements of the sellers and it did not know, nor did it have reason to know, the seller's statements were false. The court, in finding for the brokerage, stated an agent had the right to rely on the statements of the client, unless there was contradicting information.

Interestingly, in the Prigge case, the court opined that Prigge did not argue that South Seventh Realty should have known the true facts if it had exercised reasonable care. Had Prigge argued the agent should have known whether a building was frame and stucco or otherwise, the court's finding may have been different.

A licensee cannot be held liable for the Seller's nondisclosure of information on the Seller's Real Property Disclosure Statement, if:

1. The licensee did not know of the nondisclosure, or

2. The information is of public record readily available to the public.[26]

The licensee will be held liable for nondisclosure if the licensee knows the client made a misrepresentation and did not tell the recipient that the statement was false.[27] The courts will not allow a licensee who knew better to avoid liability by hiding behind a client's misrepresentation.[28]

c. No Duty to Investigate: Professional Inspections or Financial Condition - A licensee does not need to independently verify the accuracy of a statement concerning the property made by a duly licensed or certified professional.[29] A licensee should disclose to the client that a professional report exists if the licensee is aware of such a report; however, the licensee is exempted from any duty to independently verify the accuracy of that report.

A licensee is not required to independently investigate the financial condition of a party to the real estate transaction.[30] For example, a seller cannot claim it was the licensee's responsibility to investigate and disclose the buyer's credit; nor can a buyer claim it was the licensee's responsibility to investigate and disclose the seller's financial condition.

There is a caveat to these exemptions – should a licensee independently verify the accuracy of an inspection or investigate the financial condition of a party, the licensee then assumes the liability for any inaccuracies in the disclosure. A licensee cannot escape responsibility for misinformation or inaccuracy by claiming he or she was not legally obligated to disclose it in the first place and therefore, should not be held liable for the inadequate or inaccurate disclosure.

24. NRS 645.257 (2).

25. Prigge v. South Seventh Realty, 97 Nev. 640, 637 P.2d 1222 (1981).

26. & 27. NRS 645.259 (2).

28. NRS 645.259 (2) referring to NRS 645.252.

29. & 30. NRS 645.252 (4).

At no time does an "as is" clause allow the seller or licensee to conceal or not disclose known defects.

31. NRS 113.100, NRS 113.150.

32. NRS 645.254 (2).

33. See the National Association of Realtors® Code of Ethics, (2006) Article 2, does not give a limit to keeping a client's confidences.

34. Real Estate Division form, Consent to Act, 05/01/05.

35. NRS 645.252 (1)(a).

36. NRS 645.254 (2).

d. Disclosure and the "As Is" Clause - An "as is" clause in a purchase agreement requires the buyer to take the property with no warranties of fitness or condition and with all existing defects. Since 1995, Nevada residential sellers are required to complete the mandated Sellers Real Property Disclosure form identifying all defects in the property of which they are aware.[31] A seller cannot escape this disclosure duty by inserting an "as is" clause in the purchase agreement.

A licensee should never rely on an "as is" clause to shield him or her from nondisclosure liability. A licensee must always disclose, as soon as practicable and to each party to the transaction, all material and relevant facts, data or information relating to the property. If the licensee is aware of a defect that the seller does not disclose, the licensee is bound by law to disclose the defect.

5. CLIENT CONFIDENCES AND CONSUMER PRIVACY

A licensee may not disclose the client's confidential information for one year after the revocation or termination of the brokerage agreement.[32] Some professional trade organizations require extended time frames for keeping client confidences.[33]

What constitutes a client's confidential information varies from transaction to transaction and from client to client. The Real Estate Division defines confidential information as "the client's motivation to purchase, trade or sell, which if disclosed, could harm one party's bargaining position or benefit the other."[34]

Confidential information does include any information which a reasonable person would expect, or that a client requests, to be kept confidential.

No Misinformation: The client's right to confidentiality does not allow the licensee to lie or give misinformation. If asked a direct question regarding a confidential matter, the licensee should state the information is confidential and refuse to answer.

Confidentiality is a statutory duty the licensee owes to the client. Nevertheless, at no time does a client's request for confidentiality control the licensee's disclosure duty. A licensee must disclose to all parties material and relevant facts relating to the property.[35] This affirmative duty overrides a client's instruction that the licensee not disclose relevant property facts such as defects.

Right Held by Client: The right of confidentiality is held by the client, not the licensee. That means it is the client's decision on whether confidential information may be disclosed. If there is any question, the licensee must clear it with the client before disclosure. The client may authorize the licensee to disclose information that would otherwise be confidential. Any such authorization must be in writing.[36]

Required Disclosure: When may a licensee disclose confidential information? The law authorizes the disclosure of confidential information in any one of five circumstances:

1. When a court of competent jurisdiction orders disclosure;

2. When the client authorizes in writing the disclosure;

3. When the licensee discloses information to his or her broker;[37]

4. When the information is required to be disclosed by law; and

5. When a year has passed since the termination of the brokerage agreement.

A licensee is not bound to a client's instruction to keep information confidential that the licensee is obligated by law to disclose.

Gramm-Leach-Bliley Privacy Disclosure Statement: In July 2001, the privacy disclosure provisions of the Gramm-Leach-Bliley Act (GLB Act) became effective.[38] These provisions require certain disclosures to a client when handling the client's personal financial information. The GLB Act is not relevant to most real estate transactions; however, if the broker collects the client's personal financial information for use in any mortgage loan process or other financial acquisition procedure, the GLB Act becomes applicable.

Briefly, the GLB Act applies to all businesses engaging in a "financial activity" as defined by the Act. Generally, real estate brokerage and property management services are exempt. If the licensee is involved in ancillary financial services (such as lending or various appraisal services), then the licensee is required to provide the consumer with certain disclosure information.

There is no specific GLB disclosure form; however, the Act states what information must be included in the disclosure. If a licensee believes he or she may be subject to the GLB Act, an attorney familiar with that federal law should be consulted.

37. NRS 645.253.

38. 15 USC §6801 et seq. and 12 CFR Sec. 225.

39. Hesiod, Greek didactic poet, (800 BCE) in his Works and Days.

40. NRS 113.130 (1)(a).

41. NRS 645.252 (1)(e).

B. THE WHEN, WHO, AND HOW OF DISCLOSURE

When reading disclosure laws, it is important to ask:

1. When must the disclosure be made? When is the last permissible time before licensee liability? When is the best time to disclose?

2. Who is responsible for making the disclosure and to Whom must the disclosure be made? Various statutes may make different persons responsible for disclosure. For example, NRS 113.130 requires the seller to disclose what he or she knows about the property. NRS 645.252(1) requires the licensee to disclose what the licensee knows or should reasonably know about the property.

3. How should the disclosure be made? Does the disclosure require a specific form? Is a verbal disclosure sufficient?

4. Finally, What needs to be disclosed - is it a matter concerning the property, the transaction, or the licensee's agency?

1. WHEN MUST A DISCLOSURE BE MADE

An ancient Greek once said "timing is everything."[39] Legally, this is certainly true. When a disclosure is made can be as important as making the disclosure itself. Timing is dictated by statute, contract, or general common law principles.

a. When Required by Statute - When a statute requires a disclosure it usually indicates when that disclosure must be made. Often, it will state the last permissible time for the disclosure. For example, Nevada's Seller's Real Property Disclosure Statement (SRPD) must be provided by the seller to a buyer "at least 10 days before residential property is conveyed to a purchaser."[40] Because the SRPD form is important in ensuring the buyer is aware of what the seller knows about the property, most buyer's agents require the seller to provide the SRPD within a set time frame after signing the purchase agreement.

Alternatively, a statute may identify an event that creates the disclosure requirement. When and if the event occurs, the disclosure must be made. For example, if there is a change in the licensee's relationship to a party, the licensee must disclose that change to all parties to the transaction.[41]

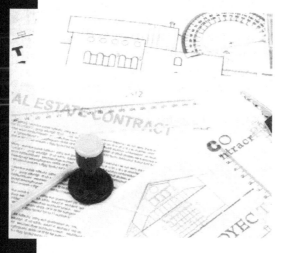

Finally, some statutes require a disclosure be made within a relative time frame. For example, the licensee is required to disclose to each party "as soon as practicable" each source from which he or she will receive compensation.[42] When is "as soon as practicable"? Nevada's Supreme Court has stated,

> clauses ... calling for notice of a liability creating event "as soon as practicable" or "promptly" or "within a reasonable time" all essentially mean the same thing. '. . . "[S]uch clauses do not require instantaneous notice of an [event], but rather call for notice within a reasonable length of time under all the facts and circumstances of each particular case." (cites omitted)[43]

b. When Required in Common Law -
Most disclosure requirements that stem from the common law have been codified (put into statute). Nevertheless, the common law provides the licensee has a duty to speak (disclose) if the information affects the desirability of the transaction from the viewpoint of the principal.[44] Common sense dictates that the disclosure should be made before the client is legally obligated, or if already obligated, as soon as possible to forestall further harm to the client.

Duty to Speak: No legal discussion of disclosures could be complete without an introduction to the licensee's legal "duty to speak" (i.e., duty to disclose) and its corresponding doctrine of equitable estoppel.

There are two ways to breach the duty to speak; first, by not telling the truth, and second, by remaining silent.[45]

It is easy to see a breach of duty when the licensee tells a lie. The more difficult issue is when a licensee is silent by either not volunteering required disclosure information, or by keeping silent when the licensee knows a party is under a mistaken belief.

When the licensee has a duty to speak, the licensee cannot remain silent or allow a party to continue under a misapprehension regarding a material fact – the licensee must affirmatively disclose and correct any misunderstanding a party has. Obviously, the licensee will only be charged with the duty to disclose if the licensee is aware of a party's misunderstanding.

Equitable Estoppel: The doctrine of equitable estoppel, very simply put, states that the law will not allow a person who has intentionally misled another to take advantage of that person's ignorance or misunderstanding. Equitable estoppel is applicable to cases of affirmative lying or silence - "silence can raise an estoppel quite as effectively as can words."[46]

In Goldstein v. Hanna, (1981)[47] Hanna sold a condominium to the Goldsteins under an option to purchase. Callahan Realty was Hanna's broker. Hanna knew Callahan gave the Goldsteins inaccurate advice about the expiration date of the option. Hanna never attempted to correct the inaccurate information. The Goldsteins, relying on that information, proceeded past the actual time frame on the option. When the Goldsteins attempted to close, Hanna refused to honor the expired option. The court held for the Goldsteins under the doctrine of equitable estoppel. It stated because Hanna was silent when he knew the Goldsteins were operating under inaccurate information, he was estopped from declaring the Goldsteins in default and he had to honor the option.

42. NRS 645.252 (1)(b).

43. American Fidelity Fire Ins. v. Adams, 97 Nev. 106, 108, 625 P.2d 88 (1981).

44. Lowe v. State Dep't of Commerce, 89 Nev. 488, 515 P.2d 388 (1973) (Justices Mowbray, J. and Thompson. C.J., dissenting).

45. Holland Realty v. NV Real Estate Comm., 84 Nev. 91, 98, 436 P.2d 422 (1968) and Goldstein v. Hanna, 97 Nev. 559, 635 P.2d 290 (1981).

46. NGA #2 Ltd. Liab. Co. v. Rains, 113 Nev. 1151, 1160, 946 P.2d 163 (1997).

47. Goldstein v. Hanna, 97 Nev. 559, 635 P.2d 290 (1981).

"Equitable" refers to just action conforming to the principles of justice and right. "Estoppel" means stopping the speaker from taking unfair advantage of another person, such as when a person relies on the speaker's false statements. The Doctrine of Equitable Estoppel means the court, in the name of justice, will not allow a speaker who has concealed facts by silence or has lied, to take advantage of a person who relied on the silence or lie. Paraphrased - Black's Law Dictionary, 7th ed. (1999).

48. Webster's New Collegiate Dictionary, 11th edition, 2004.

49. NRS 645.315, NAC 645.610 (1)(b).

50. NAC 645.610.

51. NRS 645.613.

52. NRS 645.252 (1).

53. NRS 645.257 (2).

54. NRS 645.252.

55. NRS 645.005.

56. NRS 645.254.

c. When Advertising - Advertising is the calling of public attention to a product or service by emphasizing desirable qualities so as to arouse a desire to buy or to patronize.[48] Nevada law provides that the licensee must make certain disclosures when advertising the licensee's services or property.[49] These disclosures include:

1. The identification of the licensee's licensed status;

2. Disclosing when the licensee is a principal;[50] and

3. Identifying the licensee's brokerage.[51]

d. When a Party Does Not Disclose - A licensee must disclose what the licensee knows about a property regardless of a seller's similar responsibility to disclose.[52] Even though a licensee cannot be held liable for knowing what the seller knows about a property,[53] the licensee is responsible if the licensee knew, or reasonably should have known, of a material defect or relevant fact that a seller did not include on the Seller's Real Property Disclosure (SRPD) form. The licensee will not be allowed to avoid this disclosure duty by relying upon the seller's duty to disclose.

Does this mean the licensee has to verify everything on the SRPD? No, but it could be considered licensee negligence not to review the form before providing it to the buyer.

RISK REDUCTION TIP!
The prudent licensee will review the Seller's Real Property Disclosure form, completed by the seller, in order to ensure the seller has not forgotten to list a known material fact. Should a seller refuse to disclose a relevant item, the licensee should inform the seller that under the law, the licensee is required to disclose to all parties all material and relevant property facts.

---

2. WHO MUST DISCLOSE AND TO WHOM?

The corollary to "when" a disclosure must be made is "who" must disclose and to "whom."

a. Disclosure to Each Party to the Transaction – There are four major issues that must be disclosed to each party to the transaction. These are:

1.   Material facts about the property;

2.   The licensee's agency status;

3.   The licensee's compensation sources; and

4.   The licensee's interest in the transaction or property (if any).[54]

Each party is entitled to know certain facts about the licensee's agency and about the licensee's sources of compensation. Additionally, the licensee must disclose any interest the licensee has in the transaction or the property. Disclosing this information to all parties ensures everyone has sufficient facts to reasonably and intelligently proceed with the transaction with full knowledge of any conflict of interest by the licensee.

b. Disclosures Only to the Client - Traditionally, all licensees worked for the seller. As times changed, the law allowed buyers to have their own agents and to demand the undivided loyalty of that agent regardless of the agent's source of compensation.[55]

In addition to the issues above, the licensee is required to disclose to the client all material facts about the transaction.[56] When it comes to disclosing to the client facts about the transaction, the licensee is only required to disclose facts about which the licensee has actual knowledge - there is no "should have known," therefore, the licensee is not required to investigate transaction facts.

V - 11

c. Required Disclosure to Other Parties - There are potentially four other entities to whom a licensee has a disclosure duty. These are:

• The licensee's broker;

• The Nevada Real Estate Division;

• The public (by way of advertising); and

• Applicable law enforcement agencies.

The licensee's broker: The real estate salesperson or broker-salesperson performs all real estate activities through the authority of the broker. Legally, the broker represents the client and the salesperson or broker-salesperson represents the broker in all dealings with the client.[57] Since the broker ultimately represents the client, the broker is assumed to be vested with the client's confidences. Thus, the licensee is authorized to make all disclosures concerning the transaction or property to his or her broker.

The Nevada Real Estate Division (RED), as Nevada's licensing entity, has the right to require certain disclosures from the licensee. These disclosures often concern the licensee's real estate related practices and business issues, but may include specific disclosures about a transaction or property if it is the subject of a RED proceeding.[58] The RED's authority includes the ability to compel disclosure of a licensee's books and papers.[59] Failure to disclose information when validly requested by the RED, subjects the licensee to RED discipline and the possibility of criminal action.[60]

Advertising: If the licensee has a brokerage agreement in place and advertises a property, the advertisement must identify the licensee's licensed status. This disclosure must be made whether the licensee is acting as an agent or as a principal.[61] If the licensee has an ownership interest in the property, the advertisement must disclose "for sale by owner-broker" (owner-licensee, owner-salesperson, etc.).[62]

Law Enforcement: No one wants criminals loose and doing harm. The natural inclination is to cooperate with law enforcement officials when asked to provide information on a client or client's property. Should the licensee be requested to provide a client's personal information to law enforcement, the licensee should immediately direct the officer to the broker. Certain client information may be confidential and, unless the client has authorized the disclosure of that information, the broker may be liable for its unauthorized release.[63] The broker should consult with his or her legal counsel before making such disclosure to law enforcement. The broker's attorney may very reasonably and appropriately request the law enforcement officer to provide a duly court executed subpoena duces tecum (subpoena of documents) before releasing client information.

57. NRS 645.035, NRS 645.040.

58. NRS 645.195. NRS 645.400, NRS 645.580, NRS 645.610 et seq. and NRS 645.635 (5).

59. NRS 645.690 (1), NRS 645.720.

60. NAC 645.605 (11), NRS 645.990 and NRS 645.993.

61. NAC 645.637.

62. NAC 645.610.

63. NRS 645.252.

64. NRS 645.252 (3).

65. 15 USC §1843.

66. NAC 645.637.

67. NAC 645.635.

68. NRS 645.252 (1)(a).

69. Nevada Real Estate Division, Compliance Division, report for cases opened in 2004.

70. Calloway v. City of Reno, 113 Nev. 564, 577, 939 P.2d 1020 (1997).

"A disclosure made verbally is as good as the paper it is written on."
— M. Luetkehans, 2004

Only government mandated forms are presented in the Appendixes.

An indemnity clause requires the other party to answer for any liability or harm that the broker might incur.

3. HOW MUST YOU DISCLOSE?

a. Written vs. Verbal – Some disclosures require the use of a specific form, for example, the Duties Owed by a Nevada Licensee (agency disclosure form).[64] Other disclosures may not have a specific form, but the disclosure content is determined by law, for example, the Truth-in-Lending disclosures.[65] Other statutes only direct that a disclosure must be made in writing with no specific wording dictated; for example, when a licensee is acting as agent or principal.[66]

Some statutes require a disclosure, but do not indicate whether the disclosure must be in writing.[67] Finally, some disclosures fall under a generalized disclosure requirement which does not identify specifically what item must be disclosed or how the disclosure is to be made; for example, the statute that requires the licensee to disclose all material and relevant facts relating to the property.[68]

RISK REDUCTION TIP!
If a disclosure is required to be made, it should be in writing. People forget or misinterpret verbal statements. If a statute does not require a written disclosure and a question arises as to whether the disclose was made, the burden of proof falls on the individual who claims to have made the disclosure - most often, the licensee.

Failure to disclose is one of the Real Estate Division's most frequently received complaints against licensees.[69] Most licensees understand the importance of having something in writing to prove they made a disclosure. Interestingly however, unless there is a form, many licensees are hesitant about requiring a written disclosure acknowledgment. To that end, brokerages, educators, trade associations, and individual licensees have created various disclosure forms.

b. "Homemade" Disclosure Forms - Any broker providing his or her licensees with a disclosure form that is not mandated by law should have a licensed Nevada attorney review the form and give a written opinion as to the form's legal sufficiency.

Some "homemade" disclosure forms stop being disclosure forms and attempt to become indemnification forms. Indemnification (and hold harmless) forms are an attempt to remove liability from the broker and make another party responsible. Some forms provide that should the broker be sued, the other party agrees to be responsible for any loss the broker may suffer. Even though such clauses may be legal in many contexts, they are strictly construed by the courts and any ambiguity is found against the drafter, in this case, the broker. [70]

RISK REDUCTION TIP!
If a broker hires an attorney to draft a disclosure form, the broker should require the attorney to provide a separate letter stating the form complies with all current laws. Such homemade forms should be periodically reviewed and the legal opinion updated every several years to ensure the form's compliance with then current law. An additional suggestion is to submit the form to the broker's errors and omissions insurance carrier for an opinion letter from the carrier (if it will provide one) approving coverage for the use of the form.

V - 13

c. Delivery and Acknowledgment – Any disclosure is ineffective unless it is delivered to the person to whom it is meant to inform. Some disclosure forms, such as the Duties Owed by a Nevada Licensee, incorporate a signature line for the recipient. Some forms only require the recipient's initials.[71] Once signed and dated, this acknowledgment serves as evidence that the disclosure was made and delivered.

It is old law in Nevada that notice to a party's agent is considered notice to the principal.[72] Delivery of a written disclosure to a party's agent is delivery to that party. Thus, unless a statute requires delivery only to a specific person, delivery to the party's agent is legally sufficient delivery.

The licensee should review everything that is delivered to him or her to ensure that no disclosure is delivered unnoticed. This helps remove liability to the client for non-disclosure.

71. NRS 116.41095.

72. Hornsilver Cases, 35 Nev. 464, 467 (1913).

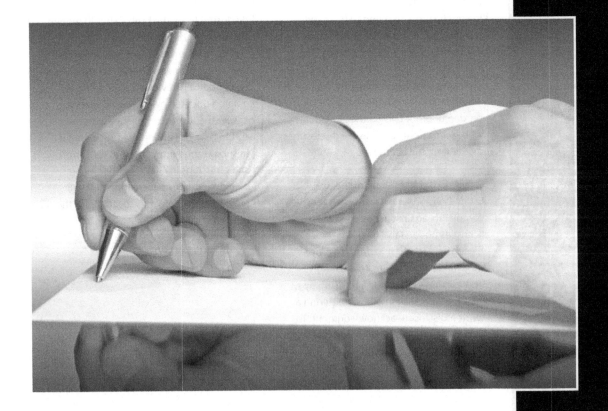

73. NRS 645.194. The Guide may be found at www.Red.state.nv.us/forms/622.pdf. Copies may be reproduced as needed; however, it may not be modified or altered in any way.

74. NRS 645.252.

75. NRS 645.252 (3).

76. NRS 645.193, NRS 645.252(1) and NAC 645.637.

77. NAC 645.650.

78. Real Estate Commission Disciplinary Fine Report 1-95 through 9-30-04.

79. For an elaboration of negligence, see II. Nevada Law on Fiduciary Duties.

80. NRS 645.252 (3).

CAUTION! Giving the Residential Disclosure Guide does not absolve the licensee from liability for not disclosing. The licensee continues to be responsible for all disclosure requirements!

Agency forms, along with many other real estate mandated forms, may be found on the internet in printable format at www.red.state.nv.us/forms/formsbytype.htm

C. WHAT MUST BE DISCLOSED

The three main areas of disclosure for a licensee are disclosures dealing with the licensee's agency, those concerning the transaction, and those relating to the property.

In all Nevada residential sales, a licensee is required to provide the client with the state mandated form Residential Disclosure Guide.[73] The Guide summarizes various disclosures, their purpose, who must provide them and when they are due. The licensee must have the client sign (acknowledge) the back page stating they received the Guide. That acknowledgement page must be retained by the broker as part of the transaction file.

1. DISCLOSURES REGARDING AGENCY

Disclosures concerning a licensee's agency status must be made to all parties to the transaction as soon as practicable.[74] Nevada requires each licensee to disclose to each client and any unrepresented party the parameters of the licensee's agency relationship on a state mandated form.[75] The forms are prepared and distributed by the Real Estate Division (RED).[76] Each form must be completed, signed and kept in the broker's transaction file for five years.[77]

Historically, all brokers worked for the seller under either a direct or sub-agency status. The broker dealing with the buyer was a sub-agent for the seller. Often, this caused confusion in the mind of buyers as they assumed that the broker working with them was representing them. Since the licensee's duties to the parties differ

depending on whether the licensee is representing a client or dealing with a non-client, the statement of agency is important. It lets each party know who is representing them and what duties an agent owes to that party.

a. Agency Disclosure Forms – A substantial number of RED disciplinary hearing cases concern agency disclosure form violations. These violations include: forms not given to clients; forms missing necessary information; forms not completed correctly; and forms lacking required signatures.[78] The Real Estate Commission, the body charged with hearing the RED's disciplinary cases, has found the incorrect execution of these forms amounts to gross negligence by the licensee. It is incumbent upon each broker to ensure the Duties Owed and Consent to Act (when applicable) forms are properly completed and signed.[79]

Before an agency relationship is established the broker is required to provide the client with a state mandated form called the "Duties Owed by a Nevada Real Estate Licensee" (Duties Owed).[80] Should the broker at any point in a transaction represent more than one party, the broker must also provide the parties with a "Consent to Act" form and receive both parties' permission before proceeding with the representation. The appropriate agency disclosure forms (Duties Owed and Consent to Act, if applicable) must be used in all real estate agency relationships regardless of the type of representation (single, multiple, or assigned) or the type of real estate transaction (purchase, lease or property management). The Duties Owed form

V - 15

must also be given when the licensee is a principal in the transaction.[81]

b. Changes in Agency Status - A licensee must disclose to all parties any change in the licensee's relationship with a party to the transaction.[82] This disclosure must be made as soon as practicable and must be in writing. If a client's consent is required, for example, when the broker represents two or more parties to the transaction that have conflicting interests (multiple representation), permission must be obtained before representation occurs – disclosure alone is insufficient to ensure consent! Any time there is a change in the identity of the parties or licensees, a new form must be completed and signed.[83]

Form Does Not Create Agency: The agency relationship is not created because a party signs either the Duties Owed or Consent to Act forms. These forms are strictly disclosure documents. Each form specifically states that it does not constitute a contract for services or an agreement to pay compensation.[84]

c. Not Required on a Referral - A licensee who refers a potential client to another licensee does not need to provide the Duties Owed disclosure form if the referring licensee's only activity is the referral.[85] For example, a seller contacts a broker about representing him in the sale of his Fallon ranch. The broker does not Regularly deal with ranch properties; therefore, he refers the client to a broker who does. The first broker is not required to provide the seller with the Duties Owed form.

2. DISCLOSURES CONCERNING THE TRANSACTION

a. Disclosure Situations - There are three main situations for disclosure regarding the real estate transaction. These are:

- Disclosure to the client of all <u>material facts concerning the transaction</u> of which the licensee has knowledge;[86]

- Disclosure to all parties of the licensee's <u>compensation sources</u>; and [87]

- Disclosure to all parties of the <u>licensee's anticipated or present interest</u> in either the transaction or the property.[88]

b. The Client and the Transaction – The law requires the licensee to disclose to the client "material facts of which the licensee has knowledge concerning the transaction."[89] What is a material fact? It is a fact that is significant or essential to the issue or matter at hand. The Nevada Supreme Court has stated,

> A fact is material … if it is one which the agent should realize would be likely to affect the judgment of the principal … [or is] likely to have a bearing upon the desirability of the transaction… .[90]

Anything impacting the physical condition, value or use of the property is material and relevant. These include facts about the escrow, title, the status of the other party's agency (ex: if there has been a change), financing and issues related to financing (ex: IRS 1031 exchanges), contingency issues (ex: sale of another property or double escrow) and any interest the licensee may have in the transaction. It also includes the disclosure of the known development of adjacent parcels.

81. NAC 645.637.

82. & 83. NRS 645.252 (1)(e).

84. See Real Estate Division forms "Duties Owed by a Nevada Real Estate Licensee" and "Consent to Act", ed.

85. Real Estate Division Position Statement, Joan Buchanan, Administrator, March 10, 1999.

86. NRS 645.254 (5).

87. NRS 645.252 (1)(b), NRS 645.633 (1)(g) and NAC 645.605 (4)(e).

88. NRS 645.252 (1)(c), NAC 645.605 (4), NAC 645.637 and NAC 645.640.

89. NRS 645.254 (5).

90. Holland Realty v. NV Real Estate Comm., 84 Nev. 91, 98, 436 P.2d 422 (1968), quoting the Restatement (Second) of Agency §390.

A new Duties Owed form should be provided to each client when there is any licensee change.

91. NRS 645.252 (4)(b).

92. NRS 645.252 (1)(b).

93. NAC 645.605 (1)(a).

94. RESPA, Real Estate Settlement Procedures Act, 12 USC §2602 (2).

95. NAC 645.605 (4)(d).

96. Judy Bendure, "Preferred Vendor Lists", Real Estate Division Open House, vol. 25, issue 1, Winter 2000, at p. 4.

97. & 98. NRS 645.633 (1)(g)

99. NRS 645.3205.

100. & 101. NAC 645.605 (4).

102. Lemon v. Landers, 81 Nev. 329, 332, 462 P.2d 648 (1965).

103. NRS 645.280.

The federal Real Estate Settlement Procedures Act (RESPA), prohibits a licensee from receiving or giving kickbacks and unearned fees even if such kickbacks or fees are disclosed. (RESPA, 12 U.S.C. § 2607)

Other Party's Ability to Perform: The licensee should disclose to the client any information of which the licensee is aware concerning the financial condition of the other party if it impacts the transaction. Nevertheless, a licensee is not required to investigate the financial condition of a party to the real estate transaction.[91] For example, if the buyer's agent learns that the seller is in bankruptcy, the agent must disclose that information to the buyer as it may impact the buyer's purchase of the property. However, the licensee is not required to investigate or discover if the seller is in bankruptcy.

c. Licensee's Compensation - A licensee must disclose to each party to a transaction (client or not), each source from which the licensee will receive compensation.[92] The statute does not require the licensee to disclose the amount of the compensation, only its source - the identity of the entity giving the compensation.[93]

The statute does not dictate when the disclosure should be made, but common law would require it be made before the transaction ends. This would ensure each party is aware of any potential conflicts of interest the licensee may have. Since the other party usually does not see the broker's employment agreement (the brokerage agreement) where both the source and amount of compensation are usually identified, compensation sources are often identified in the parties' purchase agreement. Since the purchase agreement is a contract between a seller and buyer, a better business practice is to have the licensees' sources of compensation identified in the common escrow instructions or on a separate disclosure form.

What is Compensation? Compensation is anything of value. It includes money, Goods or services.[94] It includes referral fees and other payments such as fees received from vendors to be on a broker's list of service providers.[95] Even though the broker may give a service provider list to a client without charge, the broker must disclose if a vendor paid to be on that list.[96] Compensation includes money the broker may accept or charge as a rebate or direct profit on expenditures made for the client.[97]

The Real Estate Commission may discipline any licensee found guilty of accepting, giving, or charging any undisclosed commission. This discipline can be a fine of up to $10,000 per violation and the suspension or revocation of the licensee's license.[98] A licensee may also be charged with deceitful, fraudulent or dishonest dealing if the Commission finds the licensee has not disclosed, in writing, that the licensee: [99]

- Expects to receive any direct or indirect compensation from any person for services related to the property,[100] or

- Has received compensation from more than one party.

Consent Required: If a broker anticipates receiving compensation from more than one party, the broker must disclose this to each party and obtain each party's consent.[101] Should a party refuse consent, the licensee cannot accept the compensation.

A licensee may not take an undisclosed profit at the expense of another party nor may the licensee purchase or sell the property of a client through the use of a third person without full disclosure and the client's consent.[102]

The licensee should note that disclosure alone does not make the receipt of certain compensation legal. For example, a salesperson may not accept compensation directly from a client even if that compensation is fully disclosed to all parties.[103]

V - 17

d. Licensee's Interest - A licensee must disclose to the parties in writing whenever the licensee has a personal interest in either the transaction or the property. Such disclosure ensures everyone is aware of the licensee's potential conflicting loyalties.[104]

A licensee (including permitted property managers) must disclose the licensee's affiliation with, or financial interest in, any person or entity that furnishes maintenance or other services related to the property.[105] If a licensee has an ownership interest in a business and refers clients to that business, the licensee must disclose that ownership interest.

Party to the Transaction: When a licensee is a principal, it is a material fact and must be disclosed.[106] The licensee may not acquire (purchase), lease or dispose of (sell), any time-share or real property without revealing the licensee's licensed status.[107]

Relationship with a Principal: The licensee must disclose whenever he or she has a personal relationship with a principal to the transaction.[108] The relationships that must be disclosed are when a principal is a member of the licensee's immediate family, a member of the licensee's firm, or an entity (such as a corporation, LLC, etc.) in which the licensee has an ownership interest.

Affiliated Business Relationships: Licensees are subject to federal as well as Nevada law. One federal law that addresses licensee disclosure is RESPA (Real Estate Settlement Procedures Act). It prohibits referrals from one business to another business when the businesses have joint ownership unless there is full disclosure. These intertwined businesses are Affiliated Business Arrangements.[109] A broker who has any Affiliated Business Arrangement with other real estate settlement service providers should review the RESPA statutes to determine the specifics of disclosure.

Interest in the Property: A licensee, whether acting as an agent or a principal, has an "interest in the property" whenever the licensee has or anticipates an ownership interest.[110] Failure to disclose the licensee's interest is an element in the Real Estate Commission's determination of whether the licensee is deceitful or dishonest. [111]

Any anticipated interest must be disclosed even if it is only a pass-through interest. For example, a licensee must disclose if the licensee takes title, however briefly, during a "double escrow." [112]

Disclosure in Writing: Whether the licensee's interest is in the transaction or in the property, the disclosure must be in writing – an oral disclosure does not satisfy the regulations.[113] When disclosing the licensee's interest in the property, the disclosure must state the licensee is acquiring or selling the property for him or herself and that the licensee is a broker, broker-salesperson, or salesperson. The Real Estate Division will recognize the disclosure if the licensee includes the term "agent," "licensee," or "broker, broker-salesperson, salesperson," whichever designation is appropriate. [114]

Timing: These disclosures must be made "as soon as practicable" but not later than the date and time on which any written document is signed by the parties. The Nevada Supreme Court has defined "as soon as practicable" to mean "promptly" or "within a reasonable length of time" considering the facts and circumstances of each particular case.[115]

104. NRS 645.252 (1)(b) & (c), NRS 645.633 (1)(g), NAC 645.605 (4), NAC 645.610 (1)(b), NAC 645.637 and NAC 645.640.

105. NAC 645.605 (4)(b) & (c).

106. NRS 645.252 (1)(c), NAC 645.637.

107. & 108. NAC 645.640 (1).

109. RESPA, Real Estate Settlement Procedures Act. 12 USC. § 2607.

110. NRS 645.252 (1)(c), NAC 645.637.

111. NAC 645.605 (4).

112. Alley v. NV Real Estate Div., 94 Nev. 123, 125, 575 P.2d 1334 (1978).

113. NAC 645.637.

114. NAC 645.640 (1).

115. American Fidelity Fire Ins. v. Adams, 97 Nev. 106, 108, 635 P.2d 88 (1981).

An Affiliated Business Arrangement is when two or more businesses providing various settlement services to a client are owned (in whole or part) by the same company or entity.

116. Lowe v. State Dep't of Commerce, 89 Nev. 488, 490, 515 P.2d 388 (1973) and NRS 645.252 (1)(a).

117. NRS 113.100 (1).

3. PROPERTY DISCLOSURES

Most individuals when they first think about real estate disclosure think of issues concerning the property. Property disclosures can be divided into two main areas, issues concerning the property itself, such as physical defects, and issues concerning the property's use or value. The latter would include neighborhood issues and physical components of the property that may not be a defect, but that nevertheless impact the property's use, such as out-of-code wiring in an older home. Some disclosures are mandated regardless of whether the information impacts the property. For example, buyers of residential properties built before 1978 must be given a lead-based paint disclosure without regard to the actual presence of lead-based paint.

a. Impacts the Property – What does "impacts the property" mean? Anything that affects the property's value or use in a material and relevant way impacts the property and must be disclosed.[116] All defects impact the property, but all items that impact the property may not be defects. For example, an elementary school that backs up to the property may impact it, but the presence of the school would not, in and of itself, be considered a property defect.

b. Defects: Latent and Patent – A "defect" is a condition of the property that affects its value or use in an adverse manner.[117] A patent defect is a defect that is readily observable using reasonable diligence, for example, a broken window. A licensee is independently (independent of the property owner) required to disclose patent defects of which he or she is aware. A latent defect is one that cannot be readily observed or discovered without some extraordinary activity. For example, discovery of a termite infestation behind a garage wallboard would require the wall to be removed.

The term "defect" has broad application. It contains items that are damaged (broken window, termite infestation) to items that are not damaged, but affect the property in an adverse manner. For example, an asbestos ceiling covering in an older home is a "defect" in that it affects the property's value in an adverse manner.

c. Disclosing "Everything" - It seems every few years there is a new environmental hazard that catches the public's attention. Recently, mold issues have been the front runner. Previously, it was asbestos, lead-based paint, high-Powered electric transmission lines, and radon. This is not to dismiss as a fad the very real health hazards these items may pose. Rather, it is a warning not to allow the current hazard du jour to blind the licensee from other bona fide disclosure issues.

V - 19

d. Various Non-Mandated Disclosures - Listed here are various environmental items that should be disclosed if applicable. Obviously, no list can be comprehensive. Items that have specific statutory disclosure requirements are not listed.

- Mold (hazardous)
- Agricultural uses, and those with noxious odors
- Airport flight path (see individual regional requirements)
- Encroachments
- Underground tanks (active and abandoned)
- Urea-formaldehyde
- Foam insulation (UFFI)
- Radon
- Waste Processing
- Mercury
- Earthquake Zone
- Dump (present/past)
- Arsenic
- Slide area (zone)
- Asbestos
- Landfills
- Forest fire (zone)
- Flood (zone)
- Pest Infestation
- Extensive dust (natural/construction)
- Mining (historical and present)
- Groundwater contamination

Gone are the days of "Buyer Beware" Licensee liability lies in inadequate disclosure. The fear of many licensees is that they will not catch all the potential issues, defects and hazards that should be disclosed. To address this fear, some brokers have developed "homemade" disclosure forms that attempt to disclose every possible hazard regardless of whether a particular item affects the property. As previously discussed, if used, these forms should be drafted by a licensed Nevada attorney.

Also, as previously discussed, the Nevada Real Estate Division has developed for the consumer a basic "Residential Disclosure Guide" for residential properties.[118] This is the Nevada Legislature's attempt to inform the consumer of potential disclosure issues. This booklet contains information for the consumer - it is not designed to relieve the licensee or seller of any of his or her disclosure duties.

Because no form or booklet can be all inclusive of every possible disclosure, the licensee must continually be alert to those disclosures required by law, those required when they impact the property, and those that address the concerns of the client.

e. Disclosing the Human Condition - In any discussion of disclosure, certain issues continue to be of concern to the client. These include noisy neighbors and dogs, crime, and neighborhood demographics (racial, ethnic, religious).

Noisy neighbors and dogs can be disclosed if the seller has given permission since these are things that are based in individual perception. They are also conditions that can change overnight – the dog dies, the neighbor moves. A potential buyer may not have the same experience as the current seller.

A neighborhood's crime statistics should be disclosed by an authority other than the licensee. If the client is concerned about crime in a particular neighborhood, the licensee should refer the client to the local law enforcement unit. Perception of criminal activity is too often erroneously linked with the racial or ethnic composition of an area. The licensee should always refer the client who asks about criminal activity in a neighborhood to a knowledgeable authority such as law enforcement. Repeating media reports is dangerous - even the media sometimes gets it wrong.

118. NRS 645.194.

119. 42 USA § 3604 (a), (d), (1991), & NRS 118.100

120. NRS 118.100.

121. The federal protected classes are race, color, religion, sex, national origin, handicap and familial status. 42 USC §3604 et seq., Nevada's protected classes are race, religious creed, color, national origin, disability, ancestry, familial status and sex. NRS 118.100. "Sex" does not mean sexual orientation, it refers to gender (male, female). Sexual orientation is not a protected class for housing under both federal and Nevada state law.

122. U.S. House of Representatives, Committee on the Judiciary, Report 110-711: the Fair Housing Amendments Act of 1988 at p. 24, 100th Cong., 2nd Sess. (1988).

123. The Fair Housing Act, also known as Title VIII of the Civil Rights Act of 1968. 42 USC §§3601-3619. Nevada's fair housing law is found in NRS 118.

124. NRS 40.770 (3).

Professional trade associations may have their own guidelines regarding demographic disclosure. The National Association of Realtors®, Standard of Practice 10-1 (2006), provides that its members "shall not volunteer information regarding the racial, religious or ethnic composition of any neighborhood…"

A licensee may answer the client's questions about the demographic composition of a neighborhood, but the licensee must be very careful when doing so.

There is a fine line between giving information and "steering." "Steering" occurs when a broker attempts to guide purchasers toward certain regions or neighborhoods using a protected class status.[119]

There are two types of steering: active and passive. Active steering occurs when the licensee actually attempts to persuade persons away from or toward certain neighborhoods based on a protected class status. Passive steering involves the licensee not showing or making available otherwise appropriate housing.

"Disclosures" made with the intent of steering a client to or from a neighborhood based on either the client's protected class status, or the neighborhood's protected class demographic composition, is illegal.[120]

Remember, liability is not based on the licensee's perception of whether the licensee is steering the client, but on the client's perception.

Group Homes: A common question among licensees is should they disclose a group home in the neighborhood. Disclosure depends on whether the individuals in the group home are of a Fair Housing protected class.[121] Group homes are "congregate living arrangement among non-related persons with disabilities."[122] If the disability is covered under the Fair Housing Act,[123] then the home has a protected class status and should not be disclosed - just as a licensee would not disclose that the neighbors were of a particular race, color or religion.

Various protected group homes (not to be disclosed) include homes for recovering drug and alcohol users (handicap), those with a mental illness (handicap), those with physical disabilities (handicap), pregnant teens or single mothers (familial status), and others of similar protected class status.

The disclosure rules vary for senior housing or homes for the elderly. If the housing is for individuals with mental impairment due to age, it is protected (handicap) and should not be disclosed. If the housing is for seniors only - no mental or physical impairment (age alone is not an impairment), then it can be disclosed. Age is not a protected class - at most, senior housing is an exception to the protected class of familial status.

Nevada law provides that the fact a property is located near a facility for transitional living for released offenders is not material to the transaction and does not need to be disclosed.[124]

Released offenders are persons who have been released from prison and who require assistance with reintegration into the community (NRS 449.0055).

V - 21

D. REVIEW

The licensee's duty for full and honest disclosure is an important and significant duty. Disclosure laws can be found throughout federal, state and local laws and regulations. Inadequate disclosure is a major source of liability for the licensee; therefore, it is necessary to ensure a working familiarity with the various disclosure laws and regulations. The licensee must not only be aware of what needs to be disclosed, but the when, who and how of the disclosure.

There are three main areas for disclosure, these constitute the "what" of disclosure. They are disclosures concerning the property, those concerning the licensee's agency, and those dealing with the parties' transaction.

For each disclosure the licensee must be aware of "when" the disclosure must be made, "how" the disclosure is to be made, and lastly, to "whom" the disclosure is to be made. When using non-government created disclosure forms, the broker should insure such forms will provide the brokerage with appropriate liability protection.

In addition to knowing the various disclosures, the licensee should be aware of any exceptions or exemptions to the disclosure laws and how they affect the client's confidences and general consumer privacy.

Finally, the licensee should review the following tables and forms to familiarize him or her self with the most common disclosures and their requirements, limitations and sources.

APPENDIX I

AGENCY AND TRANSACTION DISCLOSURES

EVENT REQUIRING DISCLOSURE	DISCLOSURE FORM NAME	WHAT IS BEING DISCLOSED	LEGAL CITE	RESPONSIBLE PERSON	GIVEN TO	LAST POSSIBLE TIME FOR DISCLOSURE
Creation of agency with Client.	Duties Owed to by A Nevada Licensee RED form # 525	Given to, and acknowledged by, a Client. Lists the statutory duties of a Licensee and the various levels of representation.	NRS 645.252 (3)	Licensee	Client and any unrepresented party	"As soon as practicable" but before any documents are signed by Client.
Agency for Clients with conflicting interests.	Consent to Act RED form # 524	Acknowledges authorization of Licensee from all parties for Licensee to act in a "dual agency" position. Dual agency occurs when the Licensee is acting in an agency capacity for two or more clients who have interests adverse to one other. Should either party refuse to sign, the Licensee cannot act as a dual agent.	NRS 645.252 (1)(d)	Licensee	All parties, Clients	"As soon as practicable" See text for various signing time frames.
When the Licensee's relationship to a party changes.	No Mandatory Form	Licensee must disclose any changes in his or her relationship to a party to the transaction.	NRS 645.252 (1)(e)	Licensee	All parties	"As soon as practicable."
When Licensee is acting as agent or principal.	No Mandatory Form – must be in writing.	Disclose to all parties Licensee's relationship as agent of a party, or Licensee's status as a principal.	NAC 645.637	Licensee	All parties to the transaction	Not later than the time any document is signed by parties.
When the Licensee has an interest in the transaction or the property.	No Mandatory Form	Licensee must disclose that the Licensee is a principal to the transaction or has an interest in a principal to the transaction.	NRS 645.252 (1)(c) NAC 645.640	Licensee	All parties to the transaction	"As soon as practicable."
Licensee has an interest in any escrow business or company.	No Mandatory Form	Must disclose that Licensee (or anyone associated with Licensee) has an interest in any escrow business before Licensee can deposit any money received in a real estate transaction, into such escrow company.	NAC 645.660	Licensee	All parties to the transaction	Before money is deposited.
Referral to certain settlement services providers.	Affiliated Business Arrangement Disclosure Statement	Affiliated Business Arrangement (ABA) - RESPA restricts a Licensee/ Broker from receiving a referral fee from a settlement service provider unless the Broker has an ABA with the provider. If there is an ABA, the Broker must disclose in writing the nature of the ABA relationship, a written estimate of the fees, and a notice that the consumer does not need to utilize the provider.	RESPA, 12 USC § 2607, 24 CFR Part 3500.15(d) and Reg. X	Broker/Licensee	Client/consumer	When referral is made.

AGENCY AND TRANSACTION DISCLOSURES

EVENT REQUIRING DISCLOSURE	DISCLOSURE FORM NAME	WHAT IS BEING DISCLOSED	LEGAL CITE	RESPONSIBLE PERSON	GIVEN TO	LAST POSSIBLE TIME FOR DISCLOSURE
Licensee is Inexperienced in type of transaction.	No Mandatory Form	Provides that the Real Estate Division may discipline a Licensee if there is no disclosure to Client that Licensee is providing specialized professional services outside the Licensee's field or experience or competence.	NAC 645.605 (3)	Licensee	Client	Before services are rendered.
When Licensee has a financial relationship with any entity servicing the property.	No Mandatory Form	Licensee must disclose, in writing, any interest, or contemplated interest, in any property or time share, including, but not limited to, an affiliation with or financial interest in, any person or company that furnishes services related to the property, whether Licensee is managing the property, has an interest in, or financial arrangement with such entity; or expects to receive a referral fee for referring a Client to a service provider.	NAC 645.605 (4)	Licensee	All Parties to transaction	"As soon as is practicable."
Any agency relationship.	No Mandatory Form	A Licensee who represents a Client shall disclose to the Client material facts of which the Licensee has knowledge concerning the transaction.	NRS 645.254 (3)(c)	Licensee	Client	As soon as known.
When a Broker or Brokerage engages in any "financial activity."	No Mandatory Form	Gramm-Leach-Bliley Act (Financial Privacy) – If Broker engages in any "financial activity," Broker must inform Client how the Client's "nonpublic personally identifiable information" will be used. "Financial activity" are activities involving mortgage lending or mortgage Brokering. "Non public information" is any information collected about the Client by the Broker providing the financial product or service. Most Brokerage services are not affected by this disclosure requirement.	12 USC § 1843 12 CFR § 225	Broker	Client	Before any documents are signed by Client.
When Broker includes any credit terms in **advertisement.**	No Mandatory Form – specific information must be presented when TIL "trigger terms" used	Truth in Lending – requires a Broker to provide specific information when certain credit "trigger terms" are used in advertising. Trigger terms include the amount of the down payment, amount of monthly payment, number of payments or payment period, interest rate, Annual Percentage Rate, or the amount of the finance charge.	15 USC § 1601 12 CFR part 202.2(1) (1990)	Broker	All persons	When placing advertisment.
Licensee's unsolicited **Advertising on Internet** for any service or property.	No Mandatory Form	Licensee must adhere to all disclosure requirements found in law or regulation.	NAC 645.613	Licensee Broker	All persons	When placing advertisment.

AGENCY AND TRANSACTION DISCLOSURES

EVENT REQUIRING DISCLOSURE	DISCLOSURE FORM NAME	WHAT IS BEING DISCLOSED	LEGAL CITE	RESPONSIBLE PERSON	GIVEN TO	LAST POSSIBLE TIME FOR DISCLOSURE
Advertising property when Licensee is an owner.	No Mandatory Form	A Licensee must disclose in advertisement his or her status as a Licensee and may not use "for sale (lease) by owner" without qualifying wording such as "by Broker/agent owner".	NAC 645.610	Licensee	All persons	In advertisement.
When **Advertising** the Licensee's services.	No Mandatory Form	A Licensee, (a Broker, Broker-salesperson, or salesperson) must disclose the name of the Licensee's Brokerage in any advertisement for real estate services.	NRS 645.315	Licensee	All persons	In advertisement.
When Listing Broker Accepts "other than cash" earnest money.	No Mandatory Form	A Licensee must disclose to a seller that a buyer is offering something "other than cash" as an earnest money deposit. Once disclosed, the seller may refuse to accept that type of "earnest money."	NRS 645.630 (1)(j)	Licensee	Seller	Before seller accepts Offer to Purchase.
When any deposits are accepted by Broker.	No Mandatory Form	Broker must disclose the disposition of all deposits accepted and retained by the Broker pending consummation or termination of the transaction.	NRS 645.310 (1)	Broker or owner - developer	All persons	At termination of transaction.
Close of transaction when there is no escrow holder.	No State Mandatory Form – the federal form is a HUD-1	Unless there is an escrow holder who performs these duties, Broker is responsible for disclosing to the parties in a complete, detailed closing statement all the receipts and disbursements handled by the Broker for the parties.	NRS 645.635 (4)	Broker	Seller and Buyer	Within 10 business days after the transaction is closed.
Offer or counteroffer rejected by client.	No Mandatory Form must be in writing	Licensee must disclose to other party or agent, that the licensee's client has rejected the offer or counteroffer. Licensee must attempt to have client sign notice; however, the regulation is only binding on the licensee.	NAC 645.632	Licensee	Other party or their agent.	Within reasonable time.
Sale of Residential property.	Residential Disclosure Guide	A 15-page disclosure booklet produced by the Nevada Real Estate Division for consumers of residential properties. Contains discussions on the most commonly-required state, federal and local disclosures. Last page is an acknowledgment receipt which must be filled out and held in the broker's file.	NRS 645.194	Licensee	Seller and Buyer	Not stated, but made to.

PROPERTY MANAGEMENT DISCLOSURES

EVENT Requiring DISCLOSURE	DISCLOSURE FORM NAME	WHAT IS BEING DISCLOSED	LEGAL CITE	RESPONSIBLE PERSON	GIVEN TO	LAST POSSIBLE TIME FOR Disclosure
Property tax disclosure.	No Mandatory Form	Amount of annual property taxes landlord pays for unit and the 1980 amount of property taxes for the unit.	NRS 118.165	Landlord/ property manager	Tenant/Lessee	Every July or when rent changes.
New Tenant/Lessee or new landlord.	No Mandatory Form, given to Tenant/Lessee or posted in conspicuous place.	Name and address of: 1. person managing premises, 2. person authorized to receive legal notices and demands, 3. principal or corporate owner. Additionally, the telephone number of a responsible person within the county to be called in emergencies. Information must be kept current.	NRS 118A.260 NRS 118A.270	Landlord/ property manager	Tenant/Lessee	Whenever there is a new Tenant/Lessee, new landlord, or information changes.
Termination of landlord's interest in property.	No Mandatory Form	Termination of landlord's interest in rental property by either sale, assignment, death, appointment of receiver or otherwise. Notice of new successor in interest (owner, etc.) name, address, telephone number, and statement that the Tenant/Lessee's security deposit is being transferred.	NRS 118A.244	Landlord/ property manager	Tenant/Lessee	Before transfer of deed.
Residential Property built before 1978 – lease or sale.	No Mandatory Form, but required wording and information. **Lead Paint**	Seller or landlord must provide buyer/Tenant/Lessee with the EPA disclosure booklet "Protect Your Family From Lead in Your Home" (EPA747-K-94-001), and give notice that buyer/Tenant/Lessee is allowed to perform a lead-based paint risk assessment/inspection. Buyer/Tenant/Lessee may cancel.	42 USC § 4852 (d)	Seller or Landlord	Buyer or Tenant/Lessee	As a condition of the sale or lease agreement.
Increase in rent.	No Mandatory Form	Increase in rent, amount of increase.	NRS 118A.300	Landlord/property manager	Tenant/Lessee	45 days before increase due.
Adoption or change of tenancy rules or regulations.	No Mandatory Form	Adoption of Tenant/Lessee rules and regulations. Timing may be waived by Tenant/Lessee if consents in writing.	NRS 118A.320	Landlord/property manager	Tenant/Lessee	30 days before enforcement.
Required in any written rental agreement.	No Mandatory Form but required statutes	Defines public nuisance under NRS 202.450 - 470.	NRS 118A.200 (1)	Landlord, agent, property manager	Tenant/Lessee	With any written rental agreement.

EVENT DISCLOSURE	DISCLOSURE REQUIRING NAME	FORM WHAT IS BEING DISCLOSED	LEGAL CITE	RESPONSIBLE PERSON	GIVEN TO	LAST POSSIBLE TIME FOR DISCLOSURE
New Unit in CIC – Common Interest Community.	Public Offering Statement	Identifies type of CIC (condo, cooperative, planned community), construction schedule, the CIC's bylaws, rules, regulations, C,C & Rs, financial statement, budget, service, initial or special fee, warranties, cancellation notice, judgments or lawsuits, monthly fees, CIC Information statement, date of information. Development rights of contractor. Location and description of proposed improvements. Buyer cancellation rights NRS 116.4108.	NRS 116.4102 116.4103 116.4104	Declarant or Dealer (seller)	Initial Buyer	Date offer becomes binding on buyer.
New Unit which may become Time Share.	Public Offering Statement	Same as above + number & identity of units. Total number of shares with minimum duration.	NRS 116.4105	Declarant or Dealer (seller)	Initial Buyer	Date offer becomes binding on buyer.
New Unit – Converted Building.	Public Offering Statement	Same as above + description of present condition of all structural components and mechanical, electrical installations. Useful life of each item. Outstanding uncured building code or other municipal violations and cost to repair. (Applicable to buildings with 13+ units)	NRS 116.4106	Declarant or Dealer (seller)	Initial Buyer	Date offer becomes binding on buyer.
New Unit – Converted Building in CIC.	Notice of Conversion	Notice of conversion, public offering statement, and right of Tenant/Lessee and subtenant/Lessees to acquire that unit on same or better terms than declarant offers to public.	NRS 116.4112	Declarant or seller	Existing Tenant/Lessee/ renter	120 days before Tenant/Lessees required to vacate.
Sale of any **Subdivision**,* lot, parcel, unit or interest in subdivision. *see NRS 119.110 for definition of subdivision.	Property Report As prepared by the Nevada RED	Name & address of each person owning a 10%+ interest in the subdivision. Name, occupation, address of every officer, director or owner of the subdivision. Legal description and area of lands, condition of title, public utilities, conditions of disposition of land with copies of related documents, use of land, maximum depth of fill, soil condition (with engineering reports), statement of liens for improvements, agricultural activities in area adversely affecting property. Notice of right of buyer to cancel contract.	NRS 119.182	Broker or salesman	Buyer	Before signing of any purchase contract.
Subdivision Sale of any lot, parcel, unit or interest in a subdivision.	No Mandatory Form	Location in subdivision of rights-of-way and easements for transmission lines of public utility electric lines and in all lands contiguous to it.	NRS 119.1835	Developer	Buyer	Before signing any binding agreement.
Subdivision Sale of any lot, parcel, unit or interest in a subdivision.	No Mandatory Form	Location in subdivision of rights-of-way and easements for transmission lines of public utility electric lines and in all lands contiguous to it.	NRS 119.1835	Developer	Buyer	Before signing any binding agreement.

PROPERTY DISCLOSURES

EVENT REQUIRING DISCLOSURE	DISCLOSURE FORM NAME	WHAT IS BEING DISCLOSED	LEGAL CITE	RESPONSIBLE PERSON	GIVEN TO	LAST POSSIBLE TIME FOR DISCLOSURE
When licensee becomes an Agent in a real estate transaction.	No Mandatory Form	Licensee must disclose any material and relevant facts, data or information which licensee knows, or by the exercise of reasonable care and diligence, should have known, relating to the property.	NRS 645.252 (1)(a)	Licensee	All Parties to transaction	"As soon as is practicable."
Previously unsold home + any improved lot.	No Mandatory Form	Water & sewage rates of a public utility servicing 25 to 2,000 customers. Notice must contain name, address, and telephone numbers of public utility and Div. Consumer Complaint for the Public Utilities Comm. of NV.	NRS 113.060	Seller	Buyer	Before the home is sold.
New construction – subdivided land.	No Mandatory Form - separate written document	Zoning classification & master plan designation of subdivision or parcel map. Designated land use of parcel and general land uses of adjoining parcels. Notice that the designations are subject to change. Provide instructions on how to obtain current zoning information.	NRS 113.070, Clark Co. Code 7.65.010, or 30.36.040	Seller or any person who sells land that was subdivided.	Initial Buyer	Before signing sales agreement or opening escrow, whichever is first.
Unit not occupied by buyer more than 120 days before completion.	No Mandatory Form	Provide copies of certain statutes (NRS 11.202 - .206, and NRS 40.600 - .695). These statutes deal with construction defect claims.	NRS 113.135	Seller	Initial Buyer	Upon signing sales agreement.
Unit not occupied by buyer more than 120 days before completion.	No Mandatory Form	Notice of "soil report" prepared for the property or for the subdivision in which the property is located. After receipt of notice, buyer has 5 days to request copy of the actual report and 20 days to rescind the sales agreement. Rescission right may be waived.	NRS 113.135	Seller	Initial Buyer	Upon signing sales agreement.
Sale of any land.	No Mandatory Form	Any conditions or obligations connected with any gift or other free benefit offered to potential buyers.	NRS 599A.060 (1)(d)	Seller	Customer	Not stated, but made to "prospective" customer.
Offering for sale or lease across state borders, undeveloped "subdivided" (25+ parcels) land not larger than 20 acres each.	Statement of Record, and Property Report.	Interstate Land Sales Full Disclosure Act, (ILSFDA). Administered by HUD through the Office of Interstate Land Sales Registration. Extensive and detailed requirements for disclosure items are included in the Statement of Record and Property Report. These include, but are not limited to, title condition, soil condition, availability of recreation facilities, utilities and their fees, number & type of buildings currently on site, etc. If disclosure does not adhere to all guidelines, buyer has two (2) years to rescind the contract.	15 USC § 1701-1720, 24 CFR Parts 1700-1730.100, NRS 119.119	Developer & agents.	Buyer or Lessee / Tenant/Lessee	Before any sales agreement or lease, is signed.

PROPERTY DISCLOSURES

EVENT REQUIRING DISCLOSURE	DISCLOSURE FORM NAME	WHAT IS BEING DISCLOSED	LEGAL CITE	RESPONSIBLE PERSON	GIVEN TO	LAST POSSIBLE TIME FOR DISCLOSURE
Sale of property by "seller of more than one lot created by a map of division into large parcels."	No Mandatory Form	Notice that city, county, school district and special districts are not obligated to furnish any service (specifically mentioning fire and roads), and that public utilities may not be obligated to service parcel.	NRS 119.183	Seller	Buyer	Before signing any binding agreement.
Property being sold before the final subdivision map is recorded.	No Mandatory Form	All that is required to be stated is that the final subdivision map has not been recorded.	NRS 278.350	Seller or agent	Buyer	Not stated, but made to "potential buyer."
Property subject to impact fee.	No Mandatory Form	Actual or pending impact fees. Amount of impact fee not yet paid and the name of the local government which imposed (or will impose) the fee.	NRS 278B.320	Seller	Buyer	Before property is conveyed.
HUD – FHA loan insurance, appraisal Hazard and Nuisance disclosures.	HUD adopted Fannie Mae appraisal (Form 1004)	Licensees should be aware of the various Hazards and Nuisances required to be listed on FHA appraisal Forms. These include: Airport Runway Clear Zones; Railroad tracks & other high noise sources; Flood zones (as determined under FEMA maps); Radon, Overhead high voltage transmission towers & lines; Operating & Abandoned oil & gas wells, tanks, and pressure lines; presence of asbestos, foam plastic/core materials; lead based paint; and avalanche hazard. A licensee must always disclose to all parties any condition affecting the property of which the licensee is aware, whether or not disclosed under an FHA insured appraisal (NRS 645.252.)	24 CFR part 200	Appraiser	Lender/insurer	At time of appraisal inspection or when licensee becomes aware of a H & N.
Property subject to deferred taxes.	No Mandatory Form	Lien for deferred taxes. Interestingly, the amount of lien nor the entity creating the lien is required to be disclosed. Deferred taxes statutes – NRS 361A.265, 361A.280 or 361A.283.	NRS 361A.290	Seller	Buyer	When property is sold or transferred.
After any construction by any contractor.	No Mandatory Form	Disclosure of construction defects. Written disclosure must be in understandable language, underlined and in boldfaced capital letters.	NRS 40.640 (5)	Contractor & agents	Buyer	Before purchase.

PROPERTY DISCLOSURES

EVENT REQUIRING DISCLOSURE	DISCLOSURE FORM NAME	WHAT IS BEING DISCLOSED	LEGAL CITE	RESPONSIBLE PERSON	GIVEN TO	LAST POSSIBLE TIME FOR DISCLOSURE
Any construction, remodeling, repair or other improvements on a Single-family residence (SFR).	No Mandatory Form; however, NRS 624.520 has suggested wording for Notice.	Informs owner of the Nevada "Recovery Fund" available to the property owner when a residential contractor fails to perform qualified services adequately. Notice must identify NRS 624.400 to NRS 624.560. Real Estate Licensee should be aware of this notice when representing a seller or buyer and there has been construction or contractor services on the property.	NRS 624.520	Contractor	Owner	At time of signing contract.
Whenever a general building contractor contracts with a SFR owner.	No Mandatory Form	Requires a general building contractor to provide specific information to a SFR owner about material men and subcontractors and their right to lien the property under NRS 108, Mechanics Lien laws. Real Estate Licensee should be aware of this notice when representing a seller or buyer and there has been construction or contractor services on the property.	NRS 624.600	General Building contractor	Owner	No time specified.
Title to property is unmerchantable.	No Mandatory Form	Property's title is unmerchantable. "Unmerchantable" = unmarketable, "bad title", or nonmerchantable. Property title a reasonable buyer would refuse to accept because of possible conflicting interest in or litigation over the property.	NAC 645.635	Licensee	Buyer	Before any part of purchase price is paid.
Property subject to a construction defect claim under NRS 40.600 - .695.	No Mandatory Form	Provide copies of all notices of construction defect given to contractor(s), all opinions of experts; terms of any settlement, order or judgment of defect claim; detailed report of all repairs made. ** Note ** Timing of disclosure is complicated – 30 days before COE; or if complaint is made while in escrow, w/i 24 hours of complaint; or if escrow is less then 30 days, immediately upon signing.	NRS 40.688	Claimant, Owner or Seller	Buyer	Generally, immediately upon signing sales agreement. See ** note.
Resale – Residential.	Seller's Real Property Disclosure – RED Form #547	An evaluation by the seller of the condition of property systems (plumbing, electrical, etc.) and the condition of any other aspect of the property which may effect its use or value. Information is based on what seller is aware of and is not a warranty. Includes statutes NRS 113.140 - .150(5). Non-disclosure allows buyer to rescind sales agreement. Buyer may waive all rights.	NRS 113.120 to NRS 113.150	Seller	Buyer	10 days before property conveyance or as agreed between the parties.
Resale – Home in CIC – Common Interest Community.	Required disclosures, plus Form - Before You Purchase Property … RED Form #584	Required disclosures: Resale Package Copy of declaration, rules or regulations of association, statement of monthly assessment, unpaid assessment, current operating budget, financial statement of association, summary of financial components of Reserve Study, unsatisfied judgments, status of any pending legal actions. Buyer may cancel within 5 days after receipt of resale package. Before You Purchase Property in a Common-Interest Community Did You Know…	NRS 116.4109 NRS 116.41095	Unit's owner - seller	Buyer	By parties' agreement, but before close of escrow.

PROPERTY DISCLOSURES

EVENT REQUIRING DISCLOSURE	DISCLOSURE FORM NAME	WHAT IS BEING DISCLOSED	LEGAL CITE	RESPONSIBLE PERSON	GIVEN TO	LAST POSSIBLE TIME FOR DISCLOSURE
Residential Property built before 1978 - lease or sale.	No Mandatory Form, but required wording and booklet. www.hud.gov/offices/lead/1018/selr_eng.pdf	Seller or landlord must provide buyer/Tenant/Lessee with the EPA disclosure booklet "Protect Your Family From **Lead in Your Home**" (EPA747-K-94-001), and give notice that buyer/Tenant/Lessee is allowed to perform a lead-based paint risk assessment/inspection. Buyer/Tenant/Lessee may cancel if lead is found.	42 USC § 4852 (d) 24 CFR part 35, subpart A	Seller or Landlord	Buyer or Tenant/Lessee	As a condition of the sale or lease agreement.
Revision Effective: July 1, 2009 Home or Improved or Unimproved Lot adjacent to open range.	Open Range Disclosure RED Form 551	Property is adjacent to open range on which livestock are permitted to graze or roam. Property may also be subject to county or state claims of rights-of-way granted by Congress over public lands (commonly referred to as R.S. 2477), detailed in Form 551. Identifies fencing requirements and warns about harming livestock. Open range is all unenclosed land outside cities or towns.	NRS 113.065	Seller	Buyer	Before signing sales agreement.
Buyer obtaining an FHA insured home loan.	For Your Protection Get a Home Inspection Form is HUD-92564-CN	Informs buyer about the limits of the Federal Housing Administration and suggests buyers obtain a home inspection to evaluate the physical condition of the property prior to purchase.	HUD mortgage letter 99-18	Lender or licensee	Buyer/Borrower	Before or on signing sales agreement.
Purchase of HUD-owned SFD property.	Radon Gas and Mold Notice and Release Agreement: HUD Form 9548-E(6/04)	PURCHASERS ARE HEREBY NOTIFIED AND UNDERSTAND THAT RADON GAS AND SOME MOLDS HAVE THE POTENTIAL TO CAUSE SERIOUS HEALTH PROBLEMS. Outlines HUD responsibility for home being sold "as-is" by HUD. Encourages buyers to obtain inspections.	HUD Notice 2004-8 (released may 28, 2004)	HUD-licensee	Buyer	At presentation of sales agreement.
Property in Road Maintenance District	No Mandatory Form	Notice property is within Road Maintenance District. The amount of assessments for the last two (2) years.	NRS 320.130	Seller	Buyer	Before property is sold.
Selling Used Manugactured (Mobile) Home with underly real property.	Used Manufactured/ Mobile Home Disclosure RED Form #610	Informs consumer that a manufactured home is personal property and is subject to personal property taxes unless converted. Also, instructs consumer to submit certain documents to Nevada's Manufactured Housing Division pursuant to NRS 489.521 and NRS 489.531.	NRS 645.258	Broker/Licensee	Buyer	Before property is sold.
Property was Meth Lab.	No Mandatory Form	If the property was the site of the manufacture or preparation of methamphetamine (meth). No disclosure is necessary if the property has been declared safe for habitation by a governmental agency.	NRS 40.770(6)	Licensee or seller	Buyer or tenant	Before sale or rental.
Effective: January 1, 2011	Energy Consumption Evaluation Disclosure Form to be prepared and published by the Nevada Energy Commissioner.	An evaluation of the energy consumption of property based on State-prescribed standards and information about State programs for improving energy conservation and efficiency in residential properties. Evaluation served to buyer must have been completed 5 years or less from date parties enter into an agreement to purchase. Includes statues NRS 113.115. Buyer may waive rights.	NRS 113.115	Seller	Buyer	Before close of escrow for the conveyance of property.

PROPERTY DISCLOSURES
COUNTY SPECIFIC DISCLOSURES AS OF FEBRUARY 2006

EVENT REQUIRING DISCLOSURE	DISCLOSURE FORM NAME	WHAT IS BEING DISCLOSED	LEGAL CITE	RESPONSIBLE PERSON	GIVEN TO	LAST POSSIBLE TIME FOR DISCLOSURE
Property in a subdivision subject to deed restrictions. in **Washoe County**.	No Mandatory Form	Copy of deed restrictions IF property is located in a county with a Population between 100,000 and 400,000. As of February, 2006, this is only applicable to **Washoe County**.	NRS 278.565	Seller	Buyer	Not stated, but presented to "prospective" buyer.
When the Property has a Wood Burning Stove or solid fuel burning device in **Washoe County**.		Presented at sale of any residence, or change of title of any residence in Washoe County.	Washoe Co. Health Dist. Regulation 040.051§§ A & D	Seller or agent	Buyer	Before escrow is complete or title is changed.
New construction. Currently, only **Clark County**.	No Mandatory Form	Gaming Enterprise District – (for NV counties with a Population over 400,000. As of Feb. 2006, this is only applicable to Clark County). Copy of most recent gaming enterprise district map, the location of the nearest gaming enterprise district and notice that map is subject to change.	NRS 113.080	Seller	Initial Buyer	24 hrs before signing sales agreement, time may be waived.
Selling Residential Property in **Churchill County**.	No Mandatory Form	Information sheet presented to real estate licensees titled "What Every Realtor Should Know About Water in Churchill County". Provided by the City of Fallon, 2001. Local professional associations, such as the Sierra Nevada Association of Realtors®, may have other consumer disclosure pamphlets.	Information sheet only, not required by code or statute.	Licensees	Clients	Information sheet only.
Any property subject to Lake Tahoe Regional Planning Authority.	No Mandatory Form	Lake Tahoe – Best Management Practices – Residential property at Lake Tahoe is subject to multi-jurisdictional environmental controls that regulate ground, water and air quality in the Tahoe area. Licensees need to be aware of these restrictions, called Best Management Practices, when dealing with Tahoe property.	TRPA Code of Ordinances §25.5.A	Licensees	Clients and consumers	Various.

APPENDIX II

DUTIES OWED BY A NEVADA REAL ESTATE LICENSEE
This form does not constitute a contract for services nor an agreement to pay compensation.

In Nevada, a real estate licensee is required to provide a form setting forth the duties owed by the licensee to:
    a) **Each party for whom the licensee is acting as an agent in the real estate transaction, and**
    b) **Each unrepresented party to the real estate transaction, if any.**

Licensee: The licensee in the real estate transaction is _____

whose license number is _____. The licensee is acting for [client's name(s)] _____

_____ who is/are the ☐ Seller/Landlord; ☐ Buyer/Tenant.

Broker: The broker is _____, whose

company is _____.

Licensee's Duties Owed to All Parties:
A Nevada real estate licensee shall:
1. Not deal with any party to a real estate transaction in a manner which is deceitful, fraudulent or dishonest.
2. Exercise reasonable skill and care with respect to all parties to the real estate transaction.
3. Disclose to each party to the real estate transaction as soon as practicable:
   a. Any material and relevant facts, data or information which licensee knows, or with reasonable care and diligence the licensee should know, about the property.
   b. Each source from which licensee will receive compensation.
4. Abide by all other duties, responsibilities and obligations required of the licensee in law or regulations.

Licensee's Duties Owed to the Client:
A Nevada real estate licensee shall:
1. Exercise reasonable skill and care to carry out the terms of the brokerage agreement and the licensee's duties in the brokerage agreement;
2. Not disclose, except to the licensee's broker, confidential information relating to a client for 1 year after the revocation or termination of the brokerage agreement, unless licensee is required to do so by court order or the client gives written permission;
3. Seek a sale, purchase, option, rental or lease of real property at the price and terms stated in the brokerage agreement or at a price acceptable to the client;
4. Present all offers made to, or by the client as soon as practicable, unless the client chooses to waive the duty of the licensee to present all offers and signs a waiver of the duty on a form prescribed by the Division;
5. Disclose to the client material facts of which the licensee has knowledge concerning the real estate transaction;
6. Advise the client to obtain advice from an expert relating to matters which are beyond the expertise of the licensee; and
7. Account to the client for all money and property the licensee receives in which the client may have an interest.

Duties Owed By a broker who assigns different licensees affiliated with the brokerage to separate parties.
Each licensee shall not disclose, except to the real estate broker, confidential information relating to client.

Licensee Acting for Both Parties: You understand that the licensee _____ may *or* _____ may not, in the future act
                                               (Client Inits)   *(Client Inits)*
for two or more parties who have interests adverse to each other. In acting for these parties, the licensee has a conflict of interest. Before a licensee may act for two or more parties, the licensee must give you a "Consent to Act" form to sign.

I/We acknowledge receipt of a copy of this list of licensee duties, and have read and understand this disclosure.					
Seller/Landlord	*Date*	*Time*	*Buyer/Tenant*	*Date*	*Time*
Seller/Landlord	*Date*	*Time*	*Buyer/Tenant*	*Date*	*Time*

CONSENT TO ACT

This form does not constitute a contract for services nor an agreement to pay compensation.

DESCRIPTION OF TRANSACTION: The real estate transaction is the ☐ sale and purchase *or* ☐ lease of

Property Address: _____

_____.

In Nevada, a real estate licensee may act for more than one party in a real estate transaction; however, before the licensee does so, he or she must obtain the written consent of each party. This form is that consent. Before you consent to having a licensee represent both yourself and the other party, you should read this form and understand it.

Licensee: The licensee in this real estate transaction is _____ ("Licensee") whose

license number is _____ and who is affiliated with _____ ("Brokerage").

Seller/Landlord _____
               Print Name

Buyer/Tenant _____
               Print Name

CONFLICT OF INTEREST: A licensee in a real estate transaction may legally act for two or more parties who have interests adverse to each other. In acting for these parties, the licensee has a conflict of interest.

DISCLOSURE OF CONFIDENTIAL INFORMATION: Licensee will not disclose any confidential information for one year after the revocation or termination of any brokerage agreement entered into with a party to this transaction, unless Licensee is required to do so by a court of competent jurisdiction or is given written permission to do so by that party. Confidential information includes, but is not limited to, the client's motivation to purchase, trade or sell, which if disclosed, could harm one party's bargaining position or benefit the other.

DUTIES OF LICENSEE: Licensee shall provide you with a "Duties Owed by a Nevada Real Estate Licensee" disclosure form which lists the duties a licensee owes to all parties of a real estate transaction, and those owed to the licensee's client. When representing both parties, the licensee owes the same duties to both seller and buyer. Licensee shall disclose to both Seller and Buyer all known defects in the property, any matter that must be disclosed by law, and any information the licensee believes may be material or might affect Seller's/Landlord's or Buyer's/Tenant's decisions with respect to this transaction.

NO REQUIREMENT TO CONSENT: You are not required to consent to this licensee acting on your behalf. You may
        Reject this consent and obtain your own agent;
    – Represent yourself;
        Request that the licensee's broker assign you your own licensee.

CONFIRMATION OF DISCLOSURE AND INFORMATION CONSENT

BY MY SIGNATURE BELOW, I UNDERSTAND AND CONSENT: I am giving my consent to have the above identified licensee act for both the other party and me. By signing below, I acknowledge that I understand the ramifications of this consent, and that I acknowledge that I am giving this consent without coercion.

I/We acknowledge receipt of a copy of this list of licensee duties, and have read and understand this disclosure.

Seller/Landlord	Date	Time	Buyer/Tenant	Date	Time
Seller/Landlord	Date	Time	Buyer/Tenant	Date	Time

Approved Nevada Real Estate Division
Replaces all previous editions

Page 1 of 1

524
Revised 05/01/05

| V APPENDIX II - 2

284

SELLER'S REAL PROPERTY DISCLOSURE FORM

In accordance with Nevada Law, a seller of residential real property in Nevada must disclose any and all known conditions and aspects of the property which materially affect the value or use of residential property in an adverse manner *(see NRS 113.130 and 113.140)*.

Date _____

Property address _____

Do you currently occupy or have you ever occupied this property?   YES ☐   NO ☐

☐ Check here if the Seller is exempt from the completion of this form pursuant to NRS 113.130(2).

Purpose of Statement: (1) This statement is a disclosure of the condition of the property in compliance with the Seller Real Property Disclosure Act, effective January 1, 1996. (2) This statement is a disclosure of the condition and information concerning the property known by the Seller which materially affects the value of the property. Unless otherwise advised, the Seller does not possess any expertise in construction, architecture, engineering or any other specific area related to the construction or condition of the improvements on the property or the land. Also, unless otherwise advised, the Seller has not conducted any inspection of generally inaccessible areas such as the foundation or roof. This statement is not a warranty of any kind by the Seller or by any Agent representing the Seller in this transaction and is not a substitute for any inspections or warranties the Buyer may wish to obtain.

Instructions to the Seller: (1) ANSWER ALL QUESTIONS. (2) REPORT KNOWN CONDITIONS AFFECTING THE PROPERTY. (3) ATTACH ADDITIONAL PAGES WITH YOUR SIGNATURE IF ADDITIONAL SPACE IS REQUIRED. (4) COMPLETE THIS FORM YOURSELF. (5) IF SOME ITEMS DO NOT APPLY TO YOUR PROPERTY, CHECK N/A (NOT APPLICABLE). EFFECTIVE JANUARY 1, 1996, FAILURE TO PROVIDE A PURCHASER WITH A SIGNED DISCLOSURE STATEMENT WILL ENABLE THE PURCHASER TO TERMINATE AN OTHERWISE BINDING PURCHASE AGREEMENT AND SEEK OTHER REMEDIES AS PROVIDED BY THE LAW *(see NRS 113.150)*.

Systems / Appliances: Are you aware of any problems and/or defects with any of the following:

	YES	NO	N/A		YES	NO	N/A
Electrical System	☐	☐	☐				
Plumbing	☐	☐	☐	Shower(s)	☐	☐	☐
Sewer System & line	☐	☐	☐	Sink(s)	☐	☐	☐
Septic tank & leach field	☐	☐	☐	Sauna / hot tub(s)	☐	☐	☐
Well & pump	☐	☐	☐	Built-in microwave	☐	☐	☐
Yard sprinkler system(s)	☐	☐	☐	Range / oven / hood-fan	☐	☐	☐
Fountain(s)	☐	☐	☐	Dishwasher	☐	☐	☐
Heating system	☐	☐	☐	Garbage disposal	☐	☐	☐
Cooling system	☐	☐	☐	Trash compactor	☐	☐	☐
Solar heating system	☐	☐	☐	Central vacuum	☐	☐	☐
Fireplace & chimney	☐	☐	☐	Alarm system	☐	☐	☐
Wood burning system	☐	☐	☐	owned.. ☐ leased.. ☐			
Garage door opener	☐	☐	☐	Smoke detector	☐	☐	☐
Water treatment system(s)	☐	☐	☐	Intercom	☐	☐	☐
owned.. ☐ leased.. ☐				Data Communication line(s)	☐	☐	☐
Water heater	☐	☐	☐	Satellite dish(es)	☐	☐	☐
Toilet(s)	☐	☐	☐	owned.. ☐ leased.. ☐			
Bathtub(s)	☐	☐	☐	Other _____	☐	☐	☐

EXPLANATIONS: Any "Yes" must be fully explained. Attach explanations to form.

_____
Seller(s) Initials

_____
Buyer(s) Initials

Property conditions, improvements and additional information: YES   NO   N/A

Are you aware of any of the following?:

1. **Structure:**
    (a) Previous or current moisture conditions and/or water damage? ....   ☐   ☐
    (b) Any structural defect? ....   ☐   ☐
    (c) Any construction, modification, alterations, or repairs made without
        required state, city or county building permits? ....   ☐   ☐
    (d) Whether the property is or has been the subject of a claim governed by
        NRS 40.600 to 40.695 (construction defect claims)? ....   ☐   ☐
        (If seller answers yes, FURTHER DISCLOSURE IS REQUIRED)

2. **Land / Foundation:**
    (a) Any of the improvements being located on unstable or expansive soil? ....   ☐   ☐
    (b) Any foundation sliding, settling, movement, upheaval, or earth stability problems
        that have occurred on the property? ....   ☐   ☐
    (c) Any drainage, flooding, water seepage, or high water table? ....   ☐   ☐
    (d) The property being located in a designated flood plain? ....   ☐   ☐
    (e) Whether the property is located next to or near any known future development? ..   ☐   ☐
    (f) Any encroachments, easements, zoning violations or nonconforming uses? ....   ☐   ☐
    (g) Is the property adjacent to "open range" land? ....   ☐   ☐
        (If seller answers yes, FURTHER DISCLOSURE IS REQUIRED under NRS 113.065)

3. **Roof:** Any problems with the roof? ....   ☐   ☐
4. **Pool/spa:** Any problems with structure, wall, liner, or equipment? ....   ☐   ☐   ☐
5. **Infestation:** Any history of infestation (termites, carpenter ants, etc.)? ....   ☐   ☐
6. **Environmental:** Any substances, materials, or products which may be an environmental
    hazard such as, but not limited to, asbestos, radon gas, urea formaldehyde, fuel or chemical
    storage tanks, contaminated water or soil on the property? ....   ☐   ☐
7. **Fungi / Mold:** Any previous or current fungus or mold? ....   ☐   ☐
8. Any features of the property shared in common with adjoining landowners such as walls, fences,
    road, driveways or other features whose use or responsibility for maintenance may have an effect
    on the property? ....   ☐   ☐
9. **Common Interest Communities:** Any "common areas" (facilities like pools, tennis courts,
    walkways or other areas co-owned with others) or a homeowner association which has any
    authority over the property? ....   ☐   ☐
    (a) Common Interest Community Declaration and Bylaws available? ....   ☐   ☐
    (b) Any periodic or recurring association fees? ....   ☐   ☐
    (c) Any unpaid assessments, fines or liens, and any warnings or notices that may give rise to an
        assessment, fine or lien? ....   ☐   ☐
    (d) Any litigation, arbitration, or mediation related to property or common area? ..   ☐   ☐
    (e) Any assessments associated with the property (excluding property taxes)? ......   ☐   ☐
    (f) Any construction, modification, alterations, or repairs made without
        required approval from the appropriate Common Interest Community board or committee?..   ☐   ☐
10. Any problems with water quality or water supply? ....   ☐   ☐
11. **Any other conditions** or aspects of the property which materially affect its value or
    use in an adverse manner? ....   ☐   ☐
12. **Lead-Based Paint:** Was the property constructed on or before 12/31/77? ....   ☐   ☐
    (If yes, additional Federal EPA notification and disclosure documents are required)
13. **Water source:** Municipal ☐   Community Well ☐   Domestic Well ☐   Other ☐
    If Community Well: State Engineer Well Permit # _____   Revocable ☐ Permanent ☐ Cancelled ☐
    Use of community and domestic wells may be subject to change. Contact the Nevada Division of Water Resources
    for more information regarding the future use of this well.
14. **Wastewater disposal:** Municipal Sewer ☐   Septic System ☐   Other ☐

EXPLANATIONS: Any "Yes" must be fully explained. Attach explanations to form.

_____ _____   _____ _____
Seller(s) Initials   Buyer(s) Initials

Nevada Real Estate Division   Page 2 of 4   Seller Real Property Disclosure Form
Replaces all previous versions   Revised 05/01/06   547

V APPENDIX II - 4

286

Buyers and sellers of residential property are advised to seek the advice of an attorney concerning their rights and obligations as set forth in Chapter 113 of the Nevada Revised Statutes regarding the seller's obligation to execute the Nevada Real Estate Division's approved "Seller's Real Property Disclosure Form". For your convenience, Chapter 113 of the Nevada Revised Statutes provides as follows:

CONDITION OF RESIDENTIAL PROPERTY OFFERED FOR SALE

NRS 113.100 Definitions. As used in NRS 113.100 to 113.150, inclusive, unless the context otherwise requires:

1. "Defect" means a condition that materially affects the value or use of residential property in an adverse manner.

2. "Disclosure form" means a form that complies with the regulations adopted pursuant to NRS 113.120.

3. "Dwelling unit" means any building, structure or portion thereof which is occupied as, or designed or intended for occupancy as, a residence by one person who maintains a household or by two or more persons who maintain a common household.

4. "Residential property" means any land in this state to which is affixed not less than one nor more than four dwelling units.

5. "Seller" means a person who sells or intends to sell any residential property.

(Added to NRS by 1995, 842; A 1999, 1446)

NRS 113.110 Conditions required for "conveyance of property" and to complete service of document. For the purposes of NRS 113.100 to 113.150, inclusive:

1. A "conveyance of property" occurs:

(a) Upon the closure of any escrow opened for the conveyance; or

(b) If an escrow has not been opened for the conveyance, when the purchaser of the property receives the deed of conveyance.

2. Service of a document is complete:

(a) Upon personal delivery of the document to the person being served; or

(b) Three days after the document is mailed, postage prepaid, to the person being served at his last known address.

(Added to NRS by 1995, 844)

NRS 113.120 Regulations prescribing format and contents of form for disclosing condition of property. The Real Estate Division of the Department of Business and Industry shall adopt regulations prescribing the format and contents of a form for disclosing the condition of residential property offered for sale. The regulations must ensure that the form:

1. Provides for an evaluation of the condition of any electrical, heating, cooling, plumbing and sewer systems on the property, and of the condition of any other aspects of the property which affect its use or value, and allows the seller of the property to indicate whether or not each of those systems and other aspects of the property has a defect of which the seller is aware.

2. Provides notice:

(a) Of the provisions of NRS 113.140 and subsection 5 of NRS 113.150.

(b) That the disclosures set forth in the form are made by the seller and not by his agent.

(c) That the seller's agent, and the agent of the purchaser or potential purchaser of the residential property, may reveal the completed form and its contents to any purchaser or potential purchaser of the residential property.

(Added to NRS by 1995, 842)

NRS 113.130 Completion and service of disclosure form before conveyance of property; discovery or worsening of defect after service of form; exceptions; waiver.

1. Except as otherwise provided in subsections 2 and 3:

(a) At least 10 days before residential property is conveyed to a purchaser:

(1) The seller shall complete a disclosure form regarding the residential property; and

(2) The seller or his agent shall serve the purchaser or his agent with the completed disclosure form.

(b) If, after service of the completed disclosure form but before conveyance of the property to the purchaser, a seller or his agent discovers a new defect in the residential property that was not identified on the completed disclosure form or discovers that a defect identified on the completed disclosure form has become worse than was indicated on the form, the seller or his agent shall inform the purchaser or his agent of that fact, in writing, as soon as practicable after the discovery of that fact but in no event later than the conveyance of the property to the purchaser. If the seller does not agree to repair or replace the defect, the purchaser may:

(1) Rescind the agreement to purchase the property; or

(2) Close escrow and accept the property with the defect as revealed by the seller or his agent without further recourse.

2. Subsection 1 does not apply to a sale or intended sale of residential property:

(a) By foreclosure pursuant to chapter 107 of NRS.

(b) Between any co-owners of the property, spouses or persons related within the third degree of consanguinity.

(c) Which is the first sale of a residence that was constructed by a licensed contractor.

(d) By a person who takes temporary possession or control of or title to the property solely to facilitate the sale of the property on behalf of a person who relocates to another county, state or country before title to the property is transferred to a purchaser.

3. A purchaser of residential property may waive any of the requirements of subsection 1. Any such waiver is effective only if it is made in a written document that is signed by the purchaser and notarized.

4. If a sale or intended sale of residential property is exempted from the requirements of subsection 1 pursuant to paragraph (a) of subsection 2, the trustee and the beneficiary of the deed of trust shall, not later than at the time of the conveyance of the property to the purchaser of the residential property, provide written notice to the purchaser of any defects in the property of which the trustee or beneficiary, respectively, is aware.

(Added to NRS by 1995, 842; A 1997, 349; 2003, 1339; 2005, 598)

_____   _____
        Seller(s) Initials   Buyer(s) Initials

NRS 113.135 Certain sellers to provide copies of certain provisions of NRS and give notice of certain soil reports; initial purchaser entitled to rescind sales agreement in certain circumstances; waiver of right to rescind.

1. Upon signing a sales agreement with the initial purchaser of residential property that was not occupied by the purchaser for more than 120 days after substantial completion of the construction of the residential property, the seller shall:

    (a) Provide to the initial purchaser a copy of NRS 11.202 to 11.206, inclusive, and 40.600 to 40.695, inclusive;

    (b) Notify the initial purchaser of any soil report prepared for the residential property or for the subdivision in which the residential property is located; and

    (c) If requested in writing by the initial purchaser not later than 5 days after signing the sales agreement, provide to the purchaser without cost each report described in paragraph (b) not later than 5 days after the seller receives the written request.

2. Not later than 20 days after receipt of all reports pursuant to paragraph (c) of subsection 1, the initial purchaser may rescind the sales agreement.

3. The initial purchaser may waive his right to rescind the sales agreement pursuant to subsection 2. Such a waiver is effective only if it is made in a written document that is signed by the purchaser.

    (Added to NRS by 1999, 1446)

NRS 113.140 Disclosure of unknown defect not required; form does not constitute warranty; duty of buyer and prospective buyer to exercise reasonable care.

1. NRS 113.130 does not require a seller to disclose a defect in residential property of which he is not aware.

2. A completed disclosure form does not constitute an express or implied warranty regarding any condition of residential property.

3. Neither this chapter nor chapter 645 of NRS relieves a buyer or prospective buyer of the duty to exercise reasonable care to protect himself.

    (Added to NRS by 1995, 843; A 2001, 2896)

NRS 113.150 Remedies for seller's delayed disclosure or nondisclosure of defects in property; waiver.

1. If a seller or his agent fails to serve a completed disclosure form in accordance with the requirements of NRS 113.130, the purchaser may, at any time before the conveyance of the property to the purchaser, rescind the agreement to purchase the property without any penalties.

2. If, before the conveyance of the property to the purchaser, a seller or his agent informs the purchaser or his agent, through the disclosure form or another written notice, of a defect in the property of which the cost of repair or replacement was not limited by provisions in the agreement to purchase the property, the purchaser may:

    (a) Rescind the agreement to purchase the property at any time before the conveyance of the property to the purchaser; or

    (b) Close escrow and accept the property with the defect as revealed by the seller or his agent without further recourse.

3. Rescission of an agreement pursuant to subsection 2 is effective only if made in writing, notarized and served not later than 4 working days after the date on which the purchaser is informed of the defect:

    (a) On the holder of any escrow opened for the conveyance; or

    (b) If an escrow has not been opened for the conveyance, on the seller or his agent.

4. Except as otherwise provided in subsection 5, if a seller conveys residential property to a purchaser without complying with the requirements of NRS 113.130 or otherwise providing the purchaser or his agent with written notice of all defects in the property of which the seller is aware, and there is a defect in the property of which the seller was aware before the property was conveyed to the purchaser and of which the cost of repair or replacement was not limited by provisions in the agreement to purchase the property, the purchaser is entitled to recover from the seller treble the amount necessary to repair or replace the defective part of the property, together with court costs and reasonable attorney's fees. An action to enforce the provisions of this subsection must be commenced not later than 1 year after the purchaser discovers or reasonably should have discovered the defect or 2 years after the conveyance of the property to the purchaser, whichever occurs later.

5. A purchaser may not recover damages from a seller pursuant to subsection 4 on the basis of an error or omission in the disclosure form that was caused by the seller's reliance upon information provided to the seller by:

    (a) An officer or employee of this state or any political subdivision of this state in the ordinary course of his duties; or

    (b) A contractor, engineer, land surveyor, certified inspector as defined in NRS 645D.040 or pesticide applicator, who was authorized to practice that profession in this state at the time the information was provided.

6. A purchaser of residential property may waive any of his rights under this section. Any such waiver is effective only if it is made in a written document that is signed by the purchaser and notarized.

    (Added to NRS by 1995, 842; A 1997, 350, 1797)

The above information provided on pages one (1) and two (2) of this disclosure form is true and correct to the best of seller's knowledge as of the date set forth on page one (1). **SELLER HAS DUTY TO DISCLOSE TO BUYER AS NEW DEFECTS ARE DISCOVERED AND/OR KNOWN DEFECTS BECOME WORSE** *(See NRS 113.130(1)(b))*.

Seller(s): _____   Date: _____

Seller(s): _____   Date: _____

BUYER MAY WISH TO OBTAIN PROFESSIONAL ADVICE AND INSPECTIONS OF THE PROPERTY TO MORE FULLY DETERMINE THE CONDITION OF THE PROPERTY AND ITS ENVIRONMENTAL STATUS. Buyer(s) has/have read and acknowledge(s) receipt of a copy of this Seller's Real Property Disclosure Form and copy of NRS Chapter 113.100-150, inclusive, attached hereto as pages three (3) and four (4).

Buyer(s): _____   Date: _____

Buyer(s): _____   Date: _____

Nevada Real Estate Division   Page 4 of 4   Seller Real Property Disclosure Form
Replaces all previous versions   Revised 05-01-06   517

| V APPENDIX II - 6

288

Disclosure of Information on Lead-Based Paint and/or Lead-Based Paint Hazards

Lead Warning Statement

Every purchaser of any interest in residential real property on which a residential dwelling was built prior to 1978 is notified that such property may present exposure to lead from lead-based paint that may place young children at risk of developing lead poisoning. Lead poisoning in young children may produce permanent neurological damage, including learning disabilities, reduced intelligence quotient, behavioral problems, and impaired memory. Lead poisoning also poses a particular risk to pregnant women. The seller of any interest in residential real property is required to provide the buyer with any information on lead-based paint hazards from risk assessments or inspections in the seller's possession and notify the buyer of any known lead-based paint hazards. A risk assessment or inspection for possible lead-based paint hazards is recommended prior to purchase.

Seller's Disclosure

(a) Presence of lead-based paint and/or lead-based paint hazards (check (i) or (ii) below):

    (i) _____ Known lead-based paint and/or lead-based paint hazards are present in the housing (explain)

    _____

    (ii) _____ Seller has no knowledge of lead-based paint and/or lead-based paint hazards in the housing.

(b) Records and reports available to the seller (check (i) or (ii) below):

    (i) _____ Seller has provided the purchaser with all available records and reports pertaining to lead-based paint and/or lead-based paint hazards in the housing (list documents below).

    _____

    (ii) _____ Seller has no reports or records pertaining to lead-based paint and/or lead-based paint hazards in the housing.

Purchaser's Acknowledgment (initial)

(c) _____ Purchaser has received copies of all information listed above.

(d) _____ Purchaser has received the pamphlet *Protect Your Family from Lead in Your Home.*

(e) Purchaser has (check (i) or (ii) below):

    (i) _____ received a 10-day opportunity (or mutually agreed upon period) to conduct a risk assessment or inspection for the presence of lead-based paint and/or lead-based paint hazards; or

    (ii) _____ waived the opportunity to conduct a risk assessment or inspection for the presence of lead-based paint and/or lead-based paint hazards.

Agent's Acknowledgment (initial)

(f) _____ Agent has informed the seller of the seller's obligations under 42 U.S.C. 4852(d) and is aware of his/her responsibility to ensure compliance.

Certification of Accuracy

The following parties have reviewed the information above and certify, to the best of their knowledge, that the information they have provided is true and accurate.

Seller	Date	Seller	Date
Purchaser	Date	Purchaser	Date
Agent	Date	Agent	Date

For Your Protection: Get a Home Inspection

Name of Buyer (s)

Property Address

Why a Buyer Needs a Home Inspection

A home inspection gives the buyer more detailed information about the overall condition of the home prior to purchase. In a home inspection, a qualified inspector takes an in-depth, unbiased look at your potential new home to:

- evaluate the physical condition: structure, construction, and mechanical systems
- identify items that need to be repaired or replaced
- estimate the remaining useful life of the major systems, equipment, structure, and finishes

Appraisals are Different from Home Inspections

An appraisal is different from a home inspection. Appraisals are for lenders; home inspections are for buyers.   An appraisal is required for three reasons:

- to estimate the market value of a house
- to make sure that the house meets FHA minimum property standards/requirements
- to make sure that the house is marketable

FHA Does Not Guarantee the Value or Condition of your Potential New Home

If you find problems with your new home after closing, FHA can not give or lend you money for repairs, and FHA can not buy the home back from you.

Radon Gas Testing

The United States Environmental Protection Agency and the Surgeon General of the United States have recommended that all houses should be tested for radon. For more information on radon testing, call the National Radon Information Line at 1-800-SOS-Radon or 1-800-767-7236. As with a home inspection, if you decide to test for radon, you may do so before signing your contract, or you may do so after signing the contract, as long as your contract states the sale of the home depends on your satisfaction with the results of the radon test.

Be an Informed Buyer

It is your responsibility to be an informed buyer. Be sure that what you buy is satisfactory in every respect. You have the right to carefully examine your potential new home with a qualified home inspector. You may arrange to do so before signing your contract, or may do so after signing the contract as long as your contract states that the sale of the home depends on the inspection.

I/we understand the importance of getting an independent home inspection. I/we have considered this before signing a contract with the seller for a home. Furthermore, I/we have carefully read this notice and fully understand that FHA will not perform a home inspection nor guarantee the price or condition of the property.

_____ I/We choose to have a home inspection performed.

_____ I/We choose **not** to have a home inspection performed.

X _____   X _____

Signature & Date   Signature & Date

form HUD-92564-CN (12/03)

OPEN RANGE DISCLOSURE

Assessor Parcel Number: _____

OR

Assessor's Manufactured Home ID Number: _____

Disclosure: This property is adjacent to "Open Range"

This property is adjacent to open range on which livestock are permitted to graze or roam. Unless you construct a fence that will prevent livestock from entering this property, livestock may enter the property and you will not be entitled to collect damages because livestock entered the property. *Regardless of whether you construct a fence, it is unlawful to kill, maim or injure livestock that have entered this property.*

The parcel may be subject to claims made by a county or this State of rights-of-way granted by Congress over public lands of the United States not reserved for public uses in chapter 262, section 8, 14 Statutes 253 (former 43 U.S.C. § 932, commonly referred to as R.S. 2477), and accepted by general public use and enjoyment before, on or after July 1, 1979, or other rights-of-way. Such rights-of-way may be:

(1) Unrecorded, undocumented or unsurveyed; and
(2) Used by persons, including, without limitation miners, ranchers or hunters, for access or recreational use, in a manner which interferes with the use and enjoyment of the parcel.

SELLERS: The law (NRS 113.065) requires that the seller shall:

- Disclose to the purchaser information regarding grazing on open range;
- Retain a copy of the disclosure document signed by the purchaser acknowledging the date of receipt by the purchaser of the original document;
- Provide a copy of the signed disclosure document to the purchaser; and
- Record, in the office of the county recorder in the county where the property is located, the original disclosure document that has been signed by the purchaser.

I, the below signed purchaser, acknowledge that I have received this disclosure on this date: _____ , 20 _____

_____   _____
Buyer Signature   Buyer Signature

_____   _____
Print or type name here   Print or type name here

In Witness, Whereof, I/we have hereunto set my hand/our hands this _____ day of _____ , 20 ____.

_____   _____
Seller Signature   Seller Signature

_____   _____
Print or type name here   Print or type name here

STATE OF NEVADA, COUNTY OF _____

This instrument was acknowledged before me on _____
                                                                              (date)

by _____
        Person(s) appearing before notary

by _____
        Person(s) appearing before notary

_____
        Signature of notarial officer

CONSULT AN ATTORNEY IF YOU DOUBT THIS FORM'S FITNESS FOR YOUR PURPOSE.

NOTE: Leave space within 1-inch margin blank on all sides.

Nevada Real Estate Division - Form 551

Notary Seal

Effective July 1, 2010

STATE OF NEVADA
DEPARTMENT OF BUSINESS AND INDUSTRY
REAL ESTATE DIVISION

788 Fairview Drive, Suite 200* **Carson City**, NV 89701-5453 * (775) 687-4280
2501 East Sahara Avenue, Suite 102 * **Las Vegas**, NV 89104-4137 * (702) 486-4033
e-mail: realest@red.state.nv.us   http://www.red.state.nv.us

USED MANUFACTURED/MOBILE HOME DISCLOSURE
Personal Property Taxes and Required Documents

Pursuant to Section 6, AB 114 (2005), a Real Estate Licensee is required to provide to the purchaser of a Used Manufactured or Used Mobile Home that has NOT been converted to real property the following information:

MANUFACTURER: _____	YEAR: _____
SERIAL # _____	SIZE: _____

NOTICE: The used manufactured/used mobile home you are purchasing is **PERSONAL PROPERTY** and is **subject to personal property taxes. Personal property taxes are paid through your county assessor's office.**

Personal property taxes on used manufactured/used mobile homes are required by law to be paid in full before title (certificate of ownership) is transferred and an Assessor's endorsement must be placed on the face of the title verifying the payment. Title to the manufactured/mobile home will not transfer until the assessor's endorsement is received (NRS 489.531). You may contact the county assessor to verify if the taxes on this manufactured/mobile home have been paid in full.

In this transaction, you are purchasing both personal property (the used manufactured/used mobile home) and real property (the land the used manufactured/used mobile home is located on). **As a result, you will be paying both real property taxes and personal property taxes.**

REQUIREMENT TO SUBMIT DOCUMENTS (NRS 489.521): Within 45 days after the sale of the used manufactured/used mobile home is completed, you must submit the following documents to the Manufactured Housing Division and a copy to the County Assessor of the county in which the used manufactured/used mobile home is located:

- A properly endorsed Certificate of Ownership (if the certificate of ownership has been issued in this state) or
- A properly endorsed certificate of title or other document of title issued by another state (if the certificate of ownership has not been issued in this state) and a statement with the following information (if it is not contained on the certificate or document of title):
  - the description of the used manufactured/used mobile home;
  - the names and addresses of the buyer and seller;
  - the name and address of any person who takes or retains a purchase money security interest.

  THE STATEMENT MUST BE SIGNED AND ACKNOWLEDGED BY THE BUYER AND SELLER.

If a used manufactured/used mobile home is sold pursuant to an installment contract or other agreement whereby the certificate of title or certificate of ownership does not pass immediately to the buyer upon the sale, the seller, buyer or both shall submit to the Manufactured Housing Division any information required by the regulations adopted pursuant to NRS 489.272.

NOTICE PURSUANT TO NRS 489.531: The Manufactured Housing Division shall not issue a certificate of ownership on a used manufactured/used mobile home unless the county assessor of the county in which the used manufactured/used mobile home was situated at the time of the sale has endorsed on the certificate that all personal property taxes for the fiscal year have been paid. Additionally, the certificate of ownership must contain a warning, printed or stamped on its face, to the effect that the title does not pass until the county assessor endorses on the certificate of title that all personal property taxes have been paid.

RESPONSIBILITY OF BROKER: A real estate broker who represents a client in this transaction shall take such actions as necessary to ensure that the client complies with the requirements of NRS 489.521 and NRS 489.531.

The disclosures provided above do not constitute a warranty as to title or condition of the used manufactured/mobile home information.					
Purchaser	_Date_	_Time_	_Real Estate Broker_	_Date_	_Time_
Purchaser	_Date_	_Time_	_Real Estate Licensee_	_Date_	_Time_

STATE OF NEVADA
DEPARTMENT OF BUSINESS AND INDUSTRY
REAL ESTATE DIVISION
788 Fairview Drive, Suite 200 * **Carson City**, NV 89701-5453 * (775) 687-4280
2501 East Sahara Avenue, Suite 102 * **Las Vegas**, NV 89104-4137 * (702) 486-4033
Email: realest@red.state.nv.us   http://www.red.state.nv.us

WAIVER FORM

In representing any client in an agency relationship, a real estate licensee has specific statutory duties to that client. Under Nevada law only one of these duties can be waived. NRS 645.254 requires a licensee to "present all offers made to or by the client as soon as practicable." This duty may be waived by the client.

"Presenting all offers" includes without limitation: accepting delivery of and conveying offers and counteroffers; answering a client's questions regarding offers and counteroffers; and assisting a client in preparing, communicating and negotiating offers and counteroffers.

In order to waive the duty, the client must enter into a written agreement waiving the licensee's obligation to perform the duty to present all offers. **By signing below you are agreeing that the licensee who is representing you will <u>not</u> perform the duty of presenting all offers made to or by you with regard to the property located at:**

_____.
Property Address   City

AGREEMENT TO WAIVER

By signing below I agree that the licensee who represents me shall not present any offers made to or by me, as defined above. I understand that a real estate transaction has significant legal and financial consequences. I further understand that in any proposed transaction, the other licensee(s) involved represents the interests of the other party, does not represent me and cannot perform the waived duty on my behalf. I further understand that I should seek the assistance of other professionals such as an attorney. I further understand that it is my responsibility to inform myself of the steps necessary to fulfill the terms of any purchase agreement that I may execute. I further understand that this waiver may be revoked in writing by mutual agreement between client and broker.

WAIVER NOT VALID UNTIL SIGNED BY BROKER.

_____   _____   _____   _____
Client   Date   Licensee   Date

_____   _____   _____   _____
Client   Date   Broker   Date

06/26/2007   636

V │APPENDIX II - 11

STATE OF NEVADA
DEPARTMENT OF BUSINESS AND INDUSTRY
REAL ESTATE DIVISION
788 Fairview Drive, Suite 200 * **Carson City**, NV 89701-5453 * (775) 687-4280
2501 East Sahara Avenue, Suite 102 * **Las Vegas**, NV 89104-4137 * (702) 486-4033
Email: realest@red.state.nv.us   http://www.red.state.nv.us

AUTHORIZATION TO NEGOTIATE
DIRECTLY WITH SELLER

Nevada law permits a real estate licensee to negotiate a sale or lease directly with the seller or lessor with written permission from the listing broker. This form grants that permission with respect to the below-named Seller(s) and the listed property.

- Seller agrees, and the Seller's broker authorizes, that a Buyer's agent or broker may present offers (including subsequent counteroffers) and negotiate directly with the Seller.

- "Negotiate" means (a) delivering or communicating an offer, counteroffer, or proposal; (b) discussing or reviewing the terms of any offer, counteroffer, or proposal; and/or (c) facilitating communication regarding an offer, counteroffer, or proposal and preparing any response as directed.

- Seller understands and agrees that, after accepting an offer, additional contact from the Buyer's agent may be required to obtain disclosures and other documents related to the transaction.

- Seller acknowledges and agrees that Buyer's agent does not represent the Seller, and negotiations pursuant to this authorization do not create or imply an agency relationship between the Buyer's agent and the Seller. Seller understands that he/she should seek advice from Seller's broker and/or financial advisers or legal counsel.

- Seller acknowledges that Seller's broker will provide a copy of this authorization to the Buyer's agent or broker upon request, prior to presenting an offer.

Seller's Name(s): _____

Seller's Signature(s): _____   _____/_____
                                                              Date   Time

Property Address: _____

City: _____ Zip: _____ Contract Listing Date: _____

Company Name: _____

Seller's Agent Name: _____ Signature: _____
                                                              _____/_____
                                                              Date   Time

Seller's Broker Name: _____ Signature: _____
                                                              _____/_____
                                                              Date   Time

VI. NEVADA LAW ON ADVERTISING

TABLE OF CONTENTS

1. NRS 645.254 (3)

2. NRS 598.0905

3. NAC 645.610 (3)

4. NRS 41.710

A core duty of the real estate licensee is to promote the interests of the client by seeking "a sale, purchase, option, rental or lease of real property ... at the price . . . acceptable to the client."[1] Most licensees advertise to promote either the client's property or to market the licensee's services. The public has a societal interest in promoting accurate and fair representations of the things or services being advertised. To this end, various laws regulate real estate advertising. Here, we explore the advertising laws that impact the licensee's marketing plan, whether marketing the licensee's services or the client's property.

A. ADVERTISING: WHAT IT IS AND ISN'T

"Advertisement" means the attempt by publication, dissemination, solicitation or circulation to induce, directly or indirectly, any person to enter into any obligation to lease or to acquire any title or interest in any property.[2]

Advertising includes printed materials such as business cards, stationery, signs, billboards, pre-printed forms and other documents used in a real estate transaction.[3] Advertising laws are applicable in face-to-face solicitations such as door-to-door canvassing, listing and other presentations; any live or recorded presentations; "selling" seminars; and open houses.

Advertising includes all "electronic" formats such as broadcasts made by radio, television or other electronic means, including, without limitation, unsolicited electronic mail (email) and the internet. Nevada law defines advertising by email to mean material that advertises for commercial purposes the availability or the quality of real property, goods or services, made with the intent to solicit a person to purchase such real property, goods or services.[4]

"Advertorials" are paid-for news articles and are subject to the advertising laws. It is an advertisement in the form of an editorial or feature story and is often found in the Sunday newspaper real estate section. Advertorials may focus on a specific licensee, a real estate team, a brokerage firm, or the features of a property or subdivision.

Advertising laws are applicable regardless of the type of media used. In addition, there may be specific laws for the use of certain media such as email or the internet.

What It Isn't - Not all information disseminated about a property or a licensee's services is advertising. For example, legitimate news articles and non-purchased media interviews, a licensee's or brokerage's reputation, statements made in restricted members – only multiple listing service, are not considered advertising. Though not subject to advertising laws, there may be other laws or rules that control the content of those items. For example, a multiple listing service may have rules regarding what comments may be placed on the service.

VI - 3

B. PURPOSE AND SOURCES OF ADVERTISING LAWS

Why are there advertising laws - what is their purpose? What types of laws control the licensee's advertising?

1. PRESENTING A TRUE PICTURE

The main reason advertising laws exist is to control commerce for the public good by requiring merchants to present a true picture of what is being sold. Truth in advertising is such an integral concept to our free market economy that the law provides for civil penalties for a violation[5] and has made intentional false advertising a crime.[6] A court has the authority to order such false advertising stopped through an injunctive action.[7] Interestingly, actual deception of a consumer is unnecessary (in other words, the consumer doesn't need to have been actually deceived); any statement with the tendency to deceive is subject to the law.[8]

Other laws that fall under the True Picture purpose include the federal Truth-in-Lending laws[9] and Nevada's Deceptive Trade Practices statutes.[10] Various real estate statutes require licensees to advertise in an honest and truthful manner.[11] Intentional misrepresentation, deceit or fraud by a real estate licensee is a felony criminal act subjecting the licensee to imprisonment.[12]

2. PROMOTING FAIR TRADE

Some advertising laws are designed to ensure fair trade and competition in the open market. These are the state and federal anti-trust laws. The real estate licensee is subject to both sets of laws.[13]

3. CONTROLLING UNWANTED INTRUSIONS

Recently, a number of advertising laws and restrictions were passed to protect the public against aggressive or unwanted intrusions into the public's privacy. The telemarketing laws, solicitation rules are examples of such laws.[14]

4. FOSTERING EQUAL ACCESS

Finally, many advertising laws are designed to ensure that members of various protected classes have equal access to advertised services and properties. These rules are found in the fair housing laws.[15]

5. NRS 207.174

6. NRS 207.171 "It is unlawful for any person,… to use, publish, disseminate, display or make … directly or indirectly … by any radio, television or other advertising medium, … any statement which is known or through the exercise of reasonable care should be known to be false, deceptive or misleading in order to induce any person to purchase, sell, lease, dispose of, utilize or acquire any title or interest in any real or personal property or any personal or professional services … ."

7. NRS 207.176 – An injunction is where the court orders a person to do, or to stop doing, a specific action.

8. NRS 207.173

9. 15 U.S.C. §1601 et seq.

10. NRS 598 – Deceptive Trade Practices.

11. NRS 645.630 (1)(b) A licensee shall not make false promises to influence, persuade or induce; NRS 645.633 (1)(8), a licensee shall not participate in any deceitful, fraudulent or dishonest conduct.

12. NRS 645.990 (1)(b) a person who sells or attempts to sell any interest in real property by means of intentional misrepresentation, deceit or fraud is guilty of a category D felony. A category D felony is 1-4 years in prison and a fine of not less than $5,000.

13. Federal Sherman Act, 15 U.S.C. §3 et seq. and Nevada's Unfair Trade Practices chapter NRS 598A.

14. Federal "Do Not Call" Act, 47 U.S.C.§227; and 15 U.S.C. §1601, as well as Nevada's Do Not Call laws found in NRS 228.590 and NRS 598.0918.

15. Federal Fair Housing laws 42 U.S.C. § 3604(c) (1991) and 42 U.S.C. §1982, and NRS 118, specifically made applicable to real estate licensees under NRS 645.321.

16. NRS 228.590 &
NRS 598.0918.

17. Clark County Code
30.72.040.

18. Las Vegas Municipal
Code 6.42.140-145.

19. Henderson
Municipal Code 4.72.200.

20. NRS 233B.040 (1)

21. NAC 645.690

5. SOURCES OF ADVERTISING LAW

Advertising laws are found in federal, state, county, city, and local laws, statutes, codes, and ordinances. Many of the state statutes echo federal law. For example, anti-discrimination housing laws are found in both federal and state law.

Generally, federal law is the controlling law and any state law in conflict with federal law will not be enforced. However, at times, federal law allows state law to take precedence if that law is within certain parameters. For example, the federal "Do Not Call" laws provided that a state may make "Do Not Call" laws that are more restrictive than the federal law, but it will not allow state laws that are more lenient than the federal law. Nevada's "Do Not Call" laws are more restrictive and thus are the controlling law in Nevada. Nevada real estate licensees who are "cold calling" are required to follow the stricter Nevada "Do Not Call" laws.[16]

In addition to federal and state laws and regulations, a real estate licensee may be subject to various local advertising restrictions. These restrictions range from controlling the size and placement of signs, to door-to-door solicitation hours, to the permitting and placement of handbills. For example, Clark County has a "sign" code which establishes parameters regarding the location of signs;[17] the Las Vegas Municipal Code addresses the distribution of handbills;[18] and the City of Henderson's Municipal Code restricts the hours a solicitor may knock on a residential door.[19]

There are various administrative regulations that impact a licensee's advertising. When applicable, these regulations have the force and effect of law.[20] In Nevada, the regulations are codified in the Nevada Administrative Code and the cites have the designation of NAC. The Nevada Real Estate Commission, and the Real Estate Division with Commission approval, promulgates regulations. (NRS 645.190). The Real Estate Division oversees enforcement of those regulations. If a licensee is found in violation of an advertising regulation, the RED may grant a licensee up to 10 days to correct any deficiency. After a hearing it may suspend or revoke a real estate license if the licensee fails to timely correct the noticed deficiency.[21]

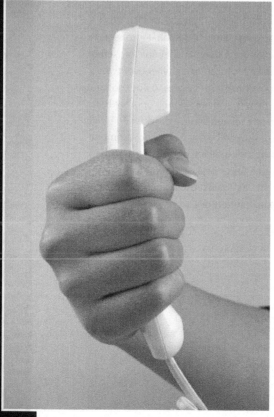

VI - 5

C. LAWS APPLICABLE TO ALL ADVERTISING

1. GENERAL RESTRICTIONS

All advertising, whether for a licensee's services or a client's property, must not be false or misleading and must provide a true and accurate picture of what is being sold.[22]

All advertising, whether for services or a client's property, and whether paid for by the licensee, the client, or the broker, is done under the auspices and supervision of the broker who retains ultimate legal control and liability for the advertising.[23]

As all real estate transactions occur under the auspices of a broker, any advertisement, whether about a licensee's services or a client's property, must indicate the brokerage firm's name in prominence to the licensee's name. In determining whether the brokerage name is "in prominence", the Real Estate Division (RED) will consider the style, size and color of the type or font used and the location of the name of the brokerage firm as it appears in the advertisement.[24]

In any advertisement, the licensee must use the name under which he or she is licensed. The use of nicknames is discouraged.

The purpose of this regulation is to provide accurate identification of the licensee to a consumer and the Real Estate Division.[25]

2. ANTI-TRUST/UNFAIR TRADE PRACTICES

The anti-trust laws cover four main areas of activity: monopolies, tying arrangements, boycotting and price fixing. The two areas that are most subject to advertising restrictions are boycotting and price fixing. The majority of anti-trust violations in advertising occur verbally with face-to-face presentations.

Boycotting occurs when the government finds there is a consensus among members of a trade or profession to isolate or limit a specific competitor's access to the market. In real estate, this has occurred when "traditional" brokerages advertised against "discount" brokerages; however, it can occur whenever two or more brokerages agree to not cooperate with a specific brokerage or other real estate related service provider.[26] Activities considered by the federal government that may indicate boycotting are when licensees or brokers publish disparaging remarks against other agents, brokerages, or a competitor's services.

Changes at the RED have modified the current advertising practice to remove the use of any nickname in advertising. This is a change from the RED position as stated in the RED Open House, Summer 2007, which stated in part that "common nicknames may be used". NAC 645.610(1)(e) states a licensee shall not advertise under a name, including a nickname, other than his or her licensed name.

27. 15 U.S.C. §1

28. See United States v. National Association of Real Estate Boards, 339 U.S. 485 (1950).

29. NRS 598

30. NRS 645.002

31. NRS 645.004

32. NAC 645.675

33. NAC 645.678

33a. In re Montgomery County Real Estate Antitrust Litigation, 452 F. Supp. 54 (D. Md. 1978).

Price fixing occurs when two or more competitors agree to a common marketing price and subsequently modify their prices to conform to that agreement.[27] Price fixing among real estate brokerages based on their association within the Realtor® boards has been an issue since the 1950s.[28]

Claims of price fixing occur when various brokers advertise their rates are the "prevailing", "common", "fixed" or "standard" rates in the area, thereby implying there is a common scheme for price fixing among competitors. Having common market rates is not, in and of itself, illegal unless two or more brokers from different brokerages have appeared to have agreed to charge the same rate.

Brokers should establish in their office policies and procedures, an independent justification for the prices the broker charges based on the broker's cost of doing business and required profit.

The licensee must be careful as an anti-trust violation can occur not only when prices are similar, but when competitors set the same terms as one another. For example, brokers agreeing to take only six-month listings and informing sellers that no broker accepts less than a six-month listing can be a violation.

The conspiracy part (two or more brokers) of an anti-trust violation claim need not be based on a formal agreement between competitors to price fix. A general casual conversation between competitors that results in common terms or prices is sufficient to warrant the charge of anti-trust.

3. DECEPTIVE TRADE PRACTICES

Licensee advertising is also covered under Nevada's Deceptive Trade Practices statutes.[29] These statutes provide that a person engages in a "deceptive trade practice" if he or she knowingly makes a false representation as to:

• the source of goods or services for sale or lease;

• the affiliation, association or certification by another entity;

• the characteristics, uses, alterations or quantities of goods or services;

• advertising goods or services without the intent to sell them as advertised;

• advertising "free" services with the intent to receive payment in undisclosed costs;

• making false or misleading statements of fact; and

• fraudulently altering any contract; or knowingly making any other false representation.

4. ADVANCED FEE AGREEMENTS

An "advanced fee" is when the broker charges a client a fee in advance of performing services.[30] In the advertising realm, most advance fee agreements occur when a broker advertises that he or she has a list of potential properties, clients or rentals available and will provide that list for a fee.[31] When a licensee takes an advanced fee, the licensee cannot advertise and imply that a buyer for the property is immediately or soon available.[32]

If a broker advertises lists of available rentals for an advance fee, the broker must have the rental property owner's permission before advertising the rental.[33]

VI - 7

A licensee taking available property information from the internet and selling that information is a violation of this regulation unless the licensee has the owner's permission.

5. THE INTERNET

The law concerning what constitutes appropriate advertising on the internet continues to evolve. Nevada statutes and regulations provide that the dissemination of unsolicited information concerning real property or the marketing of real property is "advertising" and all advertising laws are applicable.[34]

When advertising on the internet, each internet "page" should be considered a distinct advertisement and should comply with all advertising laws. For example, identifying the brokerage only on the first page of the website and not on each subsequent webpage may violate the regulation requiring each advertisement to prominently display the brokerage name.[35]

There are additional rules whenever a licensee attempts to enter into an agency relationship with a client by internet. Though not specific to advertising, these rules should be reviewed to ensure the licensee includes the necessary disclosures and adheres to the appropriate signature requirements.[36]

6. ELECTRONIC MAIL (EMAIL)

For the last several years, federal law has attempted to address the "spam" situations. The Federal Trade Commission (FTC) issued its final rules which were effective March, 2005. Those rules required the FTC to develop criteria to determine which emails are commercial. If an email is commercial, it is subject to the federal Controlling the Assault of Non-Solicited Pornography and Marketing Act of 2003 (CAN-SPAM Act).[37] The federal rules require a commercial email to contain: a legitimate

return email and physical postal address; a clear and conspicuous "opt-out" provision which must be honored by the sender within 30 days; and a notice "clear and conspicuous" that the email is an advertisement or solicitation. There is no prior or existing business relationship exemption.

If a licensee is found in violation of the FTC rules, he or she may be fined up to $250 per violation (that is per email that went out), with a maximum award of $2 million dollars. There is also the possibility of five years imprisonment if the emails were sent for the furtherance of any felony.

Nevada has its own statutes regarding advertising by email.[38] For emails, an "advertisement" is defined as an email transmittal, for commercial purpose, stating the availability of real property, goods or services. The federal law specifically preempts all state laws that expressly regulate commercial emails, even if such state's laws are more stringent than the federal law (this is unlike the federal "Do Not Call" law which allows states to have laws that are more stringent, but not less strict, than the federal law).

For all email advertisements generated by a licensee, each of the advertising rules regarding brokerage name, etc. are applicable.

7. FACSIMILE (FAX)

The federal law governing the transmittal of advertisements by facsimile (fax) is part of the Telephone Consumer Protection Act of 1991.[39] These rules prohibit the sending of unsolicited fax advertisements. "Unsolicited advertisement" is defined as "any material advertising the commercial availability or quality of any property, goods, or services which is transmitted to any person without that person's prior express invitation or permission."

34. NAC 645.613

35. NAC 645.610

36. NAC 645.613 (2)

37. 16 C.F.R. Part 316

38. NRS 41.705 et seq.

39. 47 U.S.C. §227 et seq.

40. NRS 207.325

41. For example, Clark County has a code addressing handbills (Clark County Code 12.46.010). See also Las Vegas Code 6.42.140.

42. U.S. Postal regulations are found in the Domestic Mail Manual 1.3 which provides that mail boxes may only be used for matter bearing U.S. postage. Any other use is a violation and subject to fines.

43. For example, Henderson Code 4.72.200 provides that it is unlawful for any person to knock on the door, or ring the bell, of any residence before 8:00 am or after 7 pm.

Before sending an unsolicited advertisement the sender must have the written consent or an "established business relationship" with the recipient. The written consent requirement requires the sender to have voluntarily received the recipient's fax number. In other words, purchasing the fax number from a third party would not be voluntary. An "established business relationship" is formed by the voluntary two-way communication between the recipient and fax sender based on a prior inquiry, application, purchase or transaction regarding products or services offered by the fax sender.

When a fax falls under the Act, it must have an opt-out provision allowing the recipient to stop future unsolicited advertising faxes whether an established business relationship exists or not. Finally, if the recipients does opt-out, the sender has 30 days to honor the request. The remedy for violations is $500 per fax with treble damages if the violation is willful.

The law provides that the "sender" is the individual or entity requesting the fax be sent. Therefore, if a licensee hires a third-party entity to broadcast an advertising fax, the licensee remains liable for any violations.

Nevada's statue provides that a person shall not make any unsolicited electronic or telephonic transmissions to a facsimile machine to solicit a person to purchase real property, goods or services.[40] Under Nevada law, the single exception is if there is a preexisting business relationship. This law is applicable to both business-to-individual and business-to-business transactions and real estate transactions are covered under this law. Again, for a Nevada licensee using faxes to advertise, all advertising laws apply.

8. HANDBILLS, TIME AND MAILBOX RESTRICTIONS

Licensees should be aware of some restrictions dealing with various methods of advertising. Two time tested advertising methods include the distribution of handbills and door-to-door canvassing. Many local governments have municipal codes or ordinances regarding these advertising activities.

Handbills: Sometimes, brokers and licensees will have printed handbills to pass out or put on automobiles. Many local governments have restrictions on the distribution of handbills.[41] These restrictions include filing the handbill with the local government, paying a fee, and receiving a permit number which often must be on the handbill itself. If a licensee distributes the handbills on private property, e.g., a grocery store parking lot, the prior permission of the property owner must be obtained. Neither handbills, nor any other advertising that has not gone through the U.S. mails, may be placed in mailboxes.[42]

Door-to-door canvassing: The licensee should be aware that when canvassing a neighborhood, the local government may have time restrictions as to when a residence may be solicited by either knocking on doors or hanging door bills.[43]

D. ADVERTISING BROKERAGE AND LICENSEE SERVICES

The majority of laws regarding the advertisement of a licensee's services concern providing the consumer with sufficient information in the advertisement to trace the licensee and brokerage.

1. BROKERAGE SIGNS

Each broker is required to erect a sign in a conspicuous place identifying the brokerage at the broker's place of business. The brokerage name, or the name under which the broker does business, must be clearly identified. If the broker has more than one office, each office must have a similar sign.[44] The sign must be readable from the nearest public sidewalk, street or highway. If the business is located in an office building, Hotel or apartment house, the sign must be posted on the building directory or on the exterior of the entrance to the business.[45]

2. FRANCHISES & FICTITIOUS NAMES

If a broker is advertising under the name of a franchise, the broker must incorporate in a conspicuous way the real, fictitious or corporate name under which the brokerage is licensed. If applicable, there must also be an acknowledgement that each office is independently owned and operated.[46]

A broker may not operate or advertise under a fictitious name without first registering the fictitious name and obtaining a certificate from the county

clerk.[47] This name must then be filed with the Nevada Real Estate Division and the broker may not use more than one name for each license under which the broker operates.[48]

3. TEAMS

The last decade has seen the growth of a business model in which several licensees come together as a "team" or "group" to provide real estate related services. Currently, the Real Estate Division does not require teams to register with the Division; however, the Real Estate Commissioners have established regulations regarding the formation and identification of teams, including regulations about team advertising. These are:

1. A team must have two or more members. A single person cannot be, nor advertise, as a team.

2. Team members must be employed by the same broker. A team may not be composed of members who work for different brokerages.

3. The team name must incorporate the last name of one of the team members. For example, Sally Young and Mary Smith may form "The Young Team".

4. Team names must not use a trade name nor may the team name be deceptively similar to a name under which another person or entity is lawfully doing business. The test of whether a name is

44. NRS 645.560

45. NAC 645.615. Additionally, the Division may require the broker to provide it with a photograph of the sign as proof of compliance.

46. NAC 645.610 (2)

47. NRS 602.010 et seq.

48. NAC 645.620

49. NRS 78.039. AGO 94-11 (5-25-1994)

50. AGO 42 (4-14-1955)

51. NAC 645.611

52. NAC 645.610 (1)(b)

53. NAC 645.610 (1)(b) Can't use "for sale by owner" nor "for lease by owner".

54. NAC 645.610 (1)(b) (2).

55. NAC 645.640 (2)

"deceptively similar" is whether a person of average intelligence would be misled by the name. It does not require actual deception or intent to deceive.[49]

The purposes of the regulation prohibiting deceptively similar names are: (1) the protection of vested rights to corporate names; (2) the protection of the public from deception and confusion; (3) the prevention of unnecessary litigation.[50]

In addition to these rules, any team advertising must comply with all other applicable advertising laws and regulations.[51]

4. LICENSEE STATUS

Some advertising rules require the licensee to disclose upfront the licensee's status as a real estate licensee.[52] The regulation states the licensee must provide a statement of the licensee's licensed status in any advertisement which contains the words "for sale by owner" or "for lease by owner" or similar words. The licensee who advertises to acquire, lease or dispose of any interest in a time share or real property is required to disclose in the advertisement if the licensee has an active or inactive license and his or her status as a salesperson, broker or broker-salesperson.

This restriction applies to the use of a licensee's telephone number, (or the name or telephone number of another licensee in the brokerage firm with which the licensee is associated) in any advertisement for the sale or lease of property if that sign or advertisement indicates the property is for sale or lease by an owner.[53]

If the licensee has an actual ownership interest in the property, the licensee may state the property is for sale or lease by "owner-broker" or "owner-agent", which ever is applicable.[54] This requirement to disclose the licensee's status in the advertisement is applicable if the purchaser or seller is a member of the licensee's immediate family, the licensee's firm or any member of the firm, or any entity in which the licensee has an interest as owner.[55]

5. COLD CALLING AND THE "DO NOT CALL" LAWS

Cold calling is a common real estate marketing technique. Licensees "cold call" when they solicit previously unknown individuals by telephone in order to sell their real estate services. This type of telephone solicitation is currently regulated by both the federal and state "Do Not Call" laws.[56]

Briefly, the cold calling procedure requires a person to gather a list of telephone numbers of potential customers. The licensee or broker must then register with the Federal Trade Commission (FTC). Once registered, the licensee will receive a list of restricted telephone numbers filed with the FTC. The licensee then "scrubs" (compares) his or her list against the restricted list removing any matching numbers. The remaining telephone numbers may be called. Once called, if the recipient expresses a desire not to be disturbed or called again, the licensee must put that telephone number on an internal "do not call" list. All brokers should have an office policy regarding using cold calling by their agents.

Nevada's Do Not Call laws are more restrictive than the federal law and are found in Nevada's Deceptive Trade Practices NRS 598 statutes. Nevada's Do Not Call rules include:

• No calling between 8 p.m. and 9 a.m.;

• No annoying, abusive or harassing language;

• No fair housing violations – blockbusting;

• No claiming to be information gathering when the intent is to induce a sale;

• The caller must inform the person who answers the telephone of the sales nature of the call within 30 seconds after beginning the conversation and must provide the name, address and telephone number of the business or organization.[57]

56. Federal "Do Not Call" Act, 47 U.S.C. §227; and 15 U.S.C. §1601, as well as Nevada's Do Not Call laws found in NRS 228.590 and NRS 598.0918.

57. NRS 598.0915 through NRS 598.0953.

"Block-busting"
This is the practice by which a person frightens a homeowner into selling his property at less than market value by spreading rumors that certain racial groups will move into the neighborhood. AGO 1972-71, March 24, 1972.

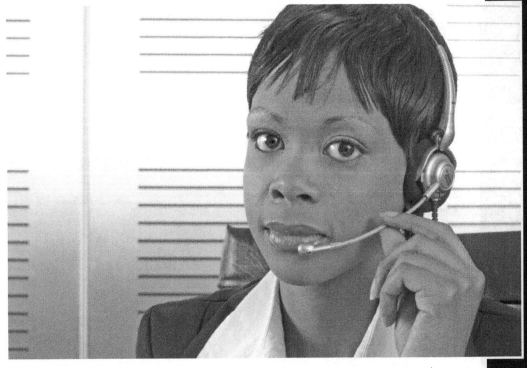

NEVADA LAW ON ADVERTISING VI - 12

58. NAC 645.600 (2)(f)

59. NRS 118

59a. NRS 645.321

60. Federal Fair Housing law 42 U.S.C. §3604(c) (1991) and 42 U.S.C. §1982; and Nevada's NRS 118, specially made applicable to real estate licensees under NRS 645.321.

61. Though not required under federal or state law, using – and abiding by – the fair housing disclaimer is a good business practice. "We list, sell and rent any property without any preference, limitation or discrimination based on race, color, religion, sex or national origin or any intention to make such a preference, limitation or discrimination."

E. THE CLIENT'S PROPERTY

Advertising a client's property encompasses laws and entities not previously dealt with when a licensee or broker advertises their services. Often, the property owner will want to share in how the property is advertised or in the very least, review what the broker proposes. When advertising a client's property the broker needs to retain control over the advertised content and process as it is the broker who retains the most liability for errors, misleading or fraudulent advertising.

In this chapter, the fair housing rules are reviewed along with the laws regarding Truth-in-Lending, Regulation Z, property signs, land, subdivisions and owner/developer regulations as they relate to advertising.

1. FAIR HOUSING

Fair housing laws, both federal and state, are often the first set of restrictions people think of when it comes to real estate advertising.

Most advertising violations by a licensee are reported to a governing entity by another licensee or real estate professional. However, the majority of fair housing violations are brought to the attention of a governing entity by a member of the public as the laws are well known to the public.

The broker always retains the ultimate liability for his or her agent's breach of advertising laws. Specifically, the Nevada Administrative Code requires the broker to supervise his or her licensees and familiarize them with the requirements of federal and state law prohibitions against discrimination.[58]

Protected Classes: There are seven federally identified protected classes. Nevada fair housing law echoes those protected classes but includes an eighth class, that of ancestry.[59] In 2011, the Nevada Legislature added gender identity or expression and sexual orientation to the protected classes. [59a] The federal protected classes are race, color, religion, sex, handicap (disability in Nevada), familial status, and national origin.[60] Most fair housing advertising violations arise from indicating, either directly or indirectly, a preference for, or a bias against, a protected class.[61]

Though each protected class may be violated in an advertising forum, the three protected classes which tend to have the greatest advertising violations are religion, familial status, and sex.

Religion: Potential violations occur when a licensee advertises only in a religious venue, or when in an advertisement, the licensee or client expresses a preference for, or bias against, certain buyers, sellers, or renters of a specific religion or belief system.

Many times the fair housing advertising violation in religion is not one of identifying a bias against a particular religion (e.g.,

VI - 13

no Muslims), but occurs when expressing a preference for a particular religion (e.g., Christians preferred).

Brokers have been found in violation of the fair housing laws when they placed signs, symbols or other indices of religion in their advertising.[62] Additionally, violations can occur when references are made in the advertising to a local religious site, e.g., "house within walking distance of Beth Shalom". An exception may be granted when the religious institution mentioned is of such national recognition that it becomes a landmark, such as the National Cathedral in Washington, D.C.

Familial Status: Familial Status refers to any adult (over 18 years of age) who is the parent, legal custodian, or other person with custody of a child or person under 18 years of age. It encompasses a wide range of relationships and is not dependant on blood or traditional parent/child legal status and includes women who may be pregnant. The term "family" includes single adults with minors.[63]

Familial status is probably the most unintentionally violated fair housing class in advertising because violations often stem from the advertiser's good intentions. For example, a Reno newspaper advertisement for a rental recently read 'house on busy street, not suitable for small children'. Regardless of the advertiser's intention, this wording is a violation of the fair housing laws. More than at any time does the old saw "describe the property, not the people", hold true. Regardless of the advertiser's intentions, the licensee should not identify people for whom the property would be perfect based on their status in a protected class.

Age is commonly assumed to be a protected class; however, it is not a protected class for housing. It is an exemption to the familial status class and is only applicable when the housing

meets certain restriction guidelines for either 55 or 65 year old or older persons. Advertising for "mature", "retired", or "settled" persons is a violation unless an exemption applies.

The licensee should be careful about allowing the client to express a fair housing violation in an indirect manner by advertising that certain properties have "children only" sections, or that children will require an additional deposit or fee. No real property advertisement should include any reference to a bias against children or a preference for childless persons.

Sex: A fair housing violation occurs when a licensee advertises a preference for a preferred gender. The term "sex" in the fair housing laws does not refer to sexual orientation; it is a reference to gender. Sexual orientation is not a protected class for residential housing federally or in Nevada.[64] An exception is made when advertising for a "shared living" arrangement. A person may advertise for a same sex roommate and certain religious/non-profit institutions may advertise accommodations for a specific gender, i.e., YMCA.

2. TRUTH-IN-LENDING/REGULATION Z

Of the myriad of federal laws that impact real estate advertising, the Truth-in-Lending laws are probably the least well known.[65] This law addresses how lenders advertise their loan information and includes what information is required to be disclosed to the public so that a consumer can intelligently compare lenders and loan programs.

Regulation Z is the federal regulation that sets forth the specifics of the Truth-in-Lending Act. [66] Its rules are applicable to all media advertising that refers to mortgage financing terms and is generally applicable in all residential credit transactions. It applies to any advertisement for any loan that is regulated by the Truth-in-Lending laws.[67] Thus, Regulation Z impacts any real estate

62. Though not a Nevada case but illustrative of the point, is Commonwealth of Virginia v. Lotz Realty Company, Inc., 376 S.E.2d 54 (Va., 1989), in which the broker Paul Lotz was found in violation of Virginia's fair housing laws when he placed signs, symbols and wording on his advertisements indicating a religious preference for clients based on a specific religion.

63. 24 C.F.R. §109.15 (i) (4-1-94)

64. Discrimination based on sexual orientation is illegal in Nevada in public accommodations (NRS 233.010) and employment (NRS 281.370, NRS 338.125, NRS 610.020, NRS 613.310).

65. 15 U.S.C. §§1601 et seq. federal Truth-in-Lending Act.

66. 12 C.F.R. §226 et seq.

67. 15 U.S.C. §1664

68. 12 C.F.R. Part 226 Known as Regulation Z.

69. The APR calculates the interest rate plus all charges. Therefore, the APR can never be less than the interest rate but is often higher than the stated interest rate.

70. A quick down-and-dirty rule of thumb is if the advertisement contains any numbers referring to credit or payment terms, it probably triggers Regulation Z; therefore, it must contain all the required information.

71. 15 U.S.C. §1640

72. NAC 645.535 (2)

73. NAC 645.610 (1)(d)

74. NAC 645.215

advertising that includes certain credit or financing "trigger" terms. The trigger terms include any reference to an amount of down payment, monthly payment, the number of payments, a specific payment period (ex: 30 years, etc.), an interest rate, an annual percentage rate (APR), or a finance charge amount.[68]

Once Regulation Z is triggered by the use of any one of the "trigger" terms, all of the following information must be contained in the advertisement: the cash price, the amount or percentage of any down payment, the term of the repayment (number of payments, amount of each payment, and the due date of each payment), the annual percentage rate and whether the APR may change.[69]

Certain statements do not trigger Regulation Z, for example, it is permissible to make such statements as "no down payment", "easy monthly payments", "pay weekly", "terms to fit your budget", "financing available", or "liberal financing terms available".[70]

The Truth-in-Lending Act, and by extension Regulation Z, is enforced by the Division of Credit Practices, Bureau of Consumer Protection, Federal Trade Commission. If an advertisement violates the Truth-in-Lending laws, a court may require an injunction, i.e., stop the problem advertising; impose a fine of not more than $5,000 per violation up to $10,000 per day for each violation; and if the advertiser is found guilty of criminal behavior, prison, for not more than 1 year. Additionally, any individuals harmed may receive their actual damages, with civil penalties of not less than $100 or more than $1,000, plus court costs and attorney fees (the government's and any harmed individual).[71]

3. "FOR SALE" SIGNS

As the real estate market slows down, competition for listings becomes more aggressive. Some assertive licensees intent on capturing any business available have placed their signs on properties not listed by their brokerage firm. The Nevada Administrative Code provides only one licensee may place a "for sale" sign on a property unless otherwise authorized by owner.[72]

A licensee may not advertise or place any sign on a property when that property is exclusively listed for sale by another broker unless the licensee obtains the prior written consent of the broker with whom the property is listed. Additionally, the listing broker cannot give or withhold such consent without the knowledge of the property's owner.[73]

4. LAND, SUBDIVISIONS, OWNER/ DEVELOPERS

There are special laws and regulations regarding the advertising of vacant or unimproved land or subdivisions. Because of the tainted history of licensees and developers selling unimproved parcels of land using fraudulent advertising, these laws have been strictly enforced.

The Real Estate Division (RED) has the authority to investigate any circumstances surrounding its suspicion that fraud, deceit or false advertising is occurring in connection with the sale, purchase, rental, lease or exchange of any vacant or unimproved land or subdivision outside the corporate limits of any city.[74] Not only may the RED investigate, but Nevada's Attorney General may take all appropriate legal action under any applicable Nevada law.

Any advertising in Nevada of a subdivision, whether that subdivision is in Nevada or another state, must be pre-approved by the Nevada Real Estate Division.[75] Advertising under the subdivision regulations additionally includes any advertisement for the retention of purchasers after the sale.[76] In advertising subdivisions, all advertising rules apply when using traditional advertising media as well as when the licensee uses any telephone solicitation,[77] promotional meetings,[78] or the offering of vacation or other gift certificates.[79]

Whenever a licensee is hired by a developer to sell subdivisions, the licensee must ensure that the advertising was submitted to and approved by the Real Estate Division.[80] Nothing in the subdivision laws of Nevada excuses a person licensed under NRS 645 from the obligations imposed in NRS and NAC 645.[81]

There are very specific laws and regulations regarding sales presentations. For example, all oral and written advertising designed to induce any attendance at or participation in a sales presentation must conspicuously include the following statement: "The purpose of (the event or activity) is to attempt to sell you property in (name of state in which property is located)."[82]

75. NRS 119.184

76. NAC 119.015

77. NAC 119.035

78. NAC 119.040

79. NAC 119.050. Under NAC 119.080 a vacation certificate is a written promise which offers accommodations in or transportation to any location as part of a program to solicit prospective purchasers to attend a sales presentation for a subdivision.

80. NAC 119.400

81. NAC 119.330 (2)

82. NAC 119.455, see also NAC 119.500 to 119.520.

F. REVIEW

If real property is the heart of real estate, advertising is its life blood. Because of the potential influence advertising has on the public and industry, various laws have been promulgated to address issues of public concern. These include the requirement that advertising presents a true picture of the thing being offered; the promotion of fair trade; control unwanted intrusions into a consumer's privacy; and fostering equal access to housing and real estate services.

52018726R00177

Made in the USA
Middletown, DE
06 July 2019